Cars, Carriers of Regionalism?

Robert Boyer, Elsie Charron, Ulrich Jürgens and Steven Tolliday (eds)
BETWEEN IMITATION AND INNOVATION: The Transfer and Hybridization of
Productive Models in the International Automobile Industry

Robert Boyer and Michel Freyssenet
The Productive Models: the Conditions of Profitability

Elsie Charron and Paul Stewart (eds), WORK AND EMPLOYMENT RELATIONS IN
THE AUTOMOBILE INDUSTRY

Jean-Pierre Durand, Paul Stewart and Juan-José Castillo (eds)
TEAMWORK IN THE AUTOMOBILE INDUSTRY: Radical Change or Passing Fashion?

Michel Freyssenet, Andrew Mair, Koichi Shimizu and Giuseppe Volpato (eds)
ONE BEST WAY? Trajectories and Industrial Models of the World's Automobile
Producers

Michel Freyssenet, Koichi Shimizu and Giuseppe Volpato (eds), GLOBALIZATION
OR REGIONALIZATION OF THE AMERICAN AND ASIAN CAR INDUSTRY?

Michel Freyssenet, Koichi Shimizu and Giuseppe Volpato (eds), GLOBALIZATION
OR REGIONALIZATION OF THE EUROPEAN CAR INDUSTRY?

John Humphrey, Yveline Lecler and Mario Sergio Salerno (eds)
GLOBAL STRATEGIES AND LOCAL REALITIES: The Auto Industry in
Emerging Markets

Yannick Lung, Jean-Jacques Chanaron, Takahiro Fujimoto and Daniel Raff (eds)
COPING WITH VARIETY: Product Variety and Production Organization in the
World Automobile Industry

Cars, Carriers of Regionalism?

Edited by

Jorge Carrillo
El Colegio de la Frontera Norte, Tijuana

Yannick Lung
Montesquieu University, Bordeaux

and

Rob van Tulder
Erasmus University, Rotterdam

in association with

GERPISA

Réseau International
International Network
Groupe d'Étude et de Recherche Permanent sur l'Industrie et les Salariés de l'Automobile
Permanent Group for the Study of the Automobile Industry and its Employees
École des Hautes Etudes en Sciences Sociales, Paris, Université d'Évry-Val d'Essonne

Selection, editorial matter and Chapter 1 © Jorge Carrillo, Yannick Lung and Rob van Tulder 2004

Individual chapters (in order) © Rob van Tulder and Denis Audet; Michel Freyssenet and Yannick Lung; Jean-Bernard Layan and Yannick Lung; Rob van Tulder; Lale Duruiz; Jorge Carrillo; Mariano F. Laplane and Fernando Sarti; Koïchi Shimokawa; Jean-Jacques Chanaron; Anthony Black and Samson Muradzikwa; Jean-Bernard Layan and Mihoub Mezouaghi; Rob van Tulder; Marc Lautier; Eric Thun; Yeong-Hyun Kim 2004

Chapter maps © Fabienne Fontanier 2004

First published 2004 by
PALGRAVE MACMILLAN
Houndmills, Basingstoke, Hampshire RG21 6XS and
175 Fifth Avenue, New York, N.Y. 10010
Companies and representatives throughout the world

PALGRAVE MACMILLAN is the global academic imprint of the Palgrave Macmillan division of St. Martin's Press, LLC and of Palgrave Macmillan Ltd. Macmillan® is a registered trademark in the United States, United Kingdom and other countries. Palgrave is a registered trademark in the European Union and other countries.

ISBN 1–4039–2144–X

This book is printed on paper suitable for recycling and made from fully managed and sustained forest sources.

A catalogue record for this book is available from the British Library.

Library of Congress Cataloging-in-Publication Data
Cars, carriers of regionalism? edited by Jorge Carrillo, Yannick Lung, Rob van Tulder.
       p. cm.
    "GERPISA Réseau International."
    Includes bibliographical references and index.
    ISBN 1–4039–2144–X (cloth)
       1. Transportation, Automotive – Case studies. 2. Automobile industry and trade – Case studies. 3. Regionalism – Case studies. I. Carrillo V., Jorge (Carrillo Viveros) II. Lung, Yannick. III. Tulder, Rob van. IV. Groupe d'études et de recherches permanent sur l'industrie et les salariés de l'automobile.
HE5611.C279 2004
338.4'7629222—dc22   2003068747

10 9 8 7 6 5 4 3 2 1
13 12 11 10 09 08 07 06 05 04

Printed and bound in Great Britain by
Antony Rowe Ltd, Chippenham and Eastbourne

Contents

List of Tables

List of Figures

List of Abbreviations

ABEIVA	Associação Brasileiva das Empresas Importadoras de Veículos Automotores
ACARA	Asociación de Concesionarias Automotrices dela. República Argentina
ADEFA	Asociación de Fábricas de Automotores
AFTA	ASEAN Free Trade Area; Arab Free Trade Area
AMIA	Asociación Mexicana de la Industria Automotriz
AMU	Arab Maghreb Union
ANFAVEA	Associação Nacional dos Fabricantes de Veículos Automotores
ANZCERTA	Australia–New Zealand Closer Economic Relations Trade Agreement (later: CER)
APEC	Asia Pacific Economic Cooperation
ASEAN	Association of South East Asian Nations
BAFTA	Baltic Free Trade Area
BLNS	Botswana, Lesotho, Namibia, and Swaziland
CACM	Central American Common Market
CARICOM	Caribbean Community
CBU	Completely built up
CCFA	Comité des constructeurs Français d'Automobiles
CEFTA	Central European Free Trade Agreement
CEMAC	Central African Economic and Monetary Union
CIS	Commonwealth of Independent States
CKD	Completely knocked down
CM	Common Market
COMESA	Common Market for Eastern and Southern Africa
CU	Customs Union
DATAINTAL	System of import/export statistics of countries in the Americas, developed by Inter-American Development Bank
DTI	Department of Trade and Industry
EAC	East African Cooperation
EC	European Communities/European Commission
ECCAS	Economic Community of Central African States
ECOWAS	Economic Community of Western African States
EEA	European Economic Area
EFTA	European Free Trade Association
EIU	Economic Intelligence Unit
EMU	Economic and Monetary Union
EPU	Economic and Political Union

ERM	Emerging Regional Market
EU	European Union
FTA	Free Trade Area
FTAA	Free Trade Area of the Americas
GATT	General Agreement on Tariffs and Trade
GCC	Gulf Cooperation Council
IPM	Integrated Peripheral Market
JRI	Japanese Research Institute
KAMA	Korean Automobiles Manufacturers Association
LAIA	Latin American Integration Association
MERCOSUR	Southern Common Market
MIDP	Motor Industry Development Programme
MRU	Mano River Union
MTAZ	Motor Trade Association of Zimbabwe
NAAMSA	National Association of Automobile Manufacturers of South Africa
NAFTA	North American Free Trade Agreement
OE	Original Equipment
OECD	Organisation for Economic Co-operation and Development
OICA	Organisation Internationale des Constructeurs Automobiles
PAM	Protected Autonomous Market
PARTA	Pacific Regional Trade Agreement
PCU	Partial Customs Union
PTA	Preferential Trade Agreement
RIA	Regional Integration Agreement
RTA	Regional Trade Agreement
SAARC	South Asian Association for Regional Cooperation
SACU	Southern African Customs Union
SADC	Southern African Development Community
SAPTA	South Asian Free Trade Area
SKD	Semi-knocked down
TAFTA	Transatlantic Free Trade Agreement
UNCTAD	United Nations Conference on Trade Aid and Development
WAEMU	West African Economic and Monetary Union
WTO	World Trade Organization

Foreword

Over the next few decades will 'lean production', and a generalized deregulation of trade, have become the norms for the international environment in which firms and political and economic spaces will be operating?

The GERPISA Group, a French-based permanent research network devoted to the study of the automobile industry and its labour force, has been transformed into an international network of researchers whose backgrounds cover a wide range of social sciences (economics, business, history, sociology, geography and political science). From 1993 to 1996, the GERPISA Group carried out its initial international programme 'The Emergence of New Industrial Models', a project in which it examined whether existing industrial models were effectively starting to converge towards the principles of 'lean production' – as had been theorized by MIT's IMVP (International Motor Vehicle Program) team. By focusing on what was happening in the automobile industry, the GERPISA Group's work was able to demonstrate the great diversity, and divergence, of the trajectories that firms have been following in recent times. Examples have been the wide spectrum of product policies; of productive organizations and labour relations; and the hybridization of production systems in the new areas towards which firms have been expanding. At the time of writing, there is no 'one best way' – there never has been, and there probably never will be. In fact, the first GERPISA research project made it possible to identify and characterize not one, but three industrial models, all of which have been in operation since the 1970s: the Toyotaist model; the Hondian model; and the Sloanian model (epitomized today by Volkswagen, not GM). The reasoning behind this conclusion is presented and discussed in the four collective books produced by the four working groups, which represent different elements of the integrated project: M. Freyssenet, A. Mair, K. Shimizu and G. Volpato (eds), *One Best Way? Trajectories and Industrial Models of the World's Automobile Producers* (Oxford and New York: Oxford University Press, 1998); R. Boyer, E. Charron, U. Jürgens and S. Tolliday (eds), *Between Imitation and Innovation: the Transfer and Hybridization of Productive Models in the International Automobile Industry* (Oxford and New York: Oxford University Press, 1998); J.P. Durand, P. Stewart and J.- J. Castillo (eds), *Teamwork in the Automobile Industry: Radical Change or Passing Fashion?* (London: Macmillan, 1999); and Y. Lung, J.- J. Chanaron, T. Fujimoto and D. Raff (eds), *Coping with Variety: Product Variety and Production Organization in the World Automobile Industry* (Aldershot: Ashgate, 1999).

This made it possible to construct theories to explain the processes that had led to this multiplicity of models. Companies follow different profit strategies – their attempts to increase their profitability cause them to favour certain policy combinations over others (for example, volume and diversity, quality, innovation and flexibility, the permanent reduction of costs, volumes, and so on). However, in order to be efficient, all of these strategies have to fit in with the environments in which they are to be applied – especially with respect to the modes of income growth and distribution that are being practised in the areas under consideration. Moreover, to form a 'productive model', developed from a 'company government compromise' between the main parties (the shareholders, management, unions, workforce and suppliers), the strategies need to be implemented coherently. This analytical framework is presented in R. Boyer and M. Freyssenet, *The Productive Models: the Conditions of Profitability* (London and New York: Palgrave, 2002).

From 1997 to 1999, GERPISA realized a second international programme 'The Automobile Industry: Between Globalization and Regionalization'. This project tested the thesis that globalization is an imperative for corporate profitability; and that it is the inevitable consequence of the deregulation of trade in the aforementioned 'new' areas. This was a logical extension to the first programme, given that 'lean production' was considered to be the most suitable model for markets that are variable and diversified, and ostensibly moving towards a single global standard. Firms are establishing themselves across the whole world; new industrialized nations are emerging, as a result of their having opened up to international trade; and more recently, certain automakers have been at the heart of some mega-mergers. All of these events have supported the thesis of globalization, a process supposedly galvanized by the fact that companies, in their efforts to benefit from economies of scale, and from improved costs structures, are continually increasing their organizational integration, and are doing this on an ever-greater geographical scale. The commercial opening of the new areas, which some expect to create a homogenization of demand, is also deemed to contribute to this process.

A previous study (J. Humphrey, Y. Leclerc and M.S. Salerno (eds), *Global Strategies and Local Realities: the Auto Industry in Emerging Markets* (London: Macmillan/New York: St Martin's Press, 2000)) constituted a first attempt to put this hypothesis to the test, and it did so by focusing on the situation in the emerging countries. The main objective was to scrutinize a concept that is being presented now as if it were self-explanatory: economic globalization. The authors who collaborated had all emphasized the diversity of the productive and spatial configurations that can be observed in the emerging countries.

This book analyses the process of regionalization of the auto industry in different areas of the world (industrialized and developing countries), considering the geographical level at which supply and demand in the auto industry get coupled, such 'automobile spaces' could be national (Japan), regional (EU or MERCOSUR) or still in balance (Russia/CIS). Two companion books aim to carry out a systematic description and analysis of the trajectories of internationalization that are being followed by the various types of firms involved in the American, Asian and European automobile industry (manufacturers, suppliers and dealers): M. Freyssenet, K. Shimizu and G. Volpato (eds), *Globalization or Regionalization of the American and Asian Car Industry?*; and, M. Freyssenet, K. Shimizu and G. Volpato (eds), *Globalization or Regionalization of the European Car Industry?* (London and New York: Palgrave, 2003). These studies identify and characterize the different processes of periodic re-heterogenization, and the conditions that are necessary if firms, and areas, are to be successful. Moreover, within this perspective, they will be particularly keen to analyse the steps being taken to allow firms' and areas' trajectories to be adjusted and hybridized – actions which in all probability will require considerable strategic and organizational inventiveness. A last book from the second GERPISA programme focuses in particular on the form and character of the internationalization of employment relationships in the automotive industry (E. Charron and P. Stewart (eds), *Work and Employment Relations in the Automobile Industry* (London/New York: Palgrave, 2004)).

GERPISA's books are not only the result of the work done by their contributors, and by the editors who have assembled and organized them. Through their participation in the international meetings, and in annual symposiums, the members of the programme's international steering committee, and the other members of the network, have contributed in varying degrees to the discussions, and to the general thought process. In addition, the books would have never seen the light of day had it not been for GERPISA's administrative staff, who take care of all of the tasks that are part of the daily life of an international network. We thank them all.

MICHEL FREYSSENET and YANNICK LUNG
Scientific co-ordinators of the GERPISA programme entitled
'The Automobile Industry between Globalization and Regionalization'

Appendix: the GERPISA International Network

The GERPISA (the Permanent Group for the Study of and Research into the Automobile Industry and its Employees) started out as a network of French economics, management, history and sociology researchers who were interested in the automobile industry. Founded by Michel Freyssenet (CNRS sociologist) and Patrick Fridenson (EHESS historian), it was transformed into an international network in 1992 in order to carry out the research programme 'Emergence of new industrial models'.

With Robert Boyer (CEPREMAP, CNRS, EHESS economist) and Michel Freyssenet supervising its scientific orientations and under the management of an international committee, the programme (1993–6) made it possible, thanks to its study of the automobile firms' (and their transplants') trajectories, productive organization and employment relationships, to demonstrate that *lean production*, which according to the authors of *The Machine that Changed the World* (Womack, Jones and Roos) was to become the industrial model of the twenty-first century, was in fact an inaccurate amalgamation of two completely different productive models, the 'Toyotian' and the 'Hondian'. Moreover, it showed that there are, have always been, and probably always will be several productive models that are capable of performing well at any one time. Shareholders, executives and employees are not only not obliged to adopt a *one best way*, they also have to devise a 'company governance compromise' covering the means that will allow them to implement one of the several profit strategies that are relevant to the economic and social environment in which they find themselves.

A second programme (1997–9) 'The automobile industry: between globalization and regionalization' and supervised and coordinated by Michel Freyssenet and Yannick Lung (Bordeaux, economist), tested the analytical framework that had been developed during the first programme in an attempt to understand better the new wave of automobile manufacturer and component-maker internationalization that had been observed over the previous decade. The outcome was that the viability of the choices being made depends primarily on the chosen profit strategies' compatibility with the growth modes in the areas in which the investments are being made.

The third programme (2000–2) has been developed under Yannick Lung's coordination, with the support of the European Union (CoCKEAS project thematic network, 5th Framework, Key Action 4: HPSE–CT–1999–00022). It focuses on the issues at stake in the 'Co-ordination of knowledge and competencies in the regional automotive systems'. Supplementing existing studies of forms of regionalization in the automobile industry, the programme analyses the sector's new contours as well as the development of new relational and co-operative modes among its actors.

In 2002, the GERPISA comprised 350 members from 27 different countries. Affiliated with the Centre de Recherches Historiques (CRH) of the Ecole des Hautes Etudes en Sciences Sociales (EHESS), and acknowledged as an 'équipe d'accueil' of the Université d'Evry–val d'Essonne by the French Ministry of National Education, it is supported by the French car companies (PSA Peugeot–Citroën and Renault), their professional association (the CCFA), and the European Union.

The international management steering committee comprises the following members: Annie Beretti, Robert Boyer (CNRS-EHESS, Paris), Juan José Castillo (Universidad Complutense, Madrid), Jorge Carrillo (Colegio de la Frontera Norte, Mexico), Jean-Jacques Chanaron (CNRS, Lyon), Elsie Charron (CNRS, Paris), Jean-Pierre Durand (Université d'Evry), Michel Freyssenet (CNRS, Paris), Patrick Fridenson (EHESS, Paris), Takahiro Fujimoto (University of Tokyo), Ulrich Jurgens (WZB, Berlin), Yveline Lecler (MRASH/IAO, Lyon), Yannick Lung (Montesquieu University, Bordeaux), Jean-Claude Monnet (Research Department, Renault), Mario Sergio Salerno (University of Sao Paolo), Koichi Shimizu (University of Okayama), Koichi Shimokawa (Hosei University, Tokyo), Paul Stewart (University of Bristol), Steve Tolliday (University of Leeds), Rob van Tulder (Erasmus University, Rotterdam), Giuseppe Volpato (Ca'Foscari University, Venice) and Karel Williams (Victoria University, Manchester).

GERPISA's publications

GERPISA edits in English and French a quarterly review *Actes du GERPISA* and a monthly newsletter *La Lettre du GERPISA*. The review combines the writings that the network's members have presented on specific topics in various work meetings.

The newsletter comments on news from the automotive world and provides up-to-date information on the network's activities. Findings from the first and second programmes have been published in a series of books:

Programme 'Emergence of new industrial models'

Freyssenet, M., Mair, A., Shimizu, K. and Volpato, G. (eds) *One Best Way? Trajectories and Industrial Models of the World's Automobile Producers.* Oxford/New York: Oxford University Press, 1998. French translation: *Quel modèle productif? Trajectoires et modèles industriels des constructeurs automobiles mondiaux.* Paris: La Découverte, 2000.

Boyer, R., Charron, E., Jürgens, U. and Tolliday, S. (eds) *Between Imitation and Innovation: the Transfer and Hybridization of Productive Models in the International Automobile Industry.* Oxford/New York: Oxford University Press, 1998.

Durand, J.P., Stewart, P. and Castillo, J.-J. (eds) *Teamwork in the Automobile Industry: Radical Change or Passing Fashion.* London: Macmillan, 1999. First edition in French: *L'avenir du travail à la chaîne.* Paris: La Découverte, 1998.

Lung, Y., Chanaron, J.-J., Fujimoto, T. and Raff, D. (eds) *Coping with Variety: Product Variety and Production Organization in the World Automobile Industry.* Aldershot: Ashgate, 1999.

Shimizu, K., *Le Toyotisme.* Paris: La Découverte, 1999.

Boyer, R. and Freyssenet, M., *The Productive Models.* London/New York: Palgrave, 2002. First edition in French: *Les modèles productifs.* Paris: La Découverte, 2000.

Boyer, R. and Freyssenet, M., *The World that Changed the Machine* (forthcoming).

Programme 'The automobile industry between globalization and regionalization'

Humphrey, J., Lecler, Y. and Salerno, M. (eds) *Global Strategies and Local Realities: the Auto industry in Emerging Markets.* London: Macmillan/New York: St Martin's Press, 2000.

Freyssenet, M., Shimizu, K. and Volpato, G. (eds) *Globalization or Regionalization of the American and Asian Car Industry?* London/New York: Palgrave Macmillan, 2003.

Freyssenet, M., Shimizu, K. and Volpato, G. (eds) *Globalization or Regionalization of the European Car Industry?* London/New York: Palgrave Macmillan, 2003.

Charron, E. and Stewart, P. (eds), *Work and Employment Relations in the Automobile Industry.* London/New York: Palgrave Macmillan, 2004.

Carillo, J., Lung, Y. and Tulder, R. van (eds), *Cars, Carriers of Regionalism?* London/New York: Palgrave Macmillan, 2004.

Programme 'Co-ordination of knowledge and competencies in the regional automotive systems'

Lung, Y. and Volpato, G. (eds), 'Reconfiguring the Auto Industry', Special Issue of *International Journal of Automotive Technology and Management*, vol. 2, no. 1, 2002.

Froud, F., Johal, S. and Williams, K. (eds), 'The Tyranny of Finance? New Agendas for Auto Research', Special Issue of *Competition and Change: The Journal of Global Business and Political Economy*, vol. 6, double issue no. 1/2, 2002.

Lung, Y. (ed.), 'The Changing Geography of the Automobile Industry', Symposium of *International Journal of Urban and Regional Research*, no. 4, 2002.

Lung, Y. and Galabrese, G. (eds), 'Designing Organizations to Manage Knowledge Creation and Coordination', Special Issue of *International Journal of Automotive Technology and Management*, vol. 3, no. 1/2, 2003.

Information on GERPISA's activities can be obtained by contacting
GERPISA réseau international. Université d'Evry-Val d'Essonne.
Rue du Facteur Cheval, 91025 Evry cedex, France
Telephone: +33 1 69 47 78 95 – Fax: +33 1 69 47 78 99
E-mail: contact@gerpisa.univ-evry.fr
Web site: http//www.gerpisa.univ-evry.fr

Notes on the Contributors

Audet, Denis, Organisation for Economic Co-operation and Development (OECD), Paris, France.

Black, Anthony, Associate Professor and Director of the School of Economics at University of Cape Town, South Africa.

Carrillo, Jorge, Dr, Full-time researcher, El Colegio de la Frontera Norte, Tijuana, Mexico.

Chanaron, Jean-Jacques, CNRS Director, GATE, Université Louis Lumière, Lyon, France.

Duruiz, Lale, Professor, Dr, Istanbul Bilgi University, Turkey.

Freyssenet, Michel, CNRS Director, GERPISA, and CSU-IRESCO, Paris, France.

Kim, Yeong-Hyun, Assistant Professor, Department of Geography, Ohio University, OH, USA.

Laplane, Mariano F., Professor of Economics, Universidade Estadual de Campinas-UNICAMP, São Paulo, Brazil.

Lautier, Marc, Senior Lecturer in Economics, Université de Rouen, France.

Layan, Jean-Bernard, Reader in Economics, Montesquieu University, Bordeaux, France.

Lung, Yannick, Professor of Economics, GERPISA co-director, Montesquieu University, Bordeaux, France.

Mezouaghi, Mihoub, Research Fellow, Institut de Recherches sur le Maghreb Contemporain (IRMC), Tunis, Tunisia.

Muradzikwa, Samson, Senior Lecturer, School of Economics, University of Cape Town, South Africa.

Sarti, Fernando, Professor of Economics, Universidade Estadual de Campinas-UNICAMP, São Paulo, Brazil.

Shimokawa, Koïchi, Emeritus Professor, Hoshei University, and Professor, Tokaigakuen University, Yokohama, Japan.

Thun, Eric, Assistant Professor of Politics and International Affairs, Princeton University, USA.

Tulder, Rob van , Professor, Erasmus University, Rotterdam, Netherlands.

1
Introduction: In Search of a Viable Automobile Space

Yannick Lung and Rob van Tulder

Introduction

Automobile firms' failed global strategies

The late twentieth century was marked by a host of strategic challenges associated with a new phase in the internationalization of the world's economies, a phenomenon commonly referred to as 'globalization'. The automobile industry found itself at the very heart of these events, mainly because of the strategies being pursued by the firms in this sector, notably automakers trying (with a greater or lesser degree of success) to implement various internationalization strategies. GERPISA has published two collective volumes that study these strategies in great detail (Freyssenet, Shimizu and Volpato, 2003a,b). These volumes highlight the problems facing those firms that have been the most committed to so-called 'world car' or 'global platform' strategies that presuppose at least a partial convergence and homogenization of markets. Since the early 1990s, Ford, with its world car (the CDW27 platform/Mondeo in Europe) and the aborted merger between its European and North American entities (the 'Ford 2000' plan) plus Fiat, with its world car targeting the emerging countries (the 178/Palio project), acted as the standard bearers for this kind of strategy. By the early twenty-first century both Ford and Fiat are suffering from the after-effects of their strategic miscalculations.

By contrast, firms that have acted more cautiously and tried to design products geared towards regional and even national markets generally find themselves in a better position. 'Think globally, act locally', the 'glocalization' slogan adopted by Honda, appears to have been a particularly effective approach. The success of Toyota's progressive internationalization strategy was based on the incremental development of an adapted regional product range and a regionally structured productive base. Toyota may have been the last of the Japanese automakers to establish facilities abroad but it now leads its counterparts in North America and Europe and has reinforced its positions in the ASEAN region. As for PSA Peugeot-Citroën, the Group's refusal to listen to the prophets of a world of recurring mergers and acquisitions and frentic globalization allowed it to bolster positions that are anchored in a fundamentally European-based geographical presence, notwithstanding recent moves into China and Brazil. Interestingly enough, Ford had once benefited from its ability to anticipate the effects of European integration – first when it created Ford of Europe in 1967, and also a few year later when it set up small car production facilities in Spain. It followed the same approach in Mexico in anticipation of the advent of NAFTA, but this time around it was unable to take advantage of the consolidated regional dynamic that the automobile industry has helped to structure and which seems to constitute an alternative to the globalization process.

The new wave of institutional regionalism

The final decade of the twentieth century also marked the start of major changes in the institutional framework of the world economy. At the same time, the liberalization of international financial markets contributed to an unprecedented number of financial crises in both developing and developed countries, leading to pleas for renewed regulation. The multilateral trading system boiled down to the establishment of the World Trade Organization (WTO) with unprecedented powers to press for further trade liberalization. However, towards the end of the 1990s non-governmental organizations (NGOs) initially frustrated a further round of trade negotiations that was supposed to start in Seattle in 1999, while developing countries barred further progress in WTO's millennium round negotiations in Cancun in 2003. Similarly, the number of bilateral agreements between countries rose at an unprecedented pace,[1] after the efforts to create a Multilateral Agreement on Investment (MAI) had failed miserably in 1998.

In the first half of the 1990s, most countries seemed to be adhering to the call for 'globalization' and to pursue multilateral strategies. Even so, some countries remained more hesitant and – despite using globalization rhetoric – adopted relatively unilateral strategies (cf. Ruigrok and Van Tulder, 1995). Certain countries moved along both tracks simultaneously. The United States, for instance, is a fervent supporter of globalization, but will not shy away from unilateralist strategies when it feels its national interests to be involved (Nye, 2002).

The second half of the 1990s extended the debate on multilateralism versus unilateralism, and has been described as the era of 'regionalism' (Scott, 1997). At the start of the twenty-first century, there is hardly any country in the world that is *not* part of a formal regional integration initiative (Ethier, 1998; Atkinson, 1999). We are currently facing a 'world of regions' (Storper, 1997). By January 2002 nearly all of the WTO's 144 members had notified participation in one or more regional integration initiatives. While over the whole 1948–1994 period the GATT (General Agreement on Tariffs and Trade) secretariat received 124 notifications of formal regional integration initiatives relating to trade in goods, the number of notifications grew dramatically, with an additional one hundred regional arrangements covering trade in goods and/or services since the formal creation of the WTO in 1995. Since the definition of the WTO of regional integration initiatives does not cover all forms of regionalism; the actual number of RIAs is even larger. Some of the regional integration agreements superseded previous arrangements, while some agreements were discontinued. Figure 1.1 summarizes the status of the notifications as registered with the WTO secretariat.

The impact of the second wave of regionalism on the dynamism of the world economy can hardly be underestimated. The WTO secretariat assesses that 43 per cent of all trade is conducted exclusively within regional trade agreements (RTAs, which excludes preferential trade agreements or partial customs unions). This is expected to rise to more than 50 per cent in 2005 when the number of RTAs in force and notified to the WTO is projected to have grown to more than 180 from 124 in 2001 (*Financial Times*, 30 November 2001). In addition, most extra-regional trade is also conducted to and from countries within a regional trade agreement, meaning that the volume of international trade that is influenced by the existence of RIAs is even higher. The effects of the regionalization trend are not merely economic. As the World Bank concludes, 'the purpose of regional integration is often political, and the economic consequences, good or bad, are side effects of the political pay-off' (quoted in *Financial Times*, 30 November 2001: v).

Rather than a scenario in which various parts of the world are linked in a homogeneous manner, a multi-polar configuration seems to have evolved in which regional integration prevails over global integration (cf. Freyssenet and

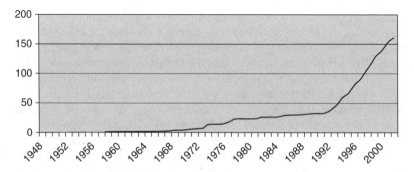

Figure 1.1 Regional trade agreements in force as notified to GATT/WTO
Source: WTO.

Lung, 2000). The constant tension between the various political and economic scenarios (regionalism, unilateralism, bilateralism, multilateralism) is likely to last well into the twenty-first century. Regionalism could be seen as a substitute for globalization, but it could also be a step towards its realization.

Addressing these issues is often considered to be the preserve of International Relations specialists and political scientists. In particular, there has been some dispute about whether regionalism is a building block or a stumbling block for globalization. The dimensions of unilateralism and bilateralism, as well as the exact nature of regionalism, are thereby rarely taken into account. These dimensions are nevertheless of increasing importance to business strategists and economic geographers. International business has to operate under these changing and rather uncertain institutional circumstances. Successful firms have often not only considered international political strategies as externally given, but have also been actively involved in shaping them. The car industry is one of the most prominent cases at hand. In most countries the car industry is still amongst the largest employers, the biggest investors in R&D and always amongst the largest traders and international investors of a country. Many of the fiercest trade disputes centred around the car industry. Some car firms have actively been helping to mould regional integration initiatives, but others have also supported multilateral and even unilateral ('go-it-alone') strategies of governments. This volume addresses the question of whether the various forms of regionalism under way – confronted with alternative strategies – could create conditions under which car manufacturers can be able to connect productive organization and markets in a sustainable/viable manner.

What are viable strategies for firms under challenging circumstances in which it is not clear whether regionalism, multilateralism or something else might prevail? For the moment regionalism seems to be viewed as a feasible 'middle way': balancing the risks of the extreme dynamism of globalization against the risk of stagnation involved in 'go-it-alone' strategies. This introductory chapter further classifies the different strategies adopted by blocks of countries in the last decade of the twentieth century. Section 2 identifies the various trade-offs that exist between multilateralism, unilateralism and regionalism. This discussion supports the particular organization of the present volume. Next, various institutional trade-offs create different possibilities for car firms to develop viable geographical strategies for a productive organization. Section 3 specifies the concept of an 'automobile space' and looks at the sources of tension and uncertainty within the various arrangements. The ultimate question of a viable automobile space depends on the interaction between company and government strategies. Finally, Section 4 explains the sequence of the volume that should enable an assessment of viable geographical and institutional strategies for the car industry in the early twenty-first century.

Multilateralism, regionalism, bilateralism, unilateralism?

The academic and policy debate on the institutional setting of the world economy in general and trade policy in particular, developed along two axes of debate that are usually presented as dyadic pairs of opposing trends: unilateralism versus multilateralism and regionalism versus multilateralism. With the growing importance of regionalism, a logical third pair of opposing trends should be added, however: unilateralism versus regionalism. This section will confront the developments on regional integration and adherence to the multilateral trade system with these three debates in order to frame the concrete debate on the car industry.

Unilateralism versus multilateralism

The traditional debate in international political economy dealt with the question whether countries should or could adopt a unilateral 'go-it-alone' strategy. In the 1920s and 1930s the disruptive effects of mercantilism and the breakdown of the closed planning economy as epitomized by communist economies has put protagonists of unilateralism at a disadvantage to the free-traders. Consequently, following the Second World War the number of countries that have become part of the GATT (later WTO) framework has rapidly increased. With the accession of China, three-quarters of the economies in the world – and most of its population – are now organized within the WTO.

Since most countries[2] have indeed become members of the United Nations, one of the clearest indications as to whether or not a country is willing to adhere to multilateralism has been its adherence to the GATT/WTO regime. But the position of the GATT as an instance of supranational multilateral rule remainded rather modest during the 1960s, 1970s and 1980s. The end of the Uruguay Round and the start of the World Trade Organization in 1995 signalled the establishment of a much more powerful supranational institution with a coherent aim of implementing multilateral free trade.

Even within the WTO framework, the unilateralism versus multilateralism debate is bound to continue. A number of important countries still follow a broadly 'go-it-alone' strategy – even despite their adherence to the multilateral framework of the WTO/GATT. Such a position could be dubbed 'unilateral multilateralism' and applies in particular to countries like China, Japan and South Korea that are members of the WTO, but are not yet very open to trade, nor part of a major regional integration initiative.

Regionalism versus multilateralism

Surfing the second wave of regionalism, the 'unilateralism versus multilateralism' debate was quickly superseded by a 'regionalism versus multilateralism' debate. The biggest fear – particularly within WTO circles – was that regionalism could substitute for globalization and thus become a stumbling block towards further global trade integration. The WTO secretariat created a special commission to monitor the process of regionalism in order to consider whether trade diversion or trade creation would emerge from booming regionalism. Leading scholars have tried to resolve this dispute by introducing the concept of 'open regionalism' (Bergsten, 1997). Closed regionalism would imply that regionalism substitutes for multilateralism/ globalism and could, on balance, lower global free trade, whereas open regionalism complements global free trade.

The clearest effort of open regionalism is no doubt the APEC initiative that explicitly embraced the concept of 'open regionalism' at its inception in 1989. The official declaration emphasized that 'the *outcome* of trade and investment liberalization in the Asia-Pacific will not only be the actual reduction of barriers among APEC economies but also between APEC economies and non-APEC economies' (Bergsten, 1997: 3).[3] However, as a consequence of the adoption of this concept, APEC is also one of the least advanced forms of regional integration.

A number of the largest APEC members – such as China, Japan and South Korea – have not entered into any other formal regional integration agreement. They can therefore be considered to be still 'going-it-alone', whilst APEC cannot (yet) be counted as a formal regional integration agreement. APEC might indeed apply for open region status, precisely because it is not a formal institutionalized region. Countries that belong to comparatively weak regional integration agreements such as India (in SAARC), can also be considered to belong to the 'go-it-alone' group. They do not face the trade-off between regionalism and multilateralism/globalism, but have engaged in a sort of 'unilateral multilateralism'.

An interesting illustration of how regionalism has prevailed over multi-lateralism or unilateralism is that hardly any of the multilateral trade dis-putes within WTO have been intra-regional in nature. In the overwhelming majority of cases, signatories of regional integration agreements abstained from WTO procedures to settle their trade disputes or only entered into relatively minor disputes (except in the case of NAFTA). Of the 242 WTO disputes in the 1995–2002 period, only nine covered disputes between members of the same RIA.

One way to overcome the multilateralism versus regionalism dispute, would be for regions to come to bilateral (inter-regional) agreements with other regions. Except for the prospective European integration process in which CEFTA countries integrate with the EU, only bilateral agreements between MERCOSUR and SACU, and between MERCOSUR and the European Union, are under negotiation (and expected to materialize in 2005).

Unilateralism versus regionalism

The debate on unilateralism versus regionalism is part and parcel of the regional integration process, not only when deciding on establishing or joining a RIA, but also for individual member countries that are already part of a RIA. Each member country faces a continuous balancing act between regional and national interests.

Regional integration agreements can range from extremely modest and shallow arrangements like preferential trade agreements (PTAs) and partial customs unions (PCUs) to very intense and deep arrangements like Economic Monetary Union (EMU) and Economic and Political Union (EPU). The rough assessments made by the WTO very often only make a distinction between free trade agreements (FTAs, which is a more shallow form of so-called 'negative' integration, and customs unions (CU, which are a deeper form of so-called 'positive' integration). As the vertical axis in Figure 1.2 indicates, FTAs and CUs occupy only the middle positions in a range of regional integration forms. An intermediate step between customs unions and monetary unions are common markets (CM).

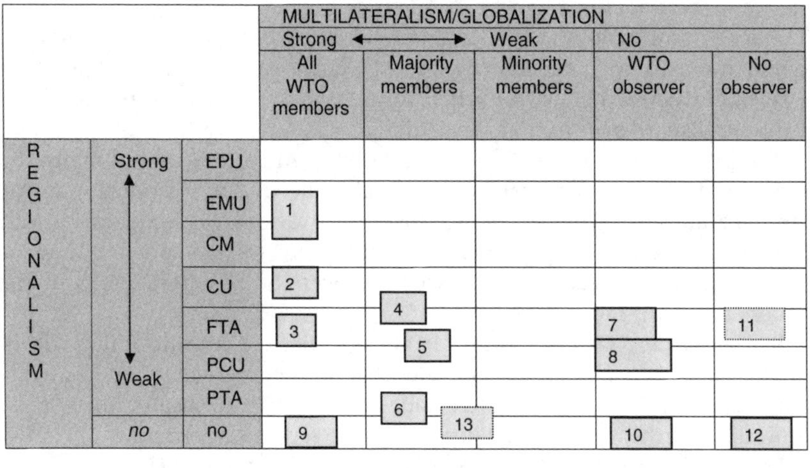

			MULTILATERALISM/GLOBALIZATION				
			Strong ◄─────► Weak			No	
			All WTO members	Majority members	Minority members	WTO observer	No observer
R E G I O N A L I S M	Strong ▲	EPU					
		EMU	1				
		CM					
		CU	2				
		FTA	3	4		7	11
		PCU		5		8	
	Weak ▼	PTA		6			
	no	no	9		13	10	12

Figure 1.2 Position of regional integration initiatives

Legend
1 = EU; with Turkey a customs union has existed since 1996
2 = MERCOSUR
3 = NAFTA, CEFTA, ANZCERTA
4 = SADC/SACU (13/14 WTO member)
5 = ASEAN/AFTA (7/10 WTO member)
6 = SAARC [INDIA] (5/7 WTO member)
7 = CIS [RUSSIA] (3/10 WTO member)
8 = AMU (3/5 WTO member)
9 = JAPAN, KOREA, CHINA (since 2002 WTO member)
10 = CHINA (1990s)
11 = SOMALIA, SYRIA, IRAQ (PART OF ARAB FREE TRADE AREA)
12 = NORTH KOREA, IRAN, TURKMENISTAN, ERITREA, 8 MICRO-STATES
13 = APEC (intended to create a free trade area by 2010).

Figure 1.2 shows the position of the 11 most important and partly overlapping regional integration agreements along the vertical axis.[4] Regions where no single strong economy (or hegemonic power) exist – in particular, Europe and MERCOSUR (with two or more strong states) – have proceeded further on the track of deeper integration than regions with one dominant state – such as NAFTA (the United States), SAARC (India), CIS (Russia). It is unclear whether the existence of a state in a hegemonic position explains the lack of integration. This is something to research further for the car industry (see the remainder of this volume).

A number of 'go-it-alone' strategies thus can materialize even within regions. The relative unilateralism of a country within a region additionally depends on the nature of bilateral agreements that have been settled within that particular region and beyond that region. Five examples can further illustrate this mechanism:

Russia in CIS [7]: within CIS there exists a customs union with a few countries, but in addition a large number of bilateral trade agreements. Russia is the spider in this web of relations.

India in SAARC [6]: SAARC is a very weak expression of regionalism in which India is clearly the leading force. Discussions on a regional Free Trade Agreement (SAFTA) are still in their initial stage and suffer from the India–Pakistan dispute over military hegemony.

The United States in NAFTA [3]: apart from NAFTA, the United States did not engage in any regional nor bilateral trade treaties.[5] Contrary to the United States, in particular Mexico has struck various bilateral treaties with outside partners in Latin America, whilst more treaties (with EC, EFTA, Japan) are under negotiation. Discussion over the Free Trade Area of the Americas (FTAA) has just begun.

South Africa in SADC [4]: South Africa has initiated a customs union within SADC with six neighbouring countries that are much smaller (SACU), while additionally striking a bilateral free trade deal with the European Commission. Both deals further reinforce its position as the region's hegemon.

Brazil and Argentina in MERCOSUR [2]: Part of the animosity between Brazil and Argentina has been over alleged efforts of Brazil in particular to make use of its economic size and establish a hegemonic position. But, the differences in relative size of both countries are not so large that a dual hegemony is unconceivable which bars an inclination to go-it-alone. Nevertheless, the tension between regionalism and unilateralism within MERCOSUR is tangible. The access of Chile to MERCOSUR might further balance the relative powers.

ASEAN [5] and the European Union [1] are clear regions without any of the countries going for a unilateral strategy for instance by separate bilateral agreements with countries or other regions. In these regions, no formal hegemon exists which reduces 'go-it-alone' or opportunistic behaviour. This is not to say, of course, that individual countries do not seek to use their bargaining space to the full, but in the trade-off between deeper and more closed regionalism and multilateralism they clearly expect to reap more benefits from a shallow form of regional integration. Figure 1.2 also positions countries and regions along a horizontal axis specifying the degree of multilateralism by the year 2002. It is possible to adopt a relatively unilateral strategy even when being a member of the WTO or belonging to a regional integration agreement. The weaker the region, the greater the changes are for unilateralism within regionalism. Under these circumstances regionalism does not substitute for unilateralism, nor for multilateralism. The most revealing cases (1 to 10) have consequently been chosen for inclusion in this volume.

Figure 1.3 summarizes the three basic strategic repertoires that countries have been adopted in the final decade of the twentieth century, thereby choosing combinations of the three axes of debate exemplified above:

Regionalism: with different trade-offs between globalism/multilateralism and open/closed regionalism. Very weak regionalism would be easiest to characterize as 'open regionalism', but it might also relate to more advanced versions of regionalism. This depends upon the exact dynamism of the particular region. Within regionalism, particular countries might choose a relatively unilateral strategy. There seems to be a difference between regionalism involving only developed countries, regionalism between developed and developing countries and regionalism between only developing countries.

'Go-it-alone' – national: where the trade-off is between unilateralism/ autarky and unilateral/multilateralism.

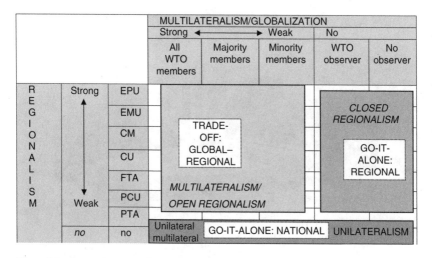

Figure 1.3 Strategic repertoires

'Go-it-alone' – **regional**: where the trade-off is basically between closed regionalism and unilateralism.

Cars ... carriers of regionalism

Regionalism in the automobile industry

Vehicle production basically occurs in zones characterized by strong processes of regionalization: for example, the EU and NAFTA accounted for more than half of the world's total automobile output in 2002. Including the other countries involved in regional trade agreements, more than 70 per cent of all automobile production is now concentrated in regional integration zones (Figure 1.4), compared with 56 per cent in 1990. The increase in the proportion of vehicle production in RTAs stems more from the rise of the phenomenon during the 1990s than from any particularly strong expansion in those zones that had already been integrated at a regional level.

More than half of all world automobile trading (56 per cent in 2000) occurs under the aegis of an RTA. Intra-regional trade within the two main industrialized zones (the European Union and NAFTA) has been particularly intensive, accounting for nearly three-quarters of all worldwide automobile trading. This activity has risen sharply in North America since the early 1990s – although it has fallen slightly in Europe. Table 1.1 indicates how, in addition to this one region (where trading had already been strongly integrated by 1990), other zones that have initiated regional integration processes have also experienced an intensification of automobile product exchange flows.

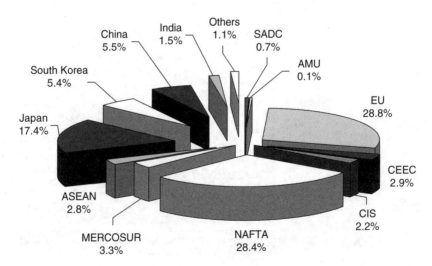

Figure 1.4 Geographical distribution of the worldwide vehicle production in 2002
Source: Organisation Internationale des Constructeurs Automobiles.

Table 1.1 Intra-regional trade in vehicles
(intra-regional [export + import] / total [export +
import])

	1990 (%)	2000 (%)
EU (European Union)	79.2	74.4
NAFTA	62.4	71.5
MERCOSUR	8.2	39.8
ASEAN	4.5	16.1
CIS	n.a.	31.9

Source: CHELEM data basis – R09 vehicles (including
automotive components).

One notable example is the integration processes in which developing
countries in Latin America (MERCOSUR) and Southeast Asia (ASEAN) have
been involved. Cross-trading within these regional areas has grown strongly,
even though intra-regional commerce remains less prevalent than in the
industrialized countries. Foreign multinationals (whether vehicle or equipment makers) predominate in these regions, a state of affairs that
is favourable to inter-regional trading with the home countries of these
MNEs (notably with Japan for ASEAN, Europe and the United States for
MERCOSUR and Europe for the CEEC and Russia).

The same trend can be detected with regard to foreign direct investment
(FDI): European carmakers invest in Europe (Ruigrok and Van Tulder, 1995;
Bélis-Bergouignan, Bordenave and Lung, 2000), US carmakers in Canada
and Mexico (which accounted for 75 per cent and 60 per cent of their automobile output in 2002, respectively) and Japanese manufacturers in Asia. In
certain cases, firms coming from other parts of the world have gone the
furthest down the road towards the regional organization of their spatial
division of labour. Their external focus enabled them to adopt a more
aggressive attitude than the national automakers could do when negotiating their internationalization process (notably in their dealings with labour
unions). For example, by acting in this manner Ford was able to become the
first truly 'Europeanized' carmaker in this part of the world (Bonin, Lung and
Tolliday, 2003) – a status that Volkswagen could only achieve by acquiring
Seat and Skoda.

The dialectics of regionalism

In practice, managers have increasingly recognized the benefit of 'political
strategies' (Baron, 2000). At the same time, politicians have begun to recognize the importance of non-state actors in regional integration (Cowles,
1995). Politicians start regionalism with a perception of the strategic response
and interests of firms, whereas business strategists envisage particular

options on an optimal configuration of the region for them. In the European integration trajectory, for instance, the Commission had clear expectations that the Internal Market would have a significant effect on economies of scale, competitiveness and competition for European firms. These expectations only partly materialized not in the last place because of a different-than-anticipated response by leading firms under which a large number of the car manufacturers (cf. Muller and Van Tulder, 2002).

Car firms have been actively helping to mould most of the regional integration initiatives in a number of ways. First, by their trade and investment decisions. In most regions and countries, a small number of car manufacturers constitute the country's largest investors, employers and traders in industrialized (EU, NAFTA) and developing areas. They thus became major stakeholders in regionalism.

Secondly, it should not come as a surprise that the car firms themselves have been amongst the strongest lobbyists for regionalism. The Single European Market would have been unthinkable without the lobbying efforts of the European Round Table of Industrialists, containing many of the leading European car manufacturers, and the formation of NAFTA was strongly supported by the Big Three US car manufacturers (and strongly opposed by their trade unions). In developing regions, like MERCOSUR, ASEAN and SADC, lobbying in favour of regionalism came in particular from foreign car manufacturers, whilst sometimes opposed by local car manufacturers that feared a 'colonisation' of the region and a frustration of local initiatives to develop an independent car industry.

Exploring the multilateral trade arena: car disputes within the WTO

Creating an automobile space implies exploring the boundaries and possibilities provided by the multilateral trade arena. In the first two years following the initiation of the WTO, trade disputes about cars were a rather prominent feature (Table 1.2). But the car industry as an area of multilateral contention quickly petered out.

Developing countries have become more actively involved in WTO as plaintiffs in general, but not with regard to the car industry (cf. Yin, 2001). Table 1.3 shows that governments from developed countries have over-proportionally used WTO dispute settlement procedures in the car industry to complain about developing countries' policies.

Table 1.4 reveals the details of the complaints. Those countries most persistently targeted by the developed countries have been 'go-it-alone' countries and/or the biggest members of a peripheral RIA: India, Indonesia (ASEAN), Poland (CEFTA), Brazil (MERCOSUR), but also Australia (ANZCERTA). None of the smaller countries of a regional integration agreement has ever been targeted in any of the dispute settlement procedures since 1995. In particular, India and Indonesia have been the target of clustered strategies by all major car-producing countries (in varying

Table 1.2 Number of trade disputes brought by the WTO, 1995–2001

Year	Total	Total acc.	Car-specific disputes	
			Total (%)	Total accumulative (%)
1995	22	22	2(9)	2(9)
1996	41	64	6(9)	8(13)
1997	45	110	3(7)	11(8)
1998	43	154	3(7)	14(9)
1999	30	185	1(3)	15(8)
2000	29	215	1(3)	16(7)
2001 (12 Dec.)	26	242	0	16(6.6)

Source: Elaborated on the basis of WTO information.

Table 1.3 Number of trade disputes, complaint requests under WTO, 1995–2001

Complaining country	Respondent country	WTO general		WTO cars	
		No. of cases	% of total	No. of cases	% of total
Developed country	Developed	87	39.5	4	23.5
	Developing	64	29.1	11	64.7
Developing country	Developed	43*	19.5	0	0
	Developing	26	11.8	2	11.8

Note: * Including 11 cases filed by both developed and developing countries.

Source: Overview of the state of WTO disputes, Jan. 15, 2001, WTO site, December 2001; Yin et al., 2001: 8.

alliances). Conversely, Canada has been targeted by Japan and the EU because of its Auto Pact with the United States. This approach – together with a formal arbitration procedure – reveals the tactics of bargaining amongst the developed countries car manufacturers to evade direct confrontation within WTO. The only case of a direct complaint of Japan, the EC and Australia with the United States was settled by consultation. No developing country filed any complaint against western countries in cars, whereas the only two cases of inter-developing countries' complaints were settled by the countries themselves (Peru and Brazil; India and Poland). The car industry mirrors the general patterns of international dispute settlement: intra-regional conflicts do not appear – implying that regionalism prevails over multilateralism – while only the developing countries that have adopted a largely 'go-it-alone' strategy are addressed through the multilateral dispute settlement procedure.

14

Table 1.4   WTO disputes on cars, 1995–December 2001

Date	Defendant	Plaintiff	Joined by … (in sequence)	Topic	Mode of settlement
22/5/95	USA	Japan	EC, Australia	'imposition of import duties on Japanese autos'	Consultation
18/10/95	Poland	India	—	'import policies for autos'	Mutually agreed solution
6/8/96	Brazil	Japan	Korea, EC/USA, Canada	'certain auto investment measures'	Consultation
14/8/96	Brazil	USA	Jap, Can, Korea, EC	'measures affecting trade and investment in the automotive sector'	Consultation
10/10/96	Indonesia	Japan	US, EC, Can, Korea	'certain measures affecting the automobile industry'	Panel, ruling, arbitration
14/10/96	Indonesia	EC	US, Jap, Korea, Can	'certain measures affecting the automobile industry'	Panel, ruling, arbitration
15/10/96	Indonesia	USA	Jap, Korea, EC, Canada	'certain automotive industry measures'	Panel, ruling, arbitration
5/12/96	Indonesia	Japan	US, EC	'certain automotive industry measures'	Panel, ruling, arbitration
17/1/97	Brazil	USA	—	'trade and investment' (complaint about specific treatment of competitors)	Consultation
20/5/97	Brazil	EC	—	'measures affecting trade and investment in the automotive sector'	Consultation

Table 1.4 Continued

Date	Defendant	Plaintiff	Joined by ...(in sequence)	Topic	Mode of settlement
17/11/97	Australia	USA	—	'subsidies ... automotive leather'	Panel
8/1/98	Peru	Brazil	—	'countervailing duty investigation against imports of buses from Brazil'	Consultation
8/7/98	Canada	Japan	EU	'certain measures affecting the automotive industry' (Auto Pact manufacturers)	Panel, appellate body
21/8/98	Canada	EC	Japan	'certain measures affecting the automotive industry'	Panel, arbitration
12/10/98	India	EC	USA	'measures affecting the automotive sector'	Panel
7/6/99	India	USA	Japan, EC	'measures affecting trade and investment in the motor vehicle sector'	Panel (request EU, US)
31/5/00	Philippines	USA	—	'measures affecting trade and investment in the motor vehicle sector'	Panel

Source: Compiled on the basis of WTO information: www.wto.org/wto/dispute/dsu.htm.

A viable 'automobile space'

The chapters in this volume should provide further evidence of the interaction between political and business strategies at national, regional and global levels. This interaction is offering the new prospect of an 'automobile space', the geographical level at which supply and demand in the auto industry can become coupled. This volume addresses the question of whether or not the various forms of regionalism under way will be able to create conditions under which car manufacturers can connect productive organization and markets in a sustainable/viable manner. A sustainable or viable (regional) automobile space implies that the new arrangements or production, of marketing of regulation and the like help to address and alleviate the sources of tension, uncertainty and instability that are at the root of the restructuring of the car industry.

A viable (regional) automobile space should create the circumstances under which virtuous growth cycles which link sophisticated supply and appropriate demand can develop. This volume considers the nature of the 'new space' developing under the influence of company and government strategies. Governments as well as firms – in a dynamic interaction – try to shape markets and production systems. It is the aim of this volume to assess the two sides of the regional reconfiguration process: the way in which governments try to influence firm strategies by striking regional integration agreements and the way in which firms influence governments through investment and lobbying strategies.

The term automobile space refers to a *geographical* level of regulation of the relationships between the supply and the demand in the auto industry, i.e. the level of connection between a productive organization and the market. New forms of automobile space are developing at various levels of analysis: local, national, macro-regional, multi-regional, global. At each level we could witness new forms of linking markets and production systems. The linkages get shaped in particular as the result of the interaction between firms and governments. Both actors have an impact on the nature and extent of markets as well as production systems.

Firms developed particular *productive models* (production organization in a network configuration) which led to the choice for a product portfolio (specialization, diversification, differentiation, niche strategies) and for particular marketing and distribution strategies (Boyer and Freyssenet, 2002). Firms also have internationalization trajectories. States have developed particular regulation regimes (industrial, technology, trade, labour market, taxation), but have also increasingly engaged in internationalization trajectories themselves by allying with other states in the forms of bilateral treaties, regional integration initiatives and/or global arrangements for instance under the auspices of the WTO. Both actors have been developing these strategies partly independent of each other, and partly in interaction with each other. Both actors thus define and design production and market space.

The redefinition of the production system and the supply and demand links has gone furthest in the European Union. The North American Free Trade Agreement (NAFTA) has acted as a clear new phase in the productive organization of the American car industry as well as of foreign investors. These two regional integration initiatives have changed the traditional automobile space which consists of the poles of the Triad: Europe, North America and Japan. The nature of the linkages between production organization and markets in Europe and North America is changing, and this has an impact on the nature of the interaction between the triad countries as well.

The regional dynamism also has repercussions for regions, countries and firms that are *not* engaged in the regions involved. Their productive organizations as well as markets are influenced by the creation of regions elsewhere. But in some cases these countries and firms from these countries have chosen to exclude themselves the regional integration processes. For instance, for various reasons Japanese and South Korean firms have not really pushed for an integration of their countries in regional integration initiatives. In the case of some developing countries (for example, China and India), the reasons not to engage in wider integration initiatives have been primarily political. Russia is trying to reconstitute its automobile space at a regional level within the Commonwealth of Independent States – without any current adherence to the multilateral trade system. The dynamism of the inter-regional interaction in terms of production organization and market integration, ultimately determines the viability of a process towards globalization in the car industry.

Layout of the volume

Regionalism is a multifaceted phenomenon. The present volume covers four dimensions of this phenomenon. In Part I (A World of Regions?), the political and firm strategic dimensions of regionalism are further specified. In Chapter 2 Van Tulder and Audet ('The Faster Lane of Regionalism'), consider the comparative political dynamics of regional integration strategies after the early 1990s. In particular, they consider whether the various regions can be dubbed 'closed' or 'open' by documenting the extent to which intra-regional flows of investment and trade have been matched by extra-regional flows in general and specifically for the car industry. Generic inernational strategies of car companies are considered in Chapter 3 by Freyssenet and Lung ('Multinational Carmakers' Regional Strategies'), who ask: What are the strategic trade-offs at the firm level between national, regional or global strategies?

Part II deals with the dynamism of Regional Integration With(in) Developed Regions. Developed regions provide the home base of some of the world's most important car manufacturers and generally have larger markets. Economies of scale and the potential of a regional division of labour are bigger. Chapter 4 first explores the dynamism within the most advanced region of the world: the European Union. Layan and Lung ('The Dynamics of Regional Integration in the European Car Industry') take the history of the European Union into consideration. The automobile space created by the original six founding fathers of the European Economic Community differed from the phase in which less developed countries were integrated. In this phase not much happened in terms of a new organization of production. After developing countries like Spain and Portugal entered the European Community, a regional division of labour was implemented which created different production system that also changed marketing strategies. Chapter 5 by Van Tulder ('Peripheral Regionalism: the Consequences of Integrating Central and Eastern Europe in the European Automobile Space') considers the tremendous changes that occurred after the fall of the Berlin Wall in the Central and Eastern European automobile space. Market and production motives developed in parallel. Despite the formation of an own regional free trade area (CEFTA), the importance of the (prospective) integration of these countries inside the European Union cannot be underestimated. Chapter 6 considers the automobile space developing in a country that wants to become a member of the European Union, that even has a customs union with the EU, but that is unlikely to enter the European Union in the next ten years. Duruiz's chapter on Turkey ('Challenges for the Turkish Car Industry on its Way to Integration with the EU') shows the peripheral and dependent route of Turkey in this respect. Are there possibilities for Turkey to link Europe to the Middle East, thereby creating its own automobile space? Chapter 7, the final chapter in Part II, looks at the dynamism of regionalism in the second most important car region in the world: NAFTA. The chapter contributed by Carillo ('Evolution and the Future of Motor Vehicle Production in the NAFTA Region') analyses the impact of the much more shallow form of regional integration that has developed in North America. The nature of regionalism has a different impact on the nature of restructuring of firms and the creation of an economic and automobile space in North America. The strategic parallels with the European Union are obvious, but the impact on a regional automobile space has been different partly because of the unilateral strategy of the United States within the North American region.

Part III focuses on Regionalism in Developing/Emerging Regions. Developing regions are frequently externally dominated. Leading producers are often subsidiaries of car producers that have their lead markets and production sites elsewhere. The chapters in this part thus document what 'dependent' regionalism might look like and what the consequences for independent policies are. Does the regional integration initiative spur developments; what are the institutional arrangements under debate to obtain such objectives? What is the likely outcome of these developments? Chapter 8 by Laplane and Sarti ('Interaction between Government and Producers') monitors the changing automobile space in MERCOSUR. The anticipated growth of the market – as well as protectionist policies – in the 1960s and 1970s favoured the development of an automobile industry, largely consisting of host-based firms from the United States and Europe. Chapter 9 by Shimokawa ('ASEAN: Developing a Division of Labour in a Developing Region') takes the dependent regionalism in the ASEAN/AFTA countries under consideration, where the dominant actors are Japanese car manufacturers. The dominant interests of Japanese firms influenced the relatively weak form of regional integration, but consecutive steps towards particular forms of deeper integration can clearly be attributed to the efforts of Japanese firms to develop a regional division of labour. Chapter 10 by Chanaron ('Recreating an Automobile Space by Regional Integration: the CIS Perspective'), shows the efforts of the Russian car industry to use the CIS region in its effort to link supply and demand beyond the too small confines of the national Russian economy. The Russian car industry provides an excellent test of the question of whether it is viable to develop an automobile independently from the western car manufacturers. Chapter 11, by Black and Muradzikwa, ('Limits to Regionalism: the Automotive Industry in SADC') analyses the dynamism of a weak region, dominated by one local hegemon that aims at deeper regional integration, but in which foreign car manufacturers prevail. Are there any prospects for a vibrant automobile space under such circumstances? The final chapter in this part, Chapter 12 by Layan and Mezouaghi ('Maghrebi Integration and the Automobile Industry: Past Failures, and New Perspectives'), considers a region that developed under the influence of the unfolding European integration process, but without any prospect of immediate integration, as in the case of CEFTA (Chapter 5).

But, as stated earlier in this introductory chapter, regionalism has not been embraced by all states. Part IV considers the challenges experienced by the four major proponents of a 'go-it-alone' strategy: Japan, South Korea, China and India. This part will address the question whether or not countries and firms can 'afford' not to be integrated in macro-regions. The first two chapters of this part will deal with developed countries that already possess an 'automobile space' linking well-developed markets with a relatively competitive production structure. Chapter 13 by Van Tulder ('The Risk of "Go-it-Alone": the Japanese Car Industry – From Boom to Bust?') documents the relatively unilateral strategy of Japan and the resulting very uncertain and rather inimical international setting in which Japanese car manufacturers had to operate. The weaker performance, and subsequently the takeover of some of the leading car producers, is related to the risks of 'go-it-alone'. But some Japanese manufacturers have also adopted an 'informal' regionalism towards China and within the ASEAN region, which might turn out to be a solution. South Korean firms and the South Korean automobile space developed much later and remained relatively weak. Their internationalization strategies targeted rather peripheral production sites and markets as part of a drastic effort to enter the global car industry. Combined with the relative isolationism of the country, these ingredients have proved to be very detrimental to the survival of an independent South Korean car industry. Chapter 14 by Lautier (' "Avoiding the Neighbours": the National/Global Development Strategy of the Korean Automobile Industry') documents the entry and the exit of the South Korean car industry.

Two developing countries have not entered any deep regional integration initiatives but should be considered 'regions' on their own. China and India contain potentially huge markets, have developed their own production expertise to various degrees and are clearly prepared to use their political leverage towards car producers in order to strike more equitable deals – for instance, through the establishment of technology transfer agreements. Chapter 15 by Thun ('Going Local') considers the Chinese experience in using foreign direct investment in specific micro-regions to develop a rapidly growing and competitive automobile space that also integrates a number of local producers. Chapter 16 on India by Kim ('Global Auto Companies' Struggles in India') analyses the competition between multinational car firms in India. Are the indigenous firms in China and India likely to survive and what does this imply for a sustainable strategy of 'go-it-alone' vis-à-vis regionalism or globalism?

Part I

A World of Regions?

2
The Faster Lane of Regionalism

Rob van Tulder and Denis Audet

Introduction[1]

The second wave of regionalism that materialized in the 1990s raised fears that the world could split into major economic blocks, more or less self-contained. RIAs are seen as a threat to a global, multilateral system of free trade (Bhagwati, 1993), since they are inherently discriminatory, giving more favourable treatment to member countries. Whether RIAs facilitate or hamper trade and investment flows within the region and with third parties provides a litmus test for assessing the direction of regional integration: is it a move towards more openness or one towards more closedness? Open regionalism can be defined as the process by which the regional opening of markets as well as the benefits of the regulations can be extended to third countries on a reciprocal or Most Favoured Nation basis (OECD, 1995: 82). It is often very difficult to assess whether this is the case, due to a variety of non-tariff barriers. This chapter will suggest that in some conditions the process of regionalism is considered to lead to more openness, since the process means that the region becomes indeed more open to extra-regional trade and investment. Yet in other circumstances, the region is de facto becoming more closed or more inward-looking – despite there being no official barriers to trade for countries not belonging to the region.[2] Closed regionalism can be defined as regionalism in which third countries have relative difficulties in reaping equal benefits of integration – for instance, when intra-regional trade substitutes for extra-regional trade. The establishment of a 'regional automobile space' implies that supply and demand structures become increasingly linked at the regional level (see the introduction to this volume). A first macroeconomic proxy for the development of regional automobile spaces can be found in researching the trade data of the countries included in RIAs and also those countries that have not been included in RIAs.

A typology of regional integration agreements

RIAs represent a wide variety of forms. Seven RIAs are the prime focus of this book: the EU, NAFTA, ASEAN, MERCOSUR, SADC, CEFTA, Maghreb. They represent the most important contemporary expressions of macroregionalism. Table 2.1 lists the accession dates of all member countries of these initiatives.

The RIAs in Table 2.1 differ significantly in a number of ways. Combining the classifications of Balassa (1961), Jovanovic (1997) and Dent (1997), one can distinguish between seven forms of regionalism representing everdeeper levels of political and economic integration (Table 2.2).

Regional integration is not necessarily a uniform process in which all countries go through the same consecutive phases. For instance, new entrants in an already established RIA often have to adapt to an already established stage of integration. Countries in a RIA can also decide to 'leap ahead' to a further phase, bypassing intermediary phases. On the other hand, sometimes countries 'leap backwards' by not participating in further (planned) steps – as, for example, in the case of European integration.

Table 2.1 Regional integration agreements and participating members

Name	*Members (accession date)*
EU (European Union)	Austria (95), Belgium (51), Denmark (73), Finland (95), France (51), Germany (51), Greece (81), Ireland (73), Italy (51), Luxembourg (51), Netherlands (51), Portugal (86), Spain (86), Sweden (95), United Kingdom (73)
NAFTA (North American Free Trade Association)	Canada, Mexico, United States (94)
ASEAN (Association of South East Asian Nations)	Brunei (84), Cambodia (99), Indonesia (67), Laos (97), Malaysia (67), Myanmar/Burma (97), Philippines (67), Singapore (67), Thailand (67), Vietnam (95)
MERCOSUR (Mercado Común del Sur)	Argentina, Brazil, Paraguay, Uruguay (1991)
SADC (South African Development Community)	Angola (92), Botswana (92), Congo (97), Lesotho (92), Malawi (92), Mauritius (95), Mozambique (92), Namibia (92), Seychelles (97), South Africa (94), Swaziland (92), Tanzania (92), Zambia (92), Zimbabwe (92)
CEFTA (Central European Free Trade Association)	Bulgaria (99), Czechoslovakia (92), Hungary (92), Poland (92), Romania (97), Slovenia (96)
AMU (Arab Maghreb Union)	Algeria, Libya, Mauritania, Morocco, Tunisia (89)
ANZCERTA (Australia–New Zealand Closer Economic Relations Trade Agreement (also: CER))	Australia, New Zealand (83)

Table 2.2 Main characteristics of regional integration

Form of integration		Main characteristics
PTA	Preferential Trade Agreement	• Mutual preferential treatment of signatories, involving lower customs duties/tariffs as due by non-signatories.
PCU	Partial Customs Union	• Application of a Common External Tariff (CET) against non-signatories. • Regular customs duties/tariffs both by signatories and non-signatories.
FTA	Free Trade Area	• Removal of (most) customs duties/tariffs for signatories. • Individual, national customs duties/tariffs against non-signatories. • Local content/rule of origin-measures.
CU	Customs Union	• Removal of (most) customs duties/tariffs for signatories: • Application of CET against non-signatories.
CM	Common Market	• Like CU, but also includes: • Free movement of factors of production (capital, goods, services, labour).
EMU	Economic and Monetary Union	• Like CM, but also includes: • Common currency.
EPU	Economic and Political Union	• Like EMU, but also includes: • Common policies on a broad range of topics, including foreign politics and military issues.

Empirical patterns

One of the main questions regarding the effect of RIAs is whether or not they are accompanied by an increase in economic activity within the region, outside the region, or both. This section of our chapter appraises the macro-level evidence about the eight regional integration initiatives for the 1984–1999 period in order to cover most relevant regime changes related to the second wave of regionalism. Traditional approaches to regionalism distinguish between two dynamic effects of integration: (1) trade/investment creation: when the volume of trade and investment is higher than before the regional integration initiative; and (2) trade/investment diversion: when the volume of trade and investment is redirected towards other countries, but does not actually increase in volume. This section considers the macroeconomic data in order to assess whether regions are becoming more 'closed' (or inward looking) or more 'open' (or outward looking), in terms of trade and investment regimes. There is both an absolute and a relative dimension to this process:

(1) *Absolute*, if trade and foreign investment flows to and from the region constitute a substantial part of GDP; a region that has for instance 25 per cent of its GDP dedicated to trade and investment flows outside the region should be considered to be more open than a region that has only 10 per cent or less of its GDP dedicated to trade;

(2) *Relative*, when extra-regional trade/investment volumes are more important than intra-regional trade/investment volumes, one can also speak of a more 'open' region. In case growth in extra-regional trade and investment volumes surpasses that of intra-regional volumes, the region can be considered relatively more closed.

Regulation regimes – including an automobile space – under open market and investment conditions differ considerably from regimes operating under more closed market and investment conditions. Open regionalism appears when economic integration in the region does not act as a substitute for economic linkages to the outside region. At its best open regionalism combines growing intra-regional flows with growing extra-regional flows. By contrast, closed regionalism appears when intra-regional trade and investment substitute for extra-regional trade and investment: the growth of intra-regional flows comes at the expense of extra-regional flows, thus contributing to a more closed nature of the region.

RIAs and the appearance of open/closed trade regimes

Figure 2.1 presents the trade data for the eight regional integration initiatives for the 1984–1999 period. For each region the most recent country membership is taken and observed for the whole period as an indication of the changing importance of the region (not necessarily the RIA). So, for instance, for the European Union, the 1984 data include the extra and intra-regional trade for the 15 member states of the EU since 1995. This measure is used in order to avoid obvious effects such as the temporary increase in intra-regional trade because of the change of members of a RIA. One has to bear in mind, therefore, that the trade data presented in Figure 2.1 are only a *minimum* measure of the changes in trade accompanied by the RIA. For individual countries the changes are even more substantial.

Absolute importance of total trade volume. The importance of trade volumes (the left axis) for each region varies. Total trade for the European Union, ANZCERTA, CEFTA, Maghreb and SADC countries is equal in value to 20–25 per cent of GDP. These regions can be characterized as being fairly open to trade, but not much more open than they were at the beginning of the 1980s. At the other extreme, MERCOSUR and NAFTA constitute relatively closed regions, with less than 10 per cent of their GDP traded outside the regions.

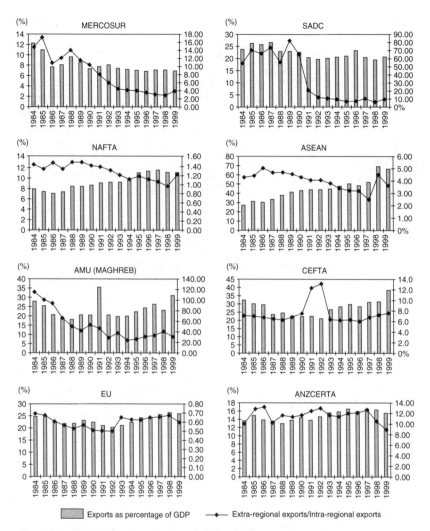

Figure 2.1 Regionalization of exports, 1984–1999

Sources: IMF DOT statistics; World Bank, own calculations.

Relative importance of the region. In taking the relative openness of a region into account, one indicator is the degree of extra-intra-regional trade. In Figure 2.1 this indicator is exemplified by the drawn line (right scale). According to this measure the most open regions are clearly Maghreb and SADC, with extra-regional trade in each case amounting to more than sixty times the intra-regional trade during the 1980s. At the end of the 1990s

ANZCERTA was in a comparable position with extra-regional trade twelve times the volume of intra-regional trade. CEFTA, MERCOSUR and ASEAN constitute a second grouping of regions with extra-regional trade worth anywhere between two and six times the value of intra-regional trade. For each of these six RIAs, the relative openness of the region implies that intra-regional economic development is vulnerable to external influences, making it equally hard to develop autonomous models (spaces of regulation). The final grouping comprises the European Union and NAFTA. For the EU countries intra-regional trade has consistently prevailed over extra-regional trade, making it by this measure the most closed region in the world. NAFTA recently balanced its outward and inward orientation.

The general dynamics of intra-/extra-regional trade flows represents declining or stabilizing extra-regional trade. So all eight regions have either remained relatively closed (developed countries) or substantially increased their relative closedness in terms of international trade (developing countries). The trade data show that some regions have become more closed or less open, but this does not necessarily imply that this process represents a step *away* from 'globalization'. Both regionalism and globalization can develop at the same time. But the more closed nature of the regions implies that, over the course of the 1990s, the process of regionalization in trade has in any case proceeded faster than the process of globalization.

RIAs and the appearance of open/closed investment regimes

Research on the effects of RIA on economic activities and foreign direct investment (FDI) has tended to focus on FDI flows between the United States, the European Union and Japan. Studies to date have been rather inconclusive: some studies, for example, have indicated that EC formation has attracted much US FDI that might otherwise have ended up elsewhere (cf. Dunning, 1992), but this has been contested. There is a gap in the literature concerning outflows of FDI after RIAs. It also remains an issue of debate what the relationship between the two dimensions (inflows and outflows) is. It may be intuitively correct to take into account the relatively increased attractiveness of the NAFTA region for US capital when considering US FDI outflows to the EU in the 1990s, but the theory and empirics are as yet inconclusive.

With these caveats in mind, this section considers some of the empirical evidence on investment flows in the regions under consideration. The stocks (i.e. accumulated flows) of *inward* and *outward* FDI as a percentage of GDP represent the best available indicator of the openness of a region or a country.

Absolute importance of total investment volume. Of all the countries included in the eight RIAs, Singapore is the country with the highest degree of openness, with inward FDI stock equal in value to 82 per cent of GDP. Taken as a whole, the ASEAN region – although there are no comprehensive regional data available – can be characterized as the most *inwardly* open region. The region embraces hardly any country with outward-oriented investment, with the exceptions of Malaysia and Singapore which perform an important 'hub' function with regard to the region.

In MERCOSUR and SADC, Brazil and Argentina, and South Africa, respectively, fulfill similar 'hub' functions, with noticeable stocks of outward FDI, primarily invested in the region. The degree of inward investment in MERCOSUR and SADC, however, remains relatively limited (around 10–15 per cent of GDP). In general, for all regions containing only developing countries, the pattern of negligible outward FDI stock and substantial inward FDI stock is visible.

The RIAs containing primarily developed countries share a number of characteristics. Their outward *and* inward stock of FDI is considerable. Only in the case of NAFTA does this lead to a balanced FDI picture. In the EU there is an outward investment surplus, whereas in ANZCERTA the inward investment by far surpasses outward investment. ANZCERTA belongs to the regions with the highest openness towards inward investments (Australia 26 per cent of GDP and New Zealand 50 per cent of GDP in 1997). The European Union countries are more open to inward investment than the NAFTA countries. Even Mexico has an inward FDI stock (12.5 per cent in 1997) that is lower than for the whole EU combined (15.2 per cent). Likewise, the external orientation of the EU in FDI is greater than that of NAFTA (almost twice the level in 1997).

Importance of the region. It has been relatively undisputed that the EU project attracted an immense inflow of FDI (Dunning, 1997). In more concrete terms: in particular, Japanese firms invested in Europe from a fear of a closed 'Fortress Europe'. Having established a sufficient presence in the EU, they substantially reduced their investment flows.

Within NAFTA, inflows of FDI in Mexico (the second largest recipient of FDI inflows in Latin America) have been directed towards manufacturing industries producing for the greater North American market. For Mexico, therefore, more than for the USA and Canada, the investment regime of NAFTA has made a difference. According to UNCTAD, the four countries of MERCOSUR all experienced a surge of FDI inflows as a result of the extension of the MERCOSUR. Intra-regional investment flows have been conducted mainly by Brazilian and Argentinean companies (three-quarters of Argentinean investments for instance; UNCTAD, 1999: 66).

Almost two-thirds of investment in the CEE countries originates in the European Union, thus further illustrating the effect of possible accession to the EU. The intra-regional investments for CEFTA are still negligible. The same can be said for SADC, though the level of South African investment outflows took up considerable pace five years after the Apartheid regime ended and international sanctions against the country were lifted (UNCTAD, 1999: 48) and after South Africa joined SADC in 1994 the effect experienced by the other countries of SADC seems to be running increasingly through the increased influence of South Africa on the region (cf. Ten Napel, 1998).

FDI flows into the ASEAN countries were severely affected by the Asian financial crisis (FDI decreased by 23 per cent in 1997–1998). Governments sought to counter the crisis not only through national measures, but also increasingly through regional measures. The effects of RIA membership in Southeast Asia have been particularly noticeable for the new entrants. By joining ASEAN, it can be hypothesized, these countries added credibility to their desire to integrate into the global economy.

The effect of ANZCERTA on the attraction of investment has also been anticipatory. For both New Zealand and Australia a substantial increase in inward investment ran parallel to the implementation of the RIA, but for both countries the effect petered out after 1995. The effect of Maghreb has clearly been the weakest of all of the RIAs under consideration. No major mutual investment projects seem to have materialized in the course of the 1990s under the auspices of the AMU.

Conclusion: a mixed picture of openness and closedness

This section has analysed the degree to which regions have become more open or more closed. It is difficult to assess to what extent these processes have exactly been triggered by the actual formalization of RIAs. What has been observed, however, are a number of parallel developments that have accompanied the second wave in RIAs, but claims about their causality lie beyond the scope of this chapter. Table 2.3 summarizes major trends in openness towards trade and investment for each of the eight RIAs.

A limited, but nevertheless telling, regional integration effect can be observed. In trade flows, regions are either stable or decreasingly open, whereas the picture is more mixed for investment flows. Trade/investment diversion and trade/investment creation can thereby go hand in hand. For some RIAs the dynamism clearly comes from within the region, for other RIAs outside influences cause the changes in the own region.

Regional integration and the automotive industry

Does the general picture as delineated in section 3 translate to the appearance of equally open or closed 'automobile spaces'? What are the consequences of those spaces for third parties? This section considers in particular the statistical evidence on new trade relations surrounding five core car regions: the EU, NAFTA, CEFTA, ANZCERTA and MERCOSUR.

Policies towards regionally integrated automotive markets

Ideally, a regionally integrated automobile space requires unhindered access for all regionally based manufacturers to rationalize production on a

Table 2.3 Summary of openness/closedness of eight RIAs

	Trade			FDI			
	Exports/GDP*	Extra-/Intra-regional	Dynamics	Inward FDI/GDP#	Outward FDI/GDP#	Extra-/Intra-regional	Dynamics
EU	Relatively open	Relatively intra-regional	Stable	Medium	High–medium	Outward open	Increasing open
NAFTA	Relatively closed	In balance	Increasing closedness	Relatively closed	Low–medium	Balanced	Stable
MERCOSUR	Relatively closed	Medium extra-regional	Increasing closedness	Medium	Closed	Inward open	Increasing open
ASEAN	Very open	Medium extra-regional	Declining openness	Very open	Closed	Inward open	Increasing openness
SADC	Relatively open	Strong extra-regional	Declining openness	Relatively closed	Closed	Inward open	Declining closedness
ANZCERTA	Relatively open	Strong extra-regional	Stable openness	Very open	Medium	Inward open	Stagnant openness
CEFTA	Relatively open	Medium extra-regional	Stable openness	Relatively open	Closed	Inward open	Increasing openness
Maghreb	Relatively open	Strong extra-regional	Declining openness	Relatively closed	Closed	Inward open	Declining closedness

Notes
* relatively open: 20–25% of GDP; relatively closed: <10%; very open: >25%.
# very open: >20%; medium: 10–20%; relatively closed: 5–10%; closed: 0–5% FDI stock as % of GDP.

Table 2.4   Rules of origin in free trade agreements

Free trade agreement	Regional content (%)	Specific rules
European Agreements*	60	Diagonal cumulation
NAFTA (1994–2002)	50–62.5	Light vehicles
	50–60	Other vehicles
MERCOSUR	58–67.5	1996–1999
CEFTA	60	Diagonal cumulation
ANZCERTA	50	

Note: * These refer to the FTAs of the EU with Central and Eastern European countries.

regional basis and to achieve efficiency gains. Rationalization and efficiency can be further enhanced under competitive pressure from manufacturers based outside the region. Still, in some cases, anti-competitive practices – that is, policies that nurture rent-seeking activities shielded behind border protection and distorting subsidies – are (temporarily) maintained. Many other obstacles to a completely free regional market exist as well – such as the absence of harmonization or mutual recognition of automobile-related standards.

Access to third parties may also be hindered when a level of tariff protection is set that is higher than existed before the formation of the RIA. In addition, the application of the rules of origin that confer duty-free status to intra-regional trade within FTAs may be excessively complex or expensive to comply with, thus providing an incentive for manufacturers to give preference to sourcing inputs from regional origins over imported inputs. Table 2.4 gives an overview of such rules of origin in existing FTAs.

Additionally, import licenses may be made conditional upon relatively opaque rules and more subtle forms of export restraint arrangements may significantly reduce import competition from third parties. All these considerations are examined below for five RIAs.

The EU's integrated automobile space

Since 1974, the EU common external tariff (CET) on imported passenger vehicles has remained unchanged at 10 per cent (Audet and Van Grasstek, 1997: 39). As a result, by the year 2000 the EU tariff was higher than prevailing tariffs in major automobile-producing countries, but lower than that in place in emerging automobile-producing countries. Despite this tariff stability, market access in the EU fluctuated in line with specific policy decisions related to the accession of new EU member states in 1995, the entry into force of several free trade agreements and a bilateral arrangement with Japan. With EU enlargement in 1995, which resulted in Sweden, Finland and Austria becoming members, the decision was taken to keep the CET tariff on passenger vehicles unchanged, even though the prevailing tariffs were lower in both Sweden (6.2 per cent) and Finland (5.3 per cent) prior to their accession – the Austrian tariff, by contrast, was 20 per cent. Countries affected by the tariff increases have obtained equivalent off-setting tariff concessions in the context of the required negotiations under Article XXIV of the WTO.

While the EU is itself a customs union, it has been very active in negotiating FTAs with numerous countries and groups of countries. The most relevant ones are the European Economic Area (EEA), several 'European Agreements' with Central and Eastern European Countries (CEECs) and several Euro-Mediterranean Agreements. In entering into these FTAs, the EU opened up its automotive market to a large number of countries, albeit on a preferential and ultimately reciprocal basis. In the same vein, the cumulative rules of origin effectively extend the application of uniform rules to a large number of countries, which ultimately provide for greater flexibility to manufacturers in securing inputs from a larger pool of countries, thereby underpinning stronger competitive conditions. The implementation of these agreements has not always been free of controversy, such as when Poland raised its duties on passenger vehicles in 1992 and modified the duty-free quota provided to the EU in the period between signing the agreement and its entry into force.

During the Uruguay Round of trade negotiations, the EU did not offer any reduction in its tariff on passenger vehicles. Rather, it agreed to phase out the application of the voluntary restraint arrangement (VRA) with Japan by 31 December 1999 (see Chapter 4). This concession was made with reference to the new measures negotiated under the WTO Safeguards Agreement that prohibit new VRAs and provide that those in effect in 1995, when the WTO entered into force, had to be phased out.[3]

Although the EU integration process started in 1957 with the Treaty of Rome, harmonization of safety standards for motor vehicles and mutual recognition of certification of conformity procedures among all EU member states was only achieved in 1993 and 1996 respectively. These were instrumental in the implementation of the EU Single Market for motor vehicles and contributed to minimizing the price differential that existed within the EU due to regulatory factors. Another key dimension of the EU regional automobile space is its competition law.[4] The European Commission has actually sanctioned car manufacturers that have infringed on the relevant EU competition law.[5]

NAFTA's integrated automobile space

Passenger vehicle imports in NAFTA countries are subjected to tariffs at the prevailing rate applicable in the importing NAFTA country. The import duty in 2000 is 2.5 per cent in the United States, 6.1 per cent in Canada and 20 per cent in Mexico – Mexico's tariff rate on passenger vehicles originating from Canada and the United States is gradually phased out (5.5 per cent in 1998). In the United States, tariffs on passenger vehicles have been relatively low, hovering at or below 3 per cent since 1974, although there is still a 25 per cent duty on light trucks. In Canada, the import tariff has been steadily declining from 17.5 per cent in 1968 to 9.2 per cent in 1994 and 6.1 per cent in 2001, as a result of Uruguay Round tariff reduction commitments.

Vehicle trade between Canada and the United States has been subject to a sequence of evolving agreements providing for bilateral duty-free trade under certain conditions. These began with the Auto Pact of 1965, and were followed by the Canada–United States Free Trade Agreement (CUSFTA) of 1989 and NAFTA in 1994. In early 2000 some allegedly discriminatory provisions of the Auto Pact, grandfathered in NAFTA, were found to be inconsistent with Canada's WTO obligations, following dispute settlement procedures requested by Japan. The related provisions allowed certain vehicle manufacturers to import in Canada vehicles duty-free in exchange for minimum commitments on local production and value-added content.[6] To comply with its WTO obligations, Canada removed the duty-free exemptions for the manufacturers in question. In moving from CUSFTA to NAFTA, higher levels of regional content were prescribed for conferring the duty-free status for intra-regional trade.[7] The higher regional content requirement acts as an incentive for manufacturers to source inputs from regional suppliers and thus disfavours inputs from third countries.

For a long period, automobile trade between the United States and Japan took place in the context of a programme of voluntary export restraint (VER). Having begun in 1981, the programme was terminated in 1994, as export levels were systematically below the restrained limits. In the meantime, Japanese manufacturers made significant investment in transplant operations in the USA. The VER was officially terminated the year before the entry into force of the WTO Safeguards Agreement, which prohibits measures of this kind.

In Mexico, automotive production and trade is highly regulated under the Automotive Decree through highly restrictive – although explicitly earmarked as temporary – trade regulations (see Chapter 7). The Decree specifies local content and trade balancing requirements to be applied by each manufacturer (OECD, 2000).[8] Imports of motor vehicles were subject to an import licence requirement and licences are only granted to manufacturers who comply with the Automobile Decree.

Under the WTO Trade-Related Investment Measures (TRIM) Agreement, developing countries, including Mexico, had until 31 December 1999 to comply with the obligations of the TRIM Agreement that forbids the application of investment measures which discriminate against foreign products or restrict quantities of imports or exports. In an act that has great significance for the automobile sector, Mexico is seeking to extend the deadline for bringing its Automotive Decree in conformity with the WTO TRIM Agreement to the end of December 2003, to correspond to the end of the transition period negotiated under NAFTA. These issues are currently pending in the WTO and are being considered in the context of the launch of a comprehensive round of multilateral trade negotiations.

Within NAFTA, technical standards for ensuring the safety of motor vehicles and for achieving environmental objectives have not been harmonized, but each party was supposed to accredit and recognize certification procedures performed by conformity assessment bodies in the territory of another party.[9] Within NAFTA, the use of technical standards as a protective device is less likely to happen because of the predominant US ownership of the automobile manufacturing capacity and the high export propensity of both Canada and Mexico to the United States. Nevertheless, the NAFTA Agreement recognizes that mutual recognition plays a key role in preventing market segmentation through regulatory procedures.

The ups and downs of integration in MERCOSUR

In MERCOSUR, the creation of the common market in 1991 raised the prospect of faster economic growth for all its members and was instrumental in the huge inflow of foreign direct investment that followed, particularly in the automotive sector. A CET for most goods entered into effect in January 1995, following the gradual elimination of import duties on intra-regional trade. Motor vehicles were considered to be too sensitive for an unconditional regional duty-free status. Instead, automotive trade was framed within a bilateral agreement between Brazil and Argentina providing for duty-free imports of vehicles and parts as long as the importer balances his foreign purchases with exports to any destination. The bilateral agreement was considered transitory until an agreement could be reached for an automobile CET.

Between 1995 and 2000, each member of MERCOSUR imposed its own external tariff. Argentina imposed a 20 per cent duty and Brazil initially imposed a 65 per cent duty on passenger vehicles. Following complaints by trading partners in late 1998 about the distorting character of investment incentives and prohibitive import duties, Brazil lowered its duty to 49 per cent and 24.5 per cent for imports by qualified manufacturers under the Brazilian auto regime (vehicles are primarily imported by manufacturers).

By the end of 2000, the long-promised automotive CET had still not been agreed upon as diverging views remained among its four members. A new bilateral agreement was reached between Brazil and Argentina whose terms had tended to an increase in current external tariffs (see Chapter 8).

Trading partners have expressed concerns about several dimensions of the Brazilian–Argentinian auto regimes, including higher local content requirements, rising from 58–60 per cent range in 1996 to 67.5 per cent in 1999, depending on the type of vehicles (WTO, 2000).

Since its inception, MERCOSUR has been prone to internal tensions and its operating rules have too often been modified as economic circumstances changed. The devaluated Brazilian real in 1999 has had a devastating impact on Brazilian automobile demand and on MERCOSUR producers struggling with considerable excess capacity. It further adversely affected the relative competitiveness of Argentinean firms and led to costly restructuring. The recent emergency measures applied by Argentina in early 2001 attest to the difficulty experienced by MERCOSUR members in setting up a stable and reliable regulatory environment for the automobile sector, one of their most important trade components. The difficulties in establishing the long-promised CET for automobile undermine the credibility of the whole arrangement. MERCOSUR members still face considerable challenges in restoring the integrity of their integration process, if they want to realize the full potential of their economic integration.

ANZCERTA's automobile space without integration

Australia and New Zealand negotiated a free trade agreement in 1983 that gradually eliminated trade barriers between the two partners, including quantitative restrictions and bilateral recourse to anti-dumping measures. Intra-regional duty-free treatment was granted on products satisfying the regional content of 50 per cent and both members continued to apply pro-hibitive import tariffs on passenger vehicles from third parties, exceeding 45 per cent until 1994. Since 1995, in the context of the Uruguay Round, Australia reduced its tariffs in stages from 27.5 to 15 per cent by the year 2000. In a similar vein, New Zealand undertook to reduce its tariffs from 30 to 15 per cent by 2000, but eliminated all automobile tariffs, including those on used vehicles, in an unexpected policy change in 1998.

Prior to New Zealand's liberalization move, there was a paradoxical situation of prohibitive import tariffs being imposed on non-regional countries with concurrently high extra-regional trade. There is virtually no bilateral trade in automobiles between the two member countries. This has masked a situation of less-than-optimal competitive conditions that have impeded the emergence of an integrated automotive market in the region. The complete liberalization of the New Zealand market has tremendously bene-fited its consumers, who are now enjoying affordable vehicle prices and wider model choice, a situation that was hardly conceivable few years ago. Virtually all New Zealand CKD plants have ceased assembly operations and some are being converted into distribution centres of reconditioned used vehicles, mainly imported from Japan (Moore, 2000).

CEFTA's peripheral automobile space

CEFTA was a peripheral FTA whose four members shared a common goal of becoming full member states of the EU. During the 1990s each benefited from duty-free access to the EU under separate European Agreements (see Chapter 5). Furthermore, the Czech and Slovak Republics established a customs union among themselves with a common external tariff (CET). CEFTA's projected date for duty-free intra-regional trade was initially set for January 2001, but it was subsequently advanced to January 2000. Passenger vehicles from third parties imported into CEFTA have been subjected to tariffs in the country of access. The Czech and the Slovak Republics impose the lowest duty in the region at 17 per cent, compared with 35 per cent in Poland and 43 per cent in Hungary. Access to the Hungarian market is further restricted by a global quota on consumer goods and an import prohibition on used vehicles older than four years old. CEFTA applies rules of origin to prevent trade diversion problems and each member qualifies under the European Agreements' diagonal cumulation of origins.

Empirical evidence in the automobile sector

Countries participating in RIAs are expected to see an increase in both their import penetration and their export propensity ratios (including intra-regional trade). The macro-level trade data referred to above already indicated that this was the case, and that regional trade integration in particular took off quicker than increases in trade on a global level. The tables below show a similar picture as regards trade data for the automobile sector in the 1990s.

Production and trade data for motor vehicles (Table 2.5) confirms that both the import penetration and the export propensity ratios increased during the period 1990–1998 for the countries in the five RIAs.

On a global basis, the export propensity of motor vehicles increased significantly, from 39.1 per cent in 1990 to 45.1 per cent in 1999. In part, this reflects the international strategy of manufacturers and the more open trade and investment environment of RIAs – in 1999, 67.6 per cent of the world production of motor vehicles took place within the five RIAs discussed above. The higher import penetration ratios between RIAs and individual countries not participating in RIAs reveal the trade dynamism induced by regional arrangements. The import penetration ratios for Japan, South Korea and China are considerably lower than the ratios for RIAs.

These import penetration ratios do not distinguish the extent to which the level and increase in the ratios are attributable to *intra-regional* trade. Table 2.6 shows the shares of total imports for passenger vehicles and parts that originate from inside the regional arrangements concerned, and are referred to as 'intra-regional imports' (the data used in Tables 2.5 and 2.6 are different and the results are not strictly comparable).[10]

The shares of intra-regional imports for passenger vehicles vary significantly between the four RIAs for which data were available. The EU's shares for both passenger vehicles and parts are the highest among the four groups and remained relatively stable during the 1985–1998 period. For NAFTA, the intra-regional import share is calculated for the period 1985 to 1998 by

Table 2.5   Import penetration and export propensity ratios for motor vehicles (%)

	Import penetration ratios*			Export propensity ratios			
	1990	*1995*	*1998*	*1990*	*1995*	*1998*	*1999*
*Countries in RIAs***							
EU countries	56.5	55.5	71.8	60.1	67.8	75.9	77.8
NAFTA countries		33.7	40.0		25.4	26.7	27.4
CEFTA countries		52.9	73.6		55.1	75.7	75.5
ANZCERTA countries	67.5	112.5	124.8		7.4	15.2	
MERCOSUR countries	−0.2	26.3	31.0	18.5	16.5	31.2	22.2
Countries							
Japan	0.9	4.5	3.6	43.2	37.2	45.1	44.2
Korea	−1.5	−0.6	9.2	26.3	38.7	69.7	53.1
China	5.6	1.4	−0.8	0.7	1.2	0.7	
India	5.4	29.0	34.2	7.4	7.7	7.5	4.4
World				39.1	39.6	46.6	45.1

Notes
* The import data refers to apparent imports obtained by adding export plus registration minus production. The import penetration ratios are obtained by dividing apparent import by production level.
** Unweighted average of single country's ratios.

Source: Estimates by the author based on data in units compiled by the Organisation Internationale des Constructeurs Automobiles (OICA).

Table 2.6   Intra-regional import ratios for passenger cars and parts (%)

	1985	*1990*	*1994*	*1998*
Passenger cars				
EU	80.5	82.3	82.9	78.6
NAFTA	37.2	39.6	49.0	51.1
CEFTA			1.7	2.1
ANCZERTA	5.5	6.4	5.1	3.5
Parts				
EU	88.4	88.2	83.8	84.3
NAFTA	73.5	59.6	63.3	69.5
CEFTA			4.5	6.3
ANCZERTA	3.9	2.9	2.2	2.3

Source: Estimates by the authors based on the COMEX database, SITC 781 and 784.

including Mexican data for the period prior to NAFTA's entry into force in 1994. Comparison of the periods before and after its entry into force shows that the passenger vehicles' intra-regional share has increased considerably. For parts, the declining share between 1985 and 1990 partly reflects the start-up phase of Japanese transplant operations that initially relied upon a high percentage of imported inputs. Despite the increasing trend in the intra-regional import shares for NAFTA, they do not measure up against the high intra-regional import shares for the EU in 1998 (in value terms, the combined *extra*-regional imports of passenger vehicles and parts in 1998 amounted to US$61.8 billion for NAFTA and $35.6 billion for the EU).

The share of intra-regional imports in CEFTA has been extremely low. Led by consumer preferences for western-produced vehicles, the brunt of the adjustment in the import composition was made at the expense of imports from Russia.

The share of intra-regional imports in ANZCERTA was also extremely low and stable during the period, which seems to be somewhat paradoxical given that for most of the period this region was shielded behind prohibitive import tariffs. Intra-regional trade within MERCOSUR is estimated to be very high, with about 80 per cent of Argentinean vehicle exports going to Brazil and about 50 per cent of Brazilian exports going to Argentina (Calmon, 1999).

Conclusion

This chapter has analysed the outlook of the second wave of regionalism. It considered to what extent regions could be considered to be closed or open. Many of the general patterns of trade and investment triggered by RIAs – as deciphered above – were confirmed in the case of the car industry. In some instances, the car industry provides a more forceful example of the processes at hand, not least because of its high visibility as an employer, as an innovator and as the producer of highly appreciated products for consumers. These factors mean that the car industry is a perfect case study for assessing the wider implications of the second wave of regionalism and of the changing positions of the countries that adopted a 'go-it-alone' strategy. The faster lane of regionalism seems indeed to be carried by the car industry.

The macroeconomic picture of comparable openness to trade for countries engaged in RIAs and those countries that 'go it alone' is more pronounced in the car industry. The openness towards trade in cars for countries inside RIAs has been higher, like the closedness of the 'go-it-alone' countries to car trade. The comparison of import penetration ratios in the automobile sector between RIAs and producing countries not participating in RIAs shows that import opportunities are effectively much higher in the regional groups. The favourable comparison equally stands when intra-regional trade is excluded for the comparison. Statistical evidence supports the view that market access in regional automotive markets is not more restrained in practice than in producing countries that have not joined regional groups. Nevertheless, due to the historic dynamism of the automotive industry and traditionally interventionist policies aimed at protecting domestic automotive industries, regional border and regulatory measures remain matters of concern for trading partners.

Because of their relatively peripheral position in the worldwide car industry, the level of intra-regional trade is minuscule in the case of some RIAs. Extra-regional import shares exceed 95 per cent of total automobile imports for both CEFTA and ANZCERTA in 1998. These numbers reveal a contrasting economic and political reality. Integration within CEFTA is secondary to the other integration process concurrently taking place between individual CEFTA members and the EU, under which most of the trade is going on. The ultimate objective of each CEFTA country is to become a full EU member state in the near future.

Within ANZCERTA, the paradoxical situation of prohibitive import tariffs imposed on third countries with concurrently high extra-regional trade masks another reality of pervasive anti-competitive conditions that have discouraged and impeded intra-regional trade. An integrated automotive market has never materialized under ANZCERTA rules. Conditions recently changed drastically, when New Zealand fully opened its automotive market to foreign competition, de facto eliminating all automotive preferential treatments for Australia.

Integrated regional automotive markets with potentially efficient scale plants can function within the EU and NAFTA. These integrated markets were built over long periods – more than thirty years in each case. The emergence of these two integrated automotive markets is not accidental and several dimensions of regional commitments have been instrumental in their realization. These include transparency and non-discrimination in the formulation of domestic regulations, a regional infrastructure for solving disputes and safeguarding the rights of their members, and undeterred political supports for the integration process.

In MERCOSUR, the integration process was enthusiastically embraced by automotive manufacturers, which have invested huge amounts in new capacity. However, market confidence was eroded by recurrent internal tensions that have entailed costly restructuring operations. MERCOSUR members still face considerable challenges in restoring the integrity of their integration process, if they want to realize the full potential of their economic integration.

Intra-regional free trade within any Free Trade Agreement is subject to rules of origin to preserve the preferential treatment of trade for its member countries, but these can be excessively complex or expensive to comply with. As a direct impact, these rules encourage manufacturers to source inputs from regional origins over imported inputs and can restrict regional competitive conditions. Rules of origin are the hidden protection instrument of choice in FTAs and third parties should be particularly vigilant when these rules are modified.

It should not come as a surprise that enhanced WTO regulation governing these rules in terms of greater transparency, uniformity, predictability and avoidance of trade restrictions, is high on the international policy agenda. Car manufacturers are adapting to this reality (see the remainder of this volume). It is likely that the regional lane of the car industry will continue to run faster than the lane of globalism, while the national lane runs slowest. It seems that the option of moving from one lane to the other is still open – with the exception of the national road. Whether the combined lanes turn out to be a highway for the car industry or a mere dirt road remains to be seen.

3

Multinational Carmakers' Regional Strategies

Michel Freyssenet and Yannick Lung

Introduction[1]

The automobile sector is often presented as the archetypal global industry. In this view, the car business is one of the main drivers behind the homogenization of the world. This chapter is an attempt to deconstruct a representation that neglects the heterogeneity of firms and areas; the great diversity of the strategies being pursued; and the inherent contradictions of the competitive process. Without purporting to analyse carmakers' internationalization strategies in their entirety,[2] it delves into issues relating to those regionalization strategies (Freyssenet and Lung, 2001) that carmakers are most likely to follow in their attempts to rebuild at a regional (supranational) level a modicum of coherency between productive systems and automobile markets – coherencies that no longer necessarily materialize at the national level that had once (during the postwar boom years) been the arena within which they could regulate themselves.

To apprehend the dynamics of regional integration, an emphasis is placed on car firms' strategies and their close interaction with certain political and institutional elements (Boyer, 1999). In the current historical context, 'regionalization' is structuring the world-space into various regions that are distinct both from the globalization (homogenization) process and from earlier and partial/parallel 'regional integration' processes. The present essay does not use an institutional definition of regional integration (Chapter 2); rather, it sees the regional integration process as one component of an automobile firm's spatial management strategy. The two aspects (institutional/ strategic) clearly interact with one another: firms' strategies respond and/or are involved in the development of an institutional compromise between sovereign states, and intergovernmental agreements can sometimes cause firms to make new choices.

This chapter will analyse carmakers' regional strategies using the analytical matrix developed by Robert Boyer and Michel Freyssenet (Boyer and Freyssenet, 2002). Section 2 will provide a historical perspective, reminding the reader of the greater or lesser extent to which carmakers have been involved in the partial regional integration processes that ran from the 1960s until the advent of the new globalization events that were so intimately associated with the 1990s. Section 3 is an attempt to analyse the regionalization process in its contemporary form, seen as an ongoing process which involves a rebuilding of spaces of regulation – and as one that is diametrically opposed to the phenomenon of globalization.

Automobile firms: drivers of regional integration?

Throughout the early 1990s, and in those areas where they had already established a presence, carmakers could often be found pursuing strategies that revolved around a principle of regional integration. Our first task is to define this process. We will then demonstrate how the automobile industry has been one of its main drivers throughout the world. We will also show that such regional integration processes can occur either in proximity to their domestic market (i.e., in neighbouring countries), or else in more distant area(s) (i.e., in developing countries). Finally, we will examine the factors that explain why the automobile industry often plays a leading role in these types of dynamics.

Regional integration as a means for creating a production system that is compatible with a given market's demand for automobiles

The regional integration process can be apprehended in car manufacturers' internationalization strategies as a set of decisions that are intended as a way of articulating at a supranational (regional) level (the region) the two conditions that are a prerequisite to profitability (Boyer and Freyssenet, 2002). On one hand, the relevancy of a particular profit strategy to the modes of growth and income sharing that exist at a macroeconomic level; and on the other, the establishment of an enterprise government compromise.

During the postwar boom years, this coherency was primarily manifested (in the Fordist regime and in its different variants) at a national level. Exports may have constituted an indispensable complement to an automobile industry's development, but a manufacturer would mainly design and develop a range of product models with its own domestic market in mind. Moreover, the government compromises that would be negotiated by the various parties concerned by such an agreement would take place in a national context, especially since at the time very little production had been internationalized. Even those American carmakers (Ford and GM) who had already developed overseas subsidiaries during the interwar period reverted after the Second World War to a system based upon autonomous activities that were geared towards a distinctive national environment. The Australian, English and German subsidiaries each had their own product; and each entity was run according to specific rules of employment relationship management – rules that were a function of each subsidiary's local, national environment. As such, in Europe, Opel and Vauxhall were run independently of one another, as were Ford UK and Ford Germany (following Ford's withdrawal from Spain and France in 1954). As a matter of fact, until the end of the 1960s, the products that Ford's various subsidiaries were offering differed from one another; and in certain external markets, the entities were rivals (Bonin, Lung and Tolliday, 2003).

At the level of the firm, the regionalization process has not been linear – but it has been affected by the various categories of tension that can exist between homogeneity and spatial differentiation. For a regionalization process to function, the manufacturer has to offer an identical range of models in the various countries comprising a particular region. This identical product range presupposes the relative homogeneity of these markets, and therefore a relative convergence, in terms of national income levels and modes of income sharing, and even further, in terms of people's lifestyles (rates and forms of urbanization, level of road transport infrastructure, role of individual transportation modes, cultural representations, and so on).

However, this regionalization process cannot be limited to its commercial dimension alone: it necessarily entails a productive internationalization, if only because of the regional division of labour that it organizes. Implanting activities in a variety of different countries is tantamount to attempting to gain proximity to one's markets by building new production plants in those countries where a firm hopes to benefit from rapid market growth. This sometimes reflects a firm's response to an opportunity to get closer to the specific, design or engineering-related resources that can be embedded in territorialized industrial complexes. To a large extent, an overseas implantation of production activities (design, manufacturing, assembly) is still motivated by the desire to benefit from spatial differentials in costs, especially labour costs (wage levels, payroll taxes, working hours and labour flexibility). What the firm is seeking to exploit is the heterogeneity of the regional space. It tries to do this by specializing its different sites in those activities that local resources (quality, costs, flexibility) are most adapted to, and by benefiting from scale economies thanks to the concentration of a specified production on each of these sites.

However, this heterogeneity is in contradiction with the alleged convergence that the markets have been undergoing. This contradiction is only a partial one, inasmuch as the broadening of a product range can help a carmaker to offer a variety of models, with a different breakdown in each of the countries that are involved (depending on variations in demand). Indeed, the automobile industry is one sector where a differentiation of goods can be found at the very core of the competitive process. This also holds for the branch's innovation aspects, with its ongoing creation of niches where the capture of additional profits becomes possible. As such, small cars and light utility vehicles are much more common in Southern Europe (Spain, Portugal, Italy) than in Northern Europe, where larger-sized models and top-of-the-range vehicles predominate (Chapter 4).

However, the heterogeneity of regional spaces' employment relationships, especially as pertains to their wage costs, must be renewed constantly if it is to serve a dynamic function. This is because economic development has created a certain convergence between those countries that the multinational firms have been focusing on – hence a reduction in wage differentials, and a search for new peripheral spaces. For the United States, Mexico now fills the same role that Canada did 20 or 30 years ago; and for the European Union, Eastern Europe has today become a pole of attraction, assuming the role that the Iberian Peninsula had filled during the 1970s.

The automobile industry as an active participant in regional integration processes

Working in a sector that is particularly sensitive to economies of scale, and where product differentiation is a significant factor, carmakers have often been one of the more active pressure groups lobbying in favour of regional integration processes. There are a number of examples of this.

Free trade in North America

In North America, the 1965 Auto Pact between Canada and the United States constituted a sectoral agreement intended to consolidate and further the integration of automobile production on both shores of the Great Lakes region. American carmakers and parts makers would benefit from the lower wage costs in Canada, whose automobile market was very similar to that of the United States. During the mid-1980s, certain Korean and Japanese operators would also start to see Canada as a launchpad for attacking the American market. It was at this time that a wave of investment began in Mexico, with the construction of engine-building plants whose production was to be exported to the United States and the greenfield creation of assembly plants in Mexico's northern states. Although the Mexican automobile market had been previously protected by import-substitution policies, there was now a shift to an export-oriented automobile policy as a result of the heavy pressure that was being exerted by the American carmakers: Mexican legislation was modified several times, leading to a relaxation of the country's control over foreign investments, as a direct result of Ford's efforts. These two waves of investment by the automobile industry were a precursor to the free-trade agreement (FTA) that was signed between Canada and United States in 1988, and extended to Mexico four years later, leading ultimately to the birth of NAFTA (Chapter 7).

European integration

In the Old World, carmakers moulded themselves to the extant European integration process in order to benefit from its localization opportunities. In the 1960s, following the Treaty of Rome, Belgium became a particularly popular site for the location of assembly plants (Renault, Volvo, VW, Opel and Ford having established operations there). Car manufacturers often anticipated and lobbied for a geographical expansion towards new spaces (England, Spain, Portugal, Eastern Europe), and for a consolidation of the economic and monetary integration that was taking place (stabilization of currency fluctuations, Euro zone as a protection against exchange risk).

American manufacturers (Ford and GM) were the first to operate on a Europe-wide scale. They achieved this by integrating their English and German subsidiaries, and by moving small car assembly plants to the Iberian Peninsula. During the 1970s, those laws that relaxed the foreign investment controls that Franco had set up in Spain, and which opened this country up to the multinationals, were baptised the 'Ford laws', because they had been adopted primarily to encourage Ford to set up operations near Valencia. The US groups created regional entities (Ford of Europe in 1967, GM Europe in 1987), thus finalizing the merger of their previously autonomous German and English subsidiaries. These entities offered a single product range, and co-ordinated all of the groups' activities (including component production sites) in an inter-site division of labour.

This strategy paid off for Ford, which became the European market leader, and increased profits by so doing. In fact, in the late 1970s, Ford Europe saved the rest of the company from bankruptcy after it had suffered major setbacks on the North American market. As for GM, once GM Europe (GME) had finally completed Opel's painful absorption of Vauxhall, GME rose to a respectable position in the European rankings, and by the early 1980s, it was beginning to turn a profit (Bordenave and Lung, 2003).

Inversely, Chrysler Europe was a failure, and when the third largest American carmaker finally decided to withdraw to its domestic market, its European activities were resold to Peugeot. This acquisition allowed PSA to reach a more significant European dimension – up to that point, the French carmaker's only European assets had been the Citroën factories in Spain, but with Chrysler Europe it was able to acquire an industrial base in Spain (Madrid) and in England (Luton). European carmakers were in fact very timid in pursuing regional integration strategies, usually limiting themselves to market access issues. With the exception of Renault (Belgium, Spain–Portugal), they tended to emphasize the consolidation of their domestic production and exportation base when building the new assembly plants that were necessitated by the market's rapid growth during the 1960s. Encouraged by regional planning policies and under pressure from labour unions, their new locations mainly benefited peripheral regions. Fiat or Alfa-Romeo stayed in Italy, VW, BMW and Mercedes in Germany,

Rover in England, Volvo or Saab in Sweden – but this did not prevent exploratory approaches in peripheral countries (Volvo in Belgium; Fiat [via Seat] and Rover in Spain).

For these reasons, the Old World's regional integration was still incomplete as the 1980s drew to a close. Most of the European automobile industry's productive base remained concentrated in carmakers' countries of origin. Even in terms of the commercial internationalization that had taken place, market integration was still an unfinished business. It is true that the product ranges that were being offered in the different countries had already converged to a certain extent. Nevertheless, significant disparities remained in new vehicle prices, and a high percentage of automobile sales were still being achieved in a carmaker's country of origin as the 1980s came to an end.

Regional integration has not been the rule everywhere

The automobile industry's integration processes may have begun in Europe and in North America as far back as the 1960s, but it is also significant that the trajectories being followed by the two most recent automobile countries to have emerged over the past 25 years, Japan and South Korea, diverged markedly (cf. Chapters 13 and 14). Japan's and Korea's automobile industries have remained nationally focussed yet, at the same time, largely export-oriented, in the sense that their mode of growth is geared towards exporting. It is true that the geopolitical environment in this region is much more disparate than in Europe or North America (due to the conflicts caused by the presence of a number of major powers in Southeast Asia) and that Asia's level of economic development is quite heterogeneous. In addition, these are young automobile industries, who had only experienced continuous growth, at least until the early 1990s for Japan (slightly later for Korea), and automobile firms that were indigenous. In this environment, the prerequisites for a regional integration centred around these two countries do not appear to have been present, despite local carmakers' active attempts to support, and to participate in, regional integration processes on the zone's periphery.

The peri-central regional integration

In Southern Hemisphere countries, automobile firms have often driven local governments' attempts to implement forms of regional integration. In South America, there had been a number of unsuccessful initiatives in this direction before the advent of MERCOSUR (Chapter 8). This common market changed the region's perspectives, leading Ford and Volkswagen to merge their Argentinian and Brazilian activities in 1987 into a joint venture, Autolatina. Abandoning their plans to export to the United States from a South American base, the two manufacturers refocused on the Argentinean and Brazilian markets, rationalizing their productive infrastructure (including the mechanical components they traded), and harmonizing their product ranges. Paradoxically, this strategy was of no benefit to VW and Ford, who saw their leadership slip away as a result of their having neglected the Brazilian market's main catalyst during the 1990s: the 'popular car' (Noberto and Uri, 2000). The association would be dissolved in 1997, and each carmaker would end up defining its own, separate strategy.

In Southeast Asia, Japanese carmakers had worked to set up a compensation system to encourage components trading between ASEAN's four main countries (Indonesia, Malaysia, the Philippines and Thailand) – with each being able to use its particular specialization in such a way as to benefit from economies of scale when producing the component. After a long period of negotiation, 1981 saw the creation of an initial scheme entitled the ASEAN Industrial Corporation (AIC). This had a relatively negligible impact, unlike the 1988 Brand to Brand Compensation (BBC) agreement that encouraged mutual trading between a carmaker's various sites in the region's different countries. The agreement, which only applied to the automobile industry, was first adopted by Mitsubishi, followed by Toyota in 1989, Nissan a year later, and Honda in 1995 (Guiheux and Lecler, 2000). The BBC was a great success: from 1991 to 1996, automobile production in these ASEAN countries almost doubled – rising from 762,000 to 1,450,000 units. In December 1995, regional integration reached a new plateau with the ASEAN Industrial Corporation Organisation (AICO), which broadened the range of activities covered by the previous scheme. It would appear that we are now moving towards a Customs Union type of regime (Common Effective Professional Tariff), which is due to come online in the year 2003 (Chapter 9).

Internationalization in a new century: between globalization and regionalization

At the dawn of a new century, a new and different approach should be taken to the issue of regionalization. This must now be analysed against an overall backdrop of economic globalization. The opening up of markets to international competition and the interpenetration of the world's economies have exacerbated automobile firms' competitive rivalry, leading to a frantic search for greater price competitiveness (lower wage costs, components prices, currency rates), and for a better performance by the factors that determine other conditions of competitiveness. These include quality (in the sense of an absence of defects); product integrity; innovation; and a broader product range (in an effort to increase variety and find new profit niches). Increased volume remains the key to greater productivity, given the rising importance of scale economics for the automobile industry (especially with the jump in R&D expenditures). Hence the search for new markets, starting with emerging countries that are growing rapidly, but which are also experiencing a great deal of volatility. Carmakers have set off on two possible paths to internationalization: globalization, on one hand, and regionalization, on the other (Freyssenet and Lung, 2000).

This section will discuss the potentialities of the carmakers' productive models (Boyer and Freyssenet, 2002) towards these two paths. In fact, the firms who have been most active in the area of regional integration are those who deem themselves to be part of a Sloanian model, starting with Ford and General Motors. Volkswagen brings a European dimension into the equation – moreover, it has concretized its preference for a Sloanian model by developing (following its purchase of SEAT and Skoda) a range of vehicles that share one and the same platform (Jürgens, 1998).

Although the other industrial models can apply a range of product variety management modes in order to cope with market segmentation issues, the Sloanian model is particularly compatible with a process of regional integration. This is because a bigger market is a prerequisite for a broader product range – the larger the market, the easier it is to create a compatibility between a 'volume-based' strategy, and a 'variety-based' one. Furthermore, enterprise government compromises allow Sloanian firms to benefit from wage differentials within a given regional space, whilst maintaining the sort of adaptability that will help them to deal with a diversified group of suppliers. Another explanation lies in the organizational learning that such firms will have developed – their experience of internationalization means that they are more capable of seizing whatever opportunities are being offered (Bélis–Bergouignan, Bordenave and Lung, 2000). This aspect demonstrates the relevance of focusing on the applicability of a Fordian model in a regionalization process – this model only constitutes one transitory form of organization in the automobile industry; that is, one possible way in which new actors can emerge (i.e., the Korean carmakers).

Globalization at the core of strategic extremes: 'volume' vs 'quality'

Globalization, when perceived as a homogeneous market for a standardized product, clearly embodies the generic vision that is to be found at the heart of the Fordian model. During the 1910s, Henry Ford's master plan with the Model T had revolved around the production of a unique car model that could be aimed at all car markets. The standardization of the product, the components, and the process led to its worldwide diffusion, Ford Motor Company moving closer to its markets. Plants for the assembly of the Ford Model T and its different variants were soon built in Europe (in England, as early as 1911), South America and Japan (Wilkins and Hill, 1964).

The Korean (Daewoo and Hyundai) carmakers' highly ambitious internationalization drives of the early 1990s reproduced this strategy, with its central focus on the search for economies of scale. This involved one or two entry-level vehicles to target both emerging and industrialized countries (in the latter, these cars were marketed to low-income households as bottom-of-the-range models) – two markets where a low price could compensate for comparatively low quality. Korean price levels for new cars are often equivalent to the prices of a top-quality second-hand car. This low price is obtained by using a strategy that is primarily volume-oriented, and thus geared towards expansion into new markets. The sudden rise in the Korean automobile firms' production capacities during the 1990s also helped bring about their decline – no independent Korean carmakers have survived now that Renault has taken over Samsung, Daimler-Chrysler Hyundai and GM Daewoo (Chapter 14).

At the other end of the scale, top-of-the-range vehicles – and particularly those manufacturers who have long been described as specialists – address a clientele that is comprised solely of high-income households. In any country, including in a manufacturer's own domestic market, this will only represent a small volume of sales. In order to achieve production volumes that are large enough to allow for economies of scale, carmakers pursuing quality-based strategies have always tended to see their market in global terms. This is feasible because of the homogeneity of a clientele that is targeted because of its level of income and cultural referents: deluxe brands (Jaguar, BMW, Mercedes, Porsche) have the same essential image across the planet. Only a small proportion of all households are concerned by this target market, a segment whose size varies from one country to the next. For these prestigious brands, the market remains a global one.

The Sloanian model: between globalization and multi-regionalization

With the Volkswagen group, we have another example of a globalization strategy that has been associated with a variety–volume strategy – VW having extended its range through both vertical and horizontal differentiation. The VW group's four generalist brands are: Audi and Seat for the sport image, Skoda and Volkswagen for the classic image. They have built up large model ranges with shared platforms, including niche vehicles such as the New Beetle or the Audi TT. This offer is completed by luxury models (the VW Phaeton) and more prestigious brands (Bugatti, Lamborghini, Bentley) that VW has taken over. Combining all of these brands, the VW group now possesses a complete product portfolio, and seems capable of occupying every conceivable product segment. Depending upon the local market, VW can combine its products in such a way as to propose an offering that has been adapted to the specific features of a composite consumer demand. Nevertheless, despite its position as the top European in the North American market (especially in the United States and in Canada) and in Japan, VW is still only a minor player in these two poles of the Triad. The German group has a presence that is essentially bi-regional: Europe and the emerging countries, especially China.

Until its alliance with General Motors, Fiat had been pursuing a multi-regionalization strategy in which the world was divided into two distinct regions: the North (primarily Europe) and the South (the emerging countries). The Italian firm has long been the most nationally oriented of all the European carmakers, having broadened its brand portfolio in its domestic market (Fiat, Alfa, Lancia, Maserati, Ferrari) without setting up operations in the other countries of the European Union. However, there have long been links with countries now classified as 'emerging' (the USSR, Turkey, Yugoslavia, Brazil). As a result, Fiat has designed a specific model that targets these emerging new markets: the Fiat 178/Palio (Camuffo and Volpato, 1999). The production of this vehicle has been organized according to a division of labour between the main protagonists (Turkey, Brazil, Poland and Morocco) in a components trade that has become widespread, and which feeds assembly and kitting plants that are spread around the world to the tune of one million units per year. Fiat has scored a few points, what with its adaptation to the emerging countries, but more with the success of the Uno in Brazil where, in contrast to the experience of VW, Fiat has been able to take advantage of the 'popular car'. The global sales of Palio are largely below target levels and, in its core market (Europe), the Italian firm has lost a great deal of market share as a result of its ageing product range. Fiat's alliance with GM, which effectively paves the way for a takeover of the Italian firm by the American giant, sanctions the failure – but it also creates new possibilities.

The difficulties associated with a strategy of trans-regionalization

It is worth studying the way in which the strategies of the two leading US carmakers (Ford and General Motors) have changed, in that this allows us to apprehend firms' uncertainties regarding the global strategies they should be following (Bordenave and Lung, 2003). From the mid-1980s onwards, Ford pursued a strategy that was based on the concept of *centres of responsibilities*, delegating and dividing the responsibility for the renewal of its models and main mechanical systems between three poles according to their core competencies: Ford North America for large vehicles, V6 and V8 engines, automatic transmissions and electronic components; Ford Europe for small and medium-sized cars, four-cylinder engines, and manual transmissions; and Mazda, in which Ford had a 25 per cent stake, for the subcompact cars to be sold and produced in Asia and North America (the new Escort was developed on the 323 platform). The structuring of Ford's space illustrated K. Ohmae's Triad concept.

In 1993, Ford accelerated its move towards a global integration of activities with the *Ford 2000* programme merging Ford's regional operations (FoE in Europe and NAAO in North America). The results of the global platforms concept that had been developed as an extension of the poles of responsibility strategy have been unsatisfactory, as illustrated by the failure of the Mondeo global platform and confirmed by the structural losses of Ford International Automotive activities since several years. Ford stopped the merger and recreated Ford Europe. The race to globalize has been a failure, and regionalization is again becoming the core of the US firm's policy.

Regionalization is also at the heart of the strategy that General Motors has been following. Considering platform sharing; GM's policy was formulated as a master plan announced in 1996. The 1996 plan simultaneously affected the three global platforms that were supposed to cover all of the manufacturer's future small and medium-sized cars. It should also be analysed in the light of GM's overall goal of reducing the number of platforms it operated (from 14 to 7). These global platforms were each named after a Greek letter – Gamma, Delta and Epsilon – and each was subdivided by type of market: A for the emerging markets, B for North America, and C for Europe. The plan is effective for the Epsilon platform (new vehicles produced since 2001), but GM abandoned its global small car Delta project platform, in order to fall back on less ambitious global objective with regional platforms policy with its partners (Bordenave and Lung, 2003).

The increased number and intensity of GM's alliances has created new problems. The US manufacturer's greater stake in Japanese carmakers such as Suzuki, Fuji Heavy and Subaru which provided it with access to Southeast Asia and allows GM to broaden its portfolio of models (adding small city cars, for example). Cross-shareholdings between GM and Fiat should lead to the rationalization of Fiat's and Opel's activities in Europe, with mechanical systems (mostly engines), purchasing, and even platforms being shared in an effort to devise a range of specific models for the GM various brands. But these alliances cast doubts over the role of GM's German subsidiary, Opel, which finds itself in the emerging countries in direct competition with its Japanese partners (where it had been market leader); and which is now a rival of its Italian partner (Fiat) in the European market. A regionalization process must be done and re-done over and over again.

The very recent association between Renault and Nissan appears to be moving towards a regionalization scheme that reproduces its precursors: a division of roles amongst the world's various regions according to the competencies and advantages that each has acquired. Renault is to be leader in Europe and in the emerging countries (outside of Asia); and it will find shelter behind its partner in the Asia-Pacific region and in North America. Renault's potential conflicts with its other partners are being kept under wraps for the moment, with the Korean firm Samsung relying on Nissan's technologies, and with Dacia in Romania undergoing a thorough restructuring. The new configuration might allow the alliance between Renault and Nissan to finally complete a project that it had first announced in the early 1990s, what with Nissan's attempt to offer a specific product range in each of the Triad's three poles, this product range being based on variants of three basic models, and on the development of a specific model in the emerging markets. For Nissan, as for the two major American carmakers, a 'volume and diversity' strategy, when extended to an international level, has had problems taking root.

The progressive internationalization of the Hondian and Toyotian models: has glocalization been a success?

In terms of the internationalization of its production, Honda has set the pace for the other Japanese carmakers. The first Japanese carmaker to have built an assembly plant in the United States, at the time of writing Honda owns a very well-balanced productive apparatus (styling and technical centres, engine and assembly plants, distribution network). In the mid-1990s, regional divisions were set up and allocated the task of co-ordinating all of these activities in North America, Europe and Asia. These divisions were required to act in such a way as to support the local production of models that had been specifically designed for a regional market, but which shared platforms and other systems with models from other regions. This was a clearly affirmed regionalization initiative, and was translated by the famous neologism 'glocalisation', coined by Honda's chairman, along with another rather successful slogan: 'Think Globally, Act Locally'. Womack, Jones and Roos (1990) even viewed the Honda as the very model of an internationalizing firm – an incarnation of the MRM (MultiRegional Motors).

Honda and Toyota have been better than their rivals in adapting to the changes that have affected the American market. Toyota took over from Honda as the top Japanese carmaker in the United States and took 10 per cent of the market share in 2002. Its controlled growth in Europe (with the opening of a new assembly plant in France in 2001) and continued strength in Asia appears to validate the concept of a progressive internationalization strategy in which a regional configuration (in Europe, North America and Southeast Asia) is articulated together with a locally adapted product range, even as it spills over into other regional markets. This organizes a division of labour at an intra- and inter-regional level without weakening a central pole's authority.

Conclusion

Although a logic of production (economies of scale) has induced automobile manufacturers to extend their area of commercialization on a global scale, it is in their articulation with a market, their getting into sync with a demand, that they have incorporated the regional tier as a level at which they can achieve a certain coherency. Except for the two extremes of the scale (bottom of the range/prestige automobiles), there are limits to the homogenization of global demand, and the failure of Ford's attempt to integrate its activities globally shows that automobile firms should be looking for more appropriate strategies – and above all, for models or innovative forms of organization that are better adapted to a particular regional space. It is not at all certain that the real challenge is to be the first to globalize – mono-regional strategies (such as the one that PSA has pursued), bi-regional, multi-regional, even trans-regional strategies, can all be relevant at a certain time, and in a given area. Is it possible to devise a productive model that allows for a combination of all of these strategies (for instance, mono-regional for certain products; multi-regional for partially overlapping market segments; global for homogeneous segments)? A certain number of carmakers seem to be looking in this direction – starting with Ford, where this approach has been broken down into light trucks in the United States; Focus-type world platforms for high-volume models; and the Premier Automotive Group for deluxe brands. Others who have started down this road include Toyota (mini city cars in Japan; Corolla/Prisma in their regional variants; and the Lexus group) and Volkswagen. To function, internationalization strategies must incorporate a regional level, and develop enterprise government compromises that enable firms to operate in this type of combinatory register whilst avoiding the incompatibilities and incoherencies that have so often been a source of tension in the past.

Translation by Alan Sitkin

Part II

Regional Integration with(in) Industrialized Regions

4

The Dynamics of Regional Integration in the European Car Industry

Jean-Bernard Layan and Yannick Lung

Introduction

In the immediate aftermath of the Second World War, Fordism experienced a golden age during which it consolidated its domination of the European automobile economy by structuring the region's producer countries into a mosaic of autonomous units. In the Fordist regime, supply and demand interactions were being played out on a national basis. However, during the final 25 years of the twentieth century, these industrial systems' national framework faded, to be replaced by a Europe-wide configuration. Nowhere has the regional integration process progressed as far as in Europe. The process of regionalization revolves on an interactive dynamic between the de facto integration process (supply- and demand-related economic factors), and the de juro integration (institutional changes). As such, the regional integration process is governed by the building of institutions, the changes in demand associated with market convergence, and the automobile firms' strategies for structuring productive spaces.

The present chapter will reconstitute the emergence of a European automobile system (de Banville and Chanaron, 1991; Lung, 2001) based on previously national automobile industries dominated by the promotion and defence of 'national champions'. Section 2 presents the various institutional phases of the regional integration. It focuses on the overall context within which the European Union first took shape; on the development and rise in automotive trade amongst the various EU member states; and on the various tools of a Europe-wide automobile policy. Section 3 analyses the demand side of the regional integration, discussing the convergence between the different European countries' automobile markets. The last two sections focus on carmakers' localization strategies: section 4 describes the regional vertical division of labour that the automobile firms have developed between European countries during the last period; and, moving beyond a static centre–periphery analysis to encompass collective learning processes, section 5 insists on the dynamic nature of the process of spatial division of labour.

The shaping of the European automobile system

The European Union constitutes a straightforward model for regional integration, in that the entire second half of the twentieth century has served to consolidate a process that had first been initiated in the aftermath of the Second World War. The EU success is manifested through its various enlargement phases, and through its furtherance of regional integration. It is reflected in the trade integration of automobile products between countries, and in the implementation of automobile policies on a European scale.

The phases of institutional integration

The Treaty of Rome, signed by six countries in 1957, included three major automobile countries: Germany, France and Italy. They were joined by Belgium, Luxembourg and the Netherlands. Belgium benefited greatly from its involvement in the new organization, as it was able to attract automaker investments (hosting many new assembly plants during the 1960s and 1970s). Amongst the major European automobile nations, only Great Britain was missing. The UK finally joined the European Economic Community in 1973, together with Ireland and Denmark. The ten-nation mark was reached in 1981 with Greece's entrance, but, more than anything else, it was the 1986 arrival of Spain and Portugal that intensified the Mediterranean orientation of Europe's automobile economy. The 1990 German reunification constituted a further enlargement of the European area, which finally reached its current 15-nation configuration in 1995 (with the addition of Austria, Finland and Sweden). However, the process is not over yet, with the further enlargement which will concern ten new countries in 2004.

The furtherance of European integration has involved participants moving beyond a Customs Union phase (first set up in 1968) to establish a fully fledged Single Market in 1993, involving all of the European Economic Community's member states. In other words, it took 25 years to fully complete the de juro institutional conditions required for a common market. Moreover, from a de facto economic point of view, a truly integrated market had not been achieved (including as regards automobile products). With the signature of the Maastricht Treaty in 1992, a new phase commenced: the implementation of an Economic and Monetary Union set up the

EU (European Union) as a replacement for the European Economic Community.

However, an ever-increasing number of domains are now covered by European prerogatives, and enlargement has not always kept pace with these developments. One example is the Euro zone, which separates the 15 member states of the European Union into two subsets – with only 12 having abandoned their domestic currency in favour of a European one. Major nations such as Great Britain remain outside this monetary integration, and given the euro versus pound sterling exchange risk, this does not bode well for the European future of the British automobile industry (both for car and for component makers). Therefore, enlargement negotiations should incorporate the various countries' integration modalities, even as the national perimeters are themselves being continually redefined. In the immediate future, however, it is clear that European integration significantly impacts the trade of automobile products, and the definition of industrial policy.

Intra-regional and intra-industry trade integration

The first indication of the success of this move towards European integration lies in the development of automobile trade between the region's member states: intra-regional trade dominates; and it has been increasing year on year. In 1980, the intra-regional trade represented 58 per cent of the EU's member states' automobile exports – by 2000, the figure had risen to 70 per cent (for a total of US$266.9 billion of automobile exports). If extra-regional trade alone is taken into account, at more than US$80 billion, the EU has become the world's second automobile exporter, just behind Japan (US$88 billion), but with a greater permeability to imports of the European market.[1] The negotiation of a voluntary exports restriction agreement with Japan in 1991 was one of the most important actions in which the European Commission has engaged to support the restructuring of the automobile industry (Vigier, 1992). At the end of the 1980s, the success of Japanese small cars in the North American and European markets constituted a major threat to these two zones' automobile industries – and certain countries (notably France and Italy) applied import quotas in an effort to limit Japanese car sales. Following the example of the voluntary exports restriction agreement that Japan and the United States had concluded during the 1980s, Europe negotiated an agreement that limited Japanese car exports to 15 per cent of the European automobile market until 1 January 2000, the market having been totally open since this date. This agreement accelerated Japanese carmakers' building of assembly plants in Europe, and it enabled regional carmakers to regain major competitive advantages – the Japanese brands' market share in Europe remains lower in 2001 (10.9 per cent) compared with 1992 (11.8 per cent) – as witnessed by the increase in their automobile exports.

Table 4.1   Gruber Lloyd Index of intra-industry trade for automobile products for EU countries

Country	1980 (%)	2000 (%)
Spain	67.45	93.08
Austria	51.54	92.79
Italy	92.64	90.53
France	73.80	89.21
Benelux	98.57	87.78
Sweden	73.98	84.76
Netherlands	58.07	84.02
Finland	40.38	81.10
United Kingdom	98.44	76.28
Portugal	31.71	74.19
Germany	45.88	63.02

For each country i, the Gruber Lloyd Index g_i is calculated from exports X_i and imports M_i

$$g_i = 1 - \frac{|X_i - M_i|}{X_i + M_i}$$

For each of the automobile countries comprising the EU, there has been a marked rise in exports. The number of cars exported outside of Europe still represents less than 20 per cent of the total number of passenger cars being produced within Europe – but there has been a significant rise in intra-European exports for the six main countries who are active in assembly operations. This trend reflects the intensification of intra-industry trade amongst EU member states (Table 4.1): cars are differentiated products, both vertically (in quality terms: German and Swedish top of the range vs Spanish bottom of the range) and horizontally (in variety terms: German–French midrange). It also reflects the rise in intra-firm trade – automobile multinational firms having established a spatial division of labour between plants located across the continent.

For the automobile industry, regional integration did not lead to a growing specialization for EU countries and geographical concentration at the national level (Maurel, 1999). Instead, the enlargement of the European automobile space has involved the diffusion of car production across an extended geographical area including new countries (such as Belgium, Spain and Portugal) to the vertical regional division of labour which has been set up by firms. But within each country, factors of geographical concentration have led to the agglomeration of automotive activities in localized systems of production. At the same time, the increasing variety of vehicle models being offered to European consumers, which stems both from the arrival of new brands (Japanese, Korean) and from the ongoing extension of the product range being offered by European carmakers, is a clear sign of the ever-greater differentiation of automobile products, both on a vertical and on a horizontal level – not to mention the growing contribution of services associated to the sale of new cars (credit and leasing, assurance, repair and maintenance, etc.) as a factor of differentiation. In the European automobile industry, regional integration is associated with the development of intra-industry trade of differentiated products and a functional specialization between countries within a vertical regional division of labour.

This rise in intra-regional trade is one of the first manifestations of regional integration processes (i.e., NAFTA and MERCOSUR) that are both extremely rapid and also reversible. The shift to an economic (and monetary) union is a more complex phenomenon, insofar as it assumes the implementation of a truly sectoral policy on a regional scale.

The development of a European automobile policy

There have been many debates about the direction of European industrial policy (Bangemann, 1992; Cohen and Lorenzi, 2000) – but for the region's automobile industry, and unlike many of the newly industrialized nations, there has been no sectoral policy. However, the continued transferral of responsibilities from national governments to the European level (that is, the principle of subsidiarity) covers a wide range of areas that amount, de facto, to a form of automobile policy within the European Union (McLaughlin and Maloney, 1999; Jürgens, 2004). The automakers' attempt to lobby Brussels (via their professional association, the European Automakers' Association, ACEA) bears witness to this.

Technological policy remains weak in Europe, compared with the United States or Japan. On the contrary, European regulation norms and standards are more important, especially regarding environmental issues (emissions, recycling end-of-life vehicles, etc.). But the crux of European industrial policy is always competition policy.

The European Commission has therefore been particularly vigilant about the aid that member states have been granting to firms, notably to automakers, in their efforts to attract new corporate investments. This incentive system is now defined at a European level within regional development and conversion policies. Indirect instruments (such as local fiscal enticement) which could falsify the rules of the competition between the various location sites are strictly regulated. This neither prevents the firms nor the authorities, i.e., the local or national governments, from engaging in lobbying activities in an attempt to become one of the 'eligible' zones for subsidies.

Regarding distribution issues, the European automobile industry has benefited from a specific status with the block exemption regulation, which excluded automobile distribution activities from the general rules that governed the terms and conditions of sales allowing exclusive and selective distribution arrangements between 1985 and 1995 – an exception that was later extended until the year 2002 (Chanaron and Jullien, 1999). The recent changes introduced in the block exemption regime[2] (July 2002) will certainly reinforce the competition within the motor vehicles' distribution area. Nevertheless, a truly European automobile market has still to be achieved, despite the efforts of the Brussels authorities, and the converging of the various markets' demands.

The markets' convergence

European consumers are faced with a wide choice of vehicles – a range that, at least with respect to its high-volume models, is basically the same throughout Europe. Yet this convergence between markets should be relativized, given the price differentials that persist between the EU member states, and the various types of differentiation which translate the different types of demand.

The rise in motorization

Europe's high unemployment and increasingly unequal income distribution have led to a drop in purchasing power for certain types of household. A section of the European population has thus been excluded from the new car market (Froud et al., 2000). Yet despite this constraint, and notwithstanding the increase in environmental awareness, the European countries' motorization rate has continued to rise strongly.

This dynamic is partially explained by the entrance of new members such as Spain, Portugal, Greece or Ireland (and conceivably, in the near future, the CEEC). Over the past 20 years, new car sales have increased by a factor of 3 in the countries located on Europe's geographical periphery, against an average growth of 50 per cent for the 15 EU member states over the same period (Table 4.2). This catch-up has been particularly rapid in Spain, where

Table 4.2   The rising motorization rates in Europe's peripheral areas (passenger cars)

Country	Sales volumes in 1980	Sales volumes in 2001
Spain	504,051	1,437,833
Greece	35,700	280,214
Ireland	93,563	164,730
Portugal	58,357	255,215
Subtotal 4 countries	691,671	2,137,992
Total EU 15	9,690,146	14,432,065

Source: Comité des Constructeurs, Français d'Automobiles.

the density of automobiles has risen from 276 per 1000 inhabitants in 1985 to 543 in 2001 (the European average being 551).

In addition, the markets' integration and increased competition have led automakers to first seek new niches, and then new market segments, to generate additional profits. This strategy is particularly profitable at the top of the range, i.e., with the generalization of monobox cars such as Renault's Espace and Scenic models. It can also be profitable in the small car segment, as demonstrated by the success of the same French automaker's Twingo model.

Price discrimination

Economists make references to the law of single price on a market. In the integrated and competitive market that Europe is supposed to become as a result of the policies that the authorities in Brussels have been pursuing, products' prices should be identical across the member states (as is the case in the United States). At present, this is far from being the case in the automobile product market – even once tax-related differences (i.e., VAT rates) are subtracted from the equation.

Despite the competitive battles raging between the different automakers, there have been clear signs of price discrimination. This epitomizes a situation of imperfect competition. The European Commission's regular reports[3] highlight price differentials amongst the various member states. In May 2002, the before-tax list price of a VW Golf was, for example, 30.5 per cent higher in Germany than in Finland. Spain, Greece, Finland and Denmark are the markets where car prices before tax are generally the lowest; in contrast, prices in the United Kingdom, Germany and Austria are the highest.

Evaluating these price differentials raises major methodological issues and structural factors (tax regimes, foreign exchange volatility, and so on) explain such divergences (Degryse and Verboven, 2000) – but there is no doubt that some discrimination is taking place. There have been controversial interpretations (Ginsburgh and Vanhamme, 1989) as regards these differentials' evolution (for better or for worse) – but they continued within the previous block exemption regulatory framework. As can be expected in a market where product differentiation prevails, firms sell their goods at a higher price in their own domestic market (where client brand loyalty basically translates into a captive market) than on external markets where devotion to a given brand is something that is difficult to build, especially when rival national carmakers are present. Pressure from consumer organizations – notably the European Office of Consumer Unions (BEUC) – has caused the European Commission to require from carmakers that they reduce their before tax price differentials to less than 30 per cent if they wish their block exemption regime to last until the year 2002. The fact that the objective of price convergence has not been reached led to changes in the Commission policy with the new regulation since 1 October 2002.

Disparities amongst national automobile demand

Even though the European automobile market's integration is still incomplete, carmakers have been clearly defining their product policies at a European level, especially since the markets' ongoing segmentation is definitively associated with the reduction in geographical disparities. By continually adding to vehicle product ranges, possibly as a result of the specification of shared platforms for each of the brands comprising an automobile group, carmakers can offer a very extensive catalogue of products for the European consumers' choice. This economic differentiation, which is both vertical and horizontal in nature, is offset by a reduction in geographical differentiation, in that more intensive cultural exchanges have led to some convergence amongst consumers (thus making it possible to launch marketing campaigns on a European market scale). By choosing and pooling the models (plus their variants) and the brands that it is offering, a carmaker can put together a vehicle range that is adapted to a local market. In this respect, and following its taking over of high-volume producers such as Seat and Skoda, and prestige marques such as Bugatti, Bentley and Lamborghini, the VW group now seems to have a complete product portfolio at its disposal (Table 4.3).

This integration does not necessarily mean that there will be a homogenization of national markets across the European Union's various member states. Although the Single Market has put an end to most regulatory disparities (this having been one reason of higher costs in Europe), there are still significant differences between the various types of national demand (see Table 4.4).

Nevertheless, market differentials of this nature pose no real problem for automakers who can use a group of products that had originally been designed for the European market (i.e., manufactured and assembled in

Table 4.3   VW's product range in Europe

Brand	Small car (B)	Lower middle range (M1)	Upper middle range (M2)	Large vehicle (H)	Luxury vehicle
Audi	A2	A3, TT	A4, S4	A6, A8	
Volkswagen	Polo, Lupo	Golf, Bora, New Beetle, Polo class	Passat,	Sharan	Touareg, Phaeton
Seat	Arosa, Ibiza	Cordoba, Vario, Leon	Toledo	Alhambra	
Skoda	Fabia	Felicia, Octavia	Superb		
Other brands					Bentley Bugatti Lamborghini

Source: Comité des Constructeurs, Français d'Automobiles.

Table 4.4 Breakdown of car sales in Europe by segment (in percentage of 2001 new car sales)

	Small car B	Lower middle range M1	Upper middle range M2	Large car H	Others (minibus, 4WD)
Northern Europe					
Sweden	12	23	24	36	5
Austria	20	38	21	15	7
Germany	21	32	18	22	7
Netherlands	29	36	19	12	4
European average	33	34	16	13	5
Southern Europe					
Spain	30	46	17	8	0
France	39	33	15	7	6
Portugal	47	36	11	6	1
Italy	53	27	10	7	5

Source: Comité des Constructeurs, Français d'Automobiles.

Europe's various countries) and adapt their local offerings to specific demand characteristics.

The affirmation of a vertical regional division of labour

European firms have long been pursuing strategies in which a clear distinction is made between protected domestic markets and two types of external markets: countries with open borders, towards which nationally manufactured products can be exported; and countries with closed borders, requiring foreign direct investment (FDI). In the case of the latter, manufacturers used to emphasize second-tier production: spare parts collection and assembly (CKD or SKD); or obsolete product manufacturing (in the cases of Eastern Europe, Spain, and Latin America). This changed completely in the early 1970s when Ford, after having integrated its German and English subsidiaries into a regional entity called Ford Europe, built a modern plant in Spain (Bordenave, 2003). The other carmakers would follow later, defining their vehicle product ranges and production organization on a continental scale and helping to create a highly coherent European automobile system (Lung, 2004). This was the beginning of an extremely hierarchical regional division of labour that created an asymmetrical polarization between the central regions, with their long-standing automobile traditions, and the peripheral regions. The 'nobility' of an activity would determine its centrality.

A major convergence in firms' productive architectures

For the past 30 years, automobiles and components makers have been progressively devising a set of coherent productive networks that are capable of functioning on a regional scale. At the same time, these firms' strategies have been profoundly influenced by the building of a European institutional framework. However, this process of regional industrial integration is, at least in part, an autonomous event. It stems from a continual rationalization of locations and activities that has coincided with firms' implantation in new European automobile countries: first in Belgium; then in the Iberian Peninsula; and more recently in Central and Eastern Europe. The growth of the regional automobile system had initially been led by firms' search for low wage areas. This integration, which had been conducted on a continental scale, unified not only firms' product ranges but also their processes, thereby leading to an ever-greater convergence between the performances that typified each productive network. It also modified the rules of competition and created the conditions for major restructuring operations: with the trend towards economic concentration in the component industry, that had long been characterized by its dispersion; and a direct financial, strategic and operational control by carmakers on their local subsidiaries.

The rationalization process associated with the integration of firms' productive networks was based on the segmentation of the productive process on a spatio-functional basis. The automobile production can be separated into several major functions (design, manufacturing, distribution), with the manufacturing stage in turn being divisible into a number of sub-systems (Bordenave and Lung, 1996). The importance of proximity for the development of knowledge and new products explains the relative concentration of R&D and this activity's need for a highly qualified workforce, meaning that it can only be carried out in Europe's metropolitan areas. This reality is not fundamentally modified when some of the segments involved in the design function are outsourced: the increasingly close cooperation between a carmaker and its suppliers' engineers during model design phases has exacerbated geographic polarization. The central financial activities are also concentrated in the major international financial centres, or in proximity to corporate headquarters. Inversely, sales activities (including the associated financial services) have to be dispersed in order to increase proximity to consumers. The distribution activities remain largely organized on a country-by-country basis to fit in with national institutional specificities.

Although the nature of the activities taking place at either end of the value chain renders them readily identifiable, the core of the productive process features agglomerative constraints that are more ambiguous in nature. In reality, manufacturing activities are subject to techno-economic agglomeration factors that limit their capacity for segmentation. Yet they are also invested with sources of scale economies related to the indivisibility of the technical production apparatus. The recent rediscovery of the crucial nature of scope economies does not mean that specialization advantages no longer count. Instead, it has encouraged firms to arbitrate between the costs and advantages of scope economies, notably by focusing on the compatibility between the various models produced at any given plant.

Firms' attempts to localize their facilities efficiently must also account for all of the costs associated with any relocation of production. First and foremost, this includes the social costs of plant closures; plus the costs that are related to the difficulties which firms can encounter in recruiting and training a workforce for their new facilities. For this reason, the European automobile system's restructuring over the past 30 years has resulted in the disappearance of only a small number of industrial plants. The European automobile industry has displayed a certain amount of geographic inertia – it is clearly concentrated along an industrial 'crescent' that extends from London to Milan to Birmingham.

A straightforward centre–periphery polarization

The older industrial regions continue to play a leading role in European automobile production. As we have seen, they play host to almost all of the activities which are deemed to be strategic: headquarters, finance, R&D. They also centralize most of the assembly operations involving top-of-the-range segments, as well as most high value added 'niche' production. The assembly of products that are drawn from the very top of the European range is basically the exclusive realm of the Germans (Mercedes, BMW, Audi) and, to a lesser extent, the Swedes (Volvo and Saab, respectively under the control of Ford and GM). Sports car assembly only occurs in Southern Germany and Northern Italy. All in all, the older automobile countries are characterized by the extreme diversification of their manufacturing activities, involving finished products as well as intermediate ones (components and organic mechanical systems).

Inversely, areas that are more geographically peripheral, and less economically developed (such as Eastern Europe, Turkey and Northern Africa) feature a narrow specialization in generic components, secondary textiles, and multiplex electrical wiring. It is also in these peripheral areas that entry-level vehicles are assembled. For example, in the late 1980s, Spain acquired a quasi-monopoly in the production of small cars (VW Polo, Ford Fiesta, Opel Corsa, Peugeot 205, Citroën AX, Renault Super 5 or Clio, etc.) and small utility vehicles (derived from passenger car platforms or other). The production zone for bottom-of-the-range products has since extended throughout Mediterranean Europe (Southern Italy, Slovenia, Turkey) as well as Central and Eastern Europe (Chapter 5). In terms of territorial hierarchy, it is significant that whenever entry-level vehicles are being produced in both a peripheral and a central location, the latter remains responsible for the special, deluxe or sporty variants. The intermediary areas (Spain, Southwest France, the new German Länder) share with the central zones the task of producing essential organic mechanical systems (engines and transmissions). These installations are often located in the immediate proximity of major vehicle assembly centres.

This hierarchy of areas and activities, closed to a centre/periphery structure, stems from convergences between firms' strategies. Above and beyond the mimetic phenomena which characterize oligopolistic competition, these strategies must account for increasingly similar economic realities: involving disparities in national (and even local) costs, standards of living, and lifestyles (Layan, 2000). Moreover, the significance of these objective factors has been reinforced by the converging cognitive representations held by decision-makers who share a number of (often arbitrary) certainties regarding territorial realities or the alleged 'nobility' of a given activity. At the same time, this vertical regional division of labour also reflects the hierarchy that exists between the actors who take part in the decision of location.

The high wage costs in (developed) Europe's core regions is definitely one of the factors behind the automobile industry's centrifugal expansion. This factorial advantage provides a partial explanation for the peripheral location of labour-intensive segments, particularly those that use a less skilled workforce: seat textiles manufacturing, wire-harnesses, electronic components assembly and, to a smaller extent, engine assembly. In reality, the peripheral localization of small car and small utility vehicle production relates to the way in which cost structures vary by product range segment: the lower the value of the vehicle and the simpler its design, the more wage costs represent as a proportion of its total value. Moreover, firms are particularly sensitive to the cost of this type of product when market entry competition is primarily price-based.

The preference of carmakers to produce small vehicles in Europe's peripheral areas can also be explained by the downscale segments' overrepresentation in the less developed markets of Southern and Central Europe. These markets' proximity affects the output's transportation costs; and, above all, it conditions the profitability of existing capacities, which is directly linked to the size of market. The uneven spatial distribution of demand thus largely explains the productive spatial hierarchy: top-of-the-range vehicles are manufactured in the central regions (where the living standards are high); and more basic vehicles are made in the more peripheral regions.

The dynamics of specialization in the European automobile system

The vertical regional division of labour exemplifies an underlying trend in the European automobile system. Nevertheless, this classical centre–periphery model is neither inevitable, nor is it written in stone. It allows for a certain number of exceptions, 'waivers', which enable us to transcend schematic analyses, and to fine-tune our understanding of regional specificities.

Higher-level activities being carried out in geographically peripheral regions

The main problem with using the aforementioned polarization to evaluate the current situation stems from the many facts that belie this notion of a European periphery which has been inserted, at a subaltern level, into the automobile sector's continental division of labour. Nowadays, the area around Barcelona (Spain) has become a top-flight automobile styling centre. In much the same way, Delphi has recently opened an engineering centre in Poland. It may also seem surprising that vehicles targeting a wealthier clientele are now being produced in zones that are located at a considerable distance from Europe's centres: the Volkswagen Group's minivan vehicles such as the VW Sharan and the Seat Alhambra, like the Ford Galaxy, are being manufactured in Setubal, Portugal – whilst Mercedes' minivans (the Vito and now the Vaneo) are being made in the company's ultra-modern factory in Vitoria (in Spain's Basque country). Moreover, many of the off-road vehicles blocking the roadside in Europe's major cities are actually being produced in Spain (Suzuki, Nissan, Ford). At the other extreme, the mini city cars being assembled in Spain (the Ford Ka, in Valencia) or in Hungary (the Suzuki Wagon R+ in Esztergom) are destined for Europe's more developed metropolitan areas as a second or third household vehicle.

The production of innovative products in peripheral areas exported to mature markets is explained by the chronological convergence of the various projects: the greenfield plants now host the new products. This convergence also demonstrates business leaders' fundamental preference for managing risk on a territorial basis, and for relocating away from the central regions their assembly of products which correspond to new and hitherto misunderstood demands. However, the risks associated with this type of behaviour can be especially high when the firms involved are not leaders in their particular segment (for example, VW or Ford in the case of minivans, or Opel for city cars). In addition, this trend towards managing industrial risks in peripheral locations also applies to organizational innovations – a recurrent example being the way in which Volkswagen's foreign subsidiaries experiment with new sourcing relationships. In 1993, the VW group opened Europe's first JIT complex at the new Seat plant in Martorell (Barcelona, Spain). Later, it applied the principles of modular production (with direct onsite involvement of suppliers) at Skoda's Mlada Boleslav complex in the Czech Republic before implementing it in its historical plants in Germany (Lung et al., 1999). Such choices would appear to revolve around the development of a real strategy for overcoming the obstacles to change that had cropped up in the VW German plants, where employees and their unions were not prepared to accept any degradation of their status.

The European automobile system's architecture is continually changing under the combined effect of a number of factors that can impact upon car and parts makers' localization strategies: the geographical structure of demand; changing competitive interactions; technical or organizational innovations; variations in the institutional framework. Firms are in fact continually trying to transform these changes in their environment into a competitive advantage. At the same time, the insertion of Europe's peripheral areas into a vertical regional division of labour, and carmakers' building of coherent productive networks, have radically altered the system's prevailing circumstances.

A permanent relocation of activities

The European automobile system now extends to the very edge of the continental space. Little by little, this movement has made it possible to overcome the divergences that had originally sparked the productive networks' international expansion. The opening up of markets that have long been protected, plus the radical organization of certain national industries, have led to a redistribution of comparative advantages – both in the peripheral areas, and (reactively) in the traditional automobile regions.

As we have seen, when firms first set up new plants in emerging countries, they are exploiting both a productive and a commercial advantage. They can benefit from a workforce that is both flexible and inexpensive – and at the same time, they can take advantage of markets that are expanding, and which remain comparatively closed to foreign competitors. However, even though consumers' preference for national brands usually persists, this advantage is usually short-lived: trade integration processes progressively erode such markets' commercial specificities. Over the long run, competitive advantages that revolve around cheap wages and worker passivity are condemned to die out as average income rises, and lifestyles and mindsets change.

This phenomenon has been observable in Southern Europe since the early 1990s. It explains the automobile industry's relative loss of interest in the Iberian Peninsula (at least in comparison with the 1980s). Above all, it explains the slowdown in the Portuguese automobile market, from which Renault (which closed its Setubal factory and transferred production to a new plant in Slovenia) and Ford (which abandoned its AutoEuropa joint venture with VW and closed its pickup assembly unit) have both withdrawn. In fact, during the 1990s, the search for new opportunities of this sort persuaded firms to reorient their investments, and they began to target Central and Eastern Europe (as well as Turkey). Nevertheless, during the 1990s, the Iberian Peninsula consolidated his position in the European automotive system (Lung, 2004) and it did not suffer a relocation of activities from Southern to Central and Eastern Europe (cf. Table 4.5).

At the same time, by building modern factories in the peripheral areas of Europe, the conditions determining the central regions' profitability have changed. The inter-plant competition has considerably weakened workers'

Table 4.5 Automobile production in the European Union, 1990–2000 (Countries with production over 100,000 vehicles per year)

Country	1990			2000			Change		
	Passenger cars	Industrial vehicles	Total vehicles	Passenger cars	Industrial vehicles	Total vehicles	Passenger cars	Industrial vehicles	Total vehicles
Austria	10,473	5,716	16,189	99,000	25,811	124,811	88,527	20,095	108,622
Belgium*	313,400	50,151	363,551	912,233	121,061	1,033,294	598,833	70,910	669,743
France*	3,294,815	474,178	3,768,993	2,923,093	406,943	3,330,036	−371,722	−67,235	−438,957
Germany	4,660,657	315,895	4,976,552	5,131,919	394,700	5,526,619	471,262	78,805	550,067
Italy	1,874,672	246,178	2,120,850	1,422,281	320,015	1,742,296	−452,391	73,837	−378,554
Netherlands	121,300	29,832	151,132	215,085	41,697	256,782	93,785	11,865	105,650
Portugal	60,221	77,466	137,687	193,651	55,286	248,937	133,430	−22,180	111,250
Spain	1,679,301	374,049	2,053,350	2,385,639	666,515	3,052,154	706,338	292,466	998,804
Sweden	335,853	74,415	410,268	396,170	115,164	511,334	60,317	40,749	101,066
United Kingdom	1,295,611	270,346	1,565,957	1,621,228	187,072	1,808,300	325,617	−83,274	242,343
European Union (consolidated)	13,061,853	2,688,509	15,750,362	14,906,571	2,693,033	17,599,604	1,844,718	4,524	1,849,242

Note: * Due to changes in the convention relative to the geographical allocation of vehicles production in Belgium and France occurred in 1996, data are not directly comparable between 1990 and 2000.

Source: Comité des Constructeurs, Français d'Automobiles.

ability to negotiate: workers have had to become much more flexible; and their pay packages have been eroded (all of this in an environment marked by a high level of unemployment). In fact, certain firms have now begun to view central area re-localization as something that is in their interest. After UK for Japanese transplants, three new assembly plants have been recently located in northern France: MCC-Smart (at Hambach, in the Lorraine region); SEVEL-Nord (a joint venture between PSA and Fiat); and, more recently, Toyota (the latter two being located in Valenciennes' suburbs). Like the less developed European areas, the zones chosen lack any automobile tradition, on one hand – and are eligible for European Community industrial reconversion subsidies, on the other. Ford's Halewood factory in the UK, a site of frequent English industrial disputes during the 1970s and often presented as a symbol of the British automobile industry's low productivity and deficient quality, has been reconverted into a plant for assembling the new Baby Jaguars. Amongst other things, this highlights the traditional automobile regions' capacity for learning and for mobilization.

The recent strategic reorientation by a certain number of carmakers should also be analysed in terms of the problems that these manufacturers have encountered in the newly industrialized countries in obtaining quality levels and delivery times that match international standards. However, this state of affairs should change soon, as carmakers encourage their traditional suppliers either to establish facilities near their own plants; or else, to strike up an association with local suppliers (i.e., in a joint venture). Examples include VW in the Czech Republic, or Fiat and Daewoo in Poland (Havas, 2000a). This development of partnership strategies linking carmakers and their component suppliers has led to an increase in the number of co-location decisions and a reinforcement of the automotive industry territorial embeddedness into this calculation. At the same time, this co-location does not necessarily take the form of clusters or of 'JIT complexes' (Frigant and Lung, 2002). If suppliers' parks are growing, they often only play host to the major parts makers' second rank facilities with sub-assembly or even warehouses activities rather than manufacturing (Larsson, 2002).

The reciprocal influence of localization is only perceptible at a relatively large regional level. Many suppliers to the Spanish automobile industry are concentrated in the Ebro River Valley, which constitutes an archipelago of industrial sites spread over more than 500 kilometres, running from Santander to Barcelona. The proximity constraint has in fact been greatly undermined by the constitution of continental networks. Like the sector's continued search for investment opportunities in Central Europe or in Turkey, the Spanish industry's ongoing subordination in a third rank role bears witness to the main industrial groups' renewed competence in areas where technical and organizational learning processes are in effect. In Spain, this phenomenon has created a substitution of advantages – the move up the experience curve having by and large offset the rise in labour costs. This is yet another country where product variety has risen, and where the quality of product range is growing. These trends have brought the 'Spanish specialization' closer into line with what can be found in the older auto-mobile countries. They have clearly been reinforced by the way in which the structure of the national demand has been changed as a result of the rise in average income.

Similar trends have been taking place in Eastern Europe (Hungary, the Czech Republic and, above all, Poland), where product and activity ranges have continued to widen. The building of a Delphi engineering centre, with worldwide competencies, in this region reflects the rising standard of the local competencies that firms can now call upon: initially low dynamic specializations in generic components can generate activities that increase the value being created.

Conclusion

By the early 1990s, Europe seemed to be under threat from new Japanese or Korean entrants to the global automobile market. At the time of writing, it would appear that Europe has consolidated its position as one of the auto-mobile industry's major poles: 16.9 million vehicles were assembled in 2002, representing 28.8 per cent of world production (Lung, 2002). The conver-gence of national markets, the growing political union and firms' strategies – all of these factors have combined to give shape to an automotive system that possesses a high degree of coherency at a continental level. At the same time, this deep transformation has caused changes in product ranges, the location of facilities, the number and dimension of the actors involved, and sometimes even their very nature. It has been accompanied by a clear improvement in European companies' performances, with firms now being less concerned with their territory of origin and more apt to pursue ambi-tious worldwide strategies. Those firms that had appeared to be falling behind during the globalization phase of the early 1990s seem to have now turned this apparent handicap to their advantage (thanks to alliances such as Daimler–Chrysler–Mitsubishi, or Renault–Nissan–Samsung).

At the same time, the European automobile continent has continued to change. There are signs of a potential integration of new peripheral areas, and specializations are continually being reshuffled. In the automobile industry, European regional integration dynamics have clearly opted for a continual redefinition of whatever advantages are being developed at a given moment in time – advantages that firms first seek to construct, and later to supersede. Rather than relying on a static vision which draws pre-mature conclusions as to an alleged return to specialization, concentration, or the type of spatio-functional division that is featured in a stable centre–periphery model, we should be focusing on the continued reconstruction of localization advantages, and construe this as part of a regional integration trajectory that, even if it is less clear-cut than the North American trajectory (Chapter 7), has not yet displayed some of the latter configuration's limits – and potential reversibility.

Translation by Alan Sitkin

5
Peripheral Regionalism: The Consequences of Integrating Central and Eastern Europe in the European Automobile Space

Rob van Tulder

Introduction: transition under uncertainty

Following the fall of the Berlin Wall in 1989, a breathtaking transformation took place in the Central and Eastern European (CEE) automobile space. Despite the formation of its own regional free trade area (CEFTA), the importance of the prospective integration of these countries inside the European Community/Union can hardly be overestimated. It made industrial development in those countries in general, and in the car industry in particular, subject to a process of 'peripheral regionalism'. CEE countries swapped their previous dependence on a division of labour within the Warsaw Pact economy under the aegis of the former Soviet Union, for a position in the production networks of western producers under the aegis of the European Union. As a result, they gained considerable political autonomy, but partly lost (again) economic autonomy.

The car industry has been the leading driver of this process in many countries. By 1996 the car industry, including the components industry, in leading countries like Hungary, Poland and the Czech Republic was already almost completely foreign-owned – thereby representing the highest degree of foreign capital penetration of any of the manufacturing sectors. Foreign ownership is considered by many to have positive economic effects in particular for transition economies. Some, however, also characterized the transition as the creation of a new form of 'colonialism' – even implying the downgrading of suppliers and the destruction of skills and competences (cf. Havas, 2000a: 257). The jury is still pending on this dispute, not least because the transition period is not yet at an end. The automobile industry has in any case been among the leading agents of change in Central and Eastern Europe. In 2000, of the leading thirty foreign affiliates in the manufacturing industry in the region, nine were in the motor vehicles industry (UNCTAD, 2003: 15) – with a combined sales volume of more than one-third of all foreign affiliates. Pavlínek (2002: 57) attributes it to the 'FDI-driven restructuring of passenger car manufacturing [that] output and employment in the motor vehicle sector grew more rapidly than for manufacturing as a whole in [Hungary, Poland and the Czech Republic] between 1995 and 2000.' This observation seems to suggest that development has perhaps been relatively dependent upon foreign capital, but also relatively successful – at least in these three countries. However, is this optimism warranted for the region as a whole?

This chapter assesses the outcome of peripheral regionalism as it developed in the automobile industry in Central and Eastern Europe. It assesses whether the process holds promises or risks for a future automobile space in the region. This critically depends on a number of uncertainties surrounding the enlargement of the European Union. At least three – strongly interrelated – uncertainties have been relevant: entry, institutional and strategic uncertainties.

Entry uncertainty

Uncertainty over the outcome of accession talks continued throughout the 1990s until 2002. Which countries would become members of the European Union, how fast and under what specific arrangements? The number of potential first-entry countries fluctuated between five and 15. Countries that were always most likely to be first-entry countries were Hungary, Poland, the Czech Republic, Malta and Slovenia. As a consequence, they received different, and considerably more favourable, attention from western car manufacturers than countries such as Romania or Bulgaria that had never appeared in the first pool of prospective members. In 2002 it was finally decided that ten countries would be admitted to the European Union – including all of the Baltic states. The bargaining process did not stop after the basic decision was made: even in December 2002 – days before the finalization of the accession talks – the membership of the biggest prospective member, Poland, still depended upon the outcome of ostensibly relatively banal bargaining issues – in particular, the Polish protectionist policies towards car trade.

Institutional uncertainty

Although most CEE countries applied for membership, the very nature of that very membership remained unclear. Throughout the 1990s, the European Community/Union was finalizing its 'internal market' programme, got enlarged with three additional member states and slowly moved into the direction of a Monetary Union. The number of countries that would constitute a 'eurozone' remained obscure. After finally 11 of the 15 EU member states entered the eurozone, discussions about the outlook of this institution as well as on new member states continued. Some CEE countries in the process found that they were more strict in applying EU directives and technical standards than some of the present members. Major disputes between the European Commission and first-tier accession countries centred around competition, taxation and subsidy policies. Hungary, for instance, had been the most successful in attracting foreign investment, through a variety of policy instruments – such as tax holidays for sometimes ten years. In the 1990–95 period Hungary was able to attract more foreign investment than all of the other CEE countries combined. Other countries followed suit – leading not only to fierce locational competition, but also to practices that were not allowed under EU law. As late as 2002 the European Commission complained that Hungary had failed to bring its policy on tax concession into line with EU rules (EIU, 2002: 85). Car firms have not only profited from these schemes, but have in fact actively contributed to an intensification of the locational competition/tournaments by making their investment decisions (partly) dependent on the support packages offered by local governments.

Strategic uncertainty

Many of the CEE countries had placed high hopes for economic growth on the effects of privatization and foreign investment. By many accounts, the fact that business people would press ahead with foreign direct investment in the region had been an important consideration for politicians in finally ending the repeated postponement of accession talks (*Financial Times*, 31 October 2002). The effects of foreign business strategies on the international position of the national economy depended upon the strategic aims of foreign investors: would they aim to integrate the local production in an international division of labour; would production be aimed at the domestic market or at exports? How foot-loose would the investment be and could governments impose local content requirements on the investors? Would it make a difference whether a German, American or a South Korean car firm invested in the country? Political uncertainties about the strategic intentions of international car manufacturers interacted with firm-level uncertainties about the outcome of the accession talks and the institutional course taken by the EU. Under those circumstances strategic planning was difficult.

After 1989, many observers expected that CEE countries would offer potentially lucrative future car markets. Sales were expected to reach at least three million units by the year 2000 (*Financial Times*, 11 December 1990). This expectation proved to be overly optimistic. The market for new cars around 2000 in Central and Eastern Europe (including Russia) amounted to two million units – roughly comparable to the sales volume in 1985 (CCFA, 2000).

So, car producers had to adjust their local sales prospects as well to the new market realities. However, they themselves were also reproached for contributing to lower than expected sales. By supporting the government's strategies of imposing high import barriers in the early 1990s, they could operate in relatively protected markets, which at the same time also limited effective competition in the local market, lower prices and thus hampered market growth. Initially, car production in the CEE countries declined also, to take up the growth pace after 1994. CEE absolute volumes of car production in 2000 considerably exceeded the 1990 levels (Pavlínek, 2002; Lung, 2004). In relative terms during the 1990–2000 period CEE production increased from 5.0 to 6.0 per cent of world passenger car production, and from 11.4 to 14.3 per cent in European car production (Pavlínek, 2002: 61). This increase in output was only attributable to integration in the Western European automobile space. But would there still be possibilities for CEE countries to develop their own models and technologies?

These three factors of uncertainty are related, their relevance changed over time and their impact on countries varied. Throughout the 1990s, industry observers have speculated about the configurations that could develop within the CEEC automobile space. Some stressed the continued salience of existing national and regional differences. Others stated that a new map of auto production would mature in the form of a European 'car system' (Banville and Chanaron, 1991). Bordenave and Lung (1996) anticipated that the integration of the West and Eastern European car production networks would probably involve a vertical division of labour within Europe, leading partly to the disintegration of national industries and forms of decentralization. With the benefit of hindsight, the remainder of this chapter shows what has happened and what the prospects for a viable automobile space are.

This chapter documents the 'rush to the East' and the way in which various CEE countries in the course of the 1990s, became integrated in production, sales and supply networks of car majors (next section). The international network position induces a particular 'room for manoeuvre' for individual CEE countries (following section). Assessing the potential for a viable automobile space in the CEE region is the ultimate aim of this chapter (final section).

The rush to the East

Once upon a time, the auto industry symbolized the centrally-planned economies' ambition to provide their citizens with consumption levels comparable to those of free market economies. By 1989, at least nine proud, independent producers of substantial volumes of cars existed in Central and Eastern Europe (excluding the Soviet Union): Wartburg and Trabant in the German Democratic Republic, FSM and FSO in Poland, Skoda in Czechoslovakia, Industrije Motronih Vozil (IMV) in Slovenia, Zastava Yugo

Automobili, the Serb producer of the Yugo brand, and Dacia and Oltcit in Romania. Ten years later, none of these firms had survived. Most have come under the control of western volume producers, mostly through takeovers rather than through the establishment of greenfield sites. All western car manufacturers were obviously interested in Central and Eastern Europe. The CEEC region could solve part of their overcapacity problem contained a large pool of cheap labour, could act as a laboratory for organization innovation, and created the possibility of developing a regional division of labour.

The prospect of EU membership had major repercussions for CEEC. The region became a relatively protected 'hunting ground' for companies with an EU legal identity. The legal status of European-based firm enabled those firms to evade EU local content regulation, more easily set up supplier networks and integrate them in their own regional networks. It also enabled these producers to obtain particular benefits from local governments – such as a duty-free zone at the time of entry. The Hungarian case provides an example of the different 'terms of trade' for European and non-European producers (cf. Bartlett and Seleny, 1998). Three major car manufacturers invested in the country: Suzuki, GM/Opel and Volkswagen/Audi. GM/Opel and Audi had a legal status as a European-based multinationals – combined with a continentally organized supply network. Suzuki's legal status of a Japanese-based multinational prevented it from obtaining a duty-free zone and forced the firm to increase local sourcing with Hungarian sub-component firms in order to adhere to EU rules. Three rival investment strategies appeared in the CEEC region: (1) frontrunners, (2) latecomers and (3) peripheral players. The strategies developed by each group of players had distinctive *origins* in their domestic car complexes (cf. van Tulder and Ruigrok, 1998).

Frontrunner networks

Over the course of two years (1991–92), around 90 per cent of the production capacity of Central and Eastern European producers was acquired by four European car producers: Volkswagen, Opel/GM, Fiat and Renault. Many of these moves were based on long-established historical ties: for example, Fiat had worked closely with the Poles since 1966, and GM Europe had some 30 years experience in the Hungarian market. To German-based companies, the eastern part of Germany appeared to offer a logical extension of their operations. Renault had been cooperating with local producer IMV in Slovenia since 1972. Swift action was necessary because for every takeover target there were many contenders. All firms focused primarily on the volume car segment.

Aiming at maximum market share, while confronted with considerable overcapacity, prompted these firms to adopt a rapid entry strategy in the CEEC region. The Volkswagen group (with its takeover of Skoda in the Czech Republic and of Trabant in Eastern Germany) and Fiat (takeover of

FSM in Poland) adopted a rapid and rather aggressive takeover strategy. Opel/General Motors (takeover of Wartburg, 1991) was quick, but generally more hesitant than either of the leading European car complexes. Both Volkswagen and Opel – as the largest German volume producers – were quick to safeguard their interests in the German automobile space by acquiring the remnants of the East German car industry. Renault took a lucrative piece of a producer located in a relatively marginal part of the CEEC region (partnership with IMV turned into majority ownership, Slovenia; in 1999 did it take over Dacia of Romania). Traditionally, French activities in Central and Eastern Europe were largely limited to the Balkan countries. All volume producers were bidding for participation in Central European car producers by the start of the 1990s. Renault's attempted takeover of Skoda in 1990/91 failed.

Frontrunner companies acted jointly with their national governments. Even though the investments in Central and Eastern Europe are based primarily on firm-specific strategic considerations, governments in Germany (regarding former DDR), Italy (regarding Catholic Poland) and in France (with regard to Renault's failed bid for Skoda, but successful bid for IMV in Slovenia) supported investment plans for a variety of political and social reasons. The frontrunner strategy also necessitated acquiring controlling stakes in the CEEC firms in order to lock-out other contenders. No big greenfield investments were planned other than after misconstrued takeover bids.

All frontrunner firms aimed at the local market *as well as* at reimportations back into Western Europe. A *segmentation* of production inside Europe became envisaged, in which the Eastern European part of the network produces the lower end of the models. So Fiat built its Cinquecento – Fiat's smallest car – only in Poland for the whole (European) market, whereas Volkswagen built its Skoda cars only in the Czech Republic for exports to the West. GM planned to develop and produce a new range of low-cost, small cars in Central Europe – smaller than its Opel Corsa supermini. All four producers attached important value to their first production site – as a coordination point for their Central and Eastern Europe strategy. These markets still represent their most important outlet in the CEEC region. Sales of Renault in the CEEC region are strongly biased towards the tiny market of Slovenia and – since its acquisition of Dacia – towards Romania. Poland has remained the largest market for Fiat and Opel, the Czech Republic and Slovakia for Volkswagen. Other markets are in lower tiered position.

The frontrunner position also facilitated the takeover of distribution networks and therefore enabled these firms to buy their way into the local market. In most Eastern European countries, state-owned sales and service outlets were representing various makes. These 'mega-dealers' could be turned into 'single-franchise' dealers applying 'European specifications'. This strategy created additional entry barriers for late-comers. Fiat bought its way into Poland – with an original market share for Fiat of almost 50 per cent. Volkswagen bought almost 80 per cent of the Czech market and more than 70 per cent of the Slovak market (where it also commenced the production of Passat cars in 1996). Renault 'conquered' the lucrative Slovenian market, the third largest market in the Central European region. Acquiring Dacia in Romania resulted in an immediate market share of more than 70 per cent in 2000. Opel managed to earn a market share in Hungary of 13 per cent that it had not been able to achieve in any of the other CEE markets. The high share of the domestic market declined over the 1990s, but the leading position of the frontrunner firms in the national market has not been changed. Comparable observations can be made for peripheral firms (see later) that were the first to enter a country – Suzuki and Daewoo in particular. Suzuki managed to reach a 20 per cent market share in Hungary, whereas Daewoo reached market shares of 20 per cent in Poland and Romania – before the company went into insolvency.

Follower networks

The two remaining 'European' volume producers, Ford Europe and PSA, did not join the bandwagon of the frontrunner firms. PSA was keen to do so, but could not muster enough bargaining clout for successful acquisitions. Only towards the end of the 1990s did PSA's continued efforts to enter the CEE market start to pay off. By 2002, PSA had obtained a 6 per cent penetration rate (selling 110,000 units) (Loubet, 2003: 163). As a latecomer PSA relied on networks with local partners. In 2001 PSA teamed up with Toyota in order to establish a joint-venture assembly plant in the Czech Republic and, some months later, it announced another specific greenfield plant in the same country.

On the other hand, Ford Europe did not want to engage in large-scale acquisitions. Over the course of the 1990s it opened, but also (in 2000) closed operations in Belarus and Poland. Ford's non-EU status created substantial entry barriers (for example, with regard to local content requirements). The latecomers looked primarily at the region as a market and have not been prepared or capable of making a credible bid for some of the bigger companies left in the East. Because of the market-oriented nature of the investments, most of the plants operated the latecomer producers are SKD in nature. The proliferation of their production networks into Central and Eastern Europe remained limited. It can be expected that as soon as the tariff barriers with the European Union are removed (around 2004), these facilities will be wound down.

Peripheral networks

The EU car market is surrounded by direct and indirect trade barriers (see Chapter 2). The opening up of the CEEC region as well as the prospect of a free trade agreement with the European Union inspired many peripheral firms to try to enter 'through the back door'. PSA (in Romania and Poland)

and even GM/Opel (in Poland and Russia) were outpaced by more adventurous new entrants from Asia. In particular, Suzuki and Daewoo targeted Central and Eastern Europe as a production site that would allow them to overcome European trade barriers and to enter the Western European market. Both of these firms shared an interesting common feature: they were in a relatively weak position in their home countries. Only since 1992 was Daewoo capable of exporting cars. Daewoo had a 18 per cent market share in South Korea, compared to Hyundai's 52 per cent and Kia's 26 per cent. Daewoo lacked the real cash to invest in core regions, whilst its car-producing activities were loss-making. Suzuki was 15 per cent owned by General Motors and compared to Toyota it was a relatively small producer of mainly compact cars. As early as 1985 Suzuki started to negotiate setting up a production site in Hungary. Suzuki hoped to use Hungary as both a cheap production base and a springboard to Western and Central and Eastern European markets. After a series of steps by 1997 Suzuki had acquired a controlling share of 77.7 per cent in a local consortium to create Magyar Suzuki and had also negotiated a lucrative tax holiday. Daewoo acquisitions in Eastern Europe were part of an ambitious, but risky, plan to quadruple Daewoo's worldwide car production to two million by the year 2000. Very generous investment plans triggered the interest of governments in Poland (a joint venture with FSO in 1995) and Romania (the takeover of Oltcit in 1994). The company negotiators made intelligent use of the frustration of the local government with lingering negotiations with some of the large Western European car producers. As the chairman and founder of the Daewoo group, Mr Kim Woo-Choong, stated, the company denounced the intentions of the other car manufacturers 'whose operations suggest something not very different from an extension of former European colonialism' (*Financial Times*, 8 May 1996). The Daewoo strategy has been very risky not only for the firm itself, but also for the local stakeholders. Because of its limited own financial leverage, Daewoo was going public with stocks in local capital markets. The company promised to reinvest the money in 'developing local operations' as it is called (ibid.). When Daewoo ran into financial difficulties – leading to its bankruptcy in 2000 – all of its CEE partners also ran into difficulties (cf. Chapter 14). The prime problem for the peripheral producers has been to adhere to the strict and high local content (80 per cent) requirements needed to export into the European Union. For both producers this has not been either easy or without cost. Suzuki, for instance, could in Hungary achieve only 25 per cent local content by 1992 (Havas, 2000b). Both producers embarked on programmes to enhance the capacity of local producers to deliver the required quality levels – rather than bringing in the own supplier from Asia which would have meant high transaction costs. Suzuki aimed at a regional division of labour between its plants in the CEEC region and those in Western Europe (Spain). On the other hand Daewoo aimed at a regional division of labour *within* the CEEC region, because it did not have any production facilities elsewhere. In particular Daewoo, due to its much weaker domestic position even compared to Suzuki, also tried to 'define' its way out of some of the trade policy consequences, by using different definitions of local content than formally applied under EU regulation.

Supply networks

Each strategic group involved a different set-up of supply networks.

Frontrunner firms had no principal problem in adhering to EU local content rules. But in the accession discussions most local governments demanded commitment to setting up an advanced local parts suppliers industry. A promise readily made – but not always kept. By the midst of the 1990s, most frontrunner firms started to scale down the high degree of vertical integration. Frontrunner firms targeted particular supply networks in the Central European countries. In particular, Hungary was an important target because it was one of the few Central and Eastern European states with an automotive components industry that was independent from (national) vehicle assemblers. But CEEC producers could only become suppliers to western firms by entering into a joint venture with another western firm, which created other dependencies (cf. Havas, 2000b).

Follower firms did not invest in production capacity for re-imports or exports to other parts of the world. Consequently, the need to create high levels of local content remained both politically and economically limited.

The companies adopting a peripheral strategy (in particular Daewoo) have been aiming at a regional division of labour. In this scenario, local component producers had a chance of becoming first-tier suppliers of medium-tech products. Peripheral players like Suzuki and Daewoo thus differed from the other car companies in their approach to local suppliers. It creates changes for the development of local suppliers, but the suppliers run the risk of getting 'locked in' into the supply network of a lower end producer. The Hungarian production for Suzuki for instance is for a relatively dated car; furthermore, Suzuki struck supply licences with its Hungarian suppliers that precluded the Hungarian firms from supplying to other Suzuki plants outside Hungary or to other customers in Western Europe (although sales to other assemblers in Eastern Europe remained possible, in theory).

Tiers and fears in Central and Eastern Europe

Most entry strategies have been politically induced and/or facilitated. No non-European firm was initially capable of acquiring any degree of ownership in the CEEC region beyond Eastern Germany. The prospect of entering into a free-trade zone with the European Union – ultimately of becoming an EU member – raised the willingness of most CEEC governments to enter into deals with Western European producers in particular. European institutions such as the European Bank for Reconstruction and Development have taken an active stance in facilitating the plans of Western European firms. Other interest groups such as ACEA, the organization of 'European' carmakers, have closely monitored – and influenced – the terms of accession under which non-European firms made use of the CEEC region as a production site. The European Commission has been an increasingly active player in the region. The European integration process also created substantial impediments for *non-European producers* of new cars and components. Tariff barriers in all CEE countries for imports from third countries on all categories of imports of cars and components were raised, whereas tariff barriers towards EU and CEFTA countries were reduced to zero. The integration process *ex-ante* led to the adoption of 'European specifications' for instance on the basis of association agreements signed between the EU and ten Central and Eastern European countries. This process followed the effective harmonization of technical requirements for new vehicles (in 1993) and mutually recognized type-approval certification in any one member state that became implemented in the second half of the 1990s.

The association agreements had already integrated the CEEC region into most of the EU car institutions. Most CEEC governments were in a relatively weak bargaining position vis-à-vis the European Commission and the individual car producers. Governments were under pressure from consumers to get themselves the cars they had been waiting for so many years. Cars also became an important symbol that governments were serious about removing the old dominance of the Soviet Union. Therefore, all governments presented various mixtures of generous subsidy schemes, free trade zones and tax holidays in order to attract foreign direct investment. The bargaining dynamics of countries that were the object of the first takeover spread (in particular, Poland and the Czech Republic) differed from that of the other countries. Since they were not only a market but also a production site, the local governments developed more restrictive trade and industrial policies. In 1997, Poland for instance had import duties of 25 per cent on all cars imported from the European Union. In 2001, import duties had been lowered to zero in all prospective entry countries. But in the transition period, thus, producers operating from Poland even had protection from other EU producers. Those CEE countries that did not have their own car industry (Bulgaria, Albania) went for a much quicker liberalization of their markets. Countries that tried to keep an independent car industry (Romania) or wanted to build their own manufacturing capabilities (Hungary) showed a mixture of policies, that also changed over time. For instance, Hungary removed most obstacles to the private import of cars in September 1989, soon after the turnround. This policy stance represented its position as a car market, without its own production capacity. Only after a few years, however, 'various restrictive measures such as 25 per cent VAT, increased import tariffs, import quota, and technical and environmental tests for cars over

Table 5.1 Automobile production in Central and Eastern European countries, 1990–2000

	1990			2000			Change		
	Passenger cars	Industrial vehicles	Total vehicles	Passenger cars	Industrial vehicles	Total vehicles	Passenger cars	Industrial vehicles	Total vehicles
Bulgaria	14,600	8,800	23,400		500	500	-14,600	-8,300	-22,900
Yugoslavia	289,362	29,754	319,116				-160,362	-29,754	-190,116
B&H			—	2,500		2,500			
Serbia			—	9,500		9,500			
Slovenia			—	117,000		117,000			
Czechoslovakia	187,773	28,587	216,360				394,082	-895	393,187
Czech Republic				428,205	27,408	455,613			
Slovakia				153,650	284	153,934			
Hungary		9,003	9,003	148,200	3,400	151,600	148,200	-5,603	142,597
Poland	283,890	51,604	335,494	653,140	73,322	726,462	369,250	21,718	390,968
Romania	90,000	11,400	101,400	64,181	13,984	78,165	-25,819	2,584	-23,235
Total (unconsolidated)	865,625	139,148	1,004,773	1,576,376	118,898	1,695,274	710,751	-20,250	690,501

Source: Autonews.

six years' were re-introduced (Havas, 1995: 7). This new policy position was partly triggered by the wish 'to curb the outflow of foreign exchange and the influx of "moving wrecks"' (ibid.), but also neatly represented the new position of the country in which Suzuki and other Western European component manufacturers have built up local production. In the 1990s, a four-tiered structure of CEE countries developed.

First-tier countries: Eastern Germany, Czech Republic and Poland

Eastern Germany rapidly became integrated in the Western German car industry. But in particular the Czech Republic and Poland can be considered as first-tier countries. Over the 1990–2000 period the two countries became the carbuilding powerhouse of the region, with 1.2 million vehicles produced in 2000, about 70 per cent of the total production in CEE – respectively 42.9 per cent for Poland, and 26.9 per cent for the Czech Republic (Table 5.1). They function as the apex of a regional division of labour and at the cutting-edge of the internationalization strategies adopted by leading German, Italian, South Korean firms – and later even of one French car producer. They have the largest car markets, and are producing the largest volumes of cars in the region. They developed a trade surplus in units of cars (not in value), but also erected more and diverse trade barriers – largely on behalf of the car complexes that invested in these countries. The first-tier countries also became ingrained in the 'world-car' strategies of Fiat and Volkswagen, where they produce and develop lower-end versions and often only one model in the parent's product range. At the same time, both have been able to attract major investment from competing car majors, thus creating a greater room for manoeuvre and bigger changes for positive spillover due to the possible agglomeration effects related to foreign investment.

Second-tier countries: Hungary, Slovenia and Slovakia

Second-tier countries have in particular become integrated in networks of component supply. The assembly operations they contain generally share a lower local content, whereas their trade orientation is much more export oriented. They share a structural trade deficit (in units as well as in value) in finished cars. Although some of these countries have tried to adopt their own developmental strategies in the car industry, their room for manoeuvre has been smaller than was the case for the first-tier countries. *Slovenia* – which is the most affluent market due to the highest per capita income in the CEE region – became 'Renault country'. Renault's strategy in the country is to produce one brand almost exclusively (the Clio since 1996) aimed at exports to France and Italy. The share of Slovenian car production in the CEE region slightly increased from 3.5 per cent to 4.9 per cent in the 1990–2000 period (Pavlínek, 2002: 63). The two other second-tier countries can be considered to have been more successful: after 1990 both Slovakia and Hungary developed own car production capacity from scratch, growing to shares of respectively 7.3 per cent and 5.4 per cent of the CEE car market (ibid.). *Slovakia* became 'Volkswagen country', but as a clear annex to the Czech production and sales site with an even stronger export orientation.

Hungary became 'Suzuki country' (and Audi). Other assembly operations located in the country have remained relatively small, with limited value added and local contents, whilst open for locational competition in particular with the first-tier countries. Opel Hungary, for instance, stopped its largely CKD production of Astra passenger cars in 1998 – only two years after it had started production in Hungary – in favour of production in Poland. In the negotiations, Opel reaped twice the benefits of locational subsidies. The change that Suzuki leaves the country is much smaller due to the sunk cost involved in producing according to local contents. However, this depends on the alliance with General Motors of the parent company. If this alliance is strengthened, the strategic role of Suzuki could change – with the Hungarian government relatively powerless to influence this process. The Hungarian government's position as the representative of a 'second-tier' nation proved relatively weak in any case in the locational tournament with Poland over Opel's production location. In the course of the 1990s, Hungary has slowly lost most of its policy instruments by which it could attract foreign investment: import duties on finished were less effective than for the larger market of Poland and also lowered; the promotion of foreign investment by the establishment of customs-free zones lost large parts of its attractiveness in the second half, in particular to the frontrunner firms, because they can now import cars and components directly from the EU without paying any duties. In the end, Hungary will remain primarily a component producer. The components produced in Hungary are engines, which can be considered strategic inputs to the companies which they supply. Audi has largely developed these activities in Hungary: it assembles Audi TTs, produces engines and has located a technical centre in the country.

Uncertain tier status: Romania

Romania developed an 'uncertain-tier' status. Romania did not participate in the rapid opening up process of the Central European countries, nor did its government have much hope for immediate entry into the European Union. But Romania also had one of the largest car markets of the region, originally containing two relatively big car manufacturers (Dacia and Oltcit), which had not been integrated into the Comecon system. Romania could not escape from foreign inroads – however, these came later than was the case in the other countries. The takeover of Oltcit by Daewoo proved particularly problematic and shows the extreme vulnerability of the reliance on foreign capital. In the 1990–2000 period Romania's share of the CEE car market declined from 4.7 to 3.1 per cent (ibid.). The takeover of the region's last independent larger car producer with own models and areas of competence firm (Dacia) by Renault in 1999 appears to offer a more promising route. It might lift the national automobile system to a higher tier status. Dacia had its production primarily aimed at Romania and its exports beyond the CEEC in other peripheral regions. The new management of Renault assigned Dacia a comparable strategic target for 2004 as in the early 1990s: to produce a 'reliable and modern' 5000 euro vehicle, aimed at Eastern European and emerging markets (Freyssenet, 2003: 122). Renault's strategy could rejuvenate the Romanian capacity to come up with innovative (world) cars for the lower priced segment.

Third and risky tier countries

The remaining countries (Albania, Bulgaria, Croatia, Macedonia, Yugoslavia and Serbia) have become the lowest and most risky tier countries. They have only a limited component manufacturing capacity, very small markets and weakly developed skills. For instance, Bulgaria in 1997 constituted a market of only 7,000 units (*Financial Times*, 24 July 1995). Ford and Rover tried to locate some SKD assembly in the country. Most of these third-tier countries have completely – and earlier than in other countries – abolished quota and licences, but to no avail. Investment proved low value added, low local content, risky and volatile: for instance, Rover withdrew from Bulgaria in 1996. After the end of the Civil War in Yugoslavia, VW reintroduced CKD assembly in Sarajevo (Bosnia-Herzegovina) and Serbia continued to produce small amounts of old models, while simultaneously searching for new partners. None of these countries had been amongst the first wave of prospective entrants of the European Union and they were therefore suffering from internal as well external institutional uncertainty.

Conclusion: the dynamics of peripheral regionalism

This contribution has argued that the development of peripheral regionalism of the Central and Eastern European automobile space has largely run along the lines of three strategic groupings: frontrunners, followers and peripheral networks. Each of these groups of firms shared different strategic intentions for the region. Follower firms saw the region primarily as a still limited market. By contrast, peripheral firms use the region primarily as an entry into the Western European car market. Frontrunner firms adopted the most sophisticated (and also the most difficult to manage) strategy: they look at the region as a production site for cheap re-imports back into the home base, they see it as a source for lower-end world cars and components, *and* they also see the region as a market. Frontrunner firms have also attached the biggest strategic value to sales (and production) in the region. Only peripheral players had a considerable share of their European sales in the CEEC region.

The CEE countries can be considered as locations helping to increase the efficiency of MNCs by playing host the lower end of the value-added chain.

As Bellak (1997: 210) notes, however, it can place the CEECs into 'a vicious circle of change', whereas it puts pressure on the bargaining circumstances in the Western European car complexes at the same time. Do we face the creation of an independent CEE automotive space or of a 'colonized' and/or 'vertical' system? Havas (2000a: 257) asks whether there is a 'viable alternative'. Bartlett and Seleny (1998) conclude that – contrary to the Asian model – the dynamism represented by Eastern Europe's emergent car networks clearly displays a hierarchical logic. More positive assessments on the future of the CEEC auto industry almost always refer to the first-tier countries – often paying particular heed to the learning processes that have led to the upgrading of Skoda's capabilities in the Czech Republic and, to a more limited extent, Audi's capabilities in Hungary. It is still too early to assess the exact outcome of the process. In any case all of the national economies in the CEEC region have become tied into a vertical regional network of dependencies – strongly aimed at supplies and exports to the core countries of the region. The lower the position of a country in the supply chain, the higher is the likelihood of 'colonization'. Characteristics of the more dependent position of a country in such a system have been/become: (1) more intense competition with external and internal suppliers (component manufacturing is rarely single-source); (2) lower technical skills needed and a more limited technological spillover; (3) a lower local content share; (4) a limited say in the international distribution decisions; (5) a smaller impact on employment; (6) a greater possibility of relocation and therefore lower effectiveness of government-induced incentives and trade policies.

The most positive effects on local productivity and skill formation have appeared in the higher-tier countries. Lower-tiered countries that tried to stimulate the development of new car models on the basis of their own technologies failed. New models or updates of Dacia (Romania) or Yugo (Yugoslavia) were introduced in the 1990s, but they were unable to compete in the rapidly changing regional market. Pavlínek (2002: 62) concludes: 'even if they had competitive products they could not compete in the servicing of their vehicles or in financing'. In all cases the development of new models and design capacity in the CEE region has become dependent upon the strategic considerations of the foreign owners. Dacia was the last car producer to lose its independence in this respect, but perhaps regained a competitive perspective through its newly found parent from France (which also tends to include some political backing by the French state).

The tiered structure is not necessarily static. Countries can move up and down. But their room for manoeuvre has become increasingly dependent upon the investment decisions of foreign firms. As a consequence since the mid-1990s all CEE countries have intensified their locational competition. In the first half of the 1990s, only Hungary created aggressive tax incentives to attract foreign investment, with substantial success. Toyota/PSA's 2001 decision to build a plant in the Czech Republic instead of Poland was strongly influenced by the more generous availability of incentives. An increasing number of firms even switched from one country to another during the 1990s, as illustrated by the Opel Hungary example. At the same time EU state aid guidelines have been imposed on the new accession countries. In 1999, the Czech government – when testing its incentives against EU competition rules – had to slash tax breaks and grants to Skoda from US\$120 million to U\$22 million (EIU, 2002: 85). However, the European Union state aid guidelines do not rule out incentives and concessions. EU rules require that subsidies be 'indispensable to prevent the company from investing in another site. In practice this means the wealthier countries are allowed to grant more subsidies to attract car investments than poor ones' (ibid.). Because Poland is one of the poorest countries in Europe, its leading position as a car market, therefore, might not lead to a leading position in attracting foreign investment. In general, this country attracts less foreign investment per capita than other leading CEE countries and could lose its first-tier status. EU regulation will not terminate locational tournaments. The fortunes of the automobile space in Central and Eastern Europe – in particular, in the lower-tier countries – will remain capricious.

6

Challenges for the Turkish Car Industry on its Way to Integration with the European Union

Lale Duruiz

Introduction

The Turkish automotive industry had been founded as a CKD assembly industry at the beginning of the 1960s and only gradually did it turn into a manufacturing industry. The industry has experienced both import-substitution and export-oriented policy periods. In both periods, priority in the industrialization strategy was given to the development of a motorway network and this helped to establish the infrastructure. The Turkish automotive sector is adding value to the economy with 30,000 people working in car production and 150,000 in the spare parts industry, moreover it also has also had a spillover effect on many other Turkish industries.

Steps towards regional integration started with the Customs Union Agreement signed with European Union in 1995. This agreement has initiated some structural changes in the sector. The most significant one is the opening up of the Turkish market to the international competition. Following the agreement, the imports of the automobile sector have been increasing at a rate of 76.7 per cent per year, of which the EU has a share of 88 per cent. The second one is the investments of third-party firms, like Japanese and South Korean, in Turkey, which are looking for a flexible and low-cost workforce in production in order to export to the EU. The last one is the capital integration of the sector with the EU and the required institutionalization by the agreement.

The industry, with a capacity of nearly one million cars, has survived both the customs unionization process and the 1994 economic crisis. When the Asian and Russian crises of 1997–1998 are added all of these events have had a serious earthquake impact on the local automotive sector in Turkey.

Moreover, the real earthquake on 17 August 1999 also had a bad effect on the sector, since more than 80 per cent of the automotive sector is located in the earthquake zone. The previous government had taken some steps towards macroeconomic stability increasing the hopes of the producers. However, the IMF-backed stabilization programme, with a political crisis in February 2001, had ended and the Turkish lira lost nearly 80 per cent of its value against the US dollar. Household consumption was also reduced as the result of increasingly pessimistic expectations. In this market, uncertainty has become the rule rather than the exception. Periodic recessions have become a structural element of the Turkish economy and excess capacity is a normal condition of the Turkish auto industry. The volatility of demand for cars also has been increasing in the recent years.

Industrial development of the Turkish car sector

The sector's developments indicate very significant signs about how the opening, globalization and the industrial policies affect the firms' approaches to product development, technology strategy, and organization of work, managerial techniques, profit strategies and investments.

The literature argues that development policy is susceptible to fashions. During the 1950s and 1960s, when import substitution was in vogue, there was excessive optimism about what government interventions could achieve (Krueger, 1993). Now that the outward orientation is the norm, there is an equally excessive faith about what openness can accomplish. The appeal of opening up to global markets is based on a powerful promise: that international economic integration will improve economic performance. As countries reduce their tariff and non-tariff barriers to trade and open up to international capital flows, the expectation is that economic growth will increase. However, it is argued that without an investment strategy and established social institutions, macroeconomic stability cannot easily be achieved (Rodrik, 1999). Successful economies combine a certain degree of openness with policies that are conducive to investment, macroeconomic stability, and the prudent management of capital inflows.

The Turkish automotive industry had initially lived through the import-substitution policy. The industry had been founded as montage (CKD or SKD) industry at the beginning of the 1960s and only turned into a manufacturing industry over a number of years. In 1950s the total vehicle park was 13,400 and the growth rate was around 17 per cent and was supplied by imports. In 1964, Turkey's First Five-Year Development Plan included a regulation of protection of the industry balancing the localization ratio with foreign exchange. Passenger car production started in 1966 with Ford-Otosan's fibre-glass-bodied Anadol model through a unique dealer–assembler agreement with the Reliant Motor Company of Britain (Duruiz, 2003). Oyak-Renault was established via a licensing agreement with Renault in

France in 1969 and Tofas was formed in cooperation with Fiat in 1968. Investment permits to both companies were issued which laid down the condition of achieving 85 per cent local content rate in the fifth year of production. As a result of the import-substitution policy, the deficiencies of the regulations were no measures for the development of components sector, no concern about development of technological capabilities and about economies of scale and scope (Duruiz and Yentürk, 1992).

Political instability and a weakening of the economy started in 1978 resulting in a huge external debt and an accelerating inflation rate. A major shortage of foreign trade due to the dramatic increase in oil prices and a decrease in Turkish workers' remittances has restricted imports both of necessary parts and components in the automotive sector.

In 1980, an export-oriented industrialization strategy was adopted and gradual liberalization of the importation of cars and gradual reduction of tariffs started. Financial support was given to the suppliers to form an internationally updated car. Import duties were lowered from 72–150 per cent in 1989 to 39 per cent in 1993. The number of the foreign investments in the automotive sector jumped to 99 in 1995, which had been 13 in 1980. The industry faces major difficulties in adjusting to the demands of global market since there was no explicit technology policy during the protection period to promote the development of the industry to internationally competitive levels. The sector has been striving for protective shields to be kept as much as possible.

Integration process with the European Union

A new period of restructuring started in the Turkish automobile industry following the Customs Unionization agreement signed with the European Union on 6 March 1995. Turkey and the EU have long been close trading partners. In 2000, Turkish had a trade deficit of about US$3 billion with the EU.

The agreement with Turkey accepts free trade rules with the EU; however, it included the protection of the industry to the third parties until 2001. It also necessitated the harmonization of the administrative and regulatory structure of the industry such as adaptation of all procedures for exporting to the EU, including standardization, measurement, accreditation, tests and documentation. The agreement also has strict regulations with regard to environmental, safety standards and exhaust emission rates.

An accreditation council is going to be established under a new law. Most of the documentation has been prepared and they are being put to action with time. Considering competition policy-related issues, the European Commission examined direct and indirect subsidies distributed in the auto sector. For example, Turkey's selective tax reduction to two non-EU investors contravening also with GATT rules had been discussed by the EU authorities and the Turkish government declared that it was an exceptional gentlemen's agreement.

By 2001, Turkey was supposed to have adopted all of the EU procedures and rules for the automotive sector, but the process of harmonizing European norms has not yet been completed. The industry views itself as being too vulnerable for immediate liberalization. The customs duties were abolished; however, another tax – entitled the Private Consumption Tax – took its place. The same agreement protects Turkish manufacturers from second-hand auto imports during the same transition period.

In conjunction with its 1 January 1996 accession to the Customs Union, Turkey has adopted a new import regime. According to this regime, companies importing vehicles should have service facilities in the seven geographical regions of Turkey, and should keep an inventory of aftermarket parts. The aim of this measure is to prevent imports of vehicles with no service or spare parts beyond the basic level. This requirement has encouraged domestic producers to offer countrywide service and spare parts guarantees in their sales promotion.

Turkey is currently a special case where the trade is liberalized but full integration is not yet accepted. This results in a disadvantageous position in comparison with the countries located on the Europe's geographical periphery – Spain, Portugal and Greece. These countries have motorway infrastructure development financed by EU funds, and a rapid rise in their income level which has directly affected their sales. At the 1998 EU Commission meeting it was decided that Turkey will benefit from the technological R&D budgets within the 5th Framework. In December 1999 Helsinki Summit announced that Turkey was as a candidate member of the EU. It is anticipated that Turkey will become a full member in 2010.

The automobile market in Turkey

With 60 million inhabitants, the market currently seems unsatisfied, with 80 cars per 1000 people (compared to the EU average of 545). The trend in local and import sales of passenger cars can be observed in Figure 6.1 changing between 200,000 and 400,000. The fluctuations in the demand for passenger cars is driven by fluctuations in GNP. The trend also shows the fluctuations in relation with the effects of the 1994 crisis and the Asian and Russian crisis during 1997–1998. The IMF-backed stabilization programme had a positive influence in the beginning where the demand has jumped above the 1993 sales for the first time in 2000 but went down sharply when the programme started to fail.

The life expectancy of automobiles is long in Turkey; the average age of a new brand car per capita of eight years is much higher than the average of two years in EU countries. This increases the importance of Turkish automotive aftermarket suppliers. Old cars have a remarkable market share, and

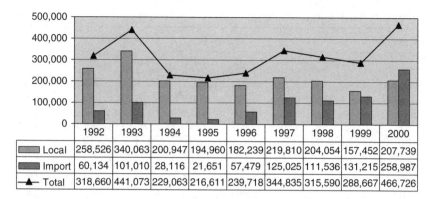

	1992	1993	1994	1995	1996	1997	1998	1999	2000
Local	258,526	340,063	200,947	194,960	182,239	219,810	204,054	157,452	207,739
Import	60,134	101,010	28,116	21,651	57,479	125,025	111,536	131,215	258,987
Total	318,660	441,073	229,063	216,611	239,718	344,835	315,590	288,667	466,726

Figure 6.1 Comparison of imports with local car sales

Source: OSD (Turkish Automotive Manufacturers' Association), Automotive Industry, December 1998 (1999 values supplied by OSD).

automobiles are kept in service for far longer than elsewhere because repair labour is cheap and readily available. Turkish mechanics are very resourceful in devising solutions to keep vehicles on the road. For this reason, the sector still negotiates strongly for a ban on used cars from the EU.

Traditionally, Turkish manufacturers have operated in two car segments – lower medium and medium models, such as the 'bird' series from Tofas, Renault 12 or Ford Taunus, which have already been phased out in their country of origin. They are producing these outdated models very cheaply. These segments account for 90 per cent of the Turkish market, whereas they represent only 40 to 60 per cent of the market in developed European economies. The Honda Civic, new Corolla and Bora are the new candidates in this segment. The majority of the import market is occupied by medium-sized four-door cars and very small number is by the luxury sports cars. Table 6.1 shows automobile market segmentation in 1998.

After the 1980s as a result of the increase in the uneven distribution of income, there has been a higher demand than expected to the luxury brands due to the symbolic status spending the significant part of their income. Changes in income concentration, household size, and urbanization, all have effects on the demands for different segments.

Production and employment

The Turkish car industry was relatively small scale during the import-substitution period but after 1984, the import liberalization policy began to influence the capacity and production. The rapid rise in the production and capacity seen after 1987 was not aimed at the domestic market rather than foreign markets, which reached its peak value as 348,095 in 1993. Following the 1994 economic crisis the sector was not able to recover fully.

Table 6.1   Turkish automobile market segmentation, 1998

Segment	Domestic		Import		Total		% of imports
	Unit	Share (%)	Unit	Share (%)	Unit	Share (%)	
A	—	0	727	0.7	727	0.2	100
B	16,144	8.0	25,208	23.6	41,352	13.4	61
C	168,818	84.2	41,287	38.6	210,105	68.3	20
D	15,651	7.8	32,151	30.1	47,802	15.5	67
E	—	0	6,381	6.0	6,381	2.1	100
G	—	0	590	0.6	590	0.2	100
H	—	0	587	0.5	587	0.2	100
Total	200,613	100	106,931	100	307,544	100	35

Segment A: Engine volume <1300cc, two-door hatchback
Segment B: 1.3–1.4 l. engine, four-door hatchback
Segment C: 1.4–1.6 l. engine, medium-sized sedan and four-door hatchback
Segment D: 1.6–1.8 l. engine
Segment E, G and H: >1.8 l. engine, imported luxury cars and sport cars.

Source: OSD (Turkish Automotive Manufacturers' Association).

Table 6.2   Turkish car production, imports and exports (units)

Year	Production	Imports	Exports	Capacity use (%)
1975	67,291			82
1980	31,529			36
1985	60,353			64
1989	118,314	7,094	8,220	83
1990	167,556	65,390	5,533	76
1991	195,574	33,651	5,790	79
1992	265,245	52,173	8,996	102
1993	348,095	101,610	6,846	118
1994	212,651	24,921	12,802	54
1995	233,414	21,651	33,163	47
1996	207,757	57,479	31,170	42
1997	242,780	121,049	22,612	44
1998	239,937	111,536	37,227	49
1999	222,041	131,215	77,459	50
2000	297,476	258,987	90,026	45

Source: OSD (Turkish Automotive Manufacturers' Association).

Some steps towards productivity increase, quality improvement and product diversity which have been in turn, important motives for new technologies, investment and increase of capacity are the main outcomes of the Customs Union Agreement. The production trend can be observed in Table 6.2.

The trend should be also examined by taking into account the share of imports after EU. The producers have shown some interest in developing new models since they have been open to global competitiveness. Since the 1980s, in addition to producing outdated models they have searched for manufacturing opportunities for the global car. 1994 investments were aiming to secure economies of scale as well as economies of scope. 2000 started with a much better sign as a result of the macroeconomic stability, promotions and government-producer purchase tax reduction. Two economic crises, in December 2000 and February 2001, led car sales to drop sharply. Only 24 per cent of the capacity was being used in 2001. This trend shows how volatile market demand has become.

In 2001, 27,000 employees were working in automobile production. Turkey has a growing population, a high number of unskilled workers and high levels of unemployment. The Turkish labour market is largely unorganized. Trade unions are not very strong. The policy of contractual worker status with no unionization rights or guarantees against layoffs has been extended since 1984. The uncertainty of demand in the car industry has meant that producers adjust the labour force accordingly by either layoffs or by introduction of short-time working. The economic crisis which caused the production to decrease around 39 per cent in 1994 resulted in workers in the sector being retired or fired. The same trend could be seen in the 2001 crisis.

Turkish car manufacturers

The Turkish Automotive industry is concentrated mainly on the Istanbul–Kocaeli–Bursa line in the Marmara Region. Annual production capacity in Turkey is around 750,000 automobiles. Even though Ford is the first to come to Turkey, Fiat and Renault have held 80–90 per cent of the market since the 1970s. Following the entrance of some other producers such as Opel and Toyota, their share in the market decreased to 40 per cent in 1999. Renault is in partnership with Oyak, The Army Mutual Assistance Organization; Fiat had made agreements with Koç Holding. Toyota has been in partnership with Sabanci Holding. Both holdings are very powerful, long-lasting industrial family groups in Turkey having strong sociopolitical networks. In 2000 Opel, which is a fairly recent factory, is being closed down as a result the fluctuations in the market. Honda/Anadolu Endustri Holding (with the Sedan) and Hyundai/Kibar Holding (with Accent) have started production in recent years.

The latest models on the production lines of Renault are the Europa (sedan, hatchback), Clio Symbol (sedan), Megane (sedan and stationwagon) and Dizel. Tofas has been producing the Palio, Siena, Doblo, Sahin, Kartal, Dogan and Uno. Export models are as Sahin to Egypt and Siena sedan to Vietnam. The firm has recently decided to end production of the 'bird' series. The Toyota factory has been producing the Corolla model and have invested US$250,000 for the factory. They had some problems with government subsidies and shifted their Yaris production to France in 1999. They are planning export of 120,000 units to the EU with a new investment of US$400,000 in 2004. The factory is outsourcing the parts and sub-systems to suppliers locating themselves near the factory in order to reduce the risks of market uncertainty. These are mostly Japanese–Turkish joint ventures and all of the first-tier suppliers are organized as a Toyota city near Izmit. Sabanci Holding pulled out of the joint venture in 2001 and Toyota got the 90 per cent share of the production firm aiming to be the third largest production unit after the United Kingdom and France.

Ford is planning to invest US$550 million dollars in its new factory, aiming to produce 150,000 units with a target of 65 per cent export achieving revenues of US$1 billion. This factory is located in the earthquake area in Gölcük, creating hopes for the local people. Total employment is planned as 4,000 people, with a further 20,000 job opportunities in the parts industry. Local content will be 50 per cent. The plant has recently started producing the Ford Transit (around 40,000 units per year) and another vehicle may also be produced. With the new model, Ford stopped the assembly of the light commercial vehicle at Genk, Belgium, and plans to relocate all the production in Turkey to re-export to the EU.

In Turkey, foreign partnerships have influenced the sector's growth, technological development and the skills of the labour force. Table 6.3 shows capacities and production, capacity usage in 2000 and the foreign partners of the manufacturing firms. The maximum capacity usage was 78 per cent recorded by the Renault factory which had a 20 per cent share of the market in 1999. The rest of the factories have been working at under 50 per cent capacity utilization. The excess capacity is the normal state for the industry. The capacity utilization has been slightly higher in the spare parts sector, at 62 per cent during the same period. The capacity usage in 2000 was 45 and 24 for the first three months of 2001.

Table 6.3   Main vehicle manufacturers in Turkey, 1999

Firms	Start year	Licence	Local firm's share	Capacity units	Cap. use (%)	Production (units)
Opel	1990	Gen. Motor	100	25,000	28.2	7,039
Otosan	1959	Ford	41	64,400	n.d.	n.d.
O.Renault	1971	Renault	51	170,000	82.4	140,159
Toyotasa	1994	Toyota	50	100,000	14.7	14,715
Tofas	1971	Fiat	38	250,000	42.3	105,775
Honda	1997	Honda	50	30,000	32.7	9,821
Hyundai	1997	Hyundai	50	120,000	16.6	19,967

Source: OSD (Turkish Automotive Manufacturers' Association).

Table 6.4 Investments in the Turkish car industry (US$ million)

Years	1992	1993	1994	1997	1998	1999
Capacity development	80.9	166.1	290.4	37	39	40
Modernization	26	89.1	109.4	79	72	30
New model development	52	97.2	225.7	71	119	114
Quality development	5.8	16.2	43.4	19	15	47
Localization	112.6	12.2	25.3	30	33	21
Others	11.6	24.3	11.9	110	85	120
Total	288.9	405.2	706.1	346	363	372

Source: OSD (Turkish Automotive Manufacturers' Association).

Investment trends

The bright years of 1992–1993 led to investment in the sector being tripled in 1994. Until 1992, five models accounted for 80 per cent of the total. New model and capacity development were the main investments in 1994 (Table 6.4). The growth of the imports and new entries were also challenging the manufacturers. However, investments on new model development dropped significantly in 1995. The government supported the investments in 1995, but the contracted market led the firms to prefer playing with financial tools. In recent years this trend has continued with a relatively higher emphasis on modernization and new model development showing that manufacturers have begun to appreciate the importance of developing a global car. After the 1993 sales, all of the producers increased the investments creating a capacity of one million vehicles. However, this capacity has never been used since the economic crisis overtook the industry shortly afterwards.

The automotive sector attracts many foreign investors. 109 foreign companies have invested in this sector over the last 12 years, importing US$1.1 billion of equipment. Germany and Italy have the largest share in automotive foreign investment; the United States, France, the United Kingdom, Switzerland and Japan follow. These foreign firms supply many different items in the sector – from pumps to diesel engines, from bolts and nuts to rims, from bodies to suspension, from electronic systems to clutches.

Imports

The imports of the automotive sector after the Customs Union Agreement have been increasing at an annual rate of 76.7 per cent. The percentage of imports to total sales was 10–20 per cent in the 1992–1996 period and this ratio jumped to nearly 52 per cent in 2000 (and the share of the EU has increased

Table 6.5 Main importers to Turkey (units)

Firms	Units imported in 2000
VW	41,354
Opel	52,044
Ford	31,307
Renault	34,310
Peugeot	14,124
Lada	12,910
Nissan	5,828
Mitsubishi	1,800
Skoda	8,121
Toyota	2,351

Source: Association for Turkish Representatives of Imported Cars.

107 per cent). Since the demand has contracted recently with the economic crisis, the imports are also likely to be affected.

After 1997, Turkey became one of the favourite import countries for the global automotive industry and approximately 38 global firms took part in the Turkish market, with Germany being the leader (Table 6.5). The structure of imports has changed fundamentally with the Customs Union: in 1993, the share of Eastern Europe was the largest, the trend has changed the whole picture and in 2000 the share of EU imports has risen from 33 to 91 per cent.

There were no significant barriers due to restrictions and regulations for import in the sector. In conjunction with its 1 January 1996 accession to the Customs Union, Turkey has now adopted a new import regime. According to this regime, companies importing vehicles should have service facilities in the seven geographical regions of Turkey, and should keep an inventory of aftermarket parts. This is to prevent imports of vehicles with no service or spare parts beyond the basic level. This requirement has encouraged domestic producers to offer countrywide service and spare parts guarantees in their sales promotion. Additionally, with the introduction of Toyota and Opel cars to the Turkish market, new plaza-type service stations have been introduced to the automobile service sector.

The imports of the spare parts sector have been relatively less affected by the Customs Union directly. The European suppliers are dominant in the import market with 75 per cent. The actual share of US products in Turkey is higher than it seems since these products pass through the European subsidiaries or affiliates. The main producers such as Honda, Toyota, Hyundai works with their own suppliers or import them rather than working with dispersed small parts producers.

Exports

The automotive sector had the 7th place among the exporting sectors of Turkey in 1998, and moved to fifth in 2000 with US$2.3 billion. Exports have been very limited in the passenger car sector, only the consequences of the customs union agreement has made the producers think about the foreign markets. The competition of the Asian firms during the crisis affected the exports from Turkey negatively in the EU market. Devaluation in 2001 and the narrowed domestic market have forced the firms towards the export and 145,400 cars have been exported in 2001.

The producers try to increase their models, especially concentrating on models produced only in Turkey for foreign markets. Internationalization permits companies to benefit from economies of scale (Freyssenet and Lung, 2000). The European producers use Turkey as a unique basis for export some niche products as Renault Megane Station Wagon, Fiat started with Tempra in 1995 and continued with the Palio Weekend and Doblo to the EU. The firm exports the 'Bird' series to Egypt and CKD and spare parts to Morocco, India, Russia, South Africa, Vietnam and Egypt. They are planning investment of 400,000 euro to produce Scudino model in 2000, which will aim at US$5 billion of exports and compete with Berlingo and Kangoo in the local market. Toyotasa, Ford-Otosan and Opel had exported small numbers around 50–100 cars in 1998. Ford's Gölcük project of US$600 million is aiming 90 per cent export products. Toyota is producing Corolla Sedan only in Turkey for European market. Hyundai Assain is planning to export the new Accent to the EU. Renault has been the most successful exporter with US$488 million during recent years.

Considering the firms, Tofas and Renault had been able to export some of their produced cars as seen in Table 6.7. Mostly exported countries can be listed as Romania, Egypt, Azerbaijan, Uzbekistan, Kurdistan, Turkmenistan, Cossack from Turkish Republics and Russia, France, Germany, Syria, Iran, Northern Turkish Republics of Cyprus, Spain, Italy, Bulgaria, Israel and Argentina. The components industry has a relatively different structure. The relative importance is seen in Table 6.6. Their exports are much higher than in the car producers sector. For example, there are firms exporting 80 per cent of their production. In general, 20–30 per cent of the production is exported. The customs union with the EU encouraged parts manufacturers to increase their market share in the EU by creating a challenge with the new standards and regulations. The annual average increase in exports after the customs union agreement is 23 per cent. The exporters are expected to increase their market share in the EU since Turkey currently has lowest labour costs than other European countries. The recent devaluation of the Turkish lira has resulted in an increased price competitiveness for exports.

Table 6.6   Exports of the Turkish automotive sector (US$)

	2000	Change (%) on 1999
Motor vehicles	621,694,696	−1
Components	1,339,924,467	13
Total exports	2,388,663,020	6

Source: OSD.

Table 6.7   Passenger car exports by firm

	1997	1998	1999	2000
Tofas	12,240	14,886	14,527	29,034
Oyak Renault	10,132	9,511	62,497	60,758
Others	186	272	435	234
Total	22,558	24,669	77,459	90,026

Source: OSD.

Conclusions

The protection years were not exploited by the Turkish automobile sector in order to establish the technological infrastructure necessary to compete in global markets. On the contrary, it enjoyed high profit margins and continued to produce outdated models for the domestic market using old production and managerial techniques. Globalization, coming in the wake of the customs union with the EU, threatened the firms and investments. As a result, efforts towards manufacturing new products, and introducing microelectronics technologies, new organization methods, and quality and ecological movements started. Competitiveness in global markets has led the firms to innovate continuously, especially in environmental and security aspects. This has created a change in the expectation of the Turkish customer as a global customer.

From 1988 to 1993, Turkey was the world's fastest-growing car market, but from the 1994 economic recession the market has been moving up and down and exhibiting very volatile demand. Fundamental change in the market structure has taken place with the agreement, with imports increasing at a rate of 76.7 per cent per year. The globalization of competition led to an erosion of the national bases of automotive industry in terms of both final markets and the decline of national producers. The great fear of manufacturers, which was that the share of imports would reach 55 per cent, was surpassed in 2001. Turkey is seen as an emerging market for the car industry, and foreign firms use an aggressive market strategy with low prices. The result has been that the structure of the import distribution has changed fundamentally, increasing the EU share to 91 per cent.

Recently Turkey has been coping with one of the worst financial crises in the republic's history – a downturn that has led to more than 500,000 people losing their jobs. The country is on the verge of an important decision: either it accepts the conditions of globalization and integration with the world or it closes its doors. The EU has discussed the fact that Turkey could be the most populous nation within the EU with all the implications that this would have for the associated voting power. On the other hand, American foreign policy makers argue that Turkey should be admitted into the EU for strategic reasons. IMF and EU's financial support has been related to Turkey's efforts to make reforms in her political and economic structures. Public sector reforms and banking sector reforms have started to occur. However, over the short term, the rates of economic growth are expected to be slow and inflation will be high. As a result, the demand for passenger cars will be low, interest rates will be high and financial tools may be preferred. Overcapacity in the world production and the aggressive marketing of importers is also likely to increase the share of imports in the market. Capacity utilization will be low and some of the factories are likely to close.

Over the long run, if political and economic stability can be established, interest rates will drop, and this will have beneficial effects on economics growth, GNP and consumption expenditure, directly affecting the demand for passenger cars. This will increase foreign direct investment, and EU membership will lead to an influx of funds and will increase revenues from tourism. All of these developments will mean that Turkey may become a key country in the Middle East and former Socialist Republics area.

7
NAFTA: The Process of Regional Integration of Motor Vehicle Production

Jorge Carrillo

In the 1980s and 1990s, the North American auto industry experienced changes that were both profound and comprehensive. There is little dispute that this great transformation of what was the historical bedrock of the industry emerged as a response to the challenges imposed by Asian manufacturers in the early 1970s. The response of the North American industry, whether it is explained by the powerful innovative forces at play, by its imposing of technological and organizational change, by new market orientation, or by the transformation of labour relations, was widely recognized as a process which had great geographical undertones and implications. Indeed, as was the case in most other regions of the world, the functional and geographical transformation of the industry went hand in hand. In North America, it was precisely this powerful impetus towards regional economic integration that help us to understand both the new ways in which the auto industry has achieved a greater competitive edge, and the possible trajectories for the region in the future. The three countries involved in the process of regional integration – the United States, Canada and Mexico – were affected by the new institutional and corporate arrangements. However, these changes could not be entirely understood when considered as separate entities, but only when their complementarities are revealed, and when their interaction is put forward as a single social system of provision, production and distribution. The purpose of this chapter is to document these changes, to explore the underlying process of economic and productive integration in North America, and to attempt to understand the future of this new industrial configuration.[1]

The first section of this chapter provides an overview of the evolution of the industry in the three countries concerned, with particular attention being paid to their institutional context. The overall structure of the industry is presented in the second part. The third section analyses the special geographical dimension of the industry with one eye on identifying the agglomeration of production within countries. The fourth section reviews the trade data between countries in light of industrial and regional restructuring. Finally, we conclude by sketching some possible scenarios about future productive integration in the North American Free Trade Agreement (NAFTA) region.

A brief overview

From the 1950s to the 1980s, each of the three NAFTA countries pursued distinct policies affecting the growth of their domestic automobile industries. At the same time certain similarities can be attributed to their common experience of global trends, and because North American auto production became increasingly integrated during this period. By the mid-1990s, the three countries had achieved a coordinated policy for increased integration, competitiveness and upgrading, even as the industry in each country had taken a different but complementary trajectory. In the year 2001 the United States produced 12.8 million vehicles, Canada 2.9 million and Mexico 1.9 million, taking the first, seventh and ninth places in the world production league table (Table 7.1).

The case of the United States

Several authors describe the US auto industry as having evolved through four stages based on the changing competitive conditions of the car corporations in the United States: (i) from 1955 to 1974, when competition was mostly between the domestic producers; (ii) from 1974 to 1984, a period characterized by the shift in the market structure as a result of the oil crises (1973 and 1979) and the introduction of Japanese imports; (iii) from 1984

Table 7.1 Vehicle production in Canada, Mexico and United States

Year	Total	Canada (%)	Mexico (%)	United States (%)	
1970	9,663,396	12.3	2.0	85.7	100
1980	9,869,454	13.9	5.0	81.2	100
1990	12,551,529	15.5	6.5	77.9	100
2000	17,698,866	16.7	10.7	72.6	100
2005	17,203,096	16.4	8.7	74.9	100

Sources: *Automotive News*; *Market Data Yearbook*; Statistics Canada; AMIA-Mexico.

to 1994, marked by the introduction of Asian transplants (mainly Japanese); and (iv) from 1995 to 2001, a period characterized by the rise of NAFTA and the growing productive integration of Mexico into North America.

From the 1950s until the 1970s the Big Three US producers (GM, Ford and Chrysler) faced relatively little international competition and were wedded to a Sloanist-style system of production, which featured a high degree of vertical integration (Boyer and Freyssenet, 2002). In the early 1970s, the changing economic and competitive situation caused some radical restructuring of the entire auto industry. Increased oil prices meant that smaller, higher mileage automobiles from Japan became increasingly popular. But Japanese competitiveness was not based solely on the style of their cars. They had also struck upon a technological paradigm for production that outperformed pure Fordism, already weakened by a precarious economic environment. Rather than vertically integrating production, Japanese automakers did the opposite in order to insulate themselves more effectively from risk. The key contribution of Japanese automakers was 'just-in-time' (JIT) processes, with multiple models, concurrent and inter-firm engineering, and continuous improvement (Womack, Jones and Roos, 1990).

In response, North American producers were forced to radically restructure their operations, adopting increasing degrees of vertical disintegration and a policy of relocating factories and suppliers that continues to this day; adopting new forms of flexible production, they outsource risk, innovation requirements, and labour problems in exchange for longer-term contracts with their suppliers. Large producers spun off many of their parts plants into new ventures, and began to buy from other suppliers. These new relations emphasized collaborative innovation, and often-geographical concentration in highly specialized areas of production.

Vertical disintegration led to changes in the geography of automobile production for both the Big Three and their suppliers. This industrial restructuring led to the modernization, conversion and closure of plants for the purpose of eliminating excess capacity and reducing operating costs.

In light of this situation, joint ventures were established between US and Japanese automakers as an additional strategy to cut costs and to transfer Japanese manufacturing techniques into North American plants. In exchange, Japanese corporations obtained financial support and deeper penetration in the North American market (Table 7.2). The growing number of these agreements is further revealed by the fact that while there were 58 Big Three and five Asian plants in 1988, by 1997 the presence of American plants had decreased by 18.3 per cent, whereas the participation of Asian and European plants had increased by 50 per cent (Asociacíon Mexicana de la Industria Automotriz). In the 1990s, in addition to the Asian plants, BMW and Mercedes-Benz opened plants in South Carolina and Alabama, respectively.

Table 7.2 New entrant vehiclemakers' investment in North America

Year	Company	Country	Location	Capacity	Products
1981	GM	Mexico	Ramos Arizpe, Coahuila	63,000	Trailblazer
1982	Honda	US	Marysville, OH	430,000	Accord, Acura TL8
1982	Ford	Mexico	Chihuahua	600,000	Engines
1983	Chrysler	Mexico	Ramos Arizpe, Coahuila	130,000	Ram pick-up
1983	Nissan	US	Smyrna, TN	240,000	Altima, 200SX, Sentra
1984	NUMMI (Toyota-GM)	US	Fremont, CA	270,000	Corolla, Prizm
1984	Nissan	Mexico	Aguascalientes, Aguas.	200,000	Tsuru, Sentra, Platina
1986	Ford (Ford–Mazda)	Mexico	Hermosillo, Sonora	165,000	Escort, Focus
1986	Honda	Canada	Alliston, ON	150,000	Civic 3-door hatchback, Acura 1.6 EL
1987	Auto Alliance (Mazda–Ford)	US	Flat Rock, MI	240,000	626, Cougar
1988	Toyota	Canada	Cambridge, ON	120,000	Corolla
1988	Diamond-Star (Mitsubishi–Chrysler)	US	Normal, IL	240,000	Eclipse, Avenger, Galant, Sebring
1988	Toyota	US	Georgetown, KY	200,000	Avalon
1989	CAMI/GM	Canada	Ingersoll, ON	200,000	Geo Metro, Swift, Sunrunner, Geo Tracker, Sideick
1989	SIA (Subaru/Isuzu)	US	Lafayette, IN	220,000	Legacy sedan and wagon, Rodeo, Amigo
1989	Honda	US	Liberty, OH	210,000	Civic, Acura CL
1991	NUMMI	US	Fremont, CA	125,000	Tacoma
1991	Saturn Corp.	US	Spring Hill, TN	300,000	Saturn coupe, sedan, wagon
1992	Volkswagen (start in 1964)	Mexico	Puebla, Puebla	350,000	Sedan,* Poniter, Golf, Jetta
1992	Nissan	US	Smyrna, TN	200,000	Frontier pick-up
1992	Nissan/Ford	US	Avalon Lake, OH	134,000	Nissan Quest, Mercury Villager
1993	Nissan	Mexico	Cuernavaca, Morelos	150,000	Frontier, Sentra, Tsuru, Megane Scenic and pick-up
1993	Nissan/Renualt	Mexico	Aguascalientes, Aguas.	250,000	Sentra, Tsuru, Tsubame wagon/van, Clio
1993	Toyota	US	Georgetown, KY	200,000	Camry
1994	GM	Mexico	Silao, Leon	100,000	Suburban, Silverado

Table 7.2   Continued

Year	Company	Country	Location	Capacity	Products
1995	BMW	Mexico	Toluca, Estado de Mexico	300	Porsche 911, 3 and 5 series
1995	Honda	Mexico	El Salto, Jalisco	15,000	Honda Accord
1995	Mercedes-Benz	Mexico	Santiago, Estado de Mexico	4,000	E, S class cars
1995	Mercedes-Benz	Mexico	Tianguistenco, Estado de Mexico	11,000	Medium trucks
1995	BMW	US	Spartanburg, NC	85,000	Z3, M5 Coupe
1998	Toyota	Canada	Cambridge, ON	120,000	Solara
1998	Mercedes-Benz	US	Vance, AL	40,000	ML 320, ML 430
1998	Toyota	US	Georgetown, KY	100,000	Sienna minivan
1998	Toyota	US	Princeton, IN	100,000	T-50 Pick-up
1999	Honda	Canada	Alliston, ON	180,000	Minivans
2000	Toyota	US	Princeton, IN	50,000	SUV
2001	GM	US	Lansing, MI		Cadillac Catera, LAV
2002*	Toyota	Mexico	Tijuana, BC	170,000	Tacoma Pickup's Cabins

Notes
*Finished in August 2003.

Sources: Micheli Thirion (1994); Carrillo, Hinojosa and Waldman (2001); Montiel Hernandez (2002); CIEMEX-WEFA, 2002; Author interviews.

The case of Canada

Canada is the seventh largest world automotive producer, assembling more vehicles on a per capita basis than any other country in the world. Nonetheless, Canada has no native assembly companies: all of the country's assemblers are American, European, or Japanese owned facilities. The industry is highly concentrated in Ontario, in close proximity to Toronto and Detroit. Although there has been auto manufacturing and some component production in Canada since before the Second World War, the modern history of the Canadian auto industry begins in 1965. As the US market became saturated and profits began to shrink, the Big Three needed to develop a lower-cost production alternative and they looked to Canada to find it. The US–Canada Auto Pact reduced tariffs in exchange for commitments on the part of the Big Three.

Despite the strong protectionist sentiments of the Canadian governments of the period, the US–Canadian Auto Pact in many ways set the stage for future trade agreements, including the Canada–US Free Trade Agreement (FTA) of 1989 and NAFTA itself (1994). The original Auto Pact virtually ensured that the Canadian industry would move in concert with the American industry in terms of employment and overseas exports – particularly to Mexico, the

Caribbean Basin, and other Latin American countries. This was originally buoyed by the near parity-valued currencies throughout the last half of the 1960s.

As the Canadian dollar devalued significantly against the US dollar during the last half of the 1970s and throughout the 1980s, it became economically advantageous to produce in Canada and the level of investment there grew rapidly.[2] The move proved to be an immediate success for the manufacturers. US–Canada official comparative data shows greater labour productivity growth in Canada than in the United States in the period 1961–92 (Weintraub, 1998). The result of this was an increased level of investment in Canada that led to massive employment in the sector, primarily in Ontario.

The case of Mexico

The modern Mexican automobile industry began in the early 1960s, under the import-substitution policy – that is, with the express purpose of serving the domestic market. For this reason, it was initially located mostly in central Mexico, where most of the country population was concentrated.

The pre-NAFTA development of Mexican institutions supporting auto production can be summarized by examining the government series of policy decrees (Layan, 2000; Humphrey and Oeter, 2000) (Table 7.3). The 1962 Auto Industry Decree initiated a period of heavy import-substitution policies on the part of the Mexican government, by imposing local-content requirements of 60 per cent on Mexican-produced automobiles.

During the last years of the import-substituting phase (1978 to 1982), the auto industry was a decisive influence on the direction of Mexican economic policy. Since automobiles could not be imported into Mexico, final assemblers interested in the national market had to make substantial investments to produce locally. The result was a strained negotiating relationship among foreign vehicle producers, national auto parts manufacturers and the government. The difficult relations between producers of vehicles and producers of parts, and the complexity of government intervention, resulted in an automotive industry that was characterized by many models and brands, low production runs, high prices and poor quality.

Furthermore, the sector impacted negatively on the national balance of payments. The sector's massive imports of components by vehicle producers (US Department of Commerce, 1995) created a yawning trade deficit that even relatively high FDI inflows could not eliminate. As a consequence, the government pressured vehicle producers to raise the local content of their vehicles and to export more parts and accessories to compensate for the trade deficit generated by the industry.

With the introduction of the first stage of the export promotion policy (1983–87), Mexican government officials began requiring greater levels of exportation from the auto industry. The vehicle producers responded by building modern, internationally competitive engine plants, which came on

Table 7.3   Evolution of the Mexican automotive industry

	Average 1978–82 (Import-substitution policy)	Average 1983–87 (Export promotion policy)	Average 1988–94 (Development of the industry and explosion of exports)	Average 1995–2000 (NAFTA)	2002
Production	477,663	351,589	871,827	1,280,347	1,821,447
Domestic	457,848	295,243	518,555	322,355	502,072
Exports	19,815	56,346	353,271	957,991	1,319,375
% cars (of total production)	62.0	67.1	75.0	67.1	62.6
% Trucks (of total production)	38.0	33.4	25.0	32.9	37.4
% Imports (of total production)	0.0	0.0	2.8	30.4	55.3
% Exports (3/1)	4.1	16.0	40.5	74.8	72.4
% 'Big Three' (Ford, GM, Chrysler)of of total production	48.1	55.5	62.2	65.1	59.4

Source: Author's elaboration based on AMIA.

stream in the early 1980s, just as the Mexican domestic demand for vehicles bottomed out. These companies had great success introducing modern technology into the new Mexican engine plants (Shaiken and Herzenberg, 1987). This success coincided with the reconsideration of existing corporate strategies due to growing import penetration by Japanese firms and other competitors. The Big Three came to the conclusion that Mexico could become a low-cost export platform for entry-level front-wheel drive four- and six-cylinder small cars, and committed to major new investments in modern small vehicle production facilities in Mexico, primarily for export to the US market, in spite of the dismal macroeconomic situation in Mexico and the depressed domestic demand for automobiles (Carrillo, Mortimore and Alonso, 1999).

The 1988–94 stage of the development of the Mexican automobile industry witnessed the explosion of vehicle exports from Mexico, with the result that the sector produced a trade surplus. Volkswagen and Nissan also made significant investments in new plants, even though their export propensities did not approach those of the US vehicle manufacturers (see Tables 7.2 and 7.3).

The institutional change during the NAFTA era

Although the process began much earlier, regional integration was accelerated with the implementation of the NAFTA in 1994, because this led to the consolidation of open market changes, especially in the institutions that govern trade (Pries, 1999). NAFTA was intended to phase out tariffs, quotas, and domestic content requirements (particularly Mexican) over a period of more than ten years. Via tough rules of origin NAFTA also created barriers to outside competitors, protecting the entire region from European and Japanese imports. Since all these changes were already in place along the US–Canadian border, it was the Mexican part of this equation that was meant to affect the whole structure of the North American industry.

Besides the Big Three, and particularly GM, had been importing large percentages of their vehicles, they supported changes in the rules of origin as part of their move towards closer supplier relations with plants clustered geographically around assembly points in North America. Furthermore, the rules of origin requirements act as a subsidy for suppliers, hastening the integration of, and protecting regional supply chains in the industry.

The rules of origin contained in NAFTA (62.5 per cent of American content) inspired further investment projects with the intention of expanding and consolidating their networks of local distributors; furthermore, despite the advantages offered to the original makers, new corporations introduced production facilities in the region (BMW, Mercedes, Honda, and Toyota) (Table 7.2).

Equally important as the emergence of new plants was the fact that existing facilities also increased their production and export levels. The production of engines reached 2.7 million and vehicles 1.82 million in 2002. The most rapid growth has been within the auto parts sector, especially in those labour-intensive products such as electric wire harnesses and interior systems. For example, Delphi has around 55 plants and employs more than 70,000 workers in Mexico. In addition to Delphi, other companies, including Yazaki, Valeo, Lear, Visteon, and Siemens, constitute most of the auto industry in Mexico, and they have established R&D centres in the country.

The tier structure in the NAFTA commodity chain

Although a strong vertical integration characterized the initial phases of the industry, following the restructuring process, a characteristic structure of suppliers emerged as the dominant form of the auto commodity chain. This production chain is generally described as a three-tier structure. Final assemblers or OEMs have a great deal of power over their suppliers (Helper and Sako, 1995; Helper, 1994), which should not be surprising considering that, despite increased competition in the automotive industry, there are a dwindling number of independent firms.[3] While 25 automobile firms existed in 1982, that number had dropped to fifteen by 1999, and is projected to fall to seven by 2010 (Sturgeon and Florida, 1999). The share of US shipments by the top eight firms has remained very high, despite a slight fall in their share of output.

These figures support the qualitative evidence that decision-making networks in the industry are extremely hierarchical and weighted towards the assemblers. Furthermore, while vertical disintegration has proceeded in the upstream aspects of production (increasing outsourcing of parts production), large firms maintain their control of the downstream marketing and consumer financing of automobiles, posing a very significant barrier to entry for new producers.

With regard to the suppliers, there are two dynamics occurring simultaneously. On the one hand, the global market for automobile parts is becoming larger in terms of both unit volume and dollar value. At the same time, all automakers have adopted a strategy of significantly reducing the number of tier-one suppliers over a very short period of time.

Outsourcing and divestment were increasing rapidly in the industry throughout the period as well. By 1995, Chrysler was purchasing almost 70 per cent of its components from external suppliers, Ford purchased 50 per cent, whereas GM maintained high levels of vertical integration, given that only 30 per cent were external suppliers. But GM had given up its entire ownership stake in Delphi, the largest North American OES parts supplier, by the end of 1999. A similar pattern is occurring with Ford and Visteon. The spin-off of Visteon and Delphi change the rate of integration of Ford and General Motors to much lower percentages. They also imposed extreme competitive pressures on suppliers, opening up contracts to bidding roundtables and demanding continual product improvement, zero-fault performance and technological innovation from suppliers. This rationalization has the effect of increasing production in low-wage areas (such as Mexico), as suppliers struggle to impose cost savings by outsourcing even smaller segments of production (Helper and Sako, 1995).

In addition, there has been a shift in the relationship between American automakers and their suppliers in the United States, Canada, and Mexico. While in the past this association relied on one-year contracts, an arms'-length link between automakers and their suppliers, and multiple sources of individual parts, higher and more selective levels of integration have now replaced this relationship. These involve the interchange of information and engineering, as well as medium- and long-run work contracts (between three and five years, according to Helper and MacDuffie, 2000). In this context, cooperation relationships may have precedence over price (Raff, 1998), although cost continues to be a very important factor. As a result, the industry works under the combined pressure of achieving high levels of cooperation, and the search for low operating costs (Cook, 1998).

In spite of the growing OES market, the number of tier-one suppliers has been falling, and this trend is expected to continue. Industry executives feel that over the next decade growth in the sector will come from companies that excel at systems integration. These are companies that engineer and supply modules or systems of parts and components to the assemblers (a process known like modularization), where Magna International and Johnson Controls are examples of companies that have achieved great success in this process in Canada, as well as Delphi and Lear in Mexico.

Agglomeration and specialization

In spite of the heated debate about deindustrialization, the actual production dynamic in the automotive heartland of North America is not as clearcut as some might insist. Obviously, over the long haul (from 1965), the share of the core area's production has been shrinking in comparison with worldwide output. Only since the arrival of Japanese transplants in the United States and Canada in the early 1980s has the world share of the core of the North American auto industry recovered.

The primary manufacturers are the traditional Big Three (GM, Ford, and Chrysler) along with newly established Japanese plants (Toyota and Honda) and a GM–Suzuki joint effort (CAMI). All of these plants are located along a 350 km strip of the Highway 401 Corridor between Detroit and Toronto, and all maintain a complex supply network, most of which is also located in the same area. As Kumar and Holmes (1997, 1998) point out, this proximity is a key reason why Canadian automotive and parts manufacturing has fared so well under JIT production techniques.

According to the list of the 150 largest vehicle manufacturers in North America, the vast majority of large-scale production, in terms of both volume and revenues, occurs in the core region between Oshawa, Ontario and the Greater Cincinnati region. This region claims 111 of the 150 largest firms and is concentrated in 94 counties (Carrillo, Hinojosa and Waldman, 2001).[4] Utilizing the geographical groupings and categorizing by product output, it becomes apparent that there is a general tendency towards regional specialization in areas other than the core (Rubenstein, 1992). Within the core area, the sheer number of manufacturers and suppliers would lead one to conclude that nearly all functions take place there. The other regions are more clearly defined (Carrillo, Hinojosa and Waldman, 2001).

By contrast, the Mexican case has been seen as a polycentric region (Pries, 1999). The crisis after the import-substitution period benefited cities in northern and central Mexico (Chihuahua, Ramos Arizpe, Torreon and Aguascalientes), as well as border cities, with the establishment or first-generation *maquiladoras* auto parts plants (Juarez, Matamoros, and Nuevo Laredo). By now, different types of automotive enterprises cover most of the Mexican territory – from Puebla to the northern border. It can generally be concluded that production specialization and territorial specialization have gone hand in hand. At the same time, some of the oldest plants were closed. Volkswagen is the only firm that did not disperse geographically. Thus, Northern Mexico rapidly developed in the field of exports during that first stage of the export promotion.

The strategies of the three large American corporations led to a new configuration of production in Mexico, via the construction of new plants and the restructuring of existing ones so that they could be integrated into the North American production system. From this viewpoint, the Mexican motor industry changed its strategic role from an internal market orientation, towards seeking efficiency in direct investments for exports, which was achieved in great part thanks to industrial relocation in greenfield zones in the northern and northern-central part of Mexico (Romijn et al., 2000)

Regarding the Canadian case, most production continues to be highly concentrated in the Ontario region, where 95 per cent of auto parts and 100 per cent of vehicle manufacturers are located (Derhak, 1998). The automotive industry carries special weight in Canada because, compared to other major national economies, the overall manufacturing base is less diversified.

Market, trade and investments

The Big Three currently concentrate most of their vehicle assembly in the United States. These firms are the largest makers in that market, collectively supplying 73 per cent of the autos purchased between 1990 and 2000. GM is in first place with 33.1 per cent of the market, followed by Ford and Chrysler with 24.8 per cent and 14.3 per cent, respectively. The US Big Three concentrated 73.9 per cent of total production in NAFTA countries in 2001 and their share in light trucks has seen an increase from 62.8 per cent to 75.3 per cent (1996–2001) (source: *Automotive News*). These numbers reflect the popularity of light trucks and sport utility vehicles (SUV) in the North American market. In the case of Mexico the US Big Three concentrated 67 per cent of total production for exports and 37 per cent the rest of the firms. However, they only concentrated 36 per cent of their production on the domestic market (see Table 7.3).

Likewise, the United States is by far the largest market for automobiles (see Table 7.4). The most salient feature of this table is the dominance of the US market, which in 2001 accounted for 85.3 per cent of passenger car sales and 89.5 per cent of the light truck sales in the three countries. The figures indicate a sporadic and slow growth in the domestic market for Mexico. In 1995, there were 1.7 people per car in United States, 2.0 in Canada, and 11.2 in Mexico (Sturgeon, 1997).

While the United States remains the engine of the auto market in North America, trade within the NAFTA region has experienced dramatic growth, even before the full implementation of the agreement. In fact, auto products trade represents about one-quarter of the North American total (Gwenell and Villareal, 1993). The explanations have been the following: (i) the easing terms of trade provided by NAFTA, (ii) Mexican peso devaluation and economic recessions; and (iii) rising demand in the United States as a result of the new cycle of economic growth begun in 1992.

Table 7.4 Automotive industry sales in Canada, Mexico and the United States

	Production (cars and trucks: units)				
Year	Canada (%)	Mexico (%)	United States (%)	Total	
1970	7.0	n.d.	93.0	10,984,241	(100)
1980	9.6	3.5	86.9	13,195,218	(100)
1990	8.2	3.4	88.3	16,014,557	(100)
2000	7.8	4.3	87.9	19,813,434	(100)
2005	7.8	5.5	86.7	19,039,530	(100)

Note to Light Trucks: Canada figures include some heavy trucks; Mexico figures include tractor trailers and buses.

Sources: *Automotive News*; *Market Data Yearbook*; Statistics Canada; AMIA-Mexico.

Currently, in the case of Mexico, the auto industry has eight final assemblers (BMW, Mercedes, Chrysler, Ford, GM, Honda, Nissan and VW), which in turn have 20 plants in 11 states around Mexico. In 2000 there were 875 auto parts companies, of which 34 per cent are subsidiaries of foreign corporations, and over 1,000 agencies in the distributor segment.

Since proximity is such an important constraint upon the location of tier-one automotive parts suppliers, this spatial reconfiguration of production in the assembly industry will continue to have a considerable impact on the location of primary parts producers. The increasing two-way trade on both sides of the US border indicates an increasing social division of labour in the manufacturing process. The boom in US imports from Mexico, along with the boom in US exports to Canada (much of which is constituted by Mexican components which are processed and re-exported to assembly plants along the 401), indicates that an increasing share of the production of all North American automobiles and trucks, especially in parts, is occurring in Mexico. Certain highly labour-intensive tasks have been completely transferred to Mexico, as in the case of wiring harnesses assembly.

Ultimately, however, the ongoing southward relocation of parts production at the current rate can only be achieved via a relocation of assembly plants. There exists the possibility of a trajectory of gradual relocation of assembly plants to Mexico, as the existing facilities grow obsolete over a span of 25 years. Given the evidence discussed above – a gradual dispersion of production from the core area over the past 15 years, a rapid growth in employment and production for export in Mexico, and that the Mexican market has the greatest growth potential in North America – this relocation remains a distant possibility, even more distant, given the overvaluation of the Mexican currency, the associated lose of competitive advantages and the emergence of China like an ideal place for assembly intensive labour parts.

Table 7.2 reveals that although there has been an upswing in investment in Mexico, there has not been a simultaneous drop in investment in United States production facilities. There is thus no indication that existing investments are being allowed to deteriorate in any way or that the pace of investment in the motor vehicle industry is declining in Canada or the United States. Although production growth will continue to occur outside the core, the figures indicate that production inside the core manufacturing area should remain broadly level.

Taking the new assembly plants in North America between 1982 and 2000 there is no trend away from locating in the United States or Canada, but there is a clear move away from locating assembly plants in the core area. With the exception of two new Canadian plants, there has been no new assembly plant construction in the core area since 1991.

In the case of Canada several of the major SIC[5] classifications actually experienced growth after the introduction of the trade agreements. This would appear to indicate that business is not necessarily leaving either the United States or Canada in favour of Mexico, but rather that the international market is growing and that there is room for all NAFTA partners to share in that growth.

Conclusions

North America is likely to remain the most important market and manufacturing region in the world. Even if innovation leadership in several areas has shifted towards firms outside the region, the leverage that sheer market size exercises over the industry will remain a powerful incentive to internalize those advances into the region, either by firm relocation, or by some form of strategic alliance with the region parts manufacturers and final assemblers. Nonetheless, if the regions leading firms have been able to remain competitive in response to the forces of globalization, this has been not only because of the powerful drive for internalization, but also because the region's industries have reorganized and restructured through a process in which market integration between the three countries has played a important and, one could argue, even definitive role.

As the region's trade barriers were brought down, and new coordinated policy arrangements were introduced across the region, especially in the heydays of open market policies between 1986 and 1995, for North American manufacturers, the ability to reorganize into productive and financially efficient networks emerges as a critical factor in regaining their competitive edge. Policy coordination, greater efficiencies in production networks, the alignment of model lines and families according to the specific advantages, not only of each country, but those between regions within each country, and the ability to remain an attractive place for foreign direct investment flows – for both export and domestic production – has made the North American region one of the most successful example of economic integration.

Nonetheless, although North American integration has meant that the region's complementarities and asymmetries have come to the fore in corporate strategic awareness, it has also awakened mounting criticism from social actors and powerful political forces in the three countries. While the question of wages and labour rights were – and remain – critical issue in this debate, increasingly, the ability to internalize within countries and regions the social and economic benefits of the industry will emerge as a matter that will require corporate attention. The asymmetries between countries are large enough to expect that the most powerful pressures will come from the US corporate boardrooms and political arenas. Even though the role of Canada and Mexico has acquired increasing strategic relevance in the industry, both will remain, with their specific differences, peripheral to the United States (for example, Lung, 2000).

Finally, it is difficult to make a definitive conclusion as to whether this North American integration has occurred as a process of downward or upward convergence. There have been both tendencies and countertendencies in the industry that make any decisive assessments difficult to sustain. The nature of productive, geographical and technological arrangements within corporate and economic networks seem complex enough to require a more careful analysis regarding the issue of convergence, and perhaps – as one could suspect from this brief review – these perceived asymmetries and complementarities are far more paradoxical and surprising than many of us are willing to admit.

Part III

Regional Integration within Emerging Regions

8
MERCOSUR: Interaction between Governments and Producers and the Sustainability of the Regional Automobile Industry

Mariano F. Laplane and Fernando Sarti

Introduction

In the years following the Second World War, South American governments implemented development policies aimed at fostering a process of rapid industrialization. During the 1950s, countries like Argentina and Brazil, which had relatively large urban middle-income classes, targeted the automobile industry to lead the process of import substitution of durable goods. It was expected that high tariff and non-tariff barriers together with a set of fiscal incentives would result in the local production of parts and components for locally assembled vehicles.

Both American and European carmakers, which were at the time in the stage of 'multi-domestic internationalization', took advantage of the incentives offered and established 'stand alone' subsidiaries in the region (Freyssenet and Lung, 2000). The pattern of foreign investment and government policies resulted in the building of national automobile production systems that were relatively autonomous from the systems in neighbouring countries and controlled by the world's leading automobile assemblers. In both Argentina and Brazil locally owned firms, supported by local governments, became successful parts suppliers.

From the 1950s to the 1980s the performance of the national systems of automobile production in South America depended upon the expansion of local demand. Exports were insignificant and restricted to smaller neighbouring South American countries that lacked their own local production capabilities. Regional integration among foreign subsidiaries was almost non-existent.

The situation began to change in the late 1980s, when automobile production in the region started to become increasingly integrated. Regional integration initially resulted from the initiative of carmakers. At the time, head companies progressively concentrated their financial resources in strengthening their market positions in developed countries where they faced challenges from Japanese competitors. Cooperation among subsidiaries in Argentina and Brazil offered an opportunity to reduce investment and production costs in a region which had become unstable and stagnant (see Laplane and Sarti, 1997; Roldan, 1997). The creation of Autolatina, by Volkswagen and Ford, which preceded the establishment of the trade agreements between Brazil and Argentina, illustrates just such a strategy.

National authorities quickly adopted bilateral trade and economic cooperation agreements as a way of promoting growth and stability, as well as building confidence in the newly elected democratic governments. During the 1970s military governments in Brazil and Argentina had been involved in a number of disputes over political and military leadership in the region. Civilian governments elected in the 1980s preferred to promote dialogue and cooperation. Once again, the automobile industry was targeted as one of the manufacturing branches to lead the process of economic recovery and bilateral cooperation. Between 1984 and 1989, Brazil and Argentina signed more than twenty bilateral protocols aiming to promote trade, several of which were related to the automobile industry.

In 1990, Uruguay and Paraguay joined Brazil and Argentina in negotiations aimed at creating a common market among the four countries. The Treaty of Asuncion, signed on 26 March 1991, was the legal instrument to implement the Common Market. On 31 December 1994, an additional Protocol to the Treaty was signed at Ouro Preto, under which the institutional structure of MERCOSUR was established.

The Ouro Preto Protocol also established that, from 1 January 1995, MERCOSUR would become a Custom Union. Nevertheless, the Custom Union Regime was not fully implemented immediately. An 'Adaptation Regime' was established which allowed restrictions to free trade within the block for some products (including vehicles and parts). A 'List of Exceptions' to the common external tariff was also agreed. The four countries decided that the Custom Union would come into full effect on 1 January 2006.

Regarding the automobile industry, it was decided that national sectoral policies would remain in place until 1 January 2000. From that date a common regional policy would establish: free trade in the region, a common external tariff and domestic content indexes. The new regional policy was also supposed to eliminate national subsidies and incentives, which could cause investment diversion among the four countries.

When the year 2000 arrived the MERCOSUR region was in the middle of a severe economic crisis. Government officials involved in the design of the new common policy for the automobile industry were not able to reach an agreement on the conditions that would allow free trade of vehicles and components to take place. After a long period of negotiation the deadline for free trade was postponed until 2006. In the meantime several mechanisms were put in place to guarantee relative balance in the automobile industry trade among MERCOSUR member countries.

The present chapter looks into developments in the automobile industry since the creation of MERCOSUR in order to assess its impact, particularly its contribution to the emergence of a regional system of automobile production. Regional integration was an explicit goal of national policies for the automobile industry in the 1990s and also became the main target of the regional policy currently in place. It seems important thus to assess to what extent this goal was achieved.

MERCOSUR and the international automobile industry

Driven by increasing competition, carmakers strengthened their presence in developing countries while simultaneously adapting their worldwide operations to the emergence of large trading blocs in the world economy (NAFTA, the European Union) during the 1990s (Freyssenet and Lung, 2000; Lung, 2000).

Investment in developing countries responded to two distinct logics. In some cases (Mexico and Eastern European countries, for instance) it was mostly a way of reducing production costs in order to serve neighbouring markets in developed countries. Such developing countries became export bases for markets in developed countries. In other cases, investments were aimed at taking advantage of the growth potential of domestic markets in developing countries (such as China and India).

The integration of the automobile markets of the four MERCOSUR countries resulted in the emergence of a new sub-regional market in Latin America. The most distinct feature of this market is that it is supplied mainly by local production. MERCOSUR therefore became simultaneously a relatively large 'emerging market' as well as a relatively large 'emerging producer'. As shown in Figure 8.1, local vehicle sales have been the main driving force of production in MERCOSUR countries since the early years of their automobile industries in the late 1950s. Except for a strong export drive in the 1980s, which was prompted by a sharp decline in local sales, production was mostly directed towards the domestic market.

This inward orientation of production remained in the 1990s, even after MERCOSUR countries had increased their openness to foreign trade. It seems clear, therefore, that investment in the car industry in MERCOSUR during this period aimed to take advantage of local market growth potential, rather than establishing an export base for developed countries.

Comparing the different modes of integration of emerging countries in the global motor industry, Humphrey, Lecler and Salerno (2001: 7) recognize

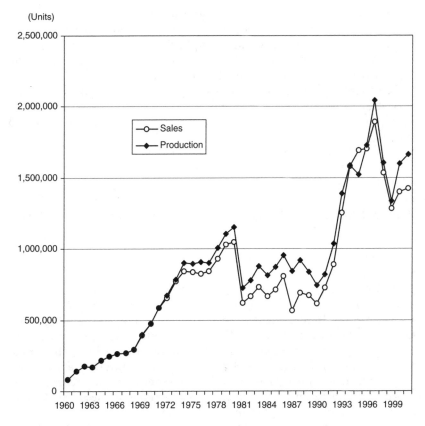

Figure 8.1 MERCOSUR: Vehicle production and domestic sales, 1960–2001
Source: ANFAVEA.

the strong link between regional supply and demand as a feature that differentiates MERCOSUR from other cases in which local car industries operate in Protected Autonomous Markets (PAMs), such as China or India, or in Integrated Peripheral Markets (IPMs), such as Mexico or Eastern Europe. MERCOSUR is classified as an Emerging Regional Market (ERM) both because of intra-regional trade flows and because of its reliance mostly on regional demand.

Given the predominantly inward orientation of supply, MERCOSUR's relative importance within the global motor industry relies mostly on the size and growth potential of the regional market. In 1997, MERCOSUR's best year for the automobile industry in the 1990s, new motor vehicles domestic sales amounted approximately to 1.9 million units in Brazil, 426,000 units in Argentina, 36,000 units in Uruguay and 30,000 units in Paraguay, totalling 2.4 million units in the trading block. Production, almost entirely concentrated in Argentina and in Brazil, reached 2.5 million units (see Table 8.1).

Table 8.1 MERCOSUR: motor vehicle domestic sales and production, 1997 and 2001, (1000 units)

	Domestic sales			Production		
	Cars and light commercials	Heavy commercials	Total	Cars and light commercials	Heavy commercials	total
1997						
Argentina	408.7	17.7	426.3	424.9	21.1	446.0
Brazil	1,873.6	69.7	1,943.4	1,984.4	85.3	2,069.7
Paraguay	26.6	3.9	30.5	—	—	—
Uruguay	34.0	2.1	36.1	5.6	—	5.6
MERCOSUR	2,342.8	93.4	2,436,3	2,414.9	106.4	2,521.4
2001						
Argentina	169.6	7.1	176.7	227.2	8.4	235.6
Brazil	1,511.2	90.1	1,601.3	1,711.3	100.7	1,812.1
Paraguay	13.4	1.2	14.6	—	—	—
Uruguay	13.4	0.8	14.3	9.7	—	9.7
MERCOSUR	1,707.6	99.1	1,806.8	1,948.1	109.2	2,057.4

Sources: ANFAVEA, ADEFA, ABEIVA.

The number of vehicles sold in 1997 placed MERCOSUR sixth in the world ranking of markets ahead of France. In the ranking of producers, MERCOSUR was in eighth place, ahead of both the United Kingdom and Italy. In 1997 MERCOSUR's output reached 4.75 per cent of the worldwide production of motor vehicles, but in 2001, the regional share of worldwide production had declined to around 3.5 per cent.

In the aftermath of the East Asian crisis the performance of the automobile industry in MERCOSUR stagnated. Regional sales and production dropped sharply and it did not return to 1997 levels over the following four years. In 2001 (see Table 8.1) sales in the trading block were down to 1.8 million units and only 2.0 million units were produced. That year MERCOSUR fell to ninth place in the ranking of producers, falling behind China.

In spite of its still fairly reduced size compared to other regional markets, the expected growth potential of the regional market prompted a sharp change in automotive firms' behaviour regarding MERCOSUR. In the second half of the 1990s, according to business figures, around US$20 to US$25 billion were invested in the trading block. As a result installed production capacity expanded to 3.5 to 4.0 million units a year and the number of assemblers and parts producers in the region also increased rapidly.

MERCOSUR became a significant arena for global oligopolistic competition in the motor industry. European assemblers held leading positions in MERCOSUR countries (Renault in Argentina, Volkswagen and Fiat in Brazil) before the trading block was established. American companies had also had interests in the region since the 1950s. Accordingly, MERCOSUR became an important space in the internationalization strategies of European and also – to a lesser extent – of American companies. Japanese carmakers, which had almost no interests in the region before MERCOSUR was established, only made marginal investments in the trading block during the 1990s.

Macroeconomic context and sectoral policies

After the decade of stagnation that resulted from the debt crisis, MERCOSUR countries introduced sharp changes in economic policy and institutions in the early 1990s. These aimed at restoring growth conditions. Market-friendly reforms were implemented with strong support from multilateral institutions (the IMF, the World Bank and the Inter-American Development Bank). Before long, significant foreign capital inflows in the form of portfolio and foreign direct investments restored the balance of foreign accounts, allowed to reduce inflation and to expand domestic demand in the region. MERCOSUR countries experienced high growth rates in the 1990s but, by 2000–2001 macroeconomic conditions had significantly deteriorated. Inflows of foreign capital dropped dramatically.

Within the general framework of market-led development, policy towards the automobile industry was a significant exception. In Argentina, Brazil and Uruguay, the automobile industry was awarded specific and very active sectoral policies (see Tigre et al., 1999). Policy intervention aimed to reactivate demand and to promote investment and local production of vehicles in a context of protection levels that were relatively lower than before. The main goals were to attain product modernization, specialization, efficient scales in production and the greater use of imported parts. Protection for local vehicle producers was lowered, but it remained higher than the levels offered to many other producers, demonstrating that the automobile industry still had strong influence on policy makers. The differential treatment granted to vehicle assemblers and to parts suppliers (mostly locally owned firms) illustrate this point. The latter were granted much lower levels of tariff protection than the former and thus locally produced parts suffered much stronger competition from imports.

In Argentina, an agreement signed in early 1991 by producers, suppliers, unions, dealers and government resulted in a 33 per cent reduction in consumer prices for locally produced cars. Strong demand recovery prompted the Argentinean government to create incentives for local car production. By the end of that year the government defined the package of incentives that would benefit the automobile industry from January 1992 onwards. The main goal was to take advantage of demand recovery in order to upgrade local production and improve export performance.

Ad valorem tariff levels were established at 22 per cent for cars and from 14 per cent to 20 per cent for components, but tariffs could be lowered to

2 per cent for imports compensated by an equivalent amount of exports of cars and/or components. The value of investments in local manufacturing facilities could also be used to compensate imports. Local content requirements were that 60 per cent of components should be produced locally.

Producers which had plants in both Argentina and Brazil (Autolatina and Fiat) were the main beneficiaries of the package, since they had already developed some degree of complementarity among their subsidiaries in both countries and could readily qualify for incentives by expanding intra-firm trade in the region.

In the early 1990 Uruguay only had small-scale vehicle assembly operations. Changes in sectoral policy aimed to reduce imports costs and to increase exports to MERCOSUR. Tariff barriers for cars were lowered from 40 per cent (in 1990) to 20 per cent (in 1993). Tariffs of 6 per cent were imposed on imports of CKD units. Local content requirements were reduced and could be substituted by export performance. Bilateral agreements signed with Argentina and with Brazil enlarged quotas for Uruguayan exports of vehicles to those markets – although quotas were in fact relatively small, with around 15,000 vehicles exported to each country, in 1997.

In Brazil, sectoral policy initially aimed to stimulate local demand (Laplane and Sarti, 1997, 2002). In the early 1990s, tax reductions were implemented for a low-price standard vehicle, the so-called 'people's car' (*carro popular*), powered by a 1,000 cc engine. At the same time, tariff protection was reduced for vehicles and for parts. The goal was to reduce tariffs for cars from 80 per cent to 35 per cent over a five-year period (1990–1994) and to 20 per cent in the year 2000.

By 1994, growing demand had become a problem. As waiting lists became larger and started to put pressure on prices, the government decided to reduce tariff barriers to 20 per cent six years ahead of schedule, in order to increase supply.

In March 1995, following an acute foreign exchange crisis, importation tariffs for consumer goods, including cars, were again raised to 70 per cent. This was supposed to be a temporary measure aiming at helping the government to adjust its exchange rate policy, but it became an important instrument in a new style of policy intervention for the auto industry. The new policy regime maintained the 70 per cent tariff barriers during 1995/96. Gradual tariff reductions were planned, starting from a 63 per cent tariff level in 1997 and reaching a 20 per cent level in the year 2000. Imports from MERCOSUR, up to 85,000 units, would be free from tariffs. A 47,500 units quota, paying 35 per cent, was established for Japanese, Korean and European car companies yet not established in Brazil.

The new policy established that tariff reductions would be granted to local producers in exchange for the exports of vehicles and components. In 1996, tariff reductions were: 50 per cent for car imports, 90 per cent for equipment imports and 85 per cent for components. Thanks to such reductions, local producers were able, in 1996, to import paying 35 per cent tariffs for cars, 2 per cent tariffs for equipment and 2.4 per cent tariffs for components. The end of 1999 would face out all incentives. At that time, tariff barriers for cars would be lowered to 20 per cent (see Laplane and Sarti, 1997).

In order to benefit from the incentives, car companies and suppliers had to qualify until the end of 1996. Nevertheless, in 1997, after the deadline had passed, the Brazilian Congress created a new 'Special Automotive Regime' which granted further incentives for carmakers willing to build new facilities in the Northern, Northeastern and Central regions of Brazil. Other state governments (Paraná, Rio Grande do Sul and Minas Gerais) had already granted similar incentives to attract investments in the automobile industry. Almost at the end of the decade, in 1999, in spite of strong reactions from other MERCOSUR countries, the Brazilian government once again created new incentives for vehicle producers, this time heavily subsidizing Ford's investment in the State of Bahía (see Rodriguez-Pose and Arbix, 2001).

National policies for the motor industry in MERCOSUR countries gave a high priority to regional integration. After the Ouro Preto Protocol was signed, in December 1994, negotiations were started to establish a common MERCOSUR policy for the automobile industry that would replace national policies. In this way the goal of regionally integrating automobile production became explicit.

It was finally agreed that until the end of the decade bilateral trade would be regulated by the establishment of quotas and compensated trade of parts and vehicles. Parts and components imported from MERCOSUR countries would be treated as 'locally produced' when assessing the 'domestic content index' and would pay no tariffs, as long as such imports were compensated with exports towards the same countries.

This arrangement proved to be mainly of benefit to assemblers that had production facilities on both sides of the border, because intra-firm trade allowed them to take full advantage of compensated trade. As a result of intra-block trade incentives, all assemblers ended up having plants on both sides of the border and establishing some kind of division of labour between their Brazilian and Argentinean subsidiaries.

The national incentives regimes expired in December 1999. After a long period of negotiation and many disagreements over the common external tariff, over subsidies and other fiscal incentives and over domestic content indexes, Argentina, Brazil and Uruguay finally reached an agreement on a new common policy at January 2001. Negotiations with Paraguay took a little longer. The 'Agreement on the MERCOSUR Automobile Policy' set February 2006 as the date to establish free trade of vehicles, parts and components within the region.

The Agreement also determined that local or national authorities could grant no further subsidies or other forms of fiscal incentives as a means of attracting new investments. It was agreed that subsidized products could not benefit from preferential treatment granted by MERCOSUR to regional producers. The goal was to avoid the practice of bidding wars between member countries.

The Common External Tariff for cars was established at 35 per cent. A timetable was established for the reduction of tariffs on the intra-regional trade of parts and components. Trade between Brazil and Argentina was supposed to remain balanced, but the Agreement allowed for increasing imbalances (ranging from 5 per cent of exports, in 2001, to 10 per cent in 2003, and higher percentages in 2004 and 2005). It was established that tariffs would be charged if unbalances exceeded the allowed levels.

The Regional Content Index was set at 60 per cent of the sales price in the domestic market, but lower levels were allowed for new models. Special rules were defined for the measurement of domestic content in Argentina and Uruguay, so as to ensure higher levels of locally produced components.

Industry's performance and market structure

Vehicle production grew rapidly in both countries during the 1960s, but followed quite different trajectories over the following decade (see Figure 8.2). In Argentina output fell because of the stagnation of the domestic market; while in Brazil, output increased fivefold. At the end of the decade, output in Brazil was four times larger than in Argentina.

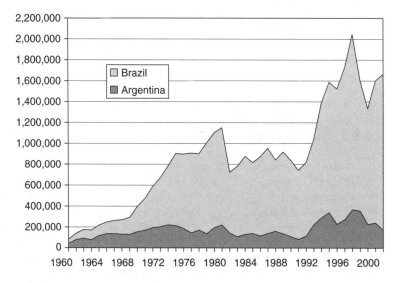

Figure 8.2   Vehicle production in MERCOSUR, 1960–2001
Sources: ANFAVEA, ADEFA.

In the 1980s, vehicle production decreased and remained stagnant in both countries, but with different consequences. Argentina's domestic market was smaller and had had a weak performance for a longer time. As a result, some assemblers (GM, Chrysler, Fiat, Peugeot, Citroën) closed their plants or transferred them to local licensees. In Brazil, carmakers and their suppliers had invested heavily in new capacity and in new models in the late 1970s. Instead of closing their plants, they reacted to the reduction of local demand in the 1980s by reducing investments and by taking advantage of strong fiscal incentives to increase exports.

During the 1990s, as macroeconomic conditions improved and as integration advanced, national and regional demand interacted positively. Increasing trade liberalization within MERCOSUR allowed national markets to become interdependent. At the beginning of the decade, the Argentinian car market recovered earlier than the Brazilian one, resulting in an increase in the export of Brazilian built cars to Argentina in 1992/93. Conversely, the demand for cars in Brazil expanded rapidly during 1996/97, fostering exports from Argentina to the Brazilian market. Once again, in 2000, when demand in Argentina shrank due to the deterioration of local economic conditions, exports to Brazil sustained local production. In other words, regional integration allowed counterbalancing fluctuations in local market conditions, stabilizing production.

The recovery of regional demand, national sectoral policies and the rules for intra-block trade established after the Ouro Preto Protocol attracted new investments in the automobile industry in the second half of the 1990s.

Investments in Argentina preceded those in Brazil, given that local demand recovered first, that many local facilities were obsolete and that most assemblers lacked capacity in Argentina to comply with domestic content indexes and compensated trade requirements established in MERCOSUR. Renault, Fiat and PSA, the leading assemblers, bought back equity control of their operations in Argentina that had been transferred to local companies (CIADEA and SEVEL) in the 1980s. Ford and Volkswagen enlarged and updated their facilities after their Autolatina joint venture ended. Fiat, GM, Chrysler and Toyota undertook greenfield investments (Table 8.2).

As a result of the regional integration in MERCOSUR, the market structure in Argentina changed significantly. Locally owned firms that had been transferred equity control by Renault, Fiat and PSA were among the leading assemblers before MERCOSUR was established. At the end of the 1990s, the European assemblers regained equity control. At the same time, newly arrived subsidiaries from assemblers that had previously only produced in Brazil (Volkswagen and GM) secured significant market shares and challenged the leaders. In the year 2000, the traditional leaders (Renault, Fiat, PSA and Ford) controlled 58 per cent of the total sales of cars and pick-ups. New entrants (Volkswagen and GM) had 24 per cent of the market (Table 8.3).

Table 8.2 MERCOSUR: main investments in vehicle production

Company	US$ million	Location	Type	Model/scale (units/year)
Argentina, 1994–8				
GM	172	Córdoba	Greenfield	Silverado/20,000
GM	400	Rosario	Greenfield	Corsa/85,000
VW	260	Pacheco	Brownfield	Golf, Polo/140,000
Ford	1,000	Pacheco	Brownfield	Escort, Ranger/80,000
Toyota	170	Zárate	Greenfield	Hilux/20,000
Fiat	600	Córdoba	Greenfield	Palio Sedan/150,000
Renault	23	Córdoba	Brownfield	Clio, Megane, Traffic/100,000
Brazil, 1996–2002				
Fiat	500	Betim	Brownfield	Engines
Ford	1,000	Camaçari	Greenfield	Amazon/240,000
GM	150	Mogi das Cruzes	Greenfield	Components
GM	600	Gravataí	Greenfield	Celta/120,000
Honda	150	Sumare	Greenfield	Civic/30,000
Toyota	150	Indaiatuba	Greenfield	Corolla/30,000
Mercedes-Benz	820	Juiz de Fora	Greenfield	Class A/40,000
VW	270	San Carlos	Greenfield	Engines
VW	750	S. Jose dos Pinhais	Greenfield	Audi A3, Golf/170,000
Renault	1,000	S. Jose dos Pinhais	Greenfield	Scenic, Clio/80,000
Renault	500	S. Jose dos Pinhais	Greenfield	Engines
PSA	600	Porto Real	Greenfield	206, Picasso/40,000
Chrysler/BMW	500	Campo Largo	Greenfield	Engines

Sources: ADEFA, ANFAVEA.

Investments in Brazil started in 1996, after the Automotive Regime was established. Brazil attracted greenfield investment from assemblers which had previously produced only in Argentina (Renault and PSA), from Japanese assemblers (Toyota and Honda) newly arrived to the region and also from leading assemblers in the local market seeking to take advantage of the incentives offered by local and state governments in new locations (Table 8.2). Despite sizable investments from new entrants, the Brazilian market remained under the tight control of the traditional leaders. In 1999, Volkswagen, Fiat and GM controlled 70 per cent of the total sales of cars and pick-ups (Table 8.3). The newly arrived Japanese (Honda and Toyota) and European (Renault and PSA) competitors still enjoyed only marginal market shares at the time. It is widely believed that newly arrived assemblers will become a real challenge to the leaders as they complete the building of their productive capacity and distribution networks. In this regard, Renault and

Table 8.3   Market share of the main carmakers in
Argentina (2000) and Brazil (1999)

Sales of cars and pick-ups (percentage)		
Brands	Brazil (%)	Argentina (%)
Fiat	25.5	10.5
Ford	9.0	14.9
General Motors	23.2	9.8
PSA	2.0	14.6
Renault	2.7	18.3
Toyota	1.3	4.2
Volkswagen	30.0	13.6
Others	6.3	14.1
Total domestic sales	100.0	100.0

Sources: ACARA, ANFAVEA.

PSA seem to have more ambitious plans than the Japanese carmakers, since their investments are larger and target the small car segment of the market, where volume can be attained and market shares can be built.

Seven years after the signature of the Ouro Preto Agreement the overall picture is one of significant convergence between the market structures in Brazil and Argentina. Both markets are under the control of the same European carmakers (or European subsidiaries of American carmakers). Locally-owned licensees that used to control the Argentinean market have been replaced by foreign carmakers. Asian carmakers have marginal positions in both markets. Some differences can still be noticed: Renault and PSA lead in Argentina, while Volkswagen and Fiat lead in Brazil.

Regional integration seems to have strengthened competition within national markets by increasing the number of leading players. This process seems to have gone furthest in Argentina where market shares seem to be more homogeneous. The Brazilian market clearly remains much more concentrated since new entrants (Renault and PSA) still need to conquer significant market shares, like Volkswagen and GM managed to do in Argentina.

Regional integration

Trade figures reveal the degree of regional integration of automobile production within MERCOSUR as well as the integration of the trading block into the global automobile industry. Intra-regional trade of motor vehicles and components grew rapidly once the Ouro Preto Protocol was signed, almost doubling in value from 1994 to 1998 (see Table 8.4). Extra-regional trade also grew, although at a slower pace.

Table 8.4 MERCOSUR: trade of motor vehicles and parts, 1994 and 1998

To/From	Exports		Imports		Balance	
	1994	1998	1994	1998	1994	1998
US$ billion						
Intra-MERCOSUR	2,185	5,180	2,275	5,278	−90	−98
Extra-MERCOSUR	1,923	2,994	5,070	6,266	−3,147	−3,272
Total	4,108	8,174	7,346	11,544	−3,238	−3,370
Percentage						
Intra-MERCOSUR	53.2	63.4	31.0	45.7	—	—
Extra-MERCOSUR	46.8	36.6	69.0	54.3	—	—
Total	100.0	100.0	100.0	100.0	—	—

Source: DATAINTAL, http://www.iadb.org/intal/

In 1994, total exports of motor vehicles and parts by MERCOSUR countries amounted to US$4.1 billion (53.2 per cent of which was made up of
intra-block trade and 46.8 per cent of extra-regional exports). In 1998, total
exports amounted to US$8.2 billion (63.4 per cent in intra-block trade and
36.6 per cent towards other countries). Imports also grew from US$7.3 billion
in 1994 to US$11.6 billion in 1998. Imports from within MERCOSUR
became increasingly important, growing from 31 per cent of total imports
in 1994 to 45.7 per cent in 1998.

The fact that intra-regional trade grew at a faster rate than overall trade
confirms the growing integration of automobile supply and demand within
the region. Trade figures confirm, thus, Humphrey, Lecler and Salerno's
characterization of MERCOSUR as an Emerging Regional Market (ERM)
(Humphrey, Lecler and Salerno, 2001: 7).

The figures in Table 8.4 also show that, in spite of its reliance mostly on
regional demand, MERCOSUR was not at all a self-sufficient 'fortress', since
the level of extra-regional trade is still very significant. Far from being an
isolated market, MERCOSUR intensified its trade links with markets outside
the region. In fact, extra-regional trade showed US$3 billion deficits in both
years, showing that the region imports more than it exports to the global
automobile industry.

Table 8.5 shows important information on the composition of trade flows
within and outside the regional market, giving some clue about the division
of labour that was established within MERCOSUR and between the regional
market and the rest of the world. Figures are from 1996, when sales
were growing and economic policies followed similar guidelines both in
Argentina and in Brazil.

Argentinean vehicle and parts exports were mainly directed to the
Brazilian market. At the same time, parts were imported mainly from Brazil,
while car imports came mostly from outside the region. Brazil exported most

Table 8.5 MERCOSUR: trade of cars and parts by destination/origin, 1996 units: US$ 1000

	Vehicle			Parts		
	Exports	*Imports*	*Balance*	*Exports*	*Imports*	*Balance*
Argentina						
Brazil	766,051	273,906	492,145	273,469	527,494	−254.025
MERCOSUR	771,682	283,489	488,193	282,261	550,135	−267,874
ROW	32,165	915,857	−883,692	71,975	448,853	−376,878
World	803,847	1,199,346	−395,499	354,236	998,988	−644,752
Brazil						
Argentina	334,119	765,094	−430,975	534,763	277,781	256,982
MERCOSUR	395,659	801,004	−405,345	573,287	280,224	293,063
ROW	223,594	760,685	−537,091	732,299	1,320,036	−587,737
World	619,253	1,561,689	−942,436	1,305,586	1,600,260	−294,674

Source: DATAINTAL.

vehicles to Argentina, while parts were shipped mainly to countries outside MERCOSUR. On the import side, Brazil bought most parts outside of the region. Brazilian car imports from within and from outside MERCOSUR were almost equally important.

As could be expected from the differences in the national market sizes, Argentina's production and trade are more dependent upon the Brazilian market than the opposite. The Brazilian market is an important destination for Argentinean exports of vehicles and parts, besides being an important supplier of parts. On the other hand, in spite of Argentina being an important trade partner, Brazil seems to be relatively less dependent upon the Argentinean market, since it had significant trade flows of vehicles and parts in both directions with countries outside MERCOSUR.

Argentina's exports growth was mostly linked to the opening up of the Brazilian market and resulted from the compensated trade requirements. Brazil already exported cars to other South American countries as well as parts to the United States before the creation of MERCOSUR.

Regional integration resulted in Argentina importing parts from Brazil, while it exported assembled cars to the Brazilian market. In this way regional integration resulted in trade creation for cars in Brazil and in parts in Argentina. Table 8.5 shows that Argentina had a surplus in trading cars with MERCOSUR (mostly with Brazil), while it ran a deficit in parts, and that Brazil's position was symmetrical to Argentina's. It had a trade surplus in trading parts with its MERCOSUR partners (mostly with Argentina), while it ran a deficit in cars. Both countries ran deficits in trading parts and vehicles with the rest of the world.

As a result of regional integration, trade in the automobile industry advanced faster than in other sectors. As Table 8.6 shows, trade of motor

Table 8.6   MERCOSUR: share of trade of motor vehicles and parts in total trade, 1994 and 1998 (%)

	Exports		Imports	
	1994	*1998*	*1994*	*1998*
Intra-MERCOSUR trade	18.3	25.5	19.2	25.8
Extra-MERCOSUR trade	3.8	4.9	10.1	8.4
Total trade	6.6	10.1	11.9	12.1

Source: DATAINTAL.

vehicles and parts amounted to 25 per cent of total intra-MERCOSUR trade in 1998. The share of the automobile industry in extra-MERCOSUR trade was much lower.

Regional integration advanced alongside the rapid modernization of products and facilities. Both newcomers and already established carmakers updated their product lines and supplied the regional market with world models. The production of outdated models, which were no longer produced in developed countries, was discontinued. Locally produced vehicles progressively incorporated safety, energy and environmental protection standards higher than those prevailing in the 1980s.

Regional integration allowed automobile production in MERCOSUR to become more specialized in comparison with the rest of the world in the production of small cars and engines. Plants in Argentina produced versions that demanded relatively smaller scales (sedan and light commercial versions, as well as versions with larger engines). Brazilian plants were mostly used to assemble 'popular cars' version with smaller engines. Pick-ups and light commercial vehicles were mostly produced in Argentina.

Each constructor followed its own regional division of labour strategy (Laplane and Sarti, 2000). Ford adopted a division of labour among its subsidiaries that resulted in the production of medium-sized models (Escort, Focus) in Argentina and smaller models (Fiesta and Ka) in Brazil. Fiat's division of labour produced different versions of the same models on the two sides of the border. VW combined both strategies, producing a medium-size sedan in Argentina (Polo Classic) as well as several versions of the Golf, which was also produced in Brazil. GM complied compensated trade requirements by assembling pick ups in Argentina and exporting to the Brazilian market while exporting Corsa models and components to Argentina.

Conclusions

The fact that regional integration was achieved so swiftly only a few years after MERCOSUR was created was a consequence of the pursuit of national sectoral policies that had pursued regional integration since the late 1980s. Intra-regional trade was promoted through bilateral trade agreements even before MERCOSUR existed. Nevertheless, MERCOSUR did made an important contribution to the regional integration of the automobile industry.

The trading block contribution was twofold. First, the overall process of economic integration gave credibility and political support to the pursuit of a policy of regional integration in the automobile industry, strengthening the confidence of foreign investors. Secondly, it provided an institutional framework within which a common policy for the automobile industry could be discussed and approved. This process was initiated after the Ouro Preto Protocol and was only concluded in 2001. During this period important steps were taken towards strengthening regional integration. These included the definition of common criteria for local content and changes in the requirements of compensated trade as macroeconomic conditions deteriorated in member countries. Institutional channels helped to restrain tensions and disagreements that emerged in the process of integration in the automobile industry. Conflicts over investment diversion caused by the 'bidding wars' in Brazil were channeled through MERCOSUR mechanisms, successfully avoiding spillovers to neighbour countries.

If MERCOSUR fostered regional integration in the automobile industry, the opposite is also true – regional integration in the motor industry contributed to the progress of MERCOSUR in different manners. First, as already mentioned, regional integration in the automobile industry started before MERCOSUR, showing that integration was feasible. Secondly, carmakers were very active as representatives of the business sector in the negotiations to implement MERCOSUR. Thirdly, and by far the most important, intra-industry trade of vehicles and parts representing 25 per cent of total intra-regional trade (as shown in Table 8.6) played a crucial role in legitimizing regional integration. Given the fact that Brazil had a much more developed manufacturing sector, other MERCOSUR members – in particular, Argentina – feared that economic integration would result in a 'vertical division of labour' by which other countries would end up exporting raw materials to and importing manufactures from Brazil. The automobile industry showed that there was also room for intra-industry trade and for a 'horizontal division of labour' within the block.

MERCOSUR and regional integration in the automobile industry reinforced each other. MERCOSUR was the carrier and was at the same time driven along by integration in the motor industry. It can only be a matter of speculation as to whether regional integration in the automobile industry could have proceeded even in the absence of MERCOSUR. It might, but it is unclear to what extent and for how long. As mentioned above, MERCOSUR provided an important institutional and political framework, which became critical as macroeconomic conditions deteriorated after the East Asian crisis.

There are reasons to believe that the political dimension of regional integration in the automobile industry will remain important in the years to come. The main challenges facing the regional automobile industry in the near future have significant political dimensions. The two main sources of tensions are: first, the stability of the present division of labour between countries in the region and, secondly, the mode of integration of MERCOSUR into the global automobile industry.

Regarding the first challenge, what is at issue is if production in Argentina (and to a lesser extent in Uruguay) will survive once compensated trade requirements currently in force are abandoned and free trade of vehicles and parts within MERCOSUR rules. As mentioned above, the current division of labour is highly complex and it is based on specialization in parts and high-volume models in Brazil and some parts and lower-volume models in Argentina. What will be the division of labour in the long run? Will it be in the interests of carmakers to concentrate production in low wage costs and larger-scale Brazilian plants after 2006? Would this imply the closure of plants in Argentina? Would it be politically feasible? Can Argentina absorb a permanent deficit in trade of vehicles and parts with Brazil?

In the last few years national governments prevented a massive transfer of automobile production from Argentina to Brazil, even when changes in macroeconomic conditions meant that production in Argentina became unprofitable. Political interest prevailed over economic interests under critical conditions. Can political interest prevail even in the long run?

Other experiences of regional integration in the automobile industry also showed that the issue of the division of labour among countries and locations is critical. Even regions where the automobile industry has been integrated for a longer time than in MERCOSUR undergo tensions because of this problem (see Part II). Conflicts of interest between business and national governments do not seem to have simple solutions. The geographical relocation of investment and jobs, especially if carried out over a short span of time, is a source of tension that may lessen regional cohesion, unless compensating mechanisms are implemented. In this regard, MERCOSUR's political channels are essential.

The other source of tension will be the mode of integration of MERCOSUR within the global automobile industry. As mentioned before, currently the trading block is firmly integrated through financial and technological flows in global industry. Yet it remains relatively autonomous regarding the world market, since most of its production is consumed within the region and most of the automobiles sold in MERCOSUR are produced in the region. It seems reasonable not to expect profound changes in the current situation in the near future, since regional demand and regional supply seem to be strongly linked.

In other words, it seems that MERCOSUR will remain in the foreseeable future an ERM, to use Humphrey, Lecler and Salerno's typology. Nevertheless, sources of tension arise from the fact that regional demand has not lived up to carmakers' expectations that led to the recent wave of investments and from negotiations for the creation of the Free Trade Area in the Americas (FTAA). The combination of these two factors seems to threaten the future of MERCOSUR as a ERM, both because its size is not as large as had been anticipated by carmakers and because it could be absorbed by the North American market.

9

ASEAN: Developing a Division of Labour in a Developing Region

Koïchi Shimokawa

Introduction: a crisis-struck region?

Asia has been widely identified by analysts as a prospective growth region for the automobile industry in the twenty-first century. Given its huge population (1.4 billion in China, 0.8 billion in India and 0.5 billion in ASEAN countries), the region has the potential to be the world's largest automobile market. In 1995, the market of the 12 most important Asian countries (excluding Korea and Japan) totalled around three and a half million cars. The automobile markets of the developed countries of the United States, Europe and Japan had reached maturity with little further growth potential, whilst the Asian region was expected to grow to more than nine million car sales by the year 2000. The four largest ASEAN markets (Thailand, Malaysia, Indonesia and the Philippines) represented approximately one-third of this market and were expected to grow by 50 per cent in the second half of the 1990s. China, India and South Korea represented the remainder of the Asia region (excluding Japan), but they had all developed 'go-it-alone' strategies (see Chapter 1 and Part IV of this volume). The ASEAN region had been more open to foreign entry.

However, although the region saw remarkable rates of industrialization and economic growth especially from the 1980s onwards, satisfactory progress is not always guaranteed, as can be seen from the 1997 currency crisis. For instance, automobile production in Thailand plummeted more than half following the baht crisis in July 1997. The financial crisis had a tremendous impact on both the automobile market and production in Asia in general and Southeast Asia in particular. Only at the beginning of 2001 did Japanese, European and American automobile manufacturers put an end to production reductions in ASEAN countries and start to increase local production again. It is also expected that a new and more innovative international division of labour will be established. The existing regional labour division was established with a focus on technology transfer and the production and supply systems aimed for the domestic markets of each Asian country. During the period of the economic crisis, most automobile manufacturers reduced their levels of production. While promoting exports outside the regions as a result of the depreciation of the countries' currencies in the regions, improvements in domestic production rates of auto parts (because of the high cost of imported parts and further promotion of intra- and inter-regional divisions of labour) were also pursued. Obviously, it can be said that the economic crisis was the turning point. Examining the future development of the automobile industry in ASEAN, which has reached a key stage, involves in particular analysing the presence and strategies of Japanese automobile manufacturers. Before the Asian international currency crisis occurred, the strategy of Japanese automobile manufacturers for the Asian markets was to expand the international divisions of labour, especially in the ASEAN countries (while also slowly establishing a foothold in the Chinese market). The international division of labour linking ASEAN countries, Taiwan and South Korea was only regionally oriented. Its aim was to develop regional divisions of labour while contributing to the domestic production in each country, on the expectation of market growth within the region. There was no assumption of a rapid price increase of imported parts due to the decline of currencies or of the export drive for completed cars. The underlying idea was to gradually develop international competitiveness through an expansion of international division of labour by AICO (the ASEAN Industrial Cooperation), expecting the establishment of AFTA (ASEAN Free Trade Area), which was scheduled for 2003.

This chapter analyses the development and the future of the car industry in the ASEAN region. It has largely been a story of regionalism under the tutelage of the Japanese car majors. So the impact in particular of Japanese firms on the shape and nature of regionalism in ASEAN will be assessed. At the beginning of the twenty-first century, Japanese automobile manufacturers are facing two options in the wake of the Asian economic crisis. One is to hold off on the expansion of the international division of labour until the economic crisis is completely over. The other is to take aggressive measures to enhance competitiveness in exports by increasing the domestic production rate, though this is a risky strategy. Additionally, this contribution considers what the prospect of ASEAN for local and/or Western car firms is.

Dependent regionalism in ASEAN

Between 80 and 90 per cent of the cars domestically produced in ASEAN countries (as well as in Taiwan) are developed by Japanese automobile manufacturers and produced by joint ventures with them. ASEAN stands out as a region within the Asian region. No other country or region allowed for comparable inroads of foreign (Japanese) producers. South Korea and China had their own policies for domestic production and strictly limited the inflow of foreign capital, especially direct investment by Japanese assemblers.

Toyota and Mitsubishi Motors started operations in ASEAN countries on a SKD (semi-knockdown) basis in the late 1960s and early 1970s in response to requests by local governments for cooperation in domestic production. Over the 1990s, Toyota and Mitsubishi Motors had the greatest leverage in the ASEAN region followed by Honda, who started with motorcycle production, and Nissan, who has begun to make efforts to catch up. As far as the automobile industry was concerned, levels of direct investment from Japan were relatively low in ASEAN countries. This is because although ASEAN countries, especially Malaysia and Thailand, positively implemented the introduction of foreign currencies in home electrical appliances and electronic equipment such as colour televisions, video tape recorders and air conditioners with regard to the automobile industry they pursued measures in favour of domestic production and domestic capital. In addition, they promoted indirect foreign investments for domestic capital rather than accepting direct foreign investment – especially from Japan.

The nature of the automobile industry has been expanding in the ASEAN region over the 1965–1995 period assisted by a combination of local and regional policies. Assembly production has been carried out in the form of SKD production (semi-knocked-down production), KD production (knocked-down production) and CKD production (complete-knocked-down production) from the early stage of imports of completed cars and repair (Figure 9.1). The domestic market was protected at the same time. However, although the protection of the domestic market has promoted technology transfers and domestic production to a certain extent, the production volume was limited and cost penalties were inevitable because of high tariffs on imported parts for the promotion of domestic production. As a result, there was a high cost dilemma, twice as high as Japanese-made, and lower quality, compared with the international standard.

In order to ease this dilemma, in 1969 the ASEAN Complementation agreement on reciprocal complementation in automobile production – strongly supported by Japanese car manufacturers – was concluded among the five founding members of ASEAN. This agreement, however, ended up as a mere desk plan since it was difficult to decide which country would produce which auto parts. The underlying cause of this failure was the low standard of industrialization of ASEAN countries and the different degrees of industrialization among the countries. Against the background of the failed ASEAN Complementation agreement, differences in the direction of the automobile industry policies for each ASEAN country emerged in the 1980s. However, the major problem lies in the difference in policy decisions among ASEAN countries as to whether they should loosen up the conditions of foreign currency introduction in order to positively invite foreign money

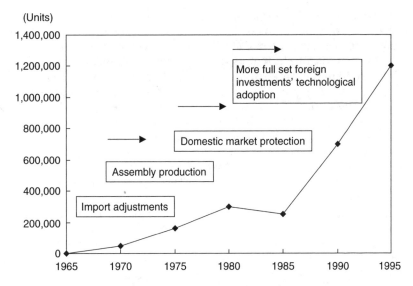

Figure 9.1   Shifts of the automobile manufacturing units of ASEAN and industrial development

Source: Small to Mid-Size Finance Corporation Investigation Dept, *Automobile Industry Trends in ASEAN and Effects to Our Domestic Small to Mid-Size Parts Manufacturers*, report by Japan Finance Corporation for Small Businesses, No. 98-1, April 1998.

to introduce more sophisticated technology for full-set production of automobiles. Other issues involved are whether they should actively prepare for free trade areas in Asia, especially AFTA (ASEAN Free Trade Area), and whether they should place emphasis on protection of domestic industries. However, experiencing trials and errors and complications, ASEAN countries saw the progress of local production of automobiles and technology transfers, and the expansion of domestic markets appeared to be under way. Then the financial crisis hit Asia.

In search of a regional division of labour

ASEAN governments have been trying to accept investments by Japanese assemblers and auto parts manufacturers in the form of joint ventures with local companies for technology transfers, although some governments have also tried pursuing policies for domestic production. Furthermore, they have also been actively seeking international divisions of labour within the region. The ASEAN nation that received the most investment from Japanese manufacturers was Thailand. In 1998, the production capacity of Thailand reached over one million, including European and US cars, and at this time Japanese manufacturers accounted for 80 per cent of local production.

In the late 1980s, when the industrialization of the four major ASEAN countries had been enhanced and the domestic automobile production plan started to get on track, the BBC (Brand of Brand Complementation) scheme was introduced. In 1982, Mitsubishi Automobile Industries had proposed to '(1) reduce the import parts tariff to half, (2) consider the import parts as the domestic parts and include in the calculation of the domestic production ratio, when each country mutually accommodates the parts with higher priority in cost.' In 1987, at the 3rd Summit, agreement was reached on promoting the BBC Plan – a commitment enshrined in the Manila Declaration. In 1988, this was approved and signed at the ASEAN Cabinet Economic Ministers Council. Under the BBC scheme, if a specific automobile manufacturer offers reciprocal complementation for parts of a specific brand car, the import tariff on the parts would be considerably reduced (Table 9.1). Some manufacturers that had been propagating the plan themselves, such as Toyota, Mitsubishi and Nissan, started to use this system. Among ASEAN countries, the concept of complementary divisions of labour was extended to parts and materials. In 1996, AICO (the ASEAN Industrial Cooperation) was established as a comprehensive and full-scale reciprocal complementation agreement to respond to the sharp reductions of import tariffs to be implemented under AFTA (ASEAN Free Trade Area), which is scheduled for 2003 (Figure 9.2).

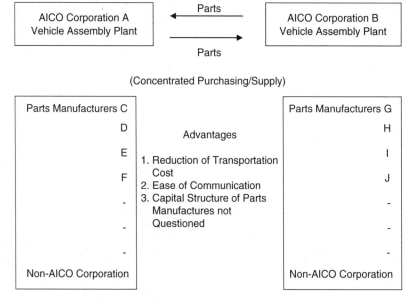

Figure 9.2 Complement of AICO arrangements

Source: Fumio Yoshimi, *Current Situation of ASEAN Automobile Industry and Strategies of Automobile Manufacturers* (unpublished).

144

Table 9.1 Comparison of BBC and AICO plans

	BBC	AICO
Contents	Expansion of mass production effects resolve obstacles for the private business plans by reducing high tariffs set to protect the domestic parts industry and reducing the vehicle production cost. This enables support for the distribution of the specific parts of the specific model of the specific brand in the local participating countries.	Promote the establishment of the infrastructure towards the trade deregulation of WTO through the trade/investment expansion in order to enhance the mutual profits and competitiveness in each country for the promotion of economic development in the ASEAN region. CEPT adoption was advanced to 2003, thus temporarily adopted the AICO Plan in 1996 in order to make adjustments for each ASEAN country for 2003. Also, ASEAN automobile industry is expected to improve in the long-term in the aspects of income and technical standards. But the recognition of the necessity of each country to reduce cost by promoting the localization and mutual complements among countries was one of the factors for the advanced adoption.
Items included	Automobile parts	Finished products/Mid-process products/Raw material
Term applicants	From October 1988 until the issue of AICO Domestic Automobile Manufacturers (Brand Owners)	Until the issue of CEPT (2003) manufacturers in each country
Authorizing party	ASEAN Office	Industrial ministry in each country.
Terms and conditions	Limited to the automobile parts. BBC products fulfill the regulation of the place of origin by PTA (ASEAN special decision). Single ASEAN content exceeds 50%. Cumulative ASEAN content exceeds 60%. Manufactured based on the International Quality Assurance Standards	Established in 'each ASEAN member country' and operate business. Minimum 30% of country's share Sharing the material, or corporations cooperate each other. Corporations conducting business established by multiple participating countries, which cooperate to manufacture AICO products. Designated parts domestic manufacturing ratio

Table 9.1 Continued

	BBC	AICO
	Competitively priced for the general market place.	exceeds 40% Approved as AICO products when the raw material import CIF amount is less than 60% of the export FOB amount.
Benefits	Domestic manufacturing approval 50% exemption of the CDK tariff.	To be included in the domestic manufacturing ratio. 0–5% performance tariff is applied (available only for the participating companies handle AICO approved parts).
Issues	Advantages and disadvantages become evident to the governments in each country due to their own domestic automobile, domestic manufacturing programmes. Each country advocate to produce more value-added parts (engines and transmissions), which leads to conflicts. BBC has the special programme for the large automobile manufacturers, thus the early shift to the CEPT is necessary. Also, more opinions are indicated for a programme to promote small to mid-size local industries. After submitting the application to the ASEAN office, opinions of each MITI of each country's must be asked. Complicated process due to the approval necessary by all ASEAN participating countries.	Each country's pace is different. Approval by the government (of importing and exporting countries) is carried out simultaneously and the importing and exporting countries need to negotiate. Both government's benefits and losses will be evident and conflicts may affect the surrounding industries such as automobile-related industries expect to have the delay in permits. In order to balance the trades, it is possible that the CKD package export, which gather the parts by the parts manufacture's under the control of each country's automobile companies, may not be approved.

Source: Small to Mid-Size Finance Corporation Investigation Dept.

AICO was supposed to help promote divisions of labour and co-operation among parts manufacturers and also to help form a network not only within the region but also beyond the region. When AICO was put into effect 19 companies – mainly Japanese – applied. But no companies actually operated under AICO. Thailand gave approval of application of AICO to a total of nine companies, including Japanese automobile manufacturers like Toyota and Honda, auto parts manufacturers (e.g. Denso Corp.) and home electrical appliance manufacturers (e.g. Matsushita Electric Industrial Co.) as well as Volvo and Goodyear. However, Malaysia and Indonesia did not give approval to any single company due to concern about the impact on domestic industries.

The ASEAN Secretariat gave approval to projects under BBC. An application under AICO required approval by the Ministry of Industry in each country. The latter delayed the implementation of AICO. According to Japanese automobile manufacturers who have applied for AICO, each country demanded a foreign currency balance (import–export balance between two countries) from each manufacturer when making application for AICO (Japan Finance Corporation for Small Business: 27). There is no doubt that the basic concept of AICO would contribute greatly to the development of a regional international division of labour in the ASEAN region if it were implemented in full. However, there were differences in expectations and degrees of domestic automobile production among the ASEAN countries. The problem of balancing auto parts trading still remained – and remains – to be solved before strengthening a regional division of labour. Furthermore, the currency crisis in 1997 discouraged each country from liberalizing the trade of important industries like the automobile industry.

The outline for the implementation of regional reciprocal complementation scheme of Toyota by BBC is shown in Figure 9.3 – Mitsubishi has

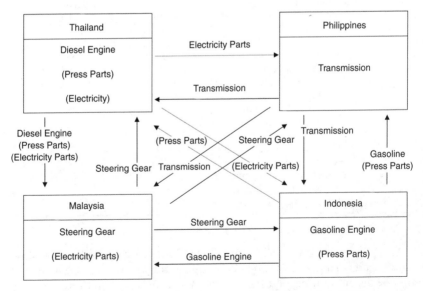

Figure 9.3 Outline of Toyota's components complementation plan, 1990
Source: Toyota Motors, *Automobile Market in Asia and Oceania*, 1990.

developed its own scheme. This figure shows how plans on a regional division of labour were initiated in the early 1990s. The currency crisis occurred when operations were starting to shift from BBC to AICO. It was believed that Japanese manufacturers will improve domestic production rates, strengthen the international divisions of labour and start exporting outside the region sooner or later because of the high cost of imported auto parts from Japan. Major Japanese automobile manufacturers also tried to establish a full-scale production system for Asian cars aided by a regional division of labour, especially in Thailand. Cars developed and produced in this manner were largely commercial vehicles adapted to road and traffic conditions in ASEAN countries. For example, Toyota developed an original commercial vehicle model Kijang which was mainly produced in Indonesia (Sugiyama and Fujimoto, 2000). The prospect of market expansion for passenger cars began to attract the attention and the production of Asian passenger car models, such as Soluna by Toyota and City by Honda, which were mainly produced in Thailand.

In the mid-1990s an international division of labour in the automobile industry in the ASEAN countries had just started to develop and it applied chiefly to a limited group of parts and components. The BBC scheme required 50 per cent ASEAN content and made it imperative to improve local content and regional divisions of labour since it is costly to import parts from Japan – for instance, due to currency fluctuations. Table 9.2 shows the general trend during the 1990–96 period based on changes in the level of imports of major products in Thailand, Malaysia, the Philippines and Indonesia. In the 1900 to 1996 period, Thailand and Malaysia saw an increase in the domestic production rates for each major auto parts category while the level of imports from Japan declined considerably. Local production of parts and components increased during this period. However, the Philippines and Indonesia experienced an increase in imports except for certain parts. In Thailand, the local production of power trains and engine supplements made some progress, reflecting the effect of local production regulations. On the other hand, the import of bodies and accessories increased, probably because the demand shifted to various passenger cars due to the rapid development of the domestic market.

With the exception of car bodies and accessories, the progress of domestic production was substantial. Thanks to the domestic production policy for national cars, Malaysia became less dependent upon imports in all areas. The Philippines became less dependent upon imports in the areas of underside parts, transmission parts and steering parts while imports of power trains, engine supplements, bodies and accessories rose. This trend implied that demand for high value added passenger cars expanded along with the political stability in the country while domestic production was not making progress in the various areas of parts production. Indonesia did not see much change on the whole, but it is noted that local production of engine supplements and

Table 9.2   Summary of parts production capability of ASEAN countries, 1990–96

	1990 to 1996	Individual items
Thailand	Generally localization progressed	—Items other than car body/ accessories showed localization. —Improved the production of power train/engine supplement equipment.
Malaysia	Localization developed for all items	—Low dependency for import on each item. —Even more development in electronic accessories in recent years.
The Philippines	Localization developed for some items	—Mainly electronic accessories, foot area, transmissions and steering parts. —Structure of the car body and accessories is easy to increase imports.
Indonesia	Little change	—Space to localize in the power train/engine supplement equipment. —Higher local production capability for the foot area parts.

Source: Small to Mid-Size Finance Corporation Investigation Dept.

power trains were lagging behind while domestic production of underside parts made progress (Japan Finance Corporation for Small Business: 39).

Structural changes after the Asia crisis

The Asian currency crisis was triggered by the Thai baht crisis in July 1997 and mainly involved ASEAN countries. It forced Japanese automobile manufacturers, who had been pursuing complementary divisions of labour mainly in ASEAN countries, to re-examine their strategy and to take temporary emergency measures. Declines in the number of units in both sales and production in 1998 were severe: Thailand dropped to one-quarter of its peak; Malaysia to 40 per cent of its peak; and Indonesia to one-sixth of its peak (cf. Table 9.3).

While devising a number of emergency measures (cf. Table 9.4), Japanese auto manufacturers also tried to implement a number of longer-term measures in order to reinforce exports from plants in Thailand and other countries preparing for the recovery period of the economy following the financial crisis.

The four ASEAN nations combined total sales for passenger cars and commercial vehicles fell to 440,000 units in 1998 from a high of 1,440,000 units in 1996, before recovering to 990,000 units in 2000 and 1,250,000 units in 2002. The shape of recovery varies strongly from country to country. Firstly, Thailand experienced a tremendous recovery in production compared to the

Table 9.3   Shift of automobile sales in four ASEAN countries, 1996–2000 (units)

	1996	1997	1998	1999	2000
Thailand	589,126	363,156	144,065	218,330	262,189
Passenger vehicle	172,730	132,060	46,300	66,858	83,106
Commercial vehicle	416,396	231,096	97,765	151,472	179,083
Malaysia	364,788	404,837	163,851	288,547	343,173
Passenger vehicle	275,615	307,907	137,691	239,647	282,103
Commercial vehicle	89,173	96,930	26,160	48,900	61,070
Indonesia	332,035	386,691	58,303	93,814	300,966
Passenger vehicle	43,914	73,215	11,941	11,012	46,931
Commercial vehicle	288,121	313,476	46,362	82,802	254,035
Philippines	162,011	144,435	80,231	74,414	83,949
Passenger vehicle	88,977	75,790	34,688	27,580	28,826
Commercial vehicle	73,034	68,675	45,543	46,834	55,123
Total	1,447,960	1,299,119	446,450	675,105	990,277
Passenger vehicle	581,236	588,942	230,620	345,097	440,966
Commercial vehicle	866,724	710,177	215,830	330,008	549,311

Source: Mori (2001).

recovery of the domestic market, mainly because manufacturers stepped up their exports. When exchange rates became favourable for exports because of the post-crisis decline of the Thai baht, manufacturers operating from Thailand followed suit in directing their excessive production capacity to exports. Thailand, which exported almost no cars before 1997, rapidly increased the share of exported cars to more than one-third (150,000 units) of the total production result (420,000 units) in 2000. Mitsubishi Motors, for example, shut down an old manufacturing site and concentrated their production in a pick-up truck factory located along the bay outside Bangkok. They used this factory as their export station – resulting in 63,541 cars being exported. Auto Alliance Thailand, a joint venture between Ford and Mazda, exported 49,977 units. Faced by a poor recovery in the local passenger car market, Toyota and Honda both built a factory to produce their versions of Asia cars (small-sized passenger cars fitted for the region) right before the economic catastrophe, shifted to exports. A large share of Thai-made automobiles is currently exported to Middle Eastern and Oceanian countries – and smaller share to African nations.

The ASEAN nation that showed the second most rapid recovery was Indonesia. From the 380,000 units sold as its peak volume in 1997, sales fell sharply to 58,000 units in 1998, but improved quickly to 300,000 units in 2000. The decline was also due to political turmoil in the country in the period 1998 to 1999, which marked a sharp decrease in domestic auto sales. The recovery is linked to a desire to quickly purchase what was restrained during that period.

Table 9.4   Japanese automobile manufacturers' strategies following the currency crisis

Temporary measures	
Production reduction	Place of origin/temporarily-terminated operation.
	Terminated outsourcing production
	Froze the investment plans
	Postponed the introduction of the new model
Reduction of employment	Temporary workers/full-time workers reduction
Measures for sales	Increase in sales price due to the raise in imported raw materials.
	Implementation of the sales promotions.
	Special implementation of Auto Loans.
Local parts	Advance payments
Manufacturer's support	Increase in the parts purchasing price
	Council to discuss the support measures by cooperative efforts among Japanese finished automobile manufacturers.
Long-term measures	*Reorganization of the production system*
Changes of purchasing	Promotion of local/regional supply purchasing.
Clients	Expansion of exports (finished car/parts)
Financial support for the local corporations	Increased investment and investment ratio by Japanese companies.
Concentration of plants	Concentrate on the domestic manufacturing centre by closing the old plants.
Technology/quality	Implement employee training in Japan.
System plants	Obtain ISO, etc.

Source: Mori (2001).

In contrast to Thailand, which adopted a liberalization policy immediately after the economic crisis, Malaysia, the third largest auto-producing nation in ASEAN, adopted a policy to protect national automobile manufacturers. This policy centres around two national car companies: Proton, protected by the preferential tax system producing comparatively lower priced cars; and Perodua, which produces compact cars similar to the Japanese minicars. Both of these firms produce cars under license and have strong technical cooperation ties with Japanese companies (Mitsubishi and Daihatsu respectively). Despite the crisis, the policy to protect and favour the national car manufacturers was still kept in place. Malaysian automobile production and sales reached an all-time peak in 1997, with 457,000 and 405,000 units respectively. There was then a sudden and steep decline to around 150,000 units in 1998, after which the figures quickly climbed in 2000 to about 80 per cent of their peak production and 85 per cent of the highest sales volumes achieved. This rapid comeback was driven by the two national auto manufacturers. Proton took a share of 52.1 per cent and Perodua took

29.2 per cent, making a combined total of 81.3 per cent. In particular, the second national manufacturer Perodua, having begun production comparatively late, did not suffer much during the economic slump.

The Malaysian government adopted a very different tactic in trying to overcome the consequences of the economic crisis. Whereas Thailand loyally followed the IMF's policy line to repreciate the baht, Malaysia, in an attempt to protect their ringgit, adopted a fixed rate system and escaped the economic disruption that may otherwise have been caused by an emergency evacuation-style measure. This approach closed off the Malaysian auto industry from international competition and resulted in very low car exports. It also delayed the liberalization policy envisaged in AFTA – the successor of ASEAN originally planned for 2003 (see Chapter 1). Thailand increased its export activities by taking advantage of the low baht rate even though it did experience the pains of domestic social disruptions. Thailand aims to became an export base in the region. The two Malaysian car projects are now faced with the problem that their production is basically aimed at the closed Malaysian market – helped by barriers to inward investment. They run the risk of lowered international competitiveness in the wake of further regional liberalization. Proton has acquired technology that allows it to design and prototype engines and even, to some extent, to design and develop new cars. In addition, suppliers with Japanese and local affiliations have also started to organize. However, problems with achieving competitive quality levels of produced cars and delivery time endure. The management at Proton is aware of the problems and has planned to implement internal reforms. Nevertheless, because of the protected nature of the national market some of the necessary reforms have been postponed. At the same time in Thailand, the inward flow of foreign capital also stopped temporarily as a result of the economic turmoil. But, as soon as the recovery period started, GM, Ford, and others increased their facilities, and megasuppliers such as Delphi and Bosch and Japanese suppliers such as Denso, Nippatsu and Yazaki followed suit. In contrast, there have been very little foreign investments by auto manufacturers in Malaysia. Of the major suppliers only Delphi made a branch facility of their Singapore factory in Malaysia.

In the light of the Asian economic environment, with the People's Republic of China successfully applying for membership of the WTO and the eventual implementation of AFTA, even though it was delayed by two or three years, it is clear that Malaysia will find it difficult to maintain its fixed rate system and protectionist policy. Therefore, on one hand, the Malaysian government has made Petronas, the national petroleum corporation with substantial financial resources, Proton's largest shareholder. The tie-up with Petronas should improve development capacity and reduce material costs. On the other hand, the government started considering the possibility of reviewing the special tax arrangements that are particularly advantageous to home-manufactured cars. Furthermore, Malaysia planned an expansion of the parts production base, based on the AICO scheme. Companies like Toyota and Honda in Malaysia started to prepare their production capacities on the expectation that the Malaysia government will ultimately embrace further liberalization measures and support the formation of AFTA.

Thailand, as it runs straight on the liberalization road, received most investments by vehicle manufacturers and suppliers from Europe and America. Japanese manufacturers are also increasing capacities to set up their export bases in Thailand (Lecler, 2002). Honda has a regional production base in Thailand for motorcycles, which they are trying to complement with a comparable regional automobile base. The plans centre around Honda's Asia car, the City. Toyota is its new Thai factory as the production base for its Asia car, the Soruna, in preparation of increased production of their very competitive and successful commercial vehicles. Both Toyota and Honda claim that they procure close to 100 per cent of their parts locally without relying on imports because of the low baht rate.

What is striking in the present situation following the Asia crisis is the overconcentration of investments and advances in Thailand. This development, however, could cause structural changes in the structure of divisions of labour in ASEAN. The concentration and integration of the parts industry are progressing rapidly in Thailand – and spreading to the other countries in the region. In 2001, there were more than sixty applications for AICO, whereas there were very few during the economic catastrophe. Not only major assemblers, but also parts manufacturers are preparing for a further regional division of labour. Presently, Thailand tends to attract all of the investments in ASEAN because the country is being shaped into an export base at the assemblers' level. However, the merits of regional complementary divisions of labour as a preparation for the possibility of full implementation of AFTA in the future have not vanished – yet.

Strategies of European and American auto manufacturers in ASEAN

Until 1997, the ASEAN car industry was dominated by Japanese automakers. Of all the automobiles produced in ASEAN nations, approximately 90 per cent were designed by Japanese manufacturers. ASEAN nations started from SKD and worked through CKD to increased levels of national content until they were able to begin full-scale mass-production plant according to the market size of each country. The types of vehicles produced also showed national characteristics. Thailand and Indonesia concentrated on multipurpose, small-sized, commercial vehicles and Malaysia on small passenger cars. By the middle of the 1990s many of the Japanese producers had started to implement a regional division of labour, following the BBC and AICO schemes and in anticipation of a further liberalization of the region under AFTA. When the 1997 Asia currency crisis appeared, the long-term strategic plans were seriously disrupted. Among the European and American automakers, on the other hand, only Volkswagen's Shanghai project ran any risk of being affected by the crisis. In contrast to their presence in China, European and American auto manufacturers did not reach any further than KD productions in the ASEAN market. The only exception was Ford Motor, who teamed up with Mazda to build a pick-up truck production facility in Thailand. Others, particularly European automakers like Renault, Peugeot, Daimler-Benz, BMW, Fiat, and Volvo, simply constructed small-scale KD factories in countries such as Indonesia, Malaysia, and Thailand in joint efforts with local capital. Hardly any joint production with Japanese passenger car firms developed. Only a local KD assembly company in Indonesia was conducting KD productions of Daihatsu and Suzuki as well as of Benz, BMW, and Fiat brand cars under the same roof.

Anticipating the recovery of the ASEAN market and its further liberalization, European and American manufacturers have adopted more aggressive activities in the region. GM followed Ford in opening their mass production facility for pick-up trucks in Thailand and is waiting for a chance to move into Indonesia if the local political situation allows. GM's current activities are autonomous, but they may choose to work with Isuzu who manufactures the most pick-up trucks in Thailand or possibly take advantage of the strong foothold of its affiliated company Suzuki in Indonesia.

The global consolidation of the car industry is additionally affecting European and American automakers' approaches to ASEAN both as a market and as a production site. The alliance between Renault and Nissan allows Renault to take advantage of Nissan's production facilities located mainly in Thailand and move toward joint materials procurement. Nissan and Renault have started to develop their own Asia car. Daimler-Chrysler – as the largest shareholder in Mitsubishi Motors – is expected to further develop its strong presence in ASEAN. Mitsubishi Motors has developed the widest range of car business in ASEAN equaling Toyota. Their problem now is how to take advantage of what they have established. Having invested in Hyundai, the largest auto manufacturer in South Korea, as well as in Mitsubishi, Daimler-Chrysler is entrusting their 'P Car Project' to the two Asian companies. Whether this develops into a fourth Asia car project – also based on a regional division of labour in the ASEAN countries such as the City and the Soruna of Honda and Toyota respectively – remains to be seen.

Furthermore, megasuppliers from Europe and America have started to make full-scale advances into ASEAN. They are stimulated by the possibility of regional complementary divisions of labour, the expectation for the market share to expand in the region in the future, and the global movements by the newly established auto group to engage in regional or even global sourcing with preferred suppliers. The European megasuppliers will start to compete with the Japanese suppliers that entered the region in an earlier phase. Bosch, with bases in Thailand, Malaysia, and Indonesia from an early stage, is now moving to enhance the capacity of each base and intra-regional cooperation. Delphi is working to expand, centring around Thailand, Malaysia, and Singapore and engulfing Indonesia. Visteon started making large-scale investments mainly in Thailand. Johnson Controls and Lear have strengthened their regional production. Valeo is likely to attempt a regional expansion of its production. In an apparent attempt to take advantage of existing Asian production bases, some of these megasuppliers have even acquired Japanese suppliers with a presence in ASEAN. For example, Bosch acquired Zexel and Jidosha Kiki K.K. and Johnson Controls purchased Ikeda Bussan. Advances into ASEAN by European and American suppliers through M&A in relation with the changes in the affiliated supplier systems in Japan, therefore, cannot be overlooked. These megasuppliers are considered not only to have developed discrete production bases across the ASEAN region but also to pursue a strategic placement of bases and integration of them under their regional and sometimes even global strategies.

Conclusion

The development of an automobile market centring around Southeast Asia can be attributed mainly to the increase in income levels in the countries, and technological transfers over a longer period by Japanese automobile and parts manufacturers that has followed along the production nationalization policies, and led to the partial development of a regional division of labour. Hit by the 1997 economic crisis just as they had started to reap proper rewards from the growing market and were preparing for full-scale regional divisions of labour, Japanese auto manufacturers were forced to reorganize their strategies extensively. The contents of the strategic reorganization included, on the one hand, factory closures, large-scale production cutbacks, and layoffs as emergency evacuation-style measures to cope with the rapid decline in automobile demand. On the other hand, given the low currency rate in the background, they started redirecting production capacities toward exports from domestic orientation and converting production facilities to export bases. Thailand provides a typical example of this redirection. However, the crisis also resulted in political and strategic divergence in the region. In particular, in Malaysia, the export position was not strengthened because of the priority that the government placed on the stability of the economy and the protection of the national car producers.

As the economic recovery in ASEAN progresses, the tendency to overconcentrate and consolidate foreign investment in the Thai auto industry continues. This development is not only confined to assemblers but can also be witnessed amongst suppliers. Whether this tendency will progress or whether the situation will settle down is closely related to political conditions in the near future. First, the question of when and how AFTA will be launched. Secondly, the domestic political stability in Indonesia and the Philippines which are considered to be very interesting prospective markets because of their large populations and the relatively low automobile saturation rates. In the short term these two nations offer little hope for rapid expansion because of their political instability. Thirdly, the position of Malaysia is particularly relevant. It adopted a protectionist stance in the second half of the 1990s by switching its free exchange currency to a fixed exchange rate system. Malaysia is bound to take a step back to exchange liberalization. At the time of writing Thailand has been the centre of the auto industry of ASEAN for some time since it has a well-developed infrastructure for supplying parts, raw materials and intermediate materials. But this position is not likely to endure in the longer run.

How will regional complementary divisions of labour among the ASEAN nations develop further? The type of regional cooperation envisaged in the BBC scheme was primarily an assembler-centred idea. Components were supplied among the assemblers to complement each other based on the brands of cars planned for each year. In contrast, the newly established AICO scheme involves suppliers as well as assemblers and attaches value to regional complementary divisions of labour among suppliers (Guiheux and Lecler, 2000). But complete self-reliance in supplies of parts, raw materials and intermediate materials has been very difficult, even though attempts were made to advance a nationalization policy in which imported goods (from Japan) were priced high due to tariffs and high yen rates. A system with complementary divisions of labour within the region can be considered to have great merits for those automotive manufacturers and suppliers that are already located in Thailand. Furthermore, once the AFTA system is established, it is likely that mutual complementarity will increase in unison with reduction of tariffs and, additionally, that divisions of labour will spread. The regional division of labour and the political choices made by future governments in the region will be strongly influenced by the presence of European and American auto manufacturers and parts suppliers. Finally, the future of the automobile space in ASEAN is under the influence of China after its entry into WTO. The affiliation of China with WTO will inevitably add momentum towards the process of liberalization under the AFTA system. If a situation develops where China allows personally owned cars and accepts foreign investments under certain conditions concerning implementation of environmental measures, it will no longer be only a dream to engage China in a wider regional division of labour in Asia. Already, in the areas of electric appliances and the electronics industry divisions of labour have developed with China. With respect to automobiles, imports of some labour-intensive, general-purpose parts from China have already started, which may lead to a price revolution for some parts. The possible scenario exists that more Japanese parts producers will focus on production in China, which – in combination with a possible appreciation of the yuan – could add to the uncertainties of the ASEAN region and change the outlook of the regional division of labour. Therefore, with China now in the WTO system and with AFTA finally having arrived in Asia, the situation will probably not allow ASEAN to remain a mere regional economic bloc, such as it has been to date.

10

Recreating an Automobile Space by Regional Integration: The CIS Perspective

Jean-Jacques Chanaron

Introduction

Nearly 40 years after Nikita S. Khrushchev's claim that the car was a product for a society dominated by the capitalist middle-class – that is 'bourgeois' – when the country was still the Soviet Union, the relationship of the people of the Commonwealth of Independent States (CIS), formed by 14 republics[1] of the former Soviet Union, to the automobile is still a question of unsatisfied passion.

After the collapse of the Soviet Union in 1990, this passion has even been reinforced by the feeling of economic freedom being made supposedly available by the long-awaited market economy. But the transition from the USSR to the CIS has proven to be much harder than had been anticipated by ordinary citizens. The global economic recession during the 1990s, culminating in the 1998 financial crisis in Russia, did shape a hectic reduction in households' consumption. But finally, to the surprise of observers on all sides, most CIS countries – and in particular Russia – remained economically viable after the serious financial crisis of the summer of 1998.

At the beginning of the twenty-first century, the future of the CIS automotive industry appears to be still in some doubt but most industry observers would expect that Russia will do its best to remain a stakeholder in the world arena:

- On the supply side, the automobile industry is still considered to be a strategic sector for employment and development of the subcontracting industry, but it has yet to be made economically and financially viable in the context of a growing competition and globalization;
- On the demand side, Russia is potentially a mass market with around 150 million inhabitants but this potential market has to be made solvent,

with respect to its historical, cultural and sociological characteristics. It might benefit from the expanding market of the whole CIS – an area which amounts to nearly 300 million inhabitants.

This chapter is based on the following assumptions:

1. The economic situation of Russia and CIS is specific and unprecedented. It is obvious that it could not be analysed by using old models of economic growth such as the Rostow's step-by-step linear and sequential economic development in which these countries would be considered as late developers behind the modern developed and industrialized countries. The current situation in the CIS is not at all that of a depressed period which would inevitably be followed by a stage of rapid growth.
2. The exclusion of Russia and other CIS countries from the international arena is simply not acceptable. This region has been one of the world leading countries for many decades and still has a highly skilled workforce. It is also a mass market with around 290 million inhabitants but it has to be made solvent, with respect to its historical, cultural and sociological characteristics.

The automotive industry in Russia and other republics of the former Soviet Union

It is probably not too dramatic to say that the fall of the Berlin Wall hastened the industry's globalization as markets long closed to major foreign automakers actively lobbied for investment. Even if many ordinary citizens may be unable to afford a new car for decades, more than 350 million

Table 10.1   Cars in use, selected countries, 2000

	Cars in use 01/01/2000	%	Cars per 1,000 inhabitants
Russian Federation	16,000,000	3.00	108.9
Ukraine	4,900,000	0.90	97.8
Belarus	1,150,000	0.20	109.5
Lithuania	980,000	0.20	272.2
Latvia	520,000	0.10	216.7
Estonia	451,000	0.10	322.1
Georgia	425,000	0.10	83.3
Azerbaijan	270,000	0.10	34.2
Moldova	170,000	*	38.4
Kyrgyzstan	140,000	*	31.1
Armenia	1,300	*	0.4
World total	535,748,400	100.00	

Source: MOTORSAT (http://perso.club-internet.fr/motorsat/1).

potential customers in the former Soviet Union and Central and Eastern Europe are enough to make any strategic planner's heart skip a beat.

Unfortunately, the outlook for the former Soviet Union is not as promising (Table 10.1). Political instability and economic contraction have combined with bureaucratic foot-dragging to reduce sales and inhibit efforts by foreign automakers to establish themselves in Russia, Ukraine, Belarus or Uzbekistan.

According to Van Tulder and Ruigrok (1998), Russia and the states of the former Soviet Union are increasingly constituting a closed car system, rather isolated from the worldwide automotive system and regarded as risky from the perspective of the investing companies, despite numerous joint ventures in vehicle and component manufacturing. At the time of writing, the well-publicized collapse of the Korean OEM Daewoo, which will inevitably affect its local operations, is likely to reinforce such isolation.

Automobile production

Russia

Since the financial and economic crisis that erupted in August 1998, the Russian automobile industry has managed to stabilize itself at a reasonably high level of output: nearly one million passenger cars were produced annually (1999–2002). This is still below the level reached by the Russian Federation before the disintegration of the former Soviet Union in 1991: from 1.7 million units produced in Russia in 1990, the total number of vehicles produced has fallen to 1.2 million in 2002. By global industry standards, of course, production volumes remain comparatively very small.

There are seven car manufacturers in Russia – namely, AvtoVAZ, its subsidiary SeAZ, JSC GAZ, Avto UAZ, JSC Moskvich, JSC Izhmach and PO EIAZ (Table 10.2). AvtoVAZ is the largest OEM and is also cooperating with KamAZ, the truck maufacturer for the assembly of the small VAZ 1111. Some other manufacturers are assembling kits supplied by foreign OEMs. This is the case of JSC Krasny Aksaj (involved in agricultural machinery) at Rostov-on-Don with Daewoo from Korea (Doninvest) – it is also assembling Citroën Berlingo and Autoagregate at Kineshma with Mahindra & Mahindra from India (jeeps). But according to the most recent figures, they are not very successful (Table 10.3).

AvtoVAZ and Gaz are far from bankrupt, at least by Russian standards. In 1997, AvtoVAZ reported a net income of US$215 million on a US$3.8 billion turnover. It is expecting to achieve a turnover of US$5 billion in 2000. In 1997 and 1999, it posted a promising pre-tax profit margin of nearly 11 per cent but an after-tax profit of less than 2 per cent. Gaz reported a 5 to 7 per cent net profit in 1997–98. Since the financial crisis in 1998, the two main OEMs, AvtoVAZ and Gaz, have managed to expand their daily working time to increase the output and match the domestic market demand. For instance, in 1999, AvtoVAZ was producing 143 cars per hour, over a 40-hour week. But this level of productivity is still very low by western standards: the factory, built by Fiat, is nearly 30 years old and its workers take about

Table 10.2   Existing car producers in Russia, 2001

Company	Type of cars	Existing cooperation	Possible cooperation
AvtoVAZ	Middle class	General Motors	GM
JSC SeAZ	Small (OKA)	AvtoVAZ	
KamAZ	Small VAZ 1111	AvtoVAZ	
Avto UAZ	4 × 4	Daimler-Chrysler	Daimler-Chrysler
JSC GAZ	Middle class	Own design	BMW, Daewoo, Fiat
JSC Moskvich	Middle class	Renault	Renault, Fiat
JSC Izhmach	Middle class	VAG	
PO EIAZ	Cargo-passenger cars	GM	
Doninvest	Middle class	Daewoo	
Avtotor	Upper class	BMW	
IzhMash	Middle class	Skoda	

Table 10.3   Production of passenger cars in Russia

	Total	AO AvtoVAZ	OAO GAZ	AO AvtoUAZ	Moskvitch
1990	1,049,000	740,000	n.a.	n.a.	n.a.
1993	955,867	656,403	105,654	57,604	95,801
1997	985,074	740,526	124,339	51,411	20,599
2000	967,493	705,561	116,319	40,250	5,543

Sources: CCFA; *Financial Times*; Chanaron (1998); *Automotive International*, January 2001.

320 hours to build a car, against an average of 28 hours in European plants. Furthermore, quality is still very low: according to the public, 'a one-year old Lada has a higher market value than a new one since the owner has repaired everything!'. But the Russian OEMs do not have sufficient cash flow to modernize their plants and renew their model range. Just before the summer of 2001, the Russian government released that AvtoVAZ will be fully privatized to allow the company to sign a strategic deal with a western OEM.

Other CIS countries

Most automobile-related activities in the other former Soviet Union republics are dealing with trucks, buses and coaches as well as agricultural machinery. The production of cars in other former Soviet Union republics is still a marginal activity. In 2002, 50,400 cars would have been manufactured in Ukraine and 22,700 in Uzbekistan (source: OICA). Belarus was expected to produce 15,000 industrial vehicles in 2002.

In Uzbekistan, the authorities, through the association of motor industry of Uzbekistan Uzavtoprom, had given priority to the component industry. Only one car manufacturer is active: UzDaewooAvto, which is indeed suffering from the current collapse of Daewoo Motor.

In Ukraine (Mezouaghi, 2001), the main car manufacturer is ZAZ – with 11,700 vehicles produced in 2000. In addition, there are LuAZ, KrymavtoGAZservis, Chernihivavtodetal, UkrVolgatekhservis and Kiev Auto Repair Plant. A deal was concluded with Skoda in 2002.

Joint-venturing

In Russia, the government is actively supporting the establishment of joint ventures, providing they derive half of the manufactured added-value from local manufacturers and suppliers during the five first years of operation (Table 10.4).

Table 10.4 Current foreign investment plans in Russia

Carmakers	Partner	Location	Investment (US$ million)	Capacity	Year	Models
BMW	ZAO Avtotor	Kaliningrad	26	10,000	1999	BMW 5-Series, Land Rover Discovery
Daewoo Citroën	Doninvest	Taganrog	n.a.	10,000	1999	Citroën Berlingo (3,000)
Fiat	OAO GAZ	Nizhny Novgorod	500	150,000	2000	Marea, Palio
Ford	Bankirshi Dom	Vsevolozhsk	150	100,000	2001	Focus
GM	AvtoVAZ		155	75,000	2002	New Lada Niva
GM	ELAZ	Yelabuga	50	50,000	1996	Chevrolet Blazer, Opel Vectra
Renault	Moscow Municipality Avtoframos	Moscow	440	120,000	1999	Megane
Skoda (VW Group)	AO Izhmash (Udmurtia)	Izhevsk	250	80,000	1999	Skoda Felicia and Fabia

Sources: FIPC (1999); 'Doninvest shifts to Citroen', *Vedomosti*, 27 October 1999; *Les Echos*, 6 March 2001.

The 50 per cent local content regulation, very badly defined in official documents, is a tough constraint since the Russian automobile component industry is currently in a parlous state. Prospects for sourcing locally are very limited. Local producers are not able yet to supply top quality products to the required technological standards. They also have tremendous difficulties in managing logistics and their own supplies from second-tier manufacturers. The golden triangle – quality, volume and just-in-time delivery – is not yet set as a standard in Russia. The only criterion which seems easy to satisfy is low price. The Russian industry – OEMs and component manufacturers – were equipped with up-to-date imported machinery in the 1970s, but there has been very little renewal since. As a result, productivity is very poor and the level of quality achieved is far from the minimal requirements desired by the customers, even in the emerging markets of Central and Eastern Europe.

In such conditions, foreign automobile manufacturers in Russia will be very reluctant to invest more if they are to re-export part of their output towards Eastern, Central or Western Europe.

Relationships with suppliers

AvtoVAZ-Lada used to be highly vertically integrated according to the industrial conglomerate industrial policy set up under the socialist government (Chanaron, 1998). Since the disintegration of the Soviet Union, the AvtoVAZ supply chain has been completely disrupted, losing most of its suppliers in Eastern Europe and in the other former Soviet Republics. Being badly affected by the cash crisis of its customers, AvtoVAZ became dependent upon barter which was once the way it transacted over 90 per cent of its business: on one hand, it was buying parts and paying utilities and commodities and on the other hand it was selling cars. Such a situation led to a spectacular rise in criminal activities (Matlack, 1999).

Foreign suppliers did establish production facilities in Russia: Delphi, Lear, Hella, Mannesmann, Bosch, for instance, are in a position to supply both local OEMs and foreign automakers and joint ventures. But again low productivity and poor quality are key obstacles to any attempts to re-export finished items. For the moment, they supply parts to assembly lines of kits. AvtoVAZ and Gaz have very limited procurements with them.

The main characteristic of the business-to-business market is its '*virtuality*'. As quoted by Gaddy and Ickes (1998),

An economy is emerging where prices are charged which no one pays in cash; where no one pays anything on time; where huge mutual debts are created that also can't be paid off in reasonable periods of time; where wages are declared and not paid; and so on ... [This creates] illusory, or virtual earnings, which in turn lead to unpaid, or virtual fiscal obligations, [with business conducted at] non market, or virtual prices. In other words, what has emerged is a 'Virtual Economy'.

A restoration of a constructive partnership with first-tier and second-tier suppliers is an absolute necessity. It is exactly the same situation in the other republics where the supply chain is completely hectic and needs a comprehensive re-engineering.

Globalizing the CIS automobile industry

AvtoVAZ, the leading Russian OEM, is already engaged into a still limited but quite innovative global expansion strategy through joint ventures or assembly licensing: Kamaz, the heavy truck manufacturer, is assembling the VAZ 1111, or Oka, the smallest Russian car, and AvtoVAZ has set up other assembly plants in Russia, namely RosLada in Syzran (80 km from its home town Togliatti), Izhmash (Lada Niva 4WD), Seaz for the VAZ 1111-Oka. RosLada built 25,000 cars in 2000.

Negotiations are currently under way for a plant in Pakistan (Karachi) to build Oka cars and for an assembly plant in Ecuador (Quito) where AvtoVAZ intends to produce VAZ 2106, its family middle-range model, and the Niva.

Gaz has also started a similar strategy, setting up a joint venture in Ukraine with KrymavtoGAZservis in Simferopol for about 3,000 cars in 2000 and for the assembly of various models in Chernygov (Chernihivavtodetal) and Kiev (Kiev Auto Repair). Gaz is also involved in Belarus through BelGazavtoservis. Similarly, Uaz has assembly agreements in Ukraine in Krasnodon and Lutsk.

The historical links with ex-Soviet Union republics such as Ukraine, Belarus and Uzbekistan have been recently reactivated thanks to the financial crisis and the rising cost of procurements from western countries. Some countries, such as Uzbekistan, are explicitly aiming to be part of the supply chain, expecting to be paid in fully built-up vehicles.

The automobile markets

The markets for cars made in the CIS

Exports

Even if the successive devaluations of the ruble have led to the price being sharply lower, exports are obviously limited not only by the poor quality of the local products but more obviously by the standard of the local products, which are old-fashioned and unable to meet the legal requirements for pollution and safety.

Two further factors limit the potential for exports:

- The main car producer within the CIS, Russia belongs to no other major trade pact, so its products enjoy no preferential treatment for customs duties;
- Russia is far from ideal as an export base, even for obvious destinations such as the European Union or the Far East, neither geographically nor

logistically, because of the long distances and the poor mass transportation infrastructures.

Domestic market

The only 'natural' market for Russian cars is the Commonwealth of Independent States, providing a real common market is set up. But the economic and political situation of the other republics is even worse than that of Russia itself.

Again, long distances and poor logistics are causing tremendous difficulties in delivering cars to CIS customers. The main obstacle remains the limitations of purchasing power. Even if demand is gradually expanding, it is as yet extremely low. Income and pricing are the two key variables.

But the dealership system also plays a crucial role, and Russia provides an illuminating example in this regard. The changes in the AvtoVAZ distribution system have followed a five-stage process since 1989:

1. The collapse of the state-run distribution system.
2. The quasi-monopoly of the All-Russian Automobile Alliance, set up in 1989 by Boris Berezovsky, a mathematician and management-systems consultant to AvtoVAZ and AvtoVAZ Chief Executive Vladimir Kadannikov, which gradually amassed a stake in AvtoVAZ now totaling 34 per cent.
3. The booming of private trading companies, up to 300 in 1996, swapping components for cars at prices as much as 30 per cent below market value. Many traders took cars without prepaying, often waiting months before settling.
4. The entry of criminal gangs collecting a $100 per car commission from trading companies, to ensure safe delivery.
5. The setting up of an official dealer network owned by the company after the raid on the Togliatti plant in October 1999 by federal troops. By the end of 1999, the number of regional sales outlets has reached 35.

The quality and the geographical spread of an efficient dealership network are key conditions to a sustainable development of the CIS automobile market.

The main market characteristics

The current car fleet

Motorstat estimates the number of cars in use at 16 million in 2000. Compared to the current population, there are 110–130 cars per 1,000 inhabitants. This fleet has nearly doubled in the 1990s, following the collapse of the Soviet Union and the gradual shift to a market economy. But this is only one-fifth of the North American figure. In the other prosperous republics, such as the Baltic ones and Ukraine and Belarus, the figures are higher or equivalent to Russia. By contrast, in the poorest republics, the figures are much lower (Table 10.1).

The other key characteristics of the car fleet in the CIS are the following:

1. This is a very old fleet: more than 50 per cent of the 20 million cars are 10 years old or more.
2. In Russia, 86 per cent are of local origin (Russia or Ukraine) and 14 per cent are imported from Europe, the United States and Japan. The share of imported cars has dramatically increased in the last ten years from nearly zero per cent in the late 1980s.
3. There is a higher concentration in Greater Moscow where the rate is 220 cars for 1,000 inhabitants and other large cities.

Since 1990, the growth of the Russian car market – the fleet has doubled in size over the past ten years – should be considered to be quite impressive, in a context of economic instability, political uncertainty, financial and monetary collapse, deteriorated demographic dynamics, endemic corruption (Council on Foreign and Defense Policy, 1998), prosperous criminal activities and increasing unemployment.

Pricing: the key issue

Pricing is a key issue. According to Russian figures, in 1999, 90 per cent of new car registrations were of models below US$7,000. Before the August 1998 crisis, 80 per cent of the market comprised models under US$10,000. This is obviously in favour of local producers while foreign importers are deeply suffering since most of them are offering models priced in the range US$12,000–US$15,000 or even higher. Even the General Motors off-road Chevrolet Blazer, assembled locally by a joint venture with Yelabuzhsky Avtomobilny Zavod (EIAZ), and in theory very appropriate to Russian country and rural roads, could not be sold for less than US$15,000: this explains why its assembly line had to be stopped due to very low levels of demand – only 2,400 units were sold in 1998.

When considering the joint ventures in project, most of them are targeting models that will be difficult to sell under the current economic and financial conditions. For example, those with Daewoo are under immediate threat due to the near-complete collapse of the Korean group.

In 1995, the imports amounted to 85,000 cars, of which 62,000 were new cars. More than 70 per cent of these were medium-sized with an engine capacity of under 1,500 cc. These data do not take into account the black market imports – mainly comprising luxury cars stolen in western countries. Since the devaluation of the ruble following the financial crisis in August 1998, the prices of imported cars have increased and they are now far too high compared to those of Russian-made cars. For instance, the small Lada Jigouli is sold for around US$2,700 and the large Volga is sold for around

US$4,000. The foreign brands have been forced to readjust their own pricing strategy. Renault, for instance, is selling its R19, assembled locally from kits by Avtoframos or imported from Turkey, at US$7,500. The Renault Megane, due to be sold at between US$14,000 and US$15,000, is a luxury good in terms of the local market: but most customers will know (through the Internet, for instance) that its performances are only those of a basic family car in Western Europe. The intention to manufacture 120,000 units per year in the near future is therefore questionable.

Experts estimate (Gorski, 1999) the 'ideal' price of a small sedan with five seats, 300–400 kg of loading space and a medium-sized engine (1,100–1,300 cm^3) at US$9,000–9,500 and a medium-sized sedan with five seats, 500–600 kg of loading space and a medium-sized engine (1,600–1,800 cm^3) at US$13,000–14,000 (including taxes). But they also state that at US$6,000, a popular car with the European standards of performances and quality will rapidly become the national leader. A Skoda Felicia is sold at between US$7,300 and US$8,100: this is then US$1,000 too expensive.

Income is obviously the main limitation. In May 2000, the average salary per month was 1,500 rubles – approximately US$55. A loaf of bread cost 5–6 rubles. It means that buying a Skoda priced at US$8,000 would require 12 years of average salary. But the worth is that prices are not any more calculated in rubles. The purchase of such a car is made much more difficult since it is no longer possible to pay in rubles. All dealers require payment in hard currency – namely US dollars – since the ruble is highly unstable. And borrowing money is very expensive. Most banks say they are lending for three months in rubles at an annualized rate of between 30 and 40 per cent. That is the reason why many Russian banks are stepping up lending.[2] And within the 'virtual economy' mentioned by Gaddy and Ickes (1998), the households are also desperate for cash to buy hard currencies in order to buy durable goods and housing.

Income distribution

When we consider income distribution, it is clear that significant problems are emerging. Transition to the market economy in Russia and other CIS republics has been associated with high economic costs and major structural changes from largely egalitarian social structures to a position characterized by greater inequality and social stratification.

The rise in income inequality is the most important new factor determining emerging class divisions in transitional societies. The distribution of income has dramatically shifted with:

- The rise of a very small class of 'new rich' individuals, a new economic elite, with very high income, including of Mafia origin, and a preference for large and expensive luxurious imported cars.
- The rapid emergence of a middle class struggling for cash which is having tremendous difficulties in buying medium-sized cars produced in Russia.

- A sharp increase in the number of people belonging to the working class, comprising blue-collar workers, farmers and peasants, and the state sector workers, who are presently completely excluded from the automobile society.
- Finally, there are socially deprived and marginalized groups.

The volume market for cars will come from the middle class. As stated by Starobin and Kravchenko (2000), analysts estimate 12 million to 30 million Russians, some 8 to 20 per cent of the nation's 145 million population, to qualify as middle class. Russia's middle class now produces some 30 per cent of the country's gross domestic product of $220 billion, calculates the Russian business magazine *Expert*. The authors remark that members of the upper strata earn as much as $7,000 a month. Families in the average of the new class enjoy what most citizens can only regard as a dream lifestyle. They can afford to own a foreign car, as opposed to a more 'breakdown-prone' Lada. They can escape to a country *dacha*.

But their status is still very fragile. According to the figures produced by Bogomolova and Tapilina (1999), over 60 per cent of households demonstrated a 'highly unstable situation' in terms of their position on the relative income scale. Forty-two per cent were at least momentarily poor and 5 per cent 'chronically poor'. Members of the middle class quake in fear that a mistaken government policy could destroy their savings. Many are eager to start new businesses, but hardly any can find a bank willing to lend them money. And they are haunted by the prospect of another national economic disaster of the same magnitude as the 1998 financial crisis. One of the key obstacles to the rise of the local domestic markets is the availability of cash. For many years, AvtoVAZ was obliged to sell its cars by barter in order to secure its own supplies or to be really paid by business customers.

Imports

Custom duties in Russia on imports vary according to the size of the engine. On average, new cars are subject to a 30 per cent import tax. But this is calculated on importers' declared prices. The State Customs Committee of the Russian Federation is limiting the possibilities for the understatement of imported cars' prices by both its instructions and by the introduction of excise rates and taxes in Euro per cubic centimetre of the engine's volume. For instance, taxes on an automobile with an engine volume of less than $1,500 \text{ cm}^3$ amount to 30 per cent of its price, but not less than 1.3 Euro for 1 cm^3. This means that taxes on such automobiles are not less than US$2,400 and, consequently, it is supposed that the price of such automobiles will be no less than US$8,000. However, average prices for new automobiles of this class are slightly lower, which could possibly be explained by the fact that a considerable number of new automobiles is imported by 'dark' dealers at understated prices in order to economize on

VAT. When adding customs tax, excise tax and VAT, there are between 70 per cent and 80 per cent total duties on imported cars.

Other republics also have excise and import taxes on cars ranging from 30 to 50 per cent. Obviously, trade within the CIS enjoys a privileged tax regime. But as far as the automotive industry is concerned, this is still only a potential advantage because of the very low level of exchange at present. Most republics have also established favourable tax regimes for foreign investments.

Conclusion: towards an industrial policy

The local environment

According to Ivashchenko and Savchenko (1997), since 1997, the core of the Russian industrial policy has been aimed at ensuring the survival of the most viable industries to provide the conditions for future economic growth, to prevent a catastrophic rise in unemployment, and to keep alive the high technological culture and the competencies of the skilled workforce.

Two of the key objectives of the industrial policy currently promoted by President Putin are, on one hand, the support to non-raw materials industries working mostly to satisfy internal demand, and, on the other hand, the promotion of industries able to export and to secure a flow of hard currencies. The automotive sector clearly belongs to that type of prioritized industries. Obviously, the automotive industry in the CIS is far behind world standards as regards quality, vehicle design, technology and productivity are concerned, even if AvtoVAZ and Gaz might be profitable in the short term. In these circumstances, how can the Russian OEMs and their local suppliers survive when facing the major global players?

Thus, the Commonwealth of Independent States is facing a triple choice:

1. To accept that all local OEMs and component suppliers are under the control of foreign investors.
2. To see its automobile industry gradually disappear.
3. To build up an independent automotive industry.

None of these three scenarios are acceptable.

The first two options are opposed to history and reality. Which state could reasonably allow foreign corporations to take over or more simply let disappear an industry which is the result of a tremendous national effort and has already survived the collapse of the Soviet Union and the financial crisis?

Is the third option really feasible? At this stage, a clear distinction should be made between Russia and the other republics.

So far, only Russia has the size and the basis for such a scenario. An independent Russian automotive industry seems possible only if a true technological and organizational trajectory might be defined as well as appropriate

strategies for national and foreign corporations and an ad hoc industrial policy. This last requirement is indeed fundamental. Without excluding any
macroeconomic policy which is needed to stabilize prices and the value of
the ruble, an industrial policy supposes specific 'meso-economic' measures
at industry or sectoral level and a microeconomic approach at firm level
which are not yet well adapted to historical and cultural characteristics of
Russia – that is, to those principles, practices and behaviours inherited from
the socialist legacy. What is needed here are new regulations and behaviours
that are able to take into account the local asset specificity and their regional
conditions of valorization.

As far as the other republics are concerned, the current output of Ukraine
and Uzbekistan is too small to offer a basis for further significant development. It is indeed difficult to convince any government that it would be
overambitious to expect the emergence of a vehicle manufacturing industry
which is still considered as a symbol of industrial development. It should be
indicated that contributing to a wider automotive system, following the
examples of Belgium and the Netherlands in the European Union, might be
a better option. Having local assembly plants belonging to a larger OEM and
component manufacturers could be a much more reasonable choice.

The viability of a Russian automotive industry within the CIS

Long-term perspectives for a CIS automobile system, that is its industry and
its market, are obviously positive. Here is a market which should be satisfied
by an appropriate supply. What is much more questionable is how the scenario many develop in the next few years:

- Would it be a sustainable and autonomous development for a nation-
  based system or an integration within the worldwide international division of labour, fatally dominated by American, Japanese or European
  global corporations?
- If this is an implication in the world automotive industry, would it be
  through cooperation and strategic alliances of equals or under the domination of foreign corporations?
- If this is a Russian way, which specific assets would be required and which
  industrial policy would be put in place?
- Would it be based on a US$5,000 car 'Assembled in Russia and other
  republics' or 'Designed in Russia'?

From recent history there is no evidence that the very cheap popular car
for emerging markets is a viable project. The Citroën FAF, launched in the
early 1970s in Sub-Saharan Africa, was a complete failure, mainly because
this model looked like 'an under-developed car' (Chanaron, 1985). In the
late 1990s, the Fiat Palio, derived from the Punto under the code name of
the '178 project' with a huge design investment of US$2 billion,[3] is marketed
at a still relatively high price. In India, its cheapest version is sold for

Rs 400,000 (US$8,600) and its top-level version is sold for US$11,000. In Brazil, the Palio Young is sold for US$7,100 with a discount given for online purchasing. In Romania, the Renault's project with Dacia has a projected price of 5,000 euros and its development is apparently taking much longer than expected.

The inherent contradiction between pricing and technical characteristics is the main dilemma. Thanks to the globalization of information through the Internet, the car for emerging markets should offer the same technical characteristics as the standards set up for the main mature markets in America, Europe and Japan. It also has to provide the same value to the customers in terms of services and quality.

As far as industrial organization is concerned, it should be made by a very efficient supply chain from design to delivery to the customers. Huge savings in costs should be obtained at every step of that value chain:

- Suppliers' price will be squeezed to the maximum. This is why, for example, Renault's suppliers are not very supportive of the Dacia project since savings might be later applicable to all purchases, including in western countries.
- Design costs will have to be reduced through 'commonalization' and standardization. This is clearly contradictory to a strategy based on product innovation.
- Manufacturing and administrative costs will have to be minimized as well. This is indeed quite easy since local labour costs are cheap, but the quest for international standards in quality and reliability might provoke an increase in cost, partly offsetting the cost reduction.
- Distribution costs will have to be substantially decreased as well. This is probably the most likely part of the value chain in which significant cost reduction could be achieved. But this might require huge changes in distribution methods and channels and this will be far from easy, particularly in emerging countries.

Within the Commonwealth of Independent States, the following conditions for a sustainable development of the automotive industry might be required regarding the industrial organization:

- Minimizing the number of decision-making centres at administrative level, through an inter-state industry coordination unit for instance.
- Unifying the OEM within one or two viable corporations, of which to date only one is obvious, that is AvtoVAZ.
- Rationalizing the flows of components and sub-systems as well as kits for assembly through an agreed specialization.

A potentially feasible scenario is depicted in Figure 10.1. This scenario could be named the '*airbus*' model in which each partner country would have to supply part of the vehicle, i.e. a major component or sub-system or a set of

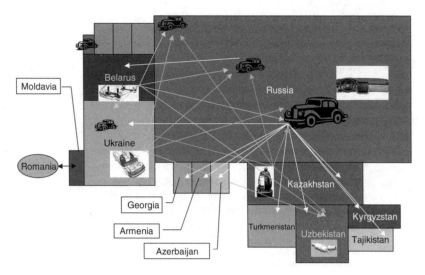

Figure 10.1 A scenario for the sustainable development of a CIS automotive industry

components which would join a common assembly line. Such a model might be feasible with a modular approach of the product for which comprehensive sub-assemblies are fixed together in the final assembly line: front-end, rear-end, cockpit, engine, gear-box, pre-assembled doors, seats, etc., minimizing the number of components to be fit during the final stage (Chanaron, 2001).

The 'political' effort to become developed should not be underestimated (Table 10.5). Some republics are far too small to be able to secure a 'very big piece of the pie'. But it might be difficult to avoid the assertion that all deserve to get a visible share. Transportation costs, synchronous delivery as well as 'transportability' might play a key role in the allocation. Seats, body panels, electric and electronic devices such as dash boards might all be manufactured not too far from the final assembly line. Mechanical components, other metal components and interior trims might be made further away.

For the OEMs and component suppliers in the CIS, this is simply a question of survival in the short term. They do have the appropriate qualified workforce. But their production organizational infrastructure are very weak. This is indeed a question of huge and urgent capital investment, which might force most of them to look for a strategic alliance with western partners which are still quite reluctant to commit themselves because of the amount of required investment.

Within the already mentioned 'airbus' scenario, such alliances are indeed perfectly feasible if they are monitored according to a transparent strategy. They might involve western and Japanese expert companies in their technology.

Table 10.5   Key success factors for the sustainable development of a common automotive industry

Domain	Main conditions
Political	• Increased multinational governance of CIS. • Agreed common industrial policy. • Agreed common market.
Managerial	• Shared vision and culture by national and local authorities. • Unified top management body. • Multinational governance mode.
Technological	• Modular design and manufacturing. • Competence-based division of tasks. • Transportability constraints.
Organizational	• Optimization of the logistic flows. • Strategic alliances with western or Japanese experts. • Centralized organizational management.

As far as the market side is concerned, if the size of the market is not to be challenged, the appropriateness of the model ranges which are currently supplied is still very much open to doubt. The volume market will be made up of middle-class families. This could not be fulfilled by expensive exclusive models. This will indeed require the redesign of specific models, derived from successful mid-range vehicles offered on western markets such as the Citroën Picasso, the Renault Scenic and Kangoo, the Opel Zafira and so on that could be used either for personal transportation or transportation of goods. A 'world car' approach might not be well adapted since local conditions and customers' requirements could be specific to Russia – including the nationalistic pride for Russian-designed and Russian-made artefacts.

The next five years will certainly be crucial. At present, most companies are very close to bankruptcy and have to define a proper strategy. Furthermore, Russian customers might well lose patience and put pressure on the government to act much more strongly in developing a more efficient industrial policy to deal with the automobile system and also to increase imports.

11

The Limits to Regionalism: The Automotive Industry in the Southern African Development Community

Anthony Black and Samson Muradzikwa

Introduction

As the southern African region moves closer towards the full implementation of the 1996 Southern African Development Community (SADC) Trade and Investment Protocol, which is intended to lead eventually to a full free trade arrangement, much closer economic ties are developing among the countries of the sub-continent. Indeed, the impetus for regional integration reflects both political imperatives and the economic necessity to consolidate southern Africa's small national economies into a market of reasonable size.[1] Even as a consolidated grouping the 14 SADC member states constitute a minor economic block with a combined regional product of approximately US$180 billion (Table 11.1). As far as the automotive industry is concerned, SADC is even less significant, accounting for less than one per cent of global output. SADC comprises economies of very varying sizes. The region is dominated by South Africa,[2] which accounts for 71 per cent of regional GDP and over 95 per cent of automotive production.[3] So while South Africa's relative size may give it some of the attributes of 'formal' or 'informal hegemony', to use the van Tulder and Audet (Chapter 2) classification the small economic size of SADC as a whole means that it is more aptly described as 'outside dominated'.

Attempts to forge regional integration in Africa have a long but undistinguished history. Weak internal transport links partly resulting from the continuing colonial pattern of transport infrastructure being developed to facilitate the export of primary commodities to the advanced countries, coupled with political fragmentation and a lack of industrial dynamism

Table 11.1   SADC member states: GDP and population, 2000

	Membership of SACU	GDP (US$ billion)	Population (millions)
Angola		8.8	12.7
Botswana	X	5.3	1.6
Dem. Rep. of Congo		4.5	51.4
Lesotho	X	0.9	2.2
Malawi		1.7	11.0
Mauritius		4.3	1.2
Mozambique		3.8	17.6
Namibia	X	1.7	3.5
Seychelles		0.6	0.1
South Africa	X	125.9	42.8
Swaziland	X	1.3	1.0
Tanzania		9.0	33.7
Zambia		2.9	10.1
Zimbabwe		7.2	12.6
Total		177.9	201.5

Source: World Bank.

have all meant that the level of internal trade between African countries has been quite limited. In southern Africa until 1994, this was massively exacerbated by the pariah status of the continent's largest economy, South Africa.[4]

Notwithstanding ongoing political rivalries and divisions, there is strong political support for regional integration. Within southern Africa, trade and investment flows have increased rapidly over the past decade. South Africa has become a very significant supplier of industrial products to the region and South African firms are also investing heavily in neighbouring countries. Large-scale infrastructure projects in transport, water and electricity supply are leading to the development of a regional rather than a national orientation. However, despite these growing links, significant growth of the industrial base of the non-South African members of SADC to supply the South African market has not yet occurred. Indeed, the large trade surplus that South Africa runs with its southern African neighbours has become an increasingly contentious issue. This trade imbalance has continued to widen in recent years, from 6:1 in 1999 to 9:1 in 2001, but is expected to decline as South African imports from the region gather pace.[5] At the institutional level the process of regional integration is also at a fairly early stage. Although some tariff reductions have already taken place, the SADC agreement aims to eliminate all import tariffs on goods traded between countries only by the end of 2007, and this arrangement excludes Angola, the Democratic Republic of Congo and the Seychelles.

Regional integration could potentially lead to greater specialization and a more efficient pattern of development in southern Africa. Certainly, a lack of specialization and the resulting lack of economies of scale is the major structural problem facing South Africa's automotive industry. This feature is even more apparent in the tiny automotive operations in other parts of the region. So regional integration is arguably essential if southern Africa – and indeed Africa as a whole – are to have any prospect of developing a sustainable automotive industry. While the argument for regional integration is clear, there are a number of factors which are likely to constrain the process:

- trade in vehicles and components is mainly in one direction, from South Africa to other SADC members. Non-South African SADC members fear the prospect of even greater automotive trade deficits with South Africa and damage to their infant automotive sectors.
- the automotive industry is small in the region and the non-South African countries add little to the overall market for new vehicles. For South African vehicle manufacturers who are already well established in southern African markets there is little perceived advantage in the short term. They are also concerned about the administrative complexities and the potential for illegal importation of new and used vehicles and components.
- a number of SADC countries do not have automotive industries and would see little benefit in joining a free trade area which may raise tariffs on extra-regional imports imposing higher costs on vehicle users.

In large groupings such as the EU and NAFTA, the automotive industry has been a powerful force behind the drive to regionalism (see Part II of this volume). In smaller groupings such as MERCOSUR and ASEAN the automotive industry has also been a driving force. However, SADC manifestly lacks the attributes even of these smaller formations. The overall market size is very small and, with only one industry and market of significance, there is little imperative at this stage to establish a system of regional specialization in the automotive industry involving all of the different countries of the region.

As we indicate in later sections, the fact that SADC is so small imposes clear limitations on the development of an integrated regional economic space in a technologically sophisticated and scale-intensive sector such as the automotive industry. It is similarly true that because of the negligible market and productive capacity in the countries of the region – with the exception of South Africa – the trajectory of automotive industry development will, at least in the short term, provide little impetus towards closer integration at the political level. However, as development proceeds its importance could be greatly enhanced.

The development of the automotive industry in southern Africa

Southern Africa constitutes a very small market and sales there have grown little since the early 1980s. The South African vehicle market is by far the largest in the region and accounted for 91 per cent of the total SADC market of 382,000 vehicles in 2000 (Table 11.2). Low growth rates in South Africa since the boom of the early 1980s are, therefore, the overriding factor accounting for the lack of expansion in the vehicle market in the region as a whole.

The second largest market in the region, Zimbabwe, has seen sporadic growth but since 1997, deteriorating political and economic conditions have resulted in a steep decline in vehicle sales. Angola's enormous potential remains unrealized due to the protracted civil war[6] and countries such as Tanzania and Zambia are only now showing some signs of emerging from a long period of economic stagnation. Economies such as Mozambique, Botswana and Mauritius are growing very rapidly, but their markets are tiny.

In 1994, the southern African region was estimated to have about seven million vehicles, with South Africa accounting for 81 per cent of the total, followed by Zimbabwe with 6 per cent. In spite of the low rate of market expansion, the vehicle park in the region is not insignificant and grew by 38 per cent over the period 1994 to 1997. This reflected both an increase in the average age of vehicles and also increased imports of used vehicles into some countries.

The average age of the South African vehicle park in 1998 was nine years, a figure which is certainly exceeded in the other SADC countries, with the possible exceptions of Mauritius and Botswana. Estimates for Zimbabwe suggest that 75 per cent of all passenger cars and 60 per cent of commercial

Table 11.2 Automotive production and sales in SADC (000 units)

	South Africa		Other SADC	
	Production	*Sales*	*Production*	*Sales*
1990	343	335	12	24
1991	315	308	13	20
1992	293	284	8	21
1993	308	298	8	23
1994	313	308	9	29
1995	389	387	10	33
1996	394	421	15	37
1997	364	399	20	44
1998	313	351	29	38
1999	326	318	31	34
2000	357	347	10	35

Note: Production in the 'Other SADC' category was mainly in Zimbabwe and since 1998 in Botswana.

Sources: NAAMSA, DTI, MTAZ.

Table 11.3 Nature of automotive operations in selected developing countries

	Assembly	Manufacture	Export	Liberalization
Brazil	1919–1956	1956–1972	1972–1990	1990–
Mexico	1925–1962	1962–1969	1969–1989	1989–
South Korea	1967–1973	1973–1977	1977–1989	1989–
South Africa	1925–1961	1961–1989	1989–1995	1995–
Zambia	1972–1991	—	—	1991–
Zimbabwe	1956–1965	1965–1994	—	1994–
Egypt	1950–1960	1960–1995	—	1985–
Kenya	1974–1994	—	—	1994–
Nigeria	1960–1970	1970–	—	—

Source: Rhys (1996).

vehicles on the roads were well over ten years old (Muradzikwa, 1999). The point here is that the ageing vehicle fleet of southern Africa creates significant aftermarket opportunities which may suggest a somewhat different trajectory of automotive development than has been the case in other more industrialized parts of the developing world.

The development of automotive production in the region has been shaped by government policies, especially tariff protection (Table 11.3). Those few countries which have tried to encourage domestic manufacture have pursued a range of policies. South Africa has followed a programme of import substitution similar to that adopted in other large developing countries, especially in Latin America. High tariffs were placed on built-up vehicles – these were later followed by increasing local content requirements. Production was initially aimed solely at the domestic market until the promotion of exports began in 1989. Since 1995, the policy has been one of phased liberalization under the Motor Industry Development Programme (MIDP).

Other African producers went through a much shallower process of local manufacture and tended to liberalize their industries before significant levels of exports had been achieved. What has remained in most cases are small-scale and inefficient assembly operations with negligible local content. In some cases such as Zambia, liberalization led to the collapse of the very small-scale assembly operations that existed. Outside of South Africa and a few countries in North Africa, the main focus of component production is on the aftermarket.

South Africa

As Table 11.4 indicates, South African vehicle manufacturers dominate production in the region. There are eight producers of light vehicles in South Africa. In 2000 they assembled 345,000 units, of which 19.5 per cent were

Table 11.4   Light vehicle assemblers operating in southern Africa

Country	Assembler	Ownership	Makes	Capacity[a]
South Africa	Nissan	Nissan (majority stake)	Nissan Fiat (under contract)	70,000
	BMW (SA)	BMW AG	BMW	60,000
	Delta	General Motors (49%) Domestic	Opel Isuzu	70,000
	Landrover	BMW AG	Landrover	15,000
	DCSA	Daimler-Chrysler	Mercedes Mitsubishi	70,000
	Ford	Ford Motor Co	Ford Mazda	70,000
	Toyota	TMC (75%) Wesco	Toyota	120,000
	VW (SA)	VW AG	VW Audi	100,000
Zimbabwe	Willowvale	Foreign/Govt.	Mazda	25,000
	Quest Motors	Domestic/ Nissan South Africa partnership	Peugeot, Nissan Land Rover	25,000
Botswana	Hyundai Motor Distributors[b]	Wheels of Africa (South Africa)	Hyundai	40,000

Notes
[a] Plant capacity figures are estimates and could be increased through more shifts.
[b] The Botswana plant has recently ceased production as a result of financial difficulties in the holding company, Wheels of Africa.

exported. Production growth has been held back by very weak internal economic conditions since the early 1980s. With falling protection, import levels have been rising and these accounted for 18.7 per cent of the light vehicle market in 2000.

Heavy protection has resulted in proliferation to the extent that most manufacturers build a variety of models – and in some cases more than one make – in a single assembly plant. All assemblers are now wholly or partly owned by the parent company in Japan, the United States or Europe. There are also 11 assemblers of medium and heavy commercial vehicles which produced approximately 12,000 vehicles in 2000.

Ford and General Motors were the first to establish a production presence in South Africa in the 1920s.[7] The domestic market expanded rapidly and the production of cars reached 87,000 units in 1960 – a level higher than any other developing country at the time. Domestic content at this stage was only 20 per cent, prompting the introduction in 1961 of the first of a series of local content programmes. Later phases of the local content programme increased local content requirements to 66 per cent for all light vehicles.

Phase VI of the local content programme, introduced in 1989, marked a substantial change of direction. This was the first attempt to address the problems of an inwardly oriented, overly fragmented industry with low volume output and associated high unit costs. Most importantly, exports by an assembler were now counted as local content and enabled it to reduce actual local content in domestically produced vehicles. Exports, particularly of components, grew extremely rapidly giving assemblers greater flexibility in their sourcing arrangements.

In 1995, Phase VI was replaced by the Motor Industry Development Programme (MIDP), which has since been extended to 2007. MIDP abolished local content requirements and introduced a tariff phase down at a steeper rate than required in terms of South Africa's WTO obligations. From previously pro-hibitive levels, tariffs are being phased down to 30 per cent for light vehicles and 25 per cent for components by 2007.[8] However, these still high nominal rates can be reduced in practice because manufacturers are entitled to import a proportion of their components duty free and are also able to offset import duties using import credits derived from the export of vehicles and compo-nents. The prime objective of the import–export complementation scheme is to assist component suppliers to generate high volumes, which make them more efficient and able to compete in the domestic market against imports.

These policy developments, together with the ending of the political and economic isolation of South Africa, have rapidly led to the industry becom-ing more internationally integrated (Black, 2001). This is apparent in the growing levels of foreign ownership and investment and the rapid expan-sion of trade – especially exports. Until the early 1990s, with the exception of the German companies (Daimler-Chrysler, BMW and Volkswagen), all local assembly operations were domestically owned and operated under licence. Much closer links have since developed between the local firm and the overseas parent/licensor. Direct equity stakes by Nissan and Toyota could be the forerunner of direct Japanese investments in the component sector. Ford now has full ownership of the local operation and General Motors has also taken a substantial equity stake.

Investment links within the region have been slower to develop. Certain South African component firms have subsidiaries in the region and South Africa tends to act as the regional headquarters for foreign firms with inter-ests in southern Africa. However, trade barriers within the region and the small scale of vehicle operations have meant that some of these operations still operate under licence. There is very little indigenous capital in the auto-motive industry outside of South Africa and investments from the region back into South Africa are negligible.

Other countries

Outside of South Africa, assembly activities in the region are very small scale, consisting of licensed operations assembling low volumes of imported completely-knocked-down (CKD) kits. Original equipment (OE) component production is also very limited. The Zimbabwean industry has the capacity to produce 50,000 vehicles per annum but only 18,000 light vehicles were assembled in the record year, 1997, and output has since declined due to the ongoing economic and political crisis.

Zimbabwe also followed a programme of import substitution, but the small-scale assembly operations that were established were unsophisticated with extremely low levels of domestic content and production remains directed primarily at the internal market. Licensing and foreign exchange restrictions together with the tiny market have hindered development. In the early 1990s, amid mounting social and economic pressure, the government launched the Economic Structural Adjustment Programme (ESAP). These economic reforms consisted of the relaxation of government controls in various sectors of the Zimbabwean economy and the liberalization of the trade environment. Although tariffs on built-up vehicles remained high, the elimination of the discretionary allocation of foreign currency and the introduction of foreign-currency-denominated accounts (FCDAs) effectively freed up the importation of vehicles and components. Imports of both vehicles and components increased rapidly. While significant local content had never been achieved, it declined further to negligible levels as a result of liberalization.[9]

Foreign exchange problems, lobbying by vehicle manufacturers[10] and a trade dispute with South Africa led to tariffs, surcharges and other taxes being adjusted sharply upwards on a range of products including vehicles in 1998.[11] With the extreme political and economic instability prevailing since 1999, the vehicle market has all but collapsed as have any plans for future investment in the short term.

In Botswana, the assembly of Hyundai vehicles under licence for the SADC market began in 1998.[12] The plant, with an initial investment of approximately R300 million and a capacity of 40,000 vehicles per year, was the largest automotive investment in SADC outside of South Africa but it ceased production in 2000 as a result of financial problems in its holding company. Diamond-rich Botswana has been one of the fastest-growing countries in the world over the past two decades and boasts political stability, a well-managed economy and attractive tax incentives. In addition, its membership of SACU (the Southern African Customs Union) and its location adjacent to the South African economic heartland of Gauteng make it a potentially favourable manufacturing location. The establishment of the Hyundai factory resulted in a few component investments in the country. Some of these continue to supply export markets.

The other member states of SADC have for the most part small-scale component sectors catering primarily for the aftermarket. For example,

Mozambique has firms producing exhausts, batteries, tyres, radiators, brake shoes and springs. Many of these plants struggle to compete against South African firms in the tiny home market or in the region and are hampered by duties on imports into South Africa. In some countries such as Swaziland and Mozambique, there are also very small-scale truck and bus assembly and body building operations but in cases such as Zambia, light vehicle assembly did not survive structural adjustment (Rhys, 1996).

The expansion of regional trade and investment

The major driver of regional integration in southern Africa is trade, especially as it is likely to foreshadow closer investment links when trade barriers are reduced. Automotive exports by SADC countries and trade within the region have expanded rapidly over the past decade. South Africa[13] accounts for over 95 per cent of total automotive exports by SADC countries and also dominates regional trade. Total automotive exports from South Africa have expanded dramatically from just R315 million in 1988 to R20 billion in 2000, of which R7.3 billion is accounted for by vehicles. There has been a major expansion in a wide range of components – especially of products such as leather seating, catalytic converters, wheels and tyres. The industry supplying leather seat covers supplies the bulk of BMW's global requirements and is an important supplier to a number of other foreign vehicle manufacturers. In addition, South Africa now supplies more than 12 per cent of the global demand for catalytic converters.

The growth in exports is the result of a number of factors. Firstly, the import–export complementation arrangements of Phase VI and the MIDP have powerfully assisted export expansion, in particular, by facilitating the integration of South Africa as a supplier of selected components to the global networks of the major carmakers. A second driver of export expansion has been falling protection and limited domestic market growth possibilities, which have forced firms into the export market. The bulk of export expansion has not been by 'traditional' component suppliers but by a rapidly emerging new group of mainly foreign-owned firms, frequently with links to global carmakers.

A share of this export expansion has been destined for SADC, a process that has accelerated since the advent of democracy in South Africa and the dropping of sanctions. But while SACU exports into SADC have increased, this has been at a much slower rate than total automotive exports. For example, SADC accounted for 9 per cent of SACU light vehicle exports in 2001, a sharp decline from the 64 per cent share in 1996 (Table 11.5). Over this period total light vehicle exports expanded from 11,000 units to 108,000 units. For medium and heavy commercial vehicle exports, which have not grown significantly in volume terms, Africa remains the dominant market, although the SADC share has declined from 89 per cent in 1996 to 57 per

Table 11.5 Destination of SACU exports (percentage share)

Country/region	1996 (%)	1997 (%)	1998 (%)	1999 (%)	2000 (%)	2001 (%)
Light vehicle (value)						
SADC	64	46	27	11	12	9
Other Africa	n.d.	n.d.	n.d.	n.d.	n.d.	n.d.
EU	4	7	41	70	53	38
NAFTA	n.d.	n.d.	n.d.	n.d.	n.d.	n.d.
Other	32	47	32	19	35	53
Total	100	100	100	100	100	100
Components						
SADC	14	13	9	8	6	
Other Africa	1	1	2	2	1	
European Union	70	71	74	74	70	
NAFTA	5	6	8	10	10	
Other	10	9	7	6	13	
Total	100	100	100	100	100	

Source: Department of Trade and Industry (2001).

cent in 2001. Likewise in components, while volumes have increased the share of total SACU components exports going to SADC, has also declined from 14 per cent in 1996 to 6 per cent in 2000 (Table 11.5).

So while SACU exports into SADC have been growing steadily, the pace of export expansion has rapidly outgrown this regional market, reflecting much closer global integration – especially with European-based carmakers. Another factor has been the collapse of the Zimbabwean market as well as the raising of tariff barriers in response to economic problems, which has slowed sales into South Africa's major regional market.

The biggest SADC markets for SACU component exports are Zimbabwe and Mozambique, which rank eighth and twelfth respectively. With the exception of Nissan CKD packs supplied to Zimbabwe, exports comprise mainly aftermarket products such as tyres, shock absorbers, filters and batteries (Table 11.6). These products are supplied either to independent distributors in the SADC countries or via distribution channels established by major South African aftermarket suppliers.

South Africa is a significant importer of vehicles and components, but very little is sourced from the region. As far as vehicles are concerned, until the early 1990s prohibitive tariff levels resulted in low levels of vehicle importation. The opening up of the economy and the phasing out of tariffs have led to an expansion of light vehicle imports mainly from Europe and the Far East. Until recently an important exception was the Hyundai plant in Botswana, which mainly served the South African market.

Imports of original equipment components increased from R7.5 billion in 1994 to R29.7 billion in 2000. Nearly 80 per cent of original equipment

Table 11.6 Percentage share of SADC countries in total SACU exports of selected components, 1999

	Zimbabwe (%)	Zambia (%)	Mozambique (%)	Angola (%)
Tyres	10	7	4	3
Engine parts	6	4	3	1
Engines	2	2	2	—
Automotive tooling	11	—	2	—
Batteries	3	8	6	1
Brake parts	5	—	—	—
Filters	24	3	3	—
Shock absorbers	10	5	1	—
Transmission shafts	3	3	—	—
Ignition equipment	13	7	1	—

Note: Only components where a significant share is exported to SADC are listed above. South Africa's two main export products (automotive leather and catalytic converters) are not exported to SADC.

Source: Department of Trade and Industry, unpublished data.

components are imported from Japan and Germany. Virtually none come from South Africa's SADC neighbours, where the small component facilities lack the required quality accreditation and are mainly geared to the aftermarket.

Survey results[14] indicate that Zimbabwean vehicle assemblers have been under severe pressure from cheaper imports. Imports of vehicles into Zimbabwe, on average, account for approximately 30 per cent of the domestic market and 70 per cent of these imports are from South Africa, with the remainder being largely second-hand imports from Japan.

Zimbabwean component producers have generally fared better than assemblers, although the effect of structural adjustment was very much contingent upon the market in which they operated. Firms reliant on the supply of original equipment components have struggled but these only constituted a small group. The aftermarket has always been important for the majority of established producers and this reliance has increased as local content levels have declined (Figure 11.1).

Zimbabwe exports little to the region or elsewhere. Survey results cite the lack of government support, political uncertainty, unfair competition from South African firms who benefit from the MIDP[15] and licensing restrictions as the factors constraining export expansion. However, aftermarket component exports have grown and by 1999, 12 per cent of component output was being exported – compared to only 3 per cent of the total in 1993. With the exception of glass, which is mainly exported to the United States, most component exports are to the relatively poorer markets of SADC such as Malawi, Mozambique and Zambia and also to markets in east and central Africa.

Automotive exports from Zimbabwe into the major regional market (SACU) have in fact been declining and by 1997 comprised only 4 per cent

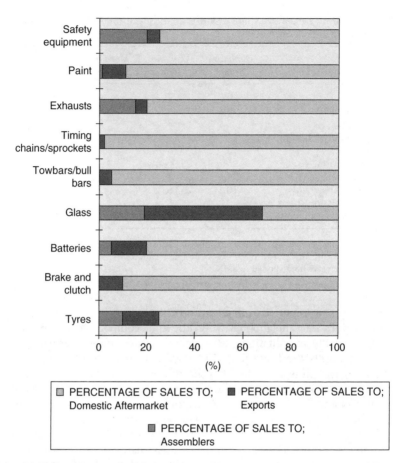

Figure 11.1   Destination of Zimbabwean component manufacturing output, 1999
Source: Survey data.

of imports from SACU into Zimbabwe – compared to 70 per cent in 1993. Apart from the more developed capacity of the South African industry, trade liberalization in Zimbabwe following structural adjustment and the assistance given to SACU automotive exports under the MIDP have contributed to this growing trade imbalance.

There have been small investments by Zimbabwean component producers in some of the other SADC countries. These investments have been targeted mainly at the aftermarket for spare parts, and in most cases consist of distributorships/dealerships of components that are manufactured in Zimbabwe.

The other countries of the region export very little but most of this is to their SADC neighbours and involves aftermarket components. Constraints remain trade barriers within SADC but also the dominance of South African production and distribution networks in the region.

Moving towards regional integration: the SADC trade protocol

It is clear from the analysis above that the integration of the automotive industry in SADC is at an early stage. South Africa exports to the rest of the region and firms based in South Africa have modest investments but the inter-linkages are minimal. Vehicle exports to the region, while important, are not, for the most part, key to the strategies of South-African-based assemblers and component exports are primarily into the aftermarket. For its part, South Africa imports little from the region. Nevertheless, the regional automotive landscape could change quite rapidly as the free trade protocols are implemented, particularly if the momentum towards higher growth rates in the region is sustained. This section concludes, therefore, by considering the likely trajectory of developments in the years ahead.

In the initial SADC protocol, which established the intention of moving towards free trade, it was recognized that South Africa's neighbours had justifiable concerns that under a free trade arrangement, the existing concentration of industrial development in the largest and most developed economy, South Africa, was likely to be accentuated. The protocol therefore allowed for additional time for neighbouring countries to open up their markets.

In the SADC trade talks, both SACU and Zimbabwe have placed their automotive industries on the list of 'sensitive' products to be negotiated separately. From a South African perspective, this is partly because of the complexities raised by the existence of the MIDP. A 1999 SACU position paper[16] sets out two proposals. Firstly, if Zimbabwe or any other SADC country adopts the MIDP in full then all MIDP rules on manufacture would apply. This would mean that no import rebate credit certificates[17] can be issued by SADC countries wishing to export into SACU (and vice versa) and that there would be no tariff barriers between SADC countries and SACU with regard to automotive products. Secondly, if Zimbabwe or any other SADC country chooses to remain outside the MIDP, then there will be no tariff concessions by SACU on either vehicle imports or automotive components. It is likely, however, that South Africa will offer a phase down of tariffs at a more rapid pace than its SADC neighbours, leading eventually to a reasonable level of free automotive trade in the region.

South African vehicle assemblers do not feel threatened by the prospect of competition from other SADC members and in this sense they would welcome the removal of trade barriers. When the SADC protocols take effect, it is likely that the vehicle operations of the global carmakers would be consolidated into a single regional entity – most probably headquartered in South Africa. However, for a number of reasons, vehicle manufacturers based in South Africa are lukewarm about the prospect of a free trade arrangement. Firstly, they currently benefit from the extremely favourable conditions of the MIDP, which effectively subsidize exports into the region. These import–export complementation arrangements would obviously have to be eliminated if a free trade arrangement was to take effect and firms feel that the removal of trade barriers into SADC markets would only partially compensate for this. More significantly, the SADC market is not perceived to be very important, at least in the short term, and in any event the market share of South African producers is already high. In addition, South African firms fear the possibility of reduced regulatory controls under a free trade scenario. While customs controls in South Africa are being improved, evasion is widespread and vehicle manufacturers are concerned that the introduction of a large free trade area would only increase these opportunities. Used vehicles imported into the BLNS countries already find their way into the South African market in large numbers.[18]

Regional integration is likely to have a much greater effect on the assembly operations of other countries in the region. The Zimbabwean industry, for instance, faces major adjustments. Low volumes, outdated plants, quality problems, restrictive licensing agreements, the absence of clear policy and the domestic economic crisis are all factors which negatively affect prospects. In 1999, vehicle prices in Zimbabwe were on average 60 per cent and 120 per cent higher than in South Africa for new and second-hand vehicles, respectively (Muradzikwa, 1999: 9).

In the course of interviews, officials of the Confederation of Zimbabwean Industry conceded that the SADC Trade protocol, while bringing about greater intra-regional trade, is likely to result in the shrinking of the automotive sector and possibly the closure of certain operations as part of the streamlining of the Zimbabwean industry. Vehicle manufacturers surveyed expected competition to increase significantly but interestingly they also anticipated the establishment of new foreign and domestic partnerships. Foreign partnerships are undoubtedly the key since they offer the possibility of expansion into the much larger South African market and beyond. But much depends upon the overall investment environment, which is currently extremely poor.

Based on survey responses, component producers stand a far better chance of withstanding – and indeed benefiting from – trade integration. Among the advantages enjoyed by Zimbabwean component manufacturers are low labour costs, an established industrial infrastructure and the central location of Zimbabwe in the SADC region. Exports have traditionally been an insignificant proportion of total output. But until the onset of the current economic crisis, trade liberalization and general economic reforms have encouraged component producers to increase exports. The aftermarket sector in particular has proven to be the most resilient and has significant growth prospects once political and economic stability is achieved.

Countries such as Mozambique, which have small component operations, face very limited prospects without access to the larger regional market. Their internal markets are insufficient to justify increased investment or production runs, which can even begin to achieve economies of scale even for aftermarket components such as exhausts. Firms in Mozambique, for example, face increasing competition from South Africa and are unable to compete on the basis of their very low volume production. Some have also lost markets to South African producers in other SADC countries. They generally feel that they have more to gain than to lose from a free trade arrangement with SACU.

The second concern for South Africa's SADC neighbours is that of trade diversion and the concomitant loss of customs revenue as well as potentially negative implications for foreign exchange usage. This clearly depends upon the duty structure which will be applied by SADC. In the automotive industry, which retains fairly high protective tariffs, it is possible that the negative impact of trade diversion would be fairly large.

While consumers could gain by paying slightly less for imported vehicles and components (they would no longer pay duty) this gain could be more than offset by the loss of customs revenue as SADC countries substitute cheaper (e.g., Japanese or European) vehicles and components with more expensively produced South African products. Complicating this calculation is the fact that a large share of SADC's current purchases of new vehicles and components are from South Africa and are effectively subsidized under the MIDP. Under a free trade arrangement, South African exporters would no longer derive MIDP benefits from vehicle or component exports to members of the free trade area and could be expected to raise prices accordingly. The extent of trade diversion would therefore depend upon the level of external tariffs on vehicles imposed by SADC, the extent of the cost premium charged by South African vehicle producers and also the treatment of second-hand vehicles.

Conclusion

The automotive industry is scale intensive and the most obvious locations for rapid development are in countries with large existing or emerging markets or in countries adjacent to such markets. The attribute of scale intensity has also placed the automotive industry at the forefront of regional integration initiatives. Market size poses a set of constraints for small economic formations such as SADC, especially as they are subjected to the pressures of globalization. So while regional economic integration is important for all members of SADC as a means of enlarging the size of the market for regional trade and attracting foreign investment, there are clear limits to this in the automotive industry in southern Africa.

From the perspective of the only significant automotive industry in the region, South Africa, trade and investment ties with the major automotive-producing regions – particularly the EU – are currently of much greater significance and in fact offer the only route to establishing reasonable production volumes. So while South Africa has pursued regional integration and is extensively involved in regional and continental[19] initiatives, it has also sought to reposition itself in relation to major entities such as the EU, for example through the recently established EU–South Africa Free Trade

Agreement.[20] National efforts to market the country as an investment location do cite access to the southern African market but they also emphasize South Africa's central location with respect to the markets of the Pacific Rim and Latin America. Trade agreements are being actively pursued with these regions. In the automotive industry, specifically, ties with countries such as Germany are being developed. The main dynamic in the automotive industry in the region, therefore, is South Africa's bid to consolidate its position as an important peripheral supplier to world markets using the leverage of its limited domestic market.

What of the implications of these extra-regional initiatives for the process of regionalism? Clearly the automotive industry in southern Africa has not yet developed a regional identity and it certainly does not constitute a viable 'automobile space' (Chapter 1). There is no developed hierarchy of production locations in the region and it is not likely in the short term that a pattern of specialization involving the region as a whole will emerge within the sector. To date regional integration has consisted primarily of an expansion in the export of vehicles and components from South Africa to other parts of the region. To a lesser extent, there has also been investment from South Africa into the region and the consolidation of the southern African subsidiaries and licensor firms affiliated to large American, European and Japanese automotive multinationals. However, this development of ownership linkages with regional headquarters based in South Africa does give an indication of the possible future shape of a regional sub-system of automotive production and distribution. South Africa's growing links with the major automotive centres could then be the conduit to global markets for such a sub-system.

In the short term, therefore, it is likely that other economic factors will be more important drivers of regionalism. For instance, in the textile and clothing industry a regional system of production is emerging involving many SADC member states at different levels.

However, the past is not necessarily a sound guide to the future and given the existence of partial or complete sanctions against South Africa until 1994, ongoing trade barriers and, until very recently, low growth rates in the region, it is hardly surprising that the linkages are relatively underdeveloped at present. Two developments, both of which are already starting to happen, are likely to change this scenario. First, in spite of the political and economic problems that currently exist, the region is on course for freer trade. This will have an important effect on the patterns of automotive investment and trade. Secondly, growth prospects for the region are now better than they have been for three decades. In the context of freer regional trade, this will encourage foreign investment and the development of new networks; and quite possibly the establishment of new locations for any of the large number of production processes which make up the automotive industry.

12
Maghrebi Integration and the Automobile Industry: Past Failures and New Perspectives

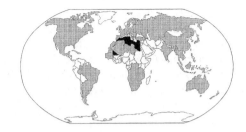

Jean-Bernard Layan and Mihoub Mezouaghi

Introduction

The purpose of this chapter is to show that the failure of regional integration in the countries of the North of Africa (henceforth called the 'Maghreb') does not constitute an insurmountable obstacle to the development of a Maghrebi automobile industry with a foothold in the Euro-Mediterranean zone. 1989 saw the creation of the Maghrebi Arab Union (MAU), a grouping of nations whose objective was to establish a free trade zone between Algeria, Libya, Morocco, Mauritania and Tunisia. The aim was to create a structure with an outlook similar to an economic and monetary union. At the time of writing this integration process has ground to a halt and its benefits have been severely curtailed. The MAU has not spawned any new opportunities, nor has it made any real contribution to the Maghrebi countries' industrial development. Although a few bilateral co-operation agreements have constituted tentative initial steps towards a regional division of labour, the absence of an integrated and stimulated institutional framework (and the low level of intra-regional trade) attests to the MAU's failure.

Contrary to expectations, the national production systems have turned out to be highly independent of one another. More specifically, three parallel trajectories can be detected within the automobile sector, as regards the region's inclusion into the European automobile space: Tunisia seems to be specializing in the production of generic components; Algeria in the building of commercial vehicles; and Morocco in the assembly of passenger cars. Currently, Libya and Mauritania feature almost no production to speak of.

Nevertheless, as these strategies are not mutually exclusive, any uncoordinated integration into the Euro-Mediterranean area would inevitably lead the national production systems to compete over the same segments, again raising doubts about the coherency of any Maghrebi automobile area that would emerge. The question is whether this area could strengthen the countries' complementarities (regarding their competencies and infrastructures) whilst limiting the negative side-effects of a confrontation between national industries. If the MAU were to be redefined at an institutional level, people could then move beyond a conception in which regional integration is seen as little more than a simple juxtaposition of national markets. The outcome could be the construction of a new framework that could tie the Maghrebi automobile area into the European one – a framework capable of reconfiguring industrial complementarities and multinational firms' actions.

After having specified in the first section the limits of regional integration in the Maghreb, in the second section we will discuss the outlook for the emergence of an automobile industry in each of the region's three producing nations, before describing, in the third section, the Maghrebi automobile area as it is today. Finally, we will attempt to sketch a redefinition of the interdependencies that exist between the Maghrebi and the European automobile areas.

The MAU – a regional integration drive that has been cut short

Maghrebi integration has stumbled over a fragile and inoperative framework of institutionalization, on one hand, and over the weakness and heterogeneity of the economic unit it represents, on the other.

A fragile and inoperative framework of institutionalization

The idea of a trilateral union (between Algeria, Morocco and Tunisia) was born in 1958 at the Tangiers Conference. The structure was supposed to materialize once Algeria had regained its independence. However, from the early 1960s onwards, this joint aspiration was already being hindered by people's varying conceptions as to what the Maghrebi entity should become – and by the particularly intense leadership rivalries that arose from the presence of a number of strong political figures of uncontested historical legitimacy. In reality, the period immediately following independence was marked by relationships that were conflictual in nature. For nearly 30 years, the relatively unfavourable regional environment and the weight of national priorities precluded any thoughts of union.

It was only towards the late 1980s that the countries began to re-evaluate their relationships. Fundamentally the Treaty of Marrakech, signed in February 1989, replaced irreconcilable regional visions and extended a converging formulation entitled the Maghrebi Arab Union so that it included Libya and Mauritania. Whether the initiative constituted a truly communitarian drive or was a largely symbolic act, it is clear that it did provide a response to a double challenge: global free trade, on one hand; and partnership with an increasingly united Europe, on the other. The countries of the

Maghreb opted for a type of regional integration that presented a twofold interest: it reinforced their negotiating position in an environment that was marked by globalization-regionalization; and it led to complementaries being created in certain strategic areas.

Today the MAU is an indisputable failure. Instead of having created a new framework for the co-ordination of national development strategies, the countries involved have continued to compete and to fight with one another. The MAU Treaty did not encourage integrated regional level actions based the countries' economic complementarities.

A regional unit that is not very homogeneous, and which has limited economic power

Despite the fact that MAU countries have shared ethnic origins, as well as the same religion, language, colonial past (with the exception of Libya), civilization and history, they have experienced diverging political and economic trajectories. This has created disparities, and accentuated the gaps in their respective levels of development.

Above and beyond differences relating to their respective sizes and specific natural resources, each country has followed a singular path. Algeria has intentionally opted for a state-driven industrialization policy that is funded by hydrocarbon-related rents and which emphasizes heavy industry. Libya, on the other hand, has been attempting a more inwardly focused style of development. The proceeds Mauritania derives from the exploitation of its mineral resources are not enough to fund development. Morocco and Tunisia have been implementing an industrialization process that is based on promoting agribusiness and light industry exports (after an unsuccessful earlier attempt at an import-substitution-based style of industrialization). Similarly, Algeria's Third World (and even socialist) orientation and Libya's radical isolationism are diametrically opposed to the neoliberal and pro-western stances that have guided Morocco and Tunisia's absorption into the world economy.

Today the MAU countries constitute a political set that is fairly heterogeneous – and which possesses relatively limited economic potential. The economies are characterized by the fact that they are running out of steam, with productivity gains being few and far between – despite the high levels of investment. The transition towards a market-based economy having become a prerequisite for accessing international funding, structural adjustment plans were adopted by Morocco and Tunisia during the 1980s, and by Algeria in the early 1990s.

After several economic reforms, the vulnerability of the Maghrebi economies remains a reality that can be expressed in three different ways:

- The economic gap with the European countries remains significant, and has in fact been increasing: average per capita income in Europe is nearly

12 times higher than in Tunisia and almost 50 times higher than in Mauritania; the cumulative GDP of the five MAU countries does not even match Portugal's.

• The MAU countries' international specialization is based on natural resources and on traditional industries: Algeria, Libya and Mauritania depend on single base products (hydrocarbons or ferrous minerals) marked by highly variable revenues, whereas Tunisia and Morocco export manufactured goods (textiles, foodstuffs or electrical products) which have low added value; these products are being sold in highly competitive markets; and they are vulnerable to cyclical economic turnrounds.
• The low volume of foreign direct investment.

All in all, the national production systems have not been able to create any real interdependencies. This is particularly true in the case of the automobile industry.

The national automobile industries' emergence trajectories

In the countries of the Maghreb, the automobile industry has been primarily structured around two types of segments: vehicle assembly and low added value components production.

Morocco's ambition to be regional leader in light vehicles assembly

The Moroccan automobile industry emphasized vehicle assembly activities from the very outset. Founded in 1959, SOMACA[1] accounts for almost all of the national output.

Over the 1990–97 period, on average 22,000 vehicles (including 65 per cent passenger cars) were assembled per annum. In Africa, only Egypt and South Africa have achieved a greater output. Note, however, the high degree of fluctuation in the number of vehicles being assembled – with the 1991 peak of 26,000 units having plummeted to a 1995 low of 13,000 units.

Morocco's automobile industry has gone through four different phases:

• During the 1960s, a number of assembly lines were set up,[2] leading to an increased number of brands and models. The domestic market was very thin, however, and the lack of local enhancement opportunities soon became an obstacle to further development.
• As such, a second phase commenced in 1970. The focus was a search for local value-added, via the promotion of subcontracting operations and import substitutions. The temporary ban on the importation of those components that could be manufactured locally (plus the setting of a local contents ratio of 40 per cent) clearly helped underpin production, to a certain extent at least. However, domestic industry suffered from a lack of technological expertise; from low economies of scale; and from too numerous models of vehicles that would end up by being abandoned no more than a few years later.

- Starting in 1982, a third phase consolidated subcontracting and export promotion orientations to the detriment of local value-added. To get manufacturers to build new assembly plants, the domestic market was protected, in the sense that new vehicle imports became subject to a license being granted. The negative side-effect of this strategy, in an environment marked by local consumers' low purchasing power, was that it encouraged the development of a market for used vehicles.
- Since the early 1990s, Moroccan strategy has shifted towards a rationalization of the number of models being assembled, and to a strengthening of the new vehicle market. Towards this end, new vehicle imports were no longer subject to licensing after 1990, with import duties being lowered from 35 per cent to 17.5 per cent by 1995. At the same time, heavy taxes were levied on used vehicle imports. These were attempts by the Moroccan authorities to encourage the development of an 'economic vehicle'.[3] They were trying to offer new vehicles at a lower price on the domestic market, thus propelling an integration of domestic generic components production operations.[4] In 1995, the Moroccan government negotiated an association with Fiat, an eight-year agreement that called for the assembly of an initial series of models (Uno, Tipo) to be followed by a second series (Palio, Siena) with production beginning in 1998 (project 178). A similar programme was launched in 1996, involving the assembly of light commercial vehicles on behalf of PSA Peugeot (C15) and Renault (Express, Kangoo). This orientation confirmed the strategic option that Morocco was pursuing, with its emphasis on light vehicle assembly (passenger cars and light commercial vehicles). The production capacities reached 60,000 units, but only 25,000 vehicles were assembled in 2002. For Fiat models alone, 13,321 vehicles were assembled in 1996, against 3,687 in 1995 but less than 90,00 in 2002. The performance is insufficient in comparison with world standards of productivity.

The privatization of SOMACA is the new key to the national policy in order to induce a real take-off of the assembling industry. The state share, 38 per cent of the SOMACA's capital, was sold to Renault in July 2003. The Renault project intends to integrate SOMACA in its worldwide platforms and to make Morocco a regional automobile pole to assemble its 5,000 euro Dacia car for emerging markets. The objective would be set at 30,000 units in 2005, rising rapidly to 45,000 units, with the intention that a part of the production will be exported to Europe, to the Middle East and to North Africa.

Another key of the recent Moroccan strategy development is the integration of the component manufacturing into the regional/world production networks.

Tunisia's positioning in generic components

The Tunisian automobile industry, like the Moroccan, entered the assembly business in the 1960s and 1970s. Domestic output, dominated by small vans and by commercial vehicles, has mainly been the concern of the Société Tunisiénne d'Industrie Automobile (the STIA). Faced with a limited national market, the Tunisian industry began to reorient its development strategy in the late 1980s (Tizaoui, 2001). At first this involved a concentration of assembly activities. In 1988 there was a suspension of small van production, which was considered to be insufficiently profitable. What remained were three assembly sites – one for large commercial vehicles (STIA) and two for buses and coaches (IMM Kairouan and Setcar). Partnerships with large commercial vehicle manufacturers (Iveco, Scania, General Motors and Renault VI being the main operators) consolidated the option that Tunisia had taken in this segment. Tax cuts were planned to underpin the production of an economic vehicle – but there was never any real political support for this orientation.

Tunisia's main efforts involved the development of a components-making industry by getting production units to specialize in the manufacturing of generic components. The domestic market was to be widely opened up to vehicle imports – even though imports were to remain subject to the granting of a license. This opening of Tunisia's automobile market to outside competition was to be offset by an increased integration of the country's textile, machinery, electrical goods and electronics production structures into the international automotive sector. Multinational firms, taking advantage of Tunisia's export promotion policies; generous fiscal and customs incentives, geographical proximity and an inexpensive workforce signed an ever-greater number of subcontracting agreements. Prime examples are Sylea-Labinal and Delphi (electrical wiring), Delafontaine (engine parts), MGI Courtier (bonnet closing mechanisms), Valeo (clutch linings) or Record France (shock absorbers). Nevertheless, limited production volumes and the absence of car manufacturers reflected a lack of local integration by production units that were primarily geared towards the export markets. Since 1993, 21 plants have been opened by global suppliers (Valeo, Delphi, UTA, Lear) to produce wire harnesses to be exported (Tizaoui, 2003).

This policy was reinforced by the 1995 signing of an agreement giving birth to a free trade zone between Tunisia and the European Union – Morocco signed a similar agreement with the EU one year later. The aim was to ensure that all automobile components destined for the European market were free of customs tariffs by 2010.

Algeria's redefinition of its industrial strategy

Algeria's desire to set up an integrated industrial base is the element that distinguishes the way in which the country developed its automobile industry. Unlike its neighbours, Algeria's development strategy revolved around linking national production to domestic demand.

A state-run firm, the Société Nationale de Véhicules Industriels (SNVI), is responsible for the production of commercial vehicles and vans (including tractors, lorries and coaches). Founded in 1981, the SNVI was developed in collaboration with Renault VI. Benefiting from a protected market, it was not integrated into any international sourcing and/or production network. From 1990 to 1997, SNVI's output averaged 3,000 vehicles per annum, with an integration rate of 70 per cent. It should be noted that output has trended downwards for the past 20 years, with a peak of 7,000 units/year having been reached during the 1983–86 period.

SNVI's further development was hindered by high production costs that were attributable to irrational management decisions and to deterioration in sales opportunities following the sharp drop in the country's purchasing power. The Algerian industrial crisis attests to the failure of its automobile sector's autonomy strategy. Industrial strategy should have been redefined in such a way as to exploit the national market's potential, thereby enabling integration into the international productive system. Indeed, if Algeria's automobile industry is to be launched again, it needs to open to foreign capital, and therefore to partnerships with global manufacturers.

If overseas carmakers were allowed to take a capital stake in SNVI (thus enabling the renovation of existing equipment and the reorganization of production), the national industry could redeploy towards vehicle assembly operations. Existing plans also make reference to the possibility of generic components being manufactured within a subcontracting framework. One example is Man, a German company that is considering externalizing its gearbox manufacturing operations to Algeria, or PSA Peugeot, which apparently intends to subcontract its engine and cable production.

Nevertheless, unlike Morocco and Tunisia, the strategy being pursued has not yet been defined to a sufficient degree (or to say the least, it remains difficult to assess) – as shown by the great deal of uncertainty surrounding Fiat's establishment of facilities in Algeria.[5]

Characteristics of the Maghrebi automobile area

The Maghrebi automobile area, far from being integrated, is characterized by its high level of segmentation – and by the attraction that the European Union exerts on each of the countries' automotive branch.

The Eurotropism of the Maghrebi automobile area

In actual fact, the different national automobile production systems have all stayed largely disconnected from one another. At the same time, they have remained firmly (and individually) linked to European industry. Moreover, regional productive integration initiatives have not been particularly convincing. For all intents and purposes, the only examples of any type of automobile industry cooperation between the Maghrebi countries was the 1988 creation of a Tunisian – Algerian factory (SAKMO) that was intended to produce diesel engines under license from Lombardini (with an annual objective of 35,000 units vs a realized output of 12,000 units in 1990). Tunisia and Algeria planned to have STIA specialize in the bottom-of-the-range (less than six tonnes) and SNVI in the top-of-the-range, an agreement that was supposed to translate into a tax- and duty-free trade in components. However, the two markets' recent shift to liberalization has caused problems for this plant, since its products are no longer sheltered from engine imports. To this can be added the foundation of a mixed Algerian–Tunisian company for the purpose of manufacturing sheet metal transformation machines in Algeria, and the impending launch of a mixed Tunisian–Moroccan company with a remit of manufacturing gearing and speed reduction mechanisms in Tunisia.

The birth of a regional zone meant to palliate the shortcomings of domestic markets that are far too thin in nature did not in fact lead to any structuring of, or linkage between, the various national automobile industries. Economies of scale and learning-related gains were less than anticipated, specifically because there was in the end little sharing of economic resources. In terms of the way in which the automobile branch's commercial trade was being structured,[6] it should be noted that in the Maghreb, commerce is still dominated by the relationships that each country maintains individually with the European Union:

- Intra-regional trade is marginal. In 2001, only 3.5 per cent of Algeria's, Morocco's and Tunisia's automotive sector exports were destined for the regional market. Relatively speaking, Algeria is the country that is most oriented towards other Maghrebi regional partners. The volumes traded remain insignificant, however.
- The European Union is the region's main supplier. In 2001 the EU was at the origin of 88.8 per cent of the automobile branch's imports in Tunisia, 76.1 per cent in Morocco and 79.8 per cent in Algeria. Nevertheless, it would appear that the Maghrebi countries have been diversifying their supply sources. There has been an increase in imports from Japan and from Southeast Asia, and to a lesser extent from Brazil and Turkey. Algeria remains the region's largest importer.
- The European Union is the main sales outlet for the Maghrebi automobile industry. In 2001 the EU absorbed 80.6 per cent of Tunisian exports, 89.2 per cent of Moroccan exports and 65 per cent of Algerian exports. This is particularly significant since between 1980 and 2001 exports increased by a factor of more than 17 for Tunisia (from US$6.2 million to US$111 million) and nearly 5 for Morocco (from US$7.6 million to US$35 million). Eighty nine per cent and 90.5 per cent respectively of exports to the European Union involved generic components. In addition, in recent years the Maghrebi automobile industry seems to have developed other sales outlets (the Gulf, Sub-Saharan Africa).

A regional market that lacks dynamism and which is highly segmented

Statistical data for the Maghrebi national markets are unreliable and/or unavailable. This is especially problematic for the Mauritanian and Libyan markets, which remain very small in absolute terms.

National motor vehicle stocks vary in size. Using data compiled by the French Carmakers' Association (CCFA), in 2000 an estimated 1.8 million vehicles were on the road in Algeria, 1.4 million in Morocco and approximately 650,000 in Tunisia (compared with 1.7 million in Egypt). French vehicles (Renault, PSA Peugeot) form the main part of this stock, the rest being mostly comprised of vehicles from Italy (Fiat), Germany (Mercedes, Volkswagen) and Japan (Toyota, Honda). Household equipment rate is very low: in 1997 the number of passenger cars per capita was 0.19 in Algeria, 0.24 in Tunisia and 0.29 in Morocco.

In addition, Maghrebi automobile stocks are characterized by a low product renewal rate, with 75 per cent of vehicles being more than 10 years old. This lack of dynamism is also seen in annual new vehicle registration statistics (only 60,400 for the whole of Morocco in 1995, compared with 31,700 in Algeria). This is clearly explained, at least in part, by the low purchasing power (and by its collapse in Algeria). However, it also translates the authorities' desire to restrict the importation of used cars. In actual fact, the recent deregulation of imports might progressively lead to a crowding out of professionals from the local marketplace, with the new market being geared towards the offering of used cars to private parties. For example, following Morocco's recent deregulation of imports, 86 per cent of all sales in 1994 were simple re-registrations.

All in all, annual sales have not developed to any significant degree. In 1998, 22,300 new vehicles were sold in Algeria (inc. 74 per cent passenger cars), a rise of 56 per cent over 1990, but a drop since 1996. In 2000, 46,300 vehicles were sold in Morocco (61.7 per cent passenger cars) and 31,200 in Tunisia (68.1 per cent passenger cars) in 1999. In these two countries, sales rose by 93.7 per cent and 97.2 per cent respectively between 1990 and 1999. Clearly, the Maghrebi countries' markets are still extremely thin – by comparison, 115,500 vehicles were sold in Egypt in 1998, an increase of 350 per cent over 1990.

The national markets' juxtaposition did not lead to the creation of a regional market. On the contrary, national regulations (such as customs barriers) reinforced the Maghrebi automobile market's segmentation and limited its growth, ultimately dissuading any global manufacturer who may have wanted to set up operations in the region.

Redefining the link between the Maghrebi and European automobile areas

Today the Maghrebi automobile industry's survival depends upon its integration with international markets – and on its absorption into the main manufacturers' productive networks. Yet even though an outward focus could well lead to new opportunities, it offers no guarantee of industrial development. The region's governments have to design support policies that leave open the possibility of an improved coordination of public interventions within an increasingly integrated Maghrebi area.

Increased trade liberalization is likely to encourage the rise of an automobile economy in the Maghreb. This will occur on two separate levels: new social categories will accede to individual motorization; and industrial expansion will take place. At the same time, the process of creating an association with the European Union will lead to a intensification of traditional relationships forged through colonial links[7] and cemented by geographical proximity. However, this process is not without risk for emerging economies.

The domestic markets' thinness means that even when integrated, national industries will not be able to offer consumers high-performance products at an acceptable cost. The design and production of a modern vehicle requires considerable material and immaterial investments, all of which imply extremely high breakeven points. It also demands productive coordination capabilities and, at a wider level, an organizational experience that only the largest global manufacturers possess. However, potential demand does exist for a means of individual transport – if only because the current deregulation trend has led to a lowering of new vehicle prices, and therefore, by extension, to a lowering of prices for the entire vehicle stock. An opening up of the Maghrebi markets would also make it possible to satisfy a need for variety that has long been underestimated. Viewed in a favourable light by consumers, such an opening would also be likely to have positive effects on the local automotive industry. The North African automobile markets' progressive integration into one large European market would in fact inevitably lead to the integration of the Maghreb's different national industries into the European automobile system. Whether this integration assumes the form of a takeover of existing production units, an establishment of new facilities by multinational firms or an increase in international subcontracting arrangements, it remains the case that national productive capacities would be modernized, and that this would allow for a considerable rise in productivity levels – and above all, in the products' and processes' quality. The experience of other emergent automobile countries (Mexico, Brazil and the Czech Republic) bears witness to this.

The main limitation for this sort of virtuous process is the region's degree of attractiveness for large companies. At a time when competitive positions are being frozen in the mature markets, large manufacturers have been displaying a renewed interest in emerging countries. In this sort of environment, the countries of the Maghreb are in the enviable situation of constituting a nearby periphery that is relatively close to the European centres. Labour costs are low in the Maghreb; workforce flexibility is high; there is considerable potential for a rise in demand; and the proximity to Western Europe facilitates access to stable and high-volume markets. The situation is very similar to the one that enabled the emergence of new 'pericentral' automobile countries such as Spain, Mexico or Central Europe (Layan, 2000).

In addition, the manufacturers' current tendency to modernize or outsource a growing proportion of their output is a factor that can lead to a mutation and relocation of the components industry. Maghrebi industries could thus benefit from the rise in the central markets' habit of sourcing from less developed nearby peripheries – and could even take advantage of the new strategies that certain carmakers have been pursuing, involving attempts to conquer the emerging markets by means of the specific products that accompany economic types of vehicles (Fiat, Ford, Renault).

All of these are favourable trends that should not mask the industrial risks faced by these fragile economies once they have opened up. The main danger is a very serious one that relates to the automobile industry's disappearance in North Africa. There are few local companies possessing the human and financial means to match international productivity and quality standards – and which are thus capable of fending off their competitors. Attempting to compensate for this weakness by getting large outside companies to undertake direct investment is a very uncertain proposition, especially given the fact that the top European firms have been recently establishing new facilities in Central Europe, Turkey and Egypt. Moreover, despite the steady erosion of the cost competitiveness of the European firms' Iberian operations, it is hard to imagine any large-scale relocation to the other side of the Mediterranean, at least in the medium term. All in all, the proximity of Western Europe is a double-edged sword – although it facilitates access to a strong and solvent demand, it also enables low-cost sourcing from European facilities, in particular from those Southern European operations that specialize in entry-level vehicles.

The second danger would be the development of an automobile business that is limited to the most mundane segments of components production (that is, electrical wiring). Of course, the immediate advantages in activity, employment and currency inflow terms are far from negligible. However, a specialization of this sort would at best involve a very progressive rate of technology transfer; learning effects would be slight; and the lock-in effects especially high. This risk of specializing in a subordinate type of activity (that is, the risk of getting involved in a type of international insertion that is of marginal interest for the European Union) is exacerbated by the possibility that the Maghrebi countries will be thrown into competition with one another. Morocco, Tunisia and Algeria have been developing parallel partnership strategies with the European Union and expecting similar types of economic fallout. Insertion into the global economy and integration into the regional division of labour of the European pole of the Triad could ultimately consolidate a sort of specialization that is wholly lacking in dynamism. Regional cooperation could ultimately constitute a fruitful answer to a framework in which each Maghrebi country has little opportunity to affect ongoing developments.

For the current power elite, free trade treaties with the European Union are tantamount to powerful drivers for economic strategies that emphasize the modernization of economic structures. First of all, such treaties enable the necessary 'updating' of industrial capabilities; and they justify a series of administrative and political reforms that – above and beyond issues such as the free circulation of capital or monetary stability – have been progressively affecting areas as diverse as intellectual property, administrative procedures, commercial justice and the system of general and/or professional training. Nevertheless, there is no doubt but that this association with the European Union, by eliminating customs barriers and by progressively tying Morocco, Tunisia and Algeria into the European system of normalization and into the Euro zone, will inevitably lead to a unification of the Maghreb region's national markets – something that the MAU was not able to achieve.

This reality offers a new vision of Maghrebi cooperation, not as something that comprises an alternative to globalization or to Euro-Mediterranean integration, but instead seeing it as a way of defining an original and fertile linkage between a high-profile regional area and the Euro-Mediterranean area within which it is encompassed. In the automotive sector, this cooperation would make it possible to encourage a modicum of differentiation within the Maghrebi market. This is a determinant factor in the development of an automotive industry in the region – and an absolute prerequisite if car manufacturers or components makers are to set up in the Maghreb those production segments that are the most intense in value-added and the most fruitful in technological fallout. If this sort of cooperation is extended to the whole of the Maghreb, it could turn current Moroccan experiments with economic cars into something viable – as has been the case in Brazil. It would also mean that this activity could be fleshed out with commercial vehicles that target a public comprising small and medium-sized businesses. At a wider level, a more closely controlled regional division of labour would make it possible to capitalize upon the experience that has been acquired in van and commercial vehicle assembly whilst enhancing upstream (parts and components) manufacturing operations. Lastly, an improvement in East–West road connections between the MAU's member countries would offer the twofold advantage of encouraging trade and simultaneously supporting the automobile market's expansion.

Conclusion

Unlike the MERCOSUR, the countries of the Maghreb have failed to set up an autonomous regional integration variant. The failure of regulation mechanisms, the absences of coordination between the different countries' industrial policies and the weakness of productive capacities and local technologies have all acted against the development of an automotive industry in this part of the world.

In the past, the national production systems' independence had brought about differentiated industrial trajectories. Now they lead to parallel insertions into the European automobile space. This uncoordinated integration into the Euro-Mediterranean area has spawned a type of competition that is as costly as it is inevitable.

And yet the building of a Maghrebi automobile area would make it possible to reinforce existing industrial and technological complementarities whilst maximizing economies of scale and learning processes. This implies a redefinition of the MAU, shifting it towards a more pragmatic approach in which relevant areas of sectoral action are identified and efficient negotiation and regulation procedures instituted. A Maghrebi development dynamic is likely to underpin the beneficial effects of the regional economies' current insertion into the international area in general – and into the Euro-Mediterranean area in particular.

So, the failure of the MAU requires a new model of South–South regional integration. In this way, the Agadir initiative, signed in 2001 by four countries (Egypt, Jordan, Morocco and Tunisia), attempts to set up before 2005 a free trade area between Arab-Mediterranean countries for promoting foreign investments and industrial complementarities. Most certainly, this process is able to loosen the market constraint but it can't succeed without a real coordination between the national policies.

Translation by Alan Sitkin

Part IV
The Challenge of 'Go It Alone'

13
The Risk of 'Go-It-Alone': The Japanese Car Industry – From Boom to Bust?

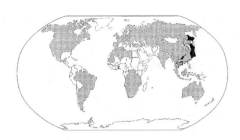

Rob van Tulder

Introduction

At the start of the 1990s, the Japanese car industry was an undisputed success story. Japanese 'lean' production practices were to be considered not only best-practice models for the car industry but also applicable to other industries as well (Womack et al., 1990; Womack and Jones, 1996). Only ten years later, at the start of the twenty-first century, the 'model' has lost most of its original radiance. Seven out of eleven firms experienced major problems throughout the 1990s and ultimately lost most of their independence to foreign owners – a unique phenomenon in postwar Japan. This chapter assesses the partial demise of the Japanese model from a political-economic perspective. The car industry has been one of the most 'politicized' of industries in Japan. Trade and restructuring policies have developed in close consultation (and dispute) with local and national governments. The car industry has been one of the most prominent carriers of the Japanese 'export model'. The success or failure of strategies of individual car firms thus can hardly be separated from the success or failure of political strategies of governments.

This chapter explores in particular the international political dimension of the Japanese car industry. The choice for a unilateral 'go-it-alone' strategy (see Chapter 1) seemed commonsensical in terms of national autonomy. Japan did not directly engage in any major and/or deep formal regional integration initiative. Rather, it engaged in a form of 'informal regionalism' (Ruigrok and Van Tulder, 1995) in an effort not to stir up new anti-Japanese political sentiments in the East Asian region. Neither did the Japanese government actively engage in creating easier entrance in its domestic system for foreign firms. For instance, it signed very few bilateral investment treaties (BITs). By way of comparison, over the whole postwar period the United States signed a total 46 bilateral investment treaties, Germany around 127, and Japan only nine – with two-thirds of these treaties signed after 1997. Japanese governments opted for relative isolation, a relatively closed market and an export orientation. In the 1980–90 period inward foreign direct investment (FDI) stock stagnated at a very low level (0.3 per cent of GDP) (UNCTAD, 2001). In this strategy, consecutive Japanese governments were joined by most of the leading Japanese car firms. The strategy resulted in extremely low levels of foreign penetration in the Japanese automobile space and enabled the coming of age of its productive model. But, Japan's 'go-it-alone' strategy also contained a number of risks. It prompted retaliation measures by major competitors that felt endangered by the Japanese challenge. The lack of formal political and economic regionalism, at the same time, hampered some of the Japanese car manufacturers in developing a regional market of sufficient size, leaving them with the difficult task to sell their production surpluses – a vital part of their competitive strategy – in other core regions. This chapter explores to what extent the weaker performance and subsequently the takeover of some of the leading car producers can be related to the risks of Japan's go-it-alone strategy.

This chapter is organized as follows. First, the historical roots of the Japanese car industry will be linked to stages in the trade policy stance of the Japanese government and the industry. Secondly, the dialectics of this process is assessed by listing the political responses to the Japanese strategy by American and European governments – representing the most important foreign markets. Thirdly, we will assess to what extent the five leading car producers (Toyota, Nissan, Mitsubishi Motors, Mazda and Honda) adapted their strategies to the new political reality and to what extent their relative performance suffered. Finally, we will consider whether the difficulties will lead to the creation of a more open car system.

The Japanese model: building vulnerable competencies behind relatively closed borders

The first US auto plant in Japan was opened in 1925, when Ford started to assemble knock-down sets. GM soon followed suit. In 1936, however, the Japanese military government passed the Automobile Manufacturing Industry Law, which required auto producers to be licensed by the government. Only two companies were licensed: Toyota and Nissan, leaving Ford and GM no choice but to leave the country (Johnson, 1982: 131). By the end of the American occupation of Japan in 1952, US automakers had reestablished their position, holding a 44.6 per cent share of the Japanese car market. By 1955, this portion had already fallen to 8.9 per cent, and in 1960 US auto producers held a mere 1.1 per cent, as a result of strict import taxation measures, levied against foreign cars according to their engine size (Cusumano, 1985). US automakers never regained a significant position in the Japanese market.

Picturing a three-phased evolution – from craft production through mass production to lean production – Womack, Jones and Roos argued that lean production 'combines the advantages of craft production and mass production, while avoiding the high costs of the former and the rigidity of the latter' (1990: 13). Interestingly, the original concept used by the MIT team to refer to this production system was dubbed *vulnerable production*, since each of the core firm's bargaining partners are in a vulnerable position where they have little choice but to cooperate according to the conditions and vision presented by the core firm. Japanese automakers have depended upon the *unconditional cooperation* of their suppliers, of their workers, and of their dealers. In such a tense system, there can be little place for foreign entrants. Authors organized in the GERPISA network (cf., for example, Boyer and Freyssenet, 2002) further specified the diversity of productive and innovative characteristics of the Japanese automakers leading to critical observations on the original lean production concept. In any case, the Japanese car industry, in its political-economic connotation, implied a relatively closed system of production, supply and distribution that proved very difficult to enter for foreign producers. Structural control over (single-franchise) dealerships and over suppliers has been an integral part of the Japanese car industry. Structural control over suppliers also implied control over the production of auto parts and over the very lucrative aftermarket. In Japan, the aftermarket has been regulated differently from either Europe or the United States: parts deemed critical to vehicle safety ('critical parts' lists) could only be replaced at certified garages, or required individual time-consuming government inspection (USTR, 1997: 216). Foreign automotive suppliers therefore had great difficulty in competing with Japanese-owned suppliers due to the Japanese automakers' control over their dealers – even independent garages often have no choice but to use genuine parts (ibid.).

Local and national Japanese governments played a major role in developing the car industry (Ruigrok and Tate, 1996). The Ministry of International Trade and Industry (MITI) has been particularly successful in sheltering the Japanese car industry from foreign competition at an infant stage (Cusumano, 1985). Indeed, the history of Japan's external auto trade policy is closely related to the ups and downs of the Japanese auto industry, and MITI appears to have been well-informed about its domestic players' trade policy preferences (cf. Ruigrok and van Tulder, 1999). MITI, however, had not been very successful in fostering the particular shape of the Japanese car system according to its own strategic preferences. The core political position of Toyota and – to a lesser extent – Nissan have been largely undisputed. But in 1969, MITI unsuccessfully tried to discourage smaller car producers like Mazda and Mitsubishi, aiming to consolidate the Japanese car industry into three groups. After the domestic car industry had become well established in the mid-1970s, the necessity for overt trade protection measures decreased rapidly. In 1978, the Japanese government abolished all tariffs on cars – a measure not paralleled by any of the other governments at that time.

One element of the Japanese strategy was the creation of overcapacity. Overcapacity in a sector is generally ascribed to slack markets or the weak competitive position of a particular producer. By contrast, the overcapacity of the Japanese car industry was aimed at conquering export markets. Overcapacity creation forces all producers in the industry to become more efficient and to compete on scale economies. As such the creation of structural overcapacity in Japan can be considered to have been a strategic move to compete head-on with producers – particularly in the United States – that had been producing less than local markets demanded. Between 1960 and 1970, Japanese passenger car production increased almost twentyfold – from 165,000 to 3,179,000 units. By the early 1990s, almost one in every four cars in the world was produced in Japan, and more than half of this output was exported to other countries (World Motor Vehicle Data, 2000). By 1980, the volume of Japanese car production had already surpassed that of the American car industry. The domestic market size in Japan did not keep pace. In 1960, according to JAMA (2003), less than 5 per cent of domestic car production was exported. In 1976, for the first time exports of cars exceeded domestic sales. This export surplus was sustained between 1976 and 1989, when domestic demand had grown rapidly, to almost 4.5 million cars. In particular, the US market provided the opportunity to absorb a sizeable part of the overproduction (cf. Table 13.1). As a result the overcapacity in the Triad surpassed over 150 per cent in the 1980s and the whole of the car system came under pressure. At the same time Japanese firms tried to establish their own 'peripheral region' in the Pacific Rim, with primarily SKD production for local markets and later on they made efforts to engage in a regional division of labour in ASEAN (see Chapter 9 for more details). These markets never approached the size of the Triad nor did they prove a solution to overcapacity problems.

Table 13.1   Overcapacity vs undercapacity in the Triad, 1980s

		USA	Japan	European Union
1980	Production	6,377	7,038	10,401
	Sales	8,761	2,854	10,065
	Prod./sales (%)	73	247	103
1985	Production	8,185	7,646	11,040
	Sales	10,889	3,104	10,643
	Prod./sales (%)	75	246	104

Source: CCFA.

The go-it-alone export-oriented strategy of Japan was supported by an undervalued yen. This played a major role in enhancing Japan's export competitiveness and could only be exerted under relative political and monetary autonomy.

The shape and nature of retaliation

European and American car producers took up the technological and product challenges posed by the Japanese car producers (cf. Freyssenet et al., 2003a, 2003b). They also addressed the political-economic ingredients of the 'go-it-alone' strategy. Three types of retaliation strategies developed: (a) multilateral and macroeconomic-oriented retaliation measures affecting the general terms of trade; (b) bilateral home-oriented sector-specific measures to protect the home market; (c) bilateral host-oriented efforts to open up the 'closed' Japanese car market.

(a) Macroeconomic and multilateral retaliation began with the 1985 'Plaza Agreement' in which the G5 countries (an informal meeting of the finance ministers of France, Germany, Japan, the UK and the US – representing all of the major car-producing countries except Italy) agreed that the US dollar was overvalued. It also implied that the Japanese yen had been severely undervalued. GATT talks in the 1980s and early 1990s had been focusing on limiting direct trade-inhibiting policy measures. They became increasingly complemented by concerns over 'non-tariff barriers' to trade.

(b) Sector-specific retaliation aimed at protecting the domestic markets in the EU and North America have included voluntary export restraints since 1981, and stepped-up local content and specific type approval regulations. In 1984, when Nissan started its first manufacturing operation in the UK, pressure from the EU car industry (in particular from France) made it 'voluntarily' raise its own local content share to 60 per cent (Abe, 2000). The European Commission further retaliated by continuing the block exemption which facilitated the imposition of a single-franchise dealer network in Europe – even when this should be deemed anti-competitive under European law. The block exemption (see Chapter 4) not only created barriers to entry for Japanese producers, but in particular discriminated against firms operating from within the British car system where mega-dealerships had already been introduced – including most Japanese European transplants.

(c) Sector-specific retaliations aimed at opening up the 'closed' Japanese market have included the most complex, tedious and widely criticized measures. The closed Japanese market was initially not considered a major problem. Only in 1975, when Nissan became the leading car importer in the United States – thereby overtaking VW's position – did concern begin to grow. In 1992, Japanese carmakers occupied 36 per cent of the US auto market, whereas the US automakers' market share in Japan was less than a tenth of that figure. At the same time, the expansion of Japanese production in the United States did not curb the trade deficit as much as had once been hoped. In 1993, companies affiliated with Japanese producers accounted for 43 per cent of all suppliers to Japanese auto transplants in the US (Pauly and Reich, 1997: 19). In the 1990s Honda, rather than one of the Big Three, became the leading US 'exporter' of finished cars to Japan. Trade tensions between Washington and Tokyo gradually escalated. With a zero tariff on imported cars since 1978, the dispute on the access of the Japanese market slowly shifted from trade to structure. The American government reproached Japan for imposing 'structural impediments' to car imports. Following the 1993 US–Japan Framework for a New Economic Partnership, and under the mounting threat of US trade sanctions, American and Japanese trade authorities sat down several times to negotiate auto trade deals.

EU trade authorities stressed concerns that the US–Japanese deals would effectively discriminate against EU auto and auto parts imports into Japan. While US firms and governments relied primarily on political pressure, European governments and producers were more pragmatic. Volkswagen, Mercedes-Benz and BMW established exclusive dealership structures in Japan long before their American competitors. They also followed the Japanese praxis of high model variety. In 1996 European auto makers sold over one hundred different right-hand drive models in Japan – US automakers sold four models (Ruigrok and van Tulder, 1999). European manufacturers became leading auto importers into Japan, because they followed the Japanese 'rules of the game'. At the same time the European Commission started talks with the Japanese government on harmonizing standards in finished cars and components (European Commission, 2001: 31). The European Commission used its earlier external trade policy – designed to protect the Community's automobile market against 'unfair trade practices' – as a bargaining chip in negotiations with Japan. Further opening of the Japanese car market – which was more closed than the US – would result in the EU market being gradually opened to Japanese cars.

The trade policies of the United States and Europe were more often than not directly triggered by the lobbying efforts of specific groups of car producers. On numerous occasions the Big Three US car manufacturers have campaigned for US trade barriers to be erected against Japanese auto imports. Examples include the 1980 petition by Ford and Chrysler to the International Trade Commission for relief from injury by Japanese auto imports, and the 1991 request by Ford and Chrysler to the Federal government to limit the number of cars produced by Japanese transplants in the United States. In Europe, GM and Ford supported the stricter local content rules imposed upon Japanese producers, the 1991 EC–Japan treaty on Japanese transplants (implying voluntary export restraints) and the controlled expansion of production and sales in Europe, as well as the 1995 extension of the block exemption. Fiat, Peugeot-Citroën (PSA) and Renault – primarily focused on the European market – also repeatedly and successfully campaigned for anti-Japanese trade barriers. Examples are the 1991 EU–Japan treaty on Japanese transplants and the controlled expansion of Japanese production and sales in Europe, and the 1995 and 2002 extensions of the 1985 block exemption (which exempts automakers from general competition rules by allowing them to maintain a selective auto distribution system in Europe). Volkswagen (VW) usually kept a lower profile, though it has tended to support such campaigns. Mercedes-Benz and BMW have often opposed EU trade barriers, though not at all costs (Ruigrok and van Tulder, 1999). They have been the only European brands that on the one hand had gained some market share in Japan, whilst operating in a market segment not (yet) invaded by the leading Japanese producers.

The effects of retaliation

The effects of the various measures of retaliation on the Japanese car industry have been varied, interrelated and have had different implications for different carmakers.

(a) **Multilateral.** The effect of the international macroeconomic currency measures can be considered substantial. The Plaza Agreement and consecutive – less outspoken – deals have seriously affected the 'terms of trade' between the United States, Europe and Japan. In the 1980–2001 period the euro/yen ratio deteriorated by a factor of three compared to a factor of two in the case of the US$/yen ratio. In 1986 car exports from Japan reached a peak of more than 4.5 million cars (JAMA, 2003). From that point car export volumes decreased to less than three million in 1997. The deteriorated general terms of trade affected, in particular, those producers that were most dependent upon exports from Japan. So Mazda (with 60 per cent exports) was the most severely affected, whereas Honda (with only 40 per cent export dependency) was the least affected (Jetin, 2003: 35). The exports into Europe experienced larger terms of trade deterioration than those into the United States. Accordingly, firms that relied more upon the European market for their international sales – such as Nissan, Mitsubishi Motors and Mazda (Table 13.2) – have been more seriously affected.

During the 1990s Japan experienced a sustained and repeated recession that was particularly severe in 1993 and 1998. The end of the 'bubble economy', accelerated by international retaliation in many areas, was a severe blow to the Japanese car industry in general. In 1999 new vehicle sales amounted to around four million units – one million below the 1990 level (CCFA estimates). But, despite 15 years of internationalization, seeing the widespread production of factories in Europe and America, Japanese domestic auto production still outpaced domestic auto consumption by some 3.3 million units in 1996 and by an even larger amount of 3.8 million units in 1999. So the scope for reducing the US or EU trade gaps with Japan in the auto industry remained limited throughout the 1990s. The Japanese government felt that it was very difficult to persuade its domestic automakers to accelerate the reduction of domestic production capacity – doubly so during this time of sustained recession in Japan.

Since 1995, the new multilateral WTO regime has further limited the room of manoeuvre for discriminatory bilateral trade action. Europe and the United States have not brought any trade distortion complaints forward to the WTO against Japan (see Chapter 1). At the same time, the bilateral measures – such as the block exemption – have become increasingly susceptible to sanctions under WTO regulation. No major new bilateral measures have been announced since 1995. Only already implemented measures have been open for continuation.

(b) **Bilateral host-oriented measures.** Efforts to open up the Japanese car system can, on most accounts, be considered to have been ineffective. The low success rate was first due to the impossibility of opening up markets through trade measures in general. Secondly, the nature of the Japanese car system made it extremely hard to enter. Although the Japanese government for instance informed many dealerships that they are free to sell foreign motor vehicles, Japanese car dealers remained reluctant to sign franchise agreements with US automakers. Thirdly, the Japanese government (and firms) have not always been very accommodating to the implementation of the imposed measures. Following the US–Japanese agreement on autos and auto parts, Japan relaxed some requirements for certified garages and agreed to study the critical parts list. For almost each component, new rounds of negotiations had to be endured. In 1997, the four major US parts suppliers filed a petition to have brake parts removed from the lists. The Japanese Ministry of Transportation denied this petition, citing safety as the principal reason. Finally, the effectiveness of the measures was severely hampered by the inability of Europe and the United States to form a united front. EU and American interests in opening up the Japanese car market clearly diverged.

Despite progress in certain areas, the American government (USTR, 2000) had to conclude in its review of the US–Japan Automotive Framework Agreement that many of the objectives had not been met. By the end of 2001, the European Commission also signalled that the Japanese government had still been slow in adopting a number of the regulations on automobiles and components as agreed upon in 1995, for instance with regard to type approval of motors vehicles in Japan (EC, September 2001: 31). Only 30 of a total of over 100 regulations were adopted. The US government expressed only 'concern' about not achieving the earlier objectives. This shows the relative ineffectiveness of the chosen cluster of instruments, because the US automotive industry also faced a record bilateral trade deficit of US$40 billion in 1999.

(c) **Bilateral home-oriented measures.** The protection of the home market in the EU and the United States created the biggest strategic challenge to Japan's 'go-it-alone' stance. VERs had sometimes perverse effects on the competitiveness of the Japanese car industry. On the one hand VERs led to higher prices and (if sold) higher profits. For this reason, MITI continued the Japanese VERs throughout the 1980s and 1990s, even when the US government no longer asked for these restraints. On the other hand, the VERs put considerable discretionary power in the hands of MITI that had to decide upon quota allocation for individual car producers. The VERs have been particularly disadvantageous to Honda. As initially the smallest and latest entrant to the Japanese market, Honda had a weak domestic distribution network and was not well represented in the policy networks, unlike the established *Keiretsu*. Honda's weak bargaining position in Japan resulted in it being 'last in the queue for quota allocation' in a number of countries such as France, Italy and Britain (Womack et al., 1990: 216).

VERs and local content regulation forced Japanese producers to internationalize production facilities in order to jump tariffs and evade regional 'fortresses'. In order to retain their core competencies and retain low levels of vertical integration, they not only had to export production and assembly plants, but had to transplant whole networks of suppliers (cf. Bélis-Bergouignan and Lung, 1994). This has not only created immense coordination problems, but has also weakened the optimal scale of production. Whereas European firms have on average higher degrees of internationalization, their production and sales remain largely concentrated in the European region. Japanese car producers have the highest commercial presence in a second Triad pole (North America) and almost all a significant presence in a third pole (Europe) (Jetin, 2003: 19). Table 13.2 shows the spread of passenger car sales by the year 2000. The lifting of import quotas in the United States appeared much earlier than in the European Union (in 1999). The US market, therefore, has traditionally been a more interesting market to target (even though Europe is, overall, a larger market). In the US,

Table 13.2   Distribution of passenger car sales, 2000 (%)

	Total/world	Japan (%)	Asia* (%)	Western Europe (%)	North America (%)
Toyota	5,767	41	4	11	30
Nissan	2,540	29	7	21	38
Honda	2,505	31	7	7	53
Mitsubishi	1,439	38	21	15	22
Mazda	988	32	5	20	31

Note: * Includes South, Southeast and East Asia (excluding Japan).

Sources: JRI; Takayasu (2002).

Japanese companies occupy a 35 per cent market share, compared to just 10 per cent in Europe in 2002 (*FT*, 30 October 2002). The forced spread of production created substantial coordination problems. Japanese firms were forced to set up subsidiaries with high local content, and therefore relatively autonomous production. Japanese subsidiaries have the lowest degree of exports to other countries from their EU and US production bases (Jetin, 2003: 24).

The European (39 per cent of sales in 2002) and North American markets (26 per cent) represent the largest passenger car markets in the world. To find an outlet for the Japanese production surpluses there are no short-term alternatives but to sell in the United States and Europe. Depending on the terms of trade for individual firms, international activities could reap profits. But, to partly evade the retaliation of Europe and the United States, most Japanese car companies sought for a fourth region: Asia (representing 10 per cent of global passenger car sales in 2002; Table 13.2). This risk-spread strategy itself involved other risks. The Asia region had great potential but was limited in size. The expectation of two million sales by the year 2000 did not materialize. It also required that – in order to be successful – Japanese car manufacturers had to agree on regional integration in the ASEAN region. It was not until 1988 that this scheme started to materialize (Guiheux and Lecrer, 2000). At the same time, Japanese producers tried to keep the region relatively closed to foreign competitors in order to sustain their dominant status in the ASEAN market: while going for tariff reductions, they showed little or no interest in reducing the duties applied to extra-regional trade (see Chapter 2 and Yoshimatsu, 2002: 145). The 1997 Asia financial crisis proved the relative vulnerability of this strategy. As a survival strategy Japanese producers started to cut costs sharply, and tried to export passenger cars towards non-ASEAN markets. But in order not to cannibalize the already weak export position of the Japanese majors in leading markets, most of these exports were aimed at other developing countries (see also Chapter 9) which hardly provided the sales outlets for the structural problems in the Asia region. Re-importing parts back into Japan was also intended to keep the overseas sites in business (Guiheux and Lecrer, 2000) but this weakened the cohesion of the domestic supply complexes. The Asian financial crisis prompted firms that were more dependent on this region to go for ad hoc solutions – quite different to the traditional longer-term strategic orientation of Japanese car manufacturers. As a consequence Mitsubishi – with a very high share of its international sales in the region – suffered most. By contrast, Toyota – with the lowest share of total sales and production in the region – suffered least.

The profitability of domestic versus international activities provides the ultimate indicator of which Japanese producers have suffered and/or benefited most from forced internationalization. The two producers that did develop relatively concise internationalization strategies – albeit from completely different starting positions – have been the only ones able to profit from international expansion. Honda was able to reap a profit of its international activities throughout the whole period since its internationalization in the early 1970s. Toyota consistently reaped a profit from its international activities since the early 1980s (cf. Jetin, 2003). Mazda and Mitsubishi Motors almost systematically suffered losses on their international activities, but were still able to reap profits from their domestic activities throughout most of the 1985–2000 period. In the case of Mazda – and to a lesser extent Mitsubishi – losses accumulated abroad largely offset for profit made on the domestic market, leaving both companies approximately at a zero-profit line. In the case of Nissan, the effects were more dramatic. Having reaped hardly any profit on its foreign activities since the mid-1970s, the foreign losses not only started to increase throughout the 1990s, but more than offset profits made in the domestic market. In the end, Nissan suffered from real structural problems in its business, which led to losses in seven out of ten years throughout the 1990s. Kumon (2003: 158) calls this the 'Nissan paradox': Nissan did not have a firm strategy for meeting political and institutional environmental change in the 1990s and to fully exploit its global network. Nissan perhaps suffered more from its internationalization process, because it has been the most eager in moving in this direction. When Nissan entered the US market in 1960, it not only had to invest much more than originally anticipated, but it was also faced with serious barriers-to-entry in the distribution of its cars (Halberstam, 1986). When Honda more successfully entered the United States in 1983, it could profit from the earlier Nissan experience – for instance, by setting up local production. Both Honda and Toyota have been more 'forced' in their internationalization strategy – Honda because of domestic and Toyota because of foreign circumstances. Both Honda and Toyota have developed more comprehensive and cohesive internationalization strategies, which proved most successful even during the troubled 1990s. The dependence upon foreign production for overall profitability in the 1980–2000 period for Toyota and Honda had been opposed: low for Toyota (10–30 per cent) and high for Honda (on average 60 per cent). Toyota still sells more cars in Japan in 2002 than its four other competitors combined. It still has its biggest relative market in Japan. All the other Japanese producers were not capable of reaping continued and sustainable profits from the overseas operations. Profits were primarily reaped in the North American market, whereas Europe contributed almost nothing to profits of any of the Japanese producers (Jetin, 2003: 30).

Positive and negative terms of trade

In sum and as a result of the various forms of retaliation, negative 'terms of trade' were experienced in the 1980–2000 period by all Japanese firms, but in particular by those (1) aimed at Europe (Nissan, Mitsubishi Motors, Mazda), (2) with a very high Asian content (Mitsubishi Motors) and (3) with a relatively low North American content (Mitsubishi Motors). Relative positive 'terms of trade' were experienced by Japanese majors (1) with a very dominant position in the Japanese market (Toyota), (2) the biggest relative and absolute shares of their international portfolio sold in the United States (Honda) and (3) the lowest share sold in Europe (Toyota and Honda).

The outcome of the process has been very dramatic and historically unprecedented, particularly for the three core firms that have suffered most from international retaliation: Mitsubishi Motors, Mazda, Nissan – and in their wake smaller car producers like Suzuki, Isuzu and Fuji Heavy. All lost their strategic autonomy. The alliances with American and European partners for these firms has prompted these firms to 'link their global strategies with those of their partners, whether they like it or not' (Takayasu, 2002: 4) or have to deal with the fact of a 'foreign leadership' (Bungsche and Heyder, 2003). The continued weak international performance of Mazda throughout the 1990s, combined with the first losses in the domestic market in 1992/93, prompted Ford to strengthen its involvement in Mazda. It not only increased its equity stake from 25 to 33.4 per cent but also applied the authority to appoint a non-Japanese Ford-dispatched executive as Mazda's president in 1996 (Heller and Orishashi, 2003: 125). By taking a share of 36.8 per cent in Nissan in 1999, Renault also acquired and used the rights to appoint an own Chief Operating Officer – the renowned Brasilian Carlos Ghosn. Later, however, Nissan also acquired a share of Renault, which makes it much more of an alliance than the de facto takeover of Mazda. One of the results of the new 'reign' at Nissan has been that operating profits in the United States in particular were boosted in 2002. Finally, Mitsubishi Motors had already been associated with a wider number of alliance partners – in particular with Chrysler in the 1980s (12 per cent equity share) which created a modestly profitable sales outlet for Mitsubishi sales in the United States. Mitsubishi has profited more from the alliance with Chrysler than vice versa, but at the same time, the alliance also lowered Mitsubishi's international strategic room for manoeuvre in the United States and Europe. In 1999, Daimler-Chrysler took a 37.3 per cent stake in Mitsubishi and appointed a German COO.

Conclusion: sustained closedness as a by-product of retaliation?

The policy conclusion of the above analysis could be straightforward: 'go-it-alone' and setting up a relatively closed car system can initially be very successful – and is perhaps a prerequisite for development. But, a successful 'go-it-alone' strategy encounters retaliatory measures. The sustained strategic success of Toyota shows the value of being the 'leader of the pack' at home, and employing a slow, prudent and low-key internationalization strategy. The strategic success of Honda shows, perhaps paradoxically, the value of being excluded from such a system and engaging in an early and wholehearted spread of production outside the domestic automobile space.

Both car companies also show the value of an international 'go-it-alone' strategy at the firm level. Both developed relatively forced, but nevertheless coherent internationalization strategies. The failure of Nissan shows the risks of a too eager and less coherent internationalization strategy. The two remaining car majors illustrate the problem of being 'stuck in the middle' in the domestic and international political and economic arena – including alliances with other firms.

Does this imply the end of Japan's 'closed' model? Not necessarily. Toyota will not part from its support of a relatively closed home market. Ford, General Motors (buying three of the smaller car producers) and Renault were scarcely represented in Japan and previously have been amongst the staunchest supporters of retaliation against Japan. Their inroads into the Japanese car system lowered the necessity of engaging in further trade policy measures. The US government and the European Commission are becoming increasingly lenient in their attitude towards Japan. This is perhaps because leading European and American producers – after obtaining an 'inside' position in the Japanese car system – have become interested in sustaining many of the 'structural impediments' of the Japanese system. There is one caveat – none of the US and European firms acquired majority stakes in the Japanese car producers, so they could still bounce back again and regain part of their strategic independence – as happened before. In September 2003, Mr Hisakazu Imaki became the first Japanese head at Mazda after seven years in which four foreign (Ford) executives headed the company (*Financial Times*, 17 September 2003). The successor of Carlos Ghosn at Nissan is also bound to be Japanese again (*Business Week*, 17 March 2003: 31).

14

'Avoiding the Neighbours': The National/Global

Development Strategy of the Korean Automobile Industry

Marc Lautier

Introduction[1]

The South Korean automobile industry has grown extraordinarily quickly during the three last decades, with production increasing from 37,000 units to more than 2.8 million units between 1975 and 1996. At the end of this period, South Korea was ranked 5th within the world industry, with a 5.3 per cent share of global production. This development is almost unparalleled in recent history. Over the last 50 years only Japan has succeeded in building such a large automobile industry so quickly. The Korean experience is also remarkable as far as internationalization is concerned. Economic theory has traditionally insisted on the competitive advantages built on the domestic market to explain firms' international expansion (from Hymer to Chandler), notably using empirical evidence from the automobile industry (Cusumano, 1989; Maxcy, 1982; Doner, 1991; Jenkins, 1987; Sachwald, 1995). Emphasis has also been put on the advantages of developing on a regional basis.[2]

By contrast, the Korean industry initially grew with neither a domestic nor a regional market base. Its development relied on a national strategic alliance between the state and private business groups. As soon as a minimum technical capability was built, partly based on technology transfers, the industry expanded abroad, firstly through exports. The small domestic market and the limited export opportunities in East Asia pushed the Korean producers to consider the world's largest markets – the United States then Europe. The fragmentation of the Asian car market and the strong presence of Japanese producers in the region also explain the wide geographical scope of their foreign investments in the 1990s. Since the 'Asian' financial crisis, the Korean automobile industry has been engaged into an intense restructuring process.

Building a national industry

Like many of the modern East Asian industries, the Korean automobile industry was initially built without any comparative advantages. At its inception, Korean firms had no technology, no supporting industry and even demand was lacking. Offering a single explanation for such a broad development as the rise of the Korean automobile industry is always hazardous. Important here are the firms' aggressive investment strategy, backed by strong support from the government, and the use of strategic short-cuts to speed-up the catching-up time.

A national strategic industry of Korea

The automobile industry has been regarded as a major national strategic industry in Korea since the 1970s. As had been the case in Japan, Korea has used a dual trade regime, under which the country was open to imports of intermediate and equipment goods, though totally closed to final product imports (the 1962 *Automobile Industry Protection Law*, the 1969 *Automobile Industry Basic Promotion Plan*) whereas exports were promoted. The automobile policy was highly centralized by the government, with the Ministry of Trade and Industry acting as a coordinating and implementing agency. In 1973, the government 'ordered' three carmakers (Hyundai, Kia, Daewoo) to submit detailed plans to develop 'Korean cars' (Kim, 1998). The government plan was quite specific. The Korean model had to be new, under 1,500 cc, and cost less than US$2,000 to produce. The minimum plant capacity was 50,000 ... (the 1974 *Long Term Automobile Promotion Plan*). The main goal was to rapidly achieve economies of scale. Combined with relatively low wages, this could give a competitive advantage to the Korean carmakers, despite their lack of manufacturing experience and technology, and should allow them to increase both their export volumes and their share of the domestic market. The reliance on foreign inputs allowed the industry to expand rapidly in spite of its initially narrow manufacturing basis (Table 14.1). Intense technology transfers from foreign producers were also promoted in

Table 14.1 Ratio of imported inputs in the transport equipment industry (percentages)

%	1970	1975	1980	1985	1990
Intermediate product imports/production	25	25	24	18	10

Source: Bank of Korea.

order to build faster a 'national' industry. Cooperations with foreign multinationals were closely monitored by the government (Chaponniere and Lautier, 1995; Judet, 1986).

As early as 1974, Kia embarked on the production under licence of a Mazda vehicle, Saehan (formerly Daewoo Motor) launched a similar cooperation scheme with Isuzu, and Hyundai tried to open the 'technological package' by contracting with different technology suppliers. To build a 'national car', the Pony, Hyundai used an Italian design (Ital design), English engineers (from British Leyland), and core components from Japan (Mitsubishi) and England (Girling, Burman, Smith).

The 1980 crisis prompted the government to implement a rationalization plan in order to bring greater scale economies and to strengthen the industry's export orientation. Hyundai was to become specialized in passenger car production and had to develop a Korean 'world car' designed to fit advanced markets demand (Rennard, 1992). This led the company to develop the Pony 2, then the Excel, with the technical assistance of Mitsubishi Motors.

Then, increasing strategic autonomy in this context of structural dependence on foreign technology became a major objective. Hyundai has always stressed placed the greatest emphasis on the concept of self-reliance most. The company failed to complete joint-venture negotiations with Ford in 1972 and with GM in 1981, because Hyundai did not want to lose its managerial control and limit its access to export markets. While Mitsubishi soon became its main technological partner, Hyundai did manage to avoid an exclusive partnership and diversified its technology sources.[3] Furthermore Hyundai R&D investments increased rapidly in the 1990s (Kim, 1998; Lautier, 2001a).

The Korean oligopoly

The industrial policy preference for intense competition between local makers and the rivalry between *chaebols* have produced an oligopolistic industry, with four groups manufacturing cars and commercial vehicles in the 1990s (Table 14.2): The domestic leader, Hyundai, has been part of the second largest Korean *chaebol*; the Kia group has long been the second largest car producer and the largest non-*chaebol* firm in Korea. It has had technological and equity links with Mazda and Ford; Daewoo Motor operated as a 50/50 joint venture with General Motors from 1976 to 1992. Most of its model range was developed on the basis of GM/Opel products. In the early 1990s became more independent from GM technology through new partnerships with Suzuki and Honda; Ssangyong Motor pursued a niche strategy focusing on sports-utility products and negotiating a partnership with Mercedes-Benz.

The firms' aggressive investment strategies, combined with a flow of state-controlled bank financing, has engaged the automobile industry in a 'capacity-push' growth since the early 1980s.[4] Production has increased

Table 14.2 The Korean industry structure before the 'Asian' crisis (1996)

	Hyundai	*Daewoo*	*Kia*	*Ssangyong*
Company foundation	1967	1965 (as Shinjin)	1944	1954 (as Dong A)
Main partners	Mitsubishi 15%	GM 50% (from 1972 to 1992), Suzuki, Honda	Ford 9.4%; C. Itoh 2%; Mazda 7.5%	Daimler-Benz 5%
Autom. turnover (US$ million)	13,600	5,300[2]	7,800	1,370
Liabilities/equity	290%, 390% (97)	480%, 610% (97)	330%, 630% (97)	n.a.
Total production (units)	1,341,990[1]	627,815[2]	756,753[3]	76,940
Employees	49,440[1]	17,243	29,610	11,160

*Note*s
1. Including Hyundai Precision and Industrial.
2. Including Daewoo Heavy Industries.
3. Including Asia.

Sources: Companies' financial reports; KAMA; CCFA.

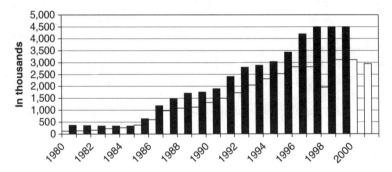

Figure 14.1 Korean production and capacity growth, 1980–2001
Sources: KAMA; EIU.

23-fold between 1980 and 1996, but capacity expansion has always been ahead of this rate (Figure 14.1). In the mid-1990s, the Korean manufacturers had created the potential for the third or fourth largest industry in the world.

Capacity utilization ratio have usually been low. The intense rivalry within the national oligopoly and firms' large ambitions have led them to introduce new models regularly in order to compete in each car segment. As a result, unitary volumes by platform and model have remained very low by world standards (McKinsey, 1998). Furthermore, a comparative study has shown that Korean makers use far fewer common parts across different models, suggesting that economies of scale are also insufficient at the component level (Ellison et al., 1995).

The late take-off of the domestic market

Since the mid-1960s, investment and exports have been the primary engines of the rapid Korean industrialization process. Real wages did also rise,[5] but from a low starting level and at a slower rate than labour productivity (Amsden, 1989). However, the purchase of consumer durables was severely constrained by the government through various austerity measures until the mid-1980s, in order to promote savings and moderate imports.

Cars, in particular, were seen as luxury items and car ownership was restricted by taxes and insurance.[6] Car use was estimated to cost about one-third of the average monthly wage in the early 1980s. Furthermore, the road network remained underdeveloped, with 47,000 km in 1980, half of them asphalted. Domestic sales had only reached 200,000 units by 1983, of which one-half were commercial vehicles. At this time there were seven cars per 1,000 people in Korea, compared with 32 in Taiwan, 58 in Malaysia and 65 per 1,000 in Brazil.

The rise in Korean consumption began in 1986–87. This process led to the fast expansion of the car market. Automobile sales rose from 230,000 units in 1985 (of which fewer than 140,000 were passenger cars) to more than 1.5 million units in 1995 (Figure 14.2). This expansion was helped by a general decrease in vehicle prices, a decline in oil prices, tax reduction and, initially, an unusually large available supply of cars as a result of the fall in Korea's sales in North America. Above all, the domestic market growth was based on the rapid wages increase that started in 1987, when many strikes prompted large firms to relax their wage policy.[7] Thus, wages increased by about 14 per cent a year in real terms between 1987 and 1991 (OECD, 1994).

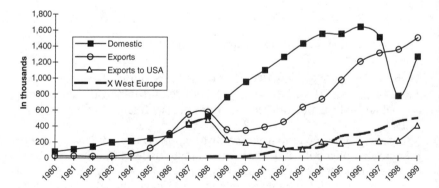

Figure 14.2   Korean automobile sales structure
Sources: KAMA, EIU.

Table 14.3 Passenger car market concentration (Herfindhal index)

	1982	1985	1988	1990	1993	1997
South Korea	0.67	0.59	0.40	0.38	0.35	0.34
USA	0.25	0.24	0.20	0.20	0.19	n.d.
Japan	0.24	0.26	0.26	0.21	0.19	n.d.
Germany	0.16	0.14	0.14	0.13	0.14	n.d.

Note: Index = 1 if Monopoly.
Sources: KAMA, Sturgeon and Florida (1999) for non-Korean data.

In the mid-1990s, after more than ten years of continuous growth, the Korean vehicle market has developed into the largest in Asia outside Japan. Growing international pressures have obliged the government to open its market at a much earlier stage of its economic development than Japan. Nevertheless, competition from imported cars has remained weak because of various barriers to foreign car purchase. In 1987, 27 cars were imported, of which 16 were Mercedes! The import figure progressively increased to 3,000 in 1990 and a little over 10,000 in 1996 (less than one per cent of the market), before it fell to 2,000–3,000 in 1998–99. Thus, whereas several reforms aimed at the improvement of market access have been implemented, according to the WTO and OECD trade policy reviews, foreign products do not yet compete on the Korean car market.[8]

The level of competition did increase within the Korean oligopoly. Hyundai's early dominance in the domestic market diminished regularly until the 1998 crisis (Table 14.3). The concentration decrease is more pronounced on a per model basis because the intense competition between producers has led to an increasing variety of models in every segment of the market. Thus, Korea began to resemble a buyer's market by the mid-1990s. Responding to the rising competition among domestic producers, Korean consumers have become much more knowledgeable and demanding, with the result that all of the firms have been pushed to upgrade the quality, technological sophistication and price competitiveness of their products. As a consequence of this fast motorization process, in the mid-1990s market growth came to an halt and replacement accounted already for 70 per cent of car sales (Chaponnière, 1997).

The export expansion

The initially limited size of the domestic market, the fierce competition among Korean carmakers, and the absolute necessity to increase volumes to pay off huge investments has forced them to seek the early expansion of their sales abroad. Hyundai initiated the internationalization of the industry by exporting its famous Pony model in the mid-1970s to Latin America and the Middle East. But sales remained weak. Korean exports took off later, when Hyundai entered the North American markets. Western Europe rapidly developed as another major market, whereas East Asia has always been a marginal export destination.

A narrow growth path in East Asia

From Japan to Southeast Asia, the Asian 'Miracles' (Judet, 1986; Wade, 1990; World Bank, 1993) have been built on trade barriers, import-substitution policies and a preference for national control on strategic industries, such as the automobile industry (Cusumano, 1989; Doner, 1991; Lautier, 1997; Odaka, 1983). Thus, export opportunities have been rare in the region for new competitors.

Additionally, car consumption has remained moderate in the developing Asian region. The whole ASEAN vehicle market is smaller than Spain's, for instance. Furthermore, market fragmentation has been high, both at the national and the regional levels. In Vietnam, 14 foreign producers have obtained assembling licences and should compete for a 20,000-unit market![9] In Thailand, about 20 carmakers have built a 1.2 million-unit capacity, whereas domestic sales have never reached half this volume. In the ASEAN, 90 per cent of all cars produced in the ASEAN region are already made through cooperation with Japanese firms or in their own facilities (Chapter 9).

China and Japan, the other two major markets in East Asia, have had their own automobile policies and have been, de facto, closed to car imports from Korea. As a consequence, sales of Korean firms in Asia have always accounted for a very limited share of their export (Table 14.4). Before the Asian financial crisis, they were already selling fewer cars in Asia than in Africa.

Barriers to export growth led Korean firms to initiate new strategies in the early 1990s in order to increase their market share. At first, they set up

Table 14.4   Automobile exports by region

% of total exports	1980	1988	1993	1998*
Asia	7	2	16	1
North America	0	89	22	19
Western Europe	22	4	21	34
Eastern Europe	0	0	4	14
Latin America	40	1.5	15	12
Oceania	0	1.5	5	9
Middle East	22	4	16	7
Africa	9	0	2	5
Export/production	20	53	31	70

Note: * Since 1994 CKD kits have been excluded from KAMA exports statistics.

Sources: KAMA; CCFA.

assembling projects, through technical and sales agreement with local partners, in a number of Asian countries. Kia pioneered this strategy and this firm has for a considerable period been the largest exporter of kits. The firm set up its first assembling operation in 1989 in Taiwan, where it supplied Ford Lio Ho with Avella kits. This is an unusual example of an 'Asian' division of labour implemented by a Korean producer. But this cooperation was fully integrated within Ford's global organization: the product was based on technical licenses from Ford's Japanese subsidiary Mazda, assembled in Ford Taiwanese facilities and sold under the Ford Aspire name. Nevertheless, it allowed Kia to gain some experience of CKD operations which has been used in other countries (Table 14.5). Hyundai has engaged more cautiously in foreign assembly operations, while Daewoo has had to wait for the end of the international limits imposed by GM before it can embark upon this new export route.

However, assembling agreements can contribute only marginally to sales growth. Korean firms soon realized that investing in manufacturing facilities abroad had become the best way to speed up their expansion. But the number of investment projects in East Asia has been limited (Table 14.5). Daewoo established modest bases in the region, in comparison with the production network it tried to build at the periphery of the European Union (cf. infra). Hyundai had planned two major operations in Asia – in Indonesia and India – but only the latter survived the Asian financial crisis. The Indonesian project was frozen in December 1997, as well as Kia's ambitious joint-venture project 'Kia-Timor'.

Table 14.5 Assembling agreements and manufacturing investments in Asia in the 1990s

Country	Kia		Hyundai		Daewoo	
	Type	*Output*	*Type*	*Output*	*Type*	*Output*
Taiwan	AA	12,000 (97)				
Philippines	AA	5,700 (97)	AA	260 (97)	JV	1,600 (96)
Vietnam	AA	400 (97)			JV(65%)	500 (98)
Iran	AA	23,000 (97)	AA	310 (97)	JV (49%)	2,600 (97)
Pakistan	AA	2,700 (96)				
Malaysia	AA	1,000 (97)			JV (15%)	n.d.
Thailand	AA		AA	11,000 (98)		
Indonesia			JV(50 %)	4,100 (97)	JV(51 %)	510 (97)
China			JV(21 %)	n.d.	JV (60%)	2,200 (97)
India			I = 100%	8,700 (98)	JV(92 %)	3,600 (97)

Note: AA = Assembling agreement (no equity investment) ; JV = joint venture, Korean firm's share; I = investment.

Source: Lautier (2001a).

As a consequence Korean firms' involvement in the Asian car industry has remained fragmented, small-scale and diffused across a very large geographical spectrum, from Taiwan to Iran.

Trade triangle: Japan, South Korea, United States

Hyundai first entered the Canadian market in 1984 and moved into the US market in 1986. The entry strategy was based on the aggressive marketing of Hyundai's recently developed Excel model.[10] This offensive benefited from an unusual window of opportunity. It was boosted by the price increases of Japanese cars brought on by the yen's rapid appreciation following the 1985 Plaza Agreement. Furthermore, the good reputation earned by the Japanese also initially benefited this new Asian producer. As a result, Hyundai sales grew at an extraordinary pace from 1985 to 1988. Whereas the firm's total exports accounted for fewer than 50,000 units in 1984, export volume reached 300,000 units in 1986 and 400,000 in 1987. At the time, nearly three-quarters of Hyundai's output was exported and the North American markets accounted for more than 90 per cent of Korean sales abroad. Kia and Daewoo soon entered the US market, but they had less marketing success than Hyundai. The two companies' products were distributed through the GM and Ford US dealer networks. In comparison, Hyundai was free of any marketing agreement and benefited from the effective support of Mitsubishi. Japanese automobile VRAs and the yen's appreciation stimulated the strategic partnership between both partners. Through its parts and components sales to Hyundai, Mitsubishi had found a way to increase indirectly its sales to US consumers at a time when its own cars exports were limited by the import quota (Rennard, 1992).

Rapid export successes in the American markets prompted Hyundai to anticipate protectionist reactions and led the company to try to consolidate its market share by investing in a large manufacturing facility in Bromont, Canada, as early as 1989. This was the first Korean automobile plant abroad. It was located in an advanced country. But Hyundai guessed wrong. The plant's total output in the five years of operation amounted to about one-fifth of the volume necessary to make it profitable, and the factory was closed in September 1993 and subsequently liquidated in 1996. The major reason for this failure was the fall of Hyundai's sales in North America. Indeed, after a promising start, sales on the US market fell almost as rapidly as they had grown. Korean exports to the United States declined regularly from 1989 to 1993. Cost increases are one explanatory factor. But the main reason for this sales drop is connected to the loss of consumer confidence in Korean products and the rapid disappearance of the reputation for high quality that they initially enjoyed.[11]

Export diversification in Western Europe

The fall in its American sales pushed the industry to diversify its exports rapidly in the late 1980s. The export structure was modified in a two-step process. At first, Korean firms developed their overseas sales almost everywhere, with the clear goal of building significant market shares in emerging countries. Accordingly, in 1993 half of all automobile exports went to Asian, South American and Middle Eastern countries (Table 14.4). Then export growth has been concentrated on mature automobile markets, mostly in Western Europe and Australia. Western Europe gradually became more important, to the point that it became the principal export destination in 1995.[12]

As a result, the Korean export structure was completely modified in less than ten years. Whereas the bulk of Korean exports were directed to North America in 1988, this region accounted for only one-fifth of its exports in 1997. Sales in Western Europe, Eastern Europe and South America have become at least as large as this.

Multinationalization strategy: from periphery to periphery

Going multinational

Manufacturing internationalization in the automobile industry has usually been driven by firms' oligopolistic advantages. In the case of Korean manufacturers (Chung, 2003), however, the reverse causal sequence gives a better explanation of their late FDI drive. It has been primarily motivated by the need to catch up rapidly with their foreign competitors in terms of size. At the time, Korean firms had not yet acquired a significant competitive advantage within the world oligopoly, in terms of product quality, productivity or technology. Accordingly, they had to keep on growing at a fast pace because volume expansion was the easiest way to catch up – at least in terms of productivity and cost (Lautier, 2001).

Despite their early export orientation and the take-off of the domestic market since the late 1980s, Korean carmakers' output remained small during the mid-1990s. They badly needed to expand their production. But the domestic market ended its rapid climb, and the traditional export markets could not absorb the large additional volumes that Korean firms had planned to sell. However, the largest emerging markets remained almost untouched by export strategies because of high trade barriers.

Besides firms' growth plans, two additional push-factors have contributed to the rise of Korean FDI projects in the 1990s. Firstly, Korean manufacturers have been subjected to rapid operational cost increase, often described as the '3 High' : high land prices, high interest rates, high labour costs. Manufacturing abroad could counterbalance domestic cost growth, especially labour costs. The change in the Daewoo Motor management structure has been a second determining factor. When it ended its relationship with GM in 1992 Daewoo was quite a small manufacturer, with a thin export network and a weak competitive position in its domestic market. Thus, expanding production abroad was the only possible way to catch-up rapidly in size with its competitors, notably Kia and Hyundai. This firm-specific reason pushed Daewoo to pioneer Korean foreign investment strategy in the 1990s.

Becoming a regional player in ... Europe

Daewoo rapidly became a major player in Central and Eastern Europe, by establishing vehicles assembly plants – and sometimes component manufacturing – in almost every important market. It set up a joint venture with Automobile Rodae in Romania, acquired FSO and FSL in Poland and took a majority stake in the Czech truck manufacturer Avia. Its commercial vehicles subsidiary in Poland was strengthened in 1998 by the acquisition of a 50 per cent stake in the British producer LDV. Furthermore, an ambitious joint venture was set-up earlier in Uzbekistan and an additional one was established in Ukraine in 1997 (Table 14.6). Daewoo had ambitious plans to develop intra-regional trade between its subsidiaries: the export of engines and transmissions from Romania to Poland; the cross-exchange of commercial vehicles between the Czech Republic and Poland; the components exports from Poland to Romania and Uzbekistan, ... At this time Hyundai had only one mature project, in Turkey, while Kia had none in the region.

Targeting new automobile consumers

The location structure of the Korean industry FDI confirm their offensive dimension. They were not aiming at preserving export market shares. On the contrary, they were clearly growth-oriented. Despite firm-specific behaviours, these FDI are all concentrated in the same world areas. Indeed, with the exception of Bromont, no large manufacturing facility was initially established either in Western Europe or North America, where the bulk of the world car demand is located, nor in South America or East Asia, where production networks had been established by advanced carmakers for some time. By focusing on emerging markets, Korean firms have implemented FDI strategies on the periphery of the core automobile countries.

Furthermore, Korean manufacturers have often invested, or have planned to invest, in the same countries. Inter-chaebols rivalry is a substantial determinant of their domestic behaviour, and it might explain also some of their international moves (Perrin, 2001). In particular, Daewoo's aggressiveness

Table 14.6　Daewoo becomes an East-European carmaker

Country	Investment date	Type of project (Daewoo's share)	Output
Uzbekistan	1992	JV (50%)	65,000 (98)
Romania	1994	JV (51%)	17,000 (98)
Czech Republic	1995	JV (50%)	4,100 (98)
Poland	1995	JV (81%)	18,000 (98)
Poland	1996	JV (85%)	160,000 (98)
Ukraine	1998	JV (50%)	24,200 (98)

Source: Lautier (2001a).

might have led Hyundai to be more active abroad. Indeed, Hyundai has tried to develop local production or assembling in several of Daewoo's invested countries.[13] Similar proximity can be found between Hyundai and Kia in Indonesia. Thus, it is clear that Korean firms have been looking for the same type of location.

The targeted markets have not been homogeneous or similar in terms of purchasing power, regulation, road conditions on growth rate. However, these countries have, at least, two common characteristics: the large growth potential of domestic automobile consumption; the lack of a strong market leadership usually combined with import protection.

By establishing large facilities in those countries, Korean firms planned to take a leadership position early on, which might allow them to become the main beneficiaries of any expected take-off in automobile demand. In these markets, they can more easily establish a favourable brand image than in mature markets, where brand recognition building is a costly activity. Indeed, the size of their investments should have allowed Hyundai and Daewoo to become the first or second largest automobile producers in several promising countries – such as India, Turkey, Romania or Poland.[14] Furthermore, the core of the Korean carmakers' product range is adapted to the taste and purchasing power of these households, for whom durable goods mass-consumption is a recent phenomenon: a modern design, over-equipped cars and a competitive price. Furthermore, most of these countries are close to the large EU market and have already negotiated free-trade or enlargement agreements. The nature of the market, rather than its world location, explains the geographical structure of Korean FDI.

From globalization makers to globalization victims

Korean firms acted as globalization makers in the 1980s and 1990s by expanding into overseas markets. They used western markets' openness to import to develop mass-export strategies, thus providing international trade with a new flow of goods, that resulted in a rapid increase of the import ratio in developed countries. Then, they were among the first car manufacturers to integrate less developed markets into the global industry through an aggressive strategy of foreign licensing and investments. The goal was to combine national control and global scope, and the instrument employed was debt-financed investments. This strategy led to an increasing financial vulnerability in the 1990s.

The Korean financial crisis and the automobile industry

In April 1997, three months before the start of the 'Asian' financial crisis in Thailand, Daewoo inaugurated a new 320,000-unit plant in Kunsan. At this time, the three main carmakers were planning to reach a seven million production capacity by the year 2000. Thus, in the car sector, as in other

Korean industries, the huge production base established during the 1990s looked excessive by the end of the decade. The emphasis on growth and outward expansion had always been based on a high debt leverage. The debt/equity ratio has been in the 500 per cent range since the mid-1970s, even for the largest groups. Along with the high level of diversification, large in-group shareholding and low profitability, it used to be a definite characteristic of Korean capitalism. Financial liberalization in the early 1990s had resulted in a rapid rise in short-term foreign loans and increased the industry financial weaknesses.[15] This vulnerability became lethal in 1997 when debt costs exploded as a result of the won's collapse. The liquidity crisis rapidly caused the collapse of the country financial system.

Car consumption and carmakers' capacity utilization declined by around 50 per cent in 1998 (Figure 14.2). Kia became the first victim of the crisis, despite its strong manufacturing and marketing achievements. The concentration of the industry had already been planned before the crisis, but it had not been implemented. Such a structural change marks a new stage in the industry modernization process, by following the trajectory of older producing countries which is a long story of mergers and concentration. Daewoo initiated the concentration process by taking over Ssangyong Motor in January 1998. Then Hyundai agreed to take over Kia and its subsidiary, Asia Motors. At the same time, operations at Samsung's new automobile plant were frozen. Thus, in less than one year the formerly competitive industry structure has now been turned into a duopoly. Since car imports remained marginal, Hyundai and Daewoo now enjoyed total control of the domestic market.

A new wave of foreign investments in Korea

The bankruptcy of the Daewoo group initiated the second stage of the restructuring process. It has relied on new investments by western automakers in the Korean industry. Daewoo's fall in August 1999 showed that the Korean *chaebols* were no longer 'too big to fail' and the end of the situation of moral hazard. This was the message sent by the government-controlled banking system to the industry. It surely accelerated the negotiations between *chaebols* and foreign investors. As a consequence, foreign direct investment (FDI) in Korea grew to US$8.8 billion in 1998, an amount equivalent to the combined FDI flow of the 1985–1995 period, and then to almost US$16 billion in 1999 and 2000.[16]

The automobile industry has been at the heart of this structural change. In April 2000, Samsung Motor became the first foreign-owned carmaker in Korea, through the sales of its manufacturing and marketing assets to Renault.[17] It took two more years for GM to buy Daewoo Motor.[18] The restructuring process also accelerated in the supplying sector with the entry of most of the world's largest components manufacturers into the industry.

In Korea, FDI has acted as a catalyst for restructuring (Beck, 1998; Lautier, 2001b). The former state-Chaebols alliance has been partly replaced by a state-led 'attractiveness' policy towards foreign firms. In the case of the automobile sector, the domestic market will become more open to competition from foreign brands. Yet, nobody should expect a genuine free trade policy to emerge in this sector. However, by producing locally, foreign carmakers will surely increase the competitive pressure on the domestic market and reduce the level of protection rents enjoyed by Hyundai and Kia.[19]

Conclusion: globalization as an alternative to regional integration?

Korean producers' foreign expansion has avoided East Asia, neither in terms of exports nor in terms of investments. High protection, fragmentation, small size, ... were the definite characteristics of the region's automobile markets when the Korean firms increased their production capacities. This explains their strategic choice to focus their exports on the large, homogeneous and unified markets of first, North-America and then Western Europe. Thus, less than 5 per cent of Korean exports were shipped to Asian countries before the financial crisis. The lack of economic integration within the region and the Japanese domination in most countries did not produce any additional incentives to establish manufacturing facilities there. Korean firms have concentrated their investments on emerging, and not yet fully exploited, markets where they could try to avoid face-to-face competition with advanced competitors. Finally, in the late 1990s seven of their ten largest foreign markets were located in Europe – by contrast none was in Asia, nor in the developed world.[20] When a regional headquarters had to be established, it was located in Warsaw, Poland, to cover Daewoo's businesses in Eastern Europe.

Besides, Korean producers emerged as credible competitors only late in the day. When they went multinational, barriers to investment and trade, control on international financial flows, transaction cost, ... were rapidly diminishing in the world economy. In this context of globalization, national market structures and firm's relative competitive advantage have become much more powerful locational determinants than proximity.

Anyhow, if a regional integration process were to intensify in Southeast Asia, it would be of benefit exclusively to local producers, including a few Japanese carmakers who already have a large regional basis. Trade and investment diversion would play a full part and the gains for newcomers would be very limited. Enlarging the region frontiers, as in the 'ASEAN + 4' scheme[21] for instance, will surely lead to higher trade and investment liberalization, but at the multilateral level not specifically at the regional one, because of the large amount of US and European investments in these countries and the high trade surpluses many of them enjoy with the United States, Canada and the European Union. Such processes will result in a higher economic integration at the world level rather than within the region. This offers the most likely scenario for the region's future.

In summary, a regional priority did not suit either the period or the expectations of these late-coming multinationals.

The causes of the industry crisis are not related to the direction of its expansion, but rather to the speed of the process. By contrast with the slow decision process which characterized Japanese firms' internationalization, Korean producers have run very fast. Indeed, they have run too fast, since obviously a consolidation of the industry was needed and firms' strategies had to be reoriented towards higher differentiation in marketing and design in the early 1990s, when their cost advantages disappeared.[22] This consolidation and a new process of modernization have begun since the financial crisis. Indeed, the new competitive and financial environment in Korea generates permanent incentives that force domestic producers to rapidly improve both their productivity and their profitability. The new constestability of the Korean market should result in strengthening the industry, of which more than 80 per cent[23] has remained Korean-owned.

15

Going Local: Foreign Investment, Local Development and the Chinese Auto Sector

Eric Thun

Introduction

For two decades, the auto industry has been at the core of China's plans to develop a modern economy. The automobile industry has an enduring appeal for developing countries, in part because it is often thought to be a symbol of a modern economy, but even more importantly because it serves as the hub of an integrated industrial structure: extensive forward and backward linkages create the potential for a substantial positive spillover effect. It is not simply about making cars, it is about developing basic manufacturing capabilities in a wide variety of industries.

This appeal was not lost on Chinese officials, and early in the process of economic reform and development, Beijing policy makers began to target the auto industry as a lynchpin of development efforts. Linkages with foreign auto manufacturers would increase the technical knowledge and management skills of joint-venture (JV) assembly plants, and this knowledge would then disseminate to the hundreds of supply firms that would be created to support the core assembly plant. All firms would develop together. This at least was the hope in 1984, when Premier Zhao Ziyang announced the need to 'switch from "self-reliance" and the all-under-one-roof mentality of small-scale development, to the cooperative industrial complex system, centred around large-scale factories based on modern technology' (Iwagaki, 1986: 11).

However, the very linkages which make the sector such an attractive development target, also increase the difficulty of coordinated development. It is not a single factory that must be constructed, but a complex network of relationships between firms, markets, and governments. An automobile consists of thousands of components that are manufactured by hundreds of firms. Because these components are part of an assembled product, each must be in a certain place at a certain time at a certain level of quality. Coordination of this process is a challenge for highly developed economies; it is a Herculean task for a government that is trying to develop an industrial base while simultaneously make the transition from centrally-planned economy to a market economy. What is the most effective manner of coordinating auto sector development?

Given the context of East Asia, it is probably unsurprising that there were many calls for the state to direct the development of strategic industries in China. However, implementation of such an approach was difficult. The central problem was that the central government usually defined 'strategic' industries according to political rather than economic criteria, and as a result, directed the resources of the financial system (via 'policy' loans) to those places and firms that were least competitive, and therefore most likely to cause political instability in the event that they failed. Even if implementing an industrial policy at the central level had been possible, such a policy would have contradicted the broader objectives of the reformist agenda: making the transition from a centrally-planned economy to the market necessitated a weakening of central control, not a strengthening. Unable to impose an industrial policy from above, the central government relied upon local governments to come up with solutions.

The central government created the space for local development efforts by protecting the domestic market with high tariff walls and imposing domestic content regulations on foreign-invested projects. Local governments were given fiscal incentives to promote the development of local industry, and were also given the autonomy to experiment with a variety of policy approaches (Hao and Lin, 1994). In other words, the local government, in cooperation with their foreign partner, had to construct an industrial model that was conducive to the development of an assembly plant and the coordinated development of a network of supply firms. The political and economic histories of each locality became critical determinants of their chosen approach, and outcomes varied widely.

In the mid-1980s three cities in China established joint-ventures (JV) assembly projects for sedans, two more were added in the early 1990s, and then numerous projects were added at the end of the 1990s. Due to space restrictions, this chapter focuses on only the three earliest localities: Beijing, Guangzhou, and Shanghai.[1] Each of these localities sought to use a JV assembly project as a mechanism for developing a network of local auto supply firms (Beijing with Chrysler, Guangzhou with Peugeot and then Honda, Shanghai with Volkswagen and then General Motors), and after two decades of development it is clear that only Shanghai has realized this objective.

By tracking the sourcing patterns of the assembly plants it is possible to determine which supply firms are the strongest. The assembly plants are intent on finding high-quality parts for the lowest possible price, and therefore their sourcing policies are a good indication of where the most competitive supply firms are located. It is true, of course, that there should be a strong preference for sourcing from local firms. First, the local government has a strong financial interest in giving business to its own parts enterprises both because it will make profits at each step of the production process and because it increases local tax revenue. Secondly, as with auto companies everywhere, supply links with firms that are in close geographical proximity are easier to manage. This is especially true in China because of the poor transportation infrastructure. Given the overwhelming preference for using local supply firms, a heavy reliance on outside suppliers is strong evidence of an extremely weak local supply base.

When each JV assembly project was created, the foreign partner initially imported 100 per cent of the components for the assembly plant. From the Chinese perspective, the objective was to gradually increase the percentage of parts that were sourced locally. Each of the JVs was forced by law to increase the domestic content of their product, and each did so. But domestic content is not an indication of *local* development because a JV might be sourcing from other regions of China. And this is exactly what happened in this instance. As of 2003, the only municipality that could rely heavily on the local auto sector was Shanghai: it sourced 88–90 per cent of domestically-sourced parts *within* the municipality of Shanghai. By comparison, in Beijing the comparable figure was 5–10 per cent and in Guangzhou it was 22 per cent (cf. Table 15.1).

Table 15.1 Percentage of components sourced locally by JV*

Joint venture	1985 (%)	1997 (%)	2003 (%)
Beijing Jeep	0	20–30	5–10
Shanghai VW	0	88–90	88–90[a]
Guangzhou Peugeot	0	20	—
Shanghai GM	—	0	60+[b]
Guangzhou Honda	—	—	22[c]

Notes
* The percentages are by component (not value), and are from interviews with the supply division of each JV. A locally sourced part is defined as being manufactured within the municipality within which the JV is located. JVs are ranked from earliest to most recent. The percentages are for the following models: Jeep Cherokee (Beijing Jeep), Santana (SVW), all Peugeot models (GZ Peugeot), Accord (GZ Honda), Buick Regal (SGM). The designation—indicates that a JV was not yet in existence. JVs are ranked from the earliest to the most recent.
[a] This number is unchanged since 1997 because it is at the highest possible level.
[b] This is the percentage by value of components sources from SAIC suppliers, all of which are within the Shanghai municipality. The percentage from all Shanghai firms is higher.
[c] This percentage is for the number of suppliers in Guangzhou. Consequently, the percentage for Guangzhou alone is probably lower. To give some indication of this, Honda is only using four former Peugeot suppliers.

Source: Author survey.

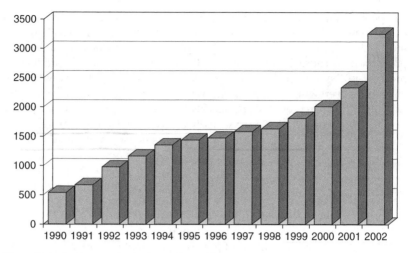

Figure 15.1   Evolution of vehicle production in China, 1990–2002 (unit: vehicles, 000s)
Source: Organisation Internationale des Constructeurs Automobiles.

Perhaps even more indicative of the weak state of supplier development in Beijing and Guangzhou was their increasing reliance on Shanghai: by 2003, for example, Beijing was sourcing only 10 per cent of its components locally, and more than 50 per cent from Shanghai. By the end of the 1990s the Chinese domestic market was growing rapidly (cf. Figure 15.1) and Shanghai, despite being far short of international standards, was the dominant force.

Why was Shanghai so much more effective in creating a strong network of local supply firms? To what degree would this further national objectives of developing an internationally competitive auto industry in China? The first purpose of this chapter is to explain the variation in local outcomes, the second purpose is to understand the implications for the national auto sector.

Developing the manufacturing capability of local firms

Understanding the relative success of Shanghai requires an examination of what might be called the micro-processes of the economic and political relations within an industrial sector (see Locke, 1995; Soskice, 1999): the relationships that exist both within and between firms and government at the sub-national level and how the politics and history of the region shape these relationships. Each of the regions in China that hoped to develop an automotive sector faced similar challenges – volumes, quality standards, and domestic content rates had to increase rapidly – yet each region adopted a different developmental approach. Comparing these regions provides an ideal opportunity to analyse how alternative regional production systems affect developmental outcomes.

Shanghai: halfway house between plan and market

The case of Shanghai demonstrates the manner in which a local government and non-market coordinating mechanisms can promote the development of firms that are struggling to adjust in a transitional economy. At the core of the development process was a foreign firm – in 1984 the Shanghai Automobile Industry Corporation (SAIC) formed a joint venture with Volkswagen (VW) – but the supply network had to consist of Chinese firms. In the very early stages of development, non-market organizing mechanisms within the local automotive sector nourished firm development in a manner that a market would not have: the local government played a pivotal role with respect to capital accumulation and investment; a hierarchically organized business group provided a structure that facilitated learning, coordination, and development among small firms; and a supplier association promoted horizontal ties between firms. In addition to nurturing firm development, these organizations allowed for the monitoring of firm development – an indispensable role in state-owned enterprises. The hierarchical corporate group monitored the performance of each firm, and the bureaucratic structure of the local government insured that top leaders were both informed and accessible. These non-market structures provided a halfway house of sorts for firms that were struggling to adjust in a transitional economy.[2]

Activist local government. When Shanghai Volkswagen (SVW) first began to search for local suppliers, no domestic firms could meet the necessary quality standards; as of 1987, two years after the start of production, only 2.7 per cent of the value of the SVW product (the Santana) consisted of parts manufactured in China (Li, 1997: 116). When it became clear that local auto sector development objectives were not being achieved, the Shanghai municipal government began to re-evaluate the problems within the sector and the capacity of individual firms to solve these problems. The response of the municipal government was to take on many of the characteristics of a local developmental state: it reorganized the bureaucratic structure so as to be able to effectively coordinate and monitor developmental efforts, it played the primary role with respect to capital accumulation and investment, and it directed the overall development process.

The first prerequisite for a successful localization drive in Shanghai was a reorganization of the municipal bureaucracy responsible for auto sector oversight. Given the manner in which many governmental structures in China are fragmented vertically along functional lines (each in its own system, or *xitong*), coordination can be achieved across separate ministries only if a coordinating office has sufficient power (Lieberthal and Oksenberg, 1988). In the auto industry, this problem of fragmented authority was particularly vexing because investment capital was extremely scarce and the widespread linkages of the industry drew a large number of governmental offices into the policy-making process. Consequently, institutional power had to be centralized not as a means of increasing leverage over foreign investors, but as a means of controlling local actors. This was achieved by means of an Automobile Industry Leading Small Group directly underneath the mayor's office and a Localization Office below that. The bureaucratic apparatus was at every level unified and coordinated in its view of how industrial development in the auto sector should proceed. The Localization Office dealt with the auto industry on a day-to-day basis – it was in a sense the head office for the local industry – and the Leading Small Group assisted by coordinating the activities of related government agencies. Importantly, it was clear from these arrangements that these industries, and the industry as a whole, would receive top-level political support when necessary (Li, 1997: 116).

The second prerequisite for increasing the capabilities of local firms was capital accumulation and investment. Managers of supply firms faced a dilemma at this stage. When the Santana assembly plant first began operations in 1985, volumes were low and consisted entirely of imported CKDs. SVW wanted to develop the local supply base, but had no money of its own to invest in supply firms. From the perspective of a supply firm, making the financial commitment necessary to forge a linkage with SVW was an extremely risky proposition. A great deal of capital was required in order to upgrade technical capabilities, current production would be disrupted, and the low volumes at SVW did not necessarily guarantee a sufficient return on the required investment.

In 1988, the Shanghai government began the process of capital accumulation by creating what it called a 'localization tax'. For every Santana automobile sold, a tax of 28,000 RMB would be levied (the price of the cars ranged from 150,000 to 200,000 RMB during this period), and the proceeds would form a localization fund controlled by the municipal government's automobile localization office. The Localization Office carried out a straightforward import-substitution policy, with import defined as any component purchased outside of the Shanghai municipality. The Localization Office examined the list of components that SVW was either importing from abroad or elsewhere in China. It determined which could most successfully be produced by Shanghai factories and coordinated the localization process. The Localization Office served to ease the risk of individual supply firms by providing access to investment capital at preferential rates, it managed their relations with the assembly plant, and it served as advocate and advisor.

Hierarchical institution. Within the Shanghai auto sector a hierarchically organized corporate structure, SAIC, coordinated relations between firms. The organizational structure of SAIC was that of a classic multidivisional enterprise: rather than using the market mechanism as a means of coordinating relations between units, salaried managers used administrative means to facilitate the flows of information and materials between manufacturing units. These manufacturing units were legally independent, and had an internal hierarchical structure that mirrored the structure of the head office.

In the initial stage of development, when the primary concern was developing manufacturing capability, the SAIC hierarchy served three critical functions.

First, the tight hierarchical structure made it possible for the head office of SAIC to maintain internal control over operations. Monthly reports from the operating divisions allowed the head office to keep apprised of enterprise operations, and control over finance and personnel allowed it direct enterprise operations. Finance was a powerful lever of control simply because the capital and assets of all enterprises within the group belonged to SAIC.

Second, the SAIC structure served as a planning base for the enterprises within the group. In terms of providing overall coordination for the auto sector, the role of SAIC overlapped with the Localization Office, and in fact it was sometimes difficult to distinguish between the two organizations: both were controlled by the municipal government and until 1995 the president of SAIC actually served concurrently as the director of the Localization Office. But while the Localization Office emphasized the broad developmental objectives in the sector, the SAIC head office was far more involved in the day-to-day operations of firms. The SAIC head office knew exactly what SVW required and it transmitted this information to the supply firms. Controlling the product mix of supply firms allowed SAIC not only to balance the growth of firms, but also ensured that there was no duplication of effort; within SAIC, each firm had a monopoly on the component that it manufactured.

Finally, the structure of SAIC facilitated learning during the development process. The hierarchical structure of management ensured that head office directives were heeded at the lower levels of the business group. Managers at supply firms reported a steady stream of 'new thinking' flowing down from SVW and the head office. Information on management and manufacturing techniques were transmitted through workshops (on techniques such as 'just-in-time' delivery and quality assurance), by means of trips that were organized to take managers to get a first-hand view of foreign auto operations (Toyota and VW), through a programme that brought retired German engineers to Shanghai to serve as short-term consultants, and by annual sessions at the SAIC Automobile Industry Training Centre. Horizontal ties proved to be just as important to supplier development as vertical, and the common ownership of firms within the SAIC group facilitated the sharing of information. The rotation of top management was one means of disseminating information throughout the group; overlapping memberships on each firm's board of directors was another. To ensure that supply firms fully utilized the resources at their disposal, both SVW and SAIC carefully monitored their development progress in a series of annual reviews. It was like having mom and dad look after you, commented several supply firm managers.

Beijing and Guangzhou: fragmented state, market-driven firms

The joint-venture projects in the municipalities of Beijing and Guangzhou, the Beijing Jeep Company (BJC) and the Guangzhou Peugeot Automobile Company (GPAC), were created during the same period as SVW, and the Chinese partners – the municipal governments – had the same objective: auto manufacturing was viewed as a lucrative sector that had the capacity to fill municipal coffers and save languishing SOEs. Over the course of a decade, however, neither city succeeded in its objective of promoting the auto sector as a core industry. In Beijing, state-owned auto supply firms continued to limp along, but in interviews none reported profits, and all complained about the complete lack of investment funds. In Guangzhou the problems were even more severe: no firms reported profits, Peugeot sold its share in the JV after a decade of frustration, some supply firms were closed down, and others were forced to shift their manufacturing to other sectors.[3] By 2003, both cities had new foreign partners (Hyundai in Beijing and Honda in Guangzhou) and radically altered localization strategies: the local governments in each locality told the new JV partners to source components from wherever the strongest suppliers were located – usually this meant Shanghai. This shift was an acknowledgement of the failure to develop a local supply base. In order to minimize their dependence on weak local suppliers, Hyundai and Honda also relied on networks of wholly foreign-owned firms.

Fragmented states. Unlike in Shanghai, the institutions and economic organizations in Beijing and Guangzhou were not structured so as to create incentives for auto sector development. Both cities used a localization tax to accumulate investment capital, but a fragmented bureaucratic structure prevented this capital from being effectively utilized.

The Guangzhou Municipal Auto Office was established in 1988 with the explicit objective of promoting the localization process at GPAC, but it was not as high in the bureaucratic hierarchy as the analogous office in Shanghai. 'We had no power to direct (*lingdao*) enterprises within other ministries', commented an official in the municipal auto office. An important consequence of this lack of control was extremely dispersed investment. Rather than concentrate on key projects, each section of the government that had auto-related industries would support its own; economies of scale were consequently extremely low and costs high.[4] The organizations governing the auto industry in Beijing were similarly fragmented.

When it is the government that is attempting to promote growth, the incentives of bureaucratic organizations must be aligned to conform with developmental objectives. The government itself must become an efficient economic organization. Not only must the state be able to ensure that investment capital reaches its intended target – protectionist policies and non-market conforming investment policies create abundant opportunities for rent-seeking – it must also be able to ensure that the capital is efficiently utilized. Local institutions in Beijing and Guangzhou were not set up to do this effectively, and the path-dependent nature of institutional change complicated the process of restructuring them.

Market-driven firms. The inability of supply firms in Beijing and Guangzhou to develop was not simply a consequence of fragmented government structures and incentives, since the corporate structures within each auto sector were equally incapable of promoting development. As in Shanghai, the supply firms in Beijing and Guangzhou were organized in corporate groups but these groups made very little investment. The problem was essentially one of property rights: all the firms were state-owned, but the head office of the corporate groups only invested in the development of supply firms that were fully-owned by the group (*quanzi qiye*) because it was from these firms that it collected profits. It neglected firms that it managed on behalf of the local government (*daiguan qiye*).

In short, these business groups appeared from the outside to be similar to Shanghai, but their internal structures led them to function in a very different manner. Rather than providing supply firms with a financial cushion during the lean years of early development, the assembly plants actually used multiple suppliers for each component as a means of using competitive pressure to force down prices. Contracts were short (one year at most), subject to frequent change, and the business for each component was split between competing firms. It was the market that governed relations between firms.

The consequences of having primarily commercial relationships between firms are not purely financial (see Helper, 1991). The suppliers – aware of the precarious nature of the relationship they had with their primary (and perhaps only) customer – were unwilling to make the investment necessary to upgrade their manufacturing capability. 'Of course we had problems,' explained a manager whose request to supply GPAC in 1986 was turned down due to poor quality standards. 'But they didn't tell us what was wrong, what their requirements were, or how to go about making necessary improvements. They simply weren't willing to work with us. Finally we said forget it.'

Conflicting interests: local and national objectives

The objective of Chinese auto sector development efforts was not simply to develop the manufacturing capability of firms in a few localities, of course, but to do so in a manner that would eventually lead to the development of internationally competitive firms. Local governments were supposed to be the means of carrying out a national industrial policy. But after a decade of development, the country was still far from this objective. In 1996, a report commissioned by the Development Research Centre of China's State Council concluded that the domestic industry was producing cars that were of inferior technology (5–15 years behind), emitted far more pollutants, and yet were still two to three times the price of comparable foreign cars. Even in Shanghai, the most competitive region in China, supply managers acknowledged that the prices paid for components were far too high relative to world markets, and their primary product, the Santana, was based on 1970s technology. Without dramatic changes, the prospects for survival in a post-WTO environment were exceedingly bleak, and two decades of painstaking development would be for naught.

The problem was that the interests of local governments did overlap with national objectives to a certain extent, but they were not identical. In fact, the same fiscal arrangements that created incentives for local governments to enthusiastically promote the development of the local auto industry, also created incentives for them to put local interests above national ones. The primacy of local interests manifested itself in both the upstream and the downstream linkages from the assembly plant. In both directions, the local governments attempted to profit from the artificially high profits that resulted from a domestic market protected from international competition, and both resulted in distorted incentives and suboptimal outcomes.

Local problems

The first, and most obvious manifestation of an overemphasis on local objectives in China, was the preponderance of local protectionism. Because of the potential for high profits in the auto sector, each locality wanted to have its own car factory. Although the factory would operate at far from efficient volumes, and quite possibly the region had neither the industrial structure nor history that was conducive to auto sector development, local protectionism allowed it to capture 'rents' which would not have been possible in an open market. The central government used tariff walls to protect the domestic market from international competition and local government used the purchasing policies of state-owned enterprises, leasing programmes, and tax policies to create advantages for local firms. The result was the most fragmented motor vehicle industry in the world. In 1995, total vehicle production in China was 1.45 million, but because this volume was spread over some 122 assembly plants, the annual average volume per firm was only 12,000 vehicles.[5] Simply put, many Chinese localities that were manufacturing cars, should not have been doing so.

A second, and somewhat more subtle form of local protectionism, involved the backward linkages from the JV assembly plants. The Chinese partner at a JV would always choose a local supplier when the option existed, not simply for the sake of convenience, but because the most critical objective from the local government's perspective was to support the development of its own firms. This strategy became a severe problem for Shanghai, the strongest auto-producing region in China in the 1990s, because it made it very difficult to lower costs.

During the first decade of development, a tightly-knit industrial structure allowed Shanghai to successfully develop the manufacturing capability of local firms; in the second decade of development, the same structure made it impossible to lower costs because the assembly plant had no means of pressuring suppliers to lower their component prices. In part this was because the assembly plant had a single supplier for the vast majority of components, but even more important were the political pressures on SAIC. The Chinese partner was wholly owned by the municipal government, and the municipal government sought to balance performance between firms and provide stable employment for workers. In stark contrast to a western corporation that seeks to cut costs, SAIC did everything possible to *avoid* downsizing during this period. It created sideline enterprises primarily for the purpose of soaking up excess labour; it avoided new technologies that would result in job losses; and it shifted workers, management, and pricing arrangements so as to help out the struggling firms. Suppliers within the SAIC group knew that they would supply SVW no matter how high their costs. As one Shanghai manager explained, 'Pricing has nothing to do with costs, it is moving money from the right pocket of SAIC to the left.' In the initial stage of development this system was not a problem, and was in fact conducive to supplier development, but as competition intensified in the late 1990s, this same system began to threaten the long-term prospects of the group.

National solutions

In an ideal world, a balance would be achieved between local governments that have the incentive to experiment with various methods of promoting industrial development and a national government that regulates competition with the domestic marketplace and forces the localities to play by the rules.[6] The fulfilment of local objectives would not come at the expense of national objectives. But the problem in China, as in so many developing countries, is that economic decentralization is the result of central government weakness, and it has proven to be extremely difficult to regulate and control local governments.

The solution has been an unusual one: the central government has, to a great extent, used foreign firms to control local governments. The central government has a great deal of leverage over the foreign firms that are desperate to gain access to the Chinese domestic market because it controls entry; local governments need the technology and management skills of foreign firms if they hope to be a top competitor in the domestic auto industry. The result has been an industrial policy of sorts, with the central government distributing foreign partners to the localities that it intends to cultivate as major players.

Rather than pay for technology through licensing – as was more the norm in Japan and Korea – the Chinese have paid for technology and managerial skills by trading access to the domestic market. With respect to the foreign partners, the central government played the MNCs off against one another. It would announce that it was going to approve one final assembly JV, and foreign firms, desperate not to be locked out of one of the last great auto markets, would claw over one another to get the contract. The bargaining process between Shanghai and General Motors (GM) was a classic example of how the central government used its leverage to access modern technology, and the cutting-edge plant clearly changed the dynamics of the industry.[7] VW responded with the Audi A6 and VW Bora in Changchun and the Passat in Shanghai; Honda introduced the Accord in Guangzhou. It was no longer possible to compete in China with outdated technology, and supply firms had to follow the lead of the assemblers. Most did so by expanding their own foreign linkages. Virtually every major supply firm within the SAIC group, for example, had a foreign partner by 2002.[8]

With respect to the localities, the central government used its regulatory control over foreign investment to distribute JV partners to centrally-sanctioned projects. Even if it could not prevent entry into the crowded sector, and did not have the means of directing firm development itself, it could bestow critical foreign partnerships to the firms that it wanted to support – an industrial policy on the cheap. Despite the high overall number of auto assemblers, by the late 1990s production was increasingly dominated by a relatively small number of major players, and inevitably the key firms were those the central government had bestowed multiple foreign partners upon.[9] By 2002, three business groups (First Auto Works, Dongfeng, and Shanghai) accounted for 57.7 per cent of total auto sector production in China.

The final contribution of increased foreign investment was to break down the barriers within localities. In effect, it served as a Trojan horse of sorts, bringing the expectations and benchmarks of the international auto industry into localities with highly protectionist instincts. The clearest manifestation of this trend was in purchasing operation in Shanghai. After Shanghai General Motors (SGM) was established, it was clear that GM expected to make purchasing decision based on a standard process of supplier evaluation and to adhere as closely as possible to a budget for every component based on the worldwide purchasing price for that part. As I have explained, SAIC usually sought to protect its own firms. Aware of both SAIC's apprehension over WTO accession and their long-term desire to become a world-class company, GM presented its own purchasing system as a model to be emulated.

The GM efforts brought results. Increasingly, there were two purchasing systems within the Shanghai supply network: the old SVW system and the new SGM system. The former was all about relationships; the latter was above-board negotiations, competition, and hard bargaining. In many cases, firms sold similar components to SVW for one price, and then at another (lower) price to SGM. SVW, of course, had no choice but to respond, and after introducing a new model of its own in 2000, it began to duplicate the SGM purchasing system. Benchmarks from abroad decreased the market distortions created by Chinese tariffs; benchmarks from other provinces decreased the power of local politics.

Conclusion

Successful auto sector development in China required that a delicate balance is maintained between multiple jurisdictions, and this balance has changed over time. In the initial state of development, the central government had to create the space for local governments to choose the most suitable means of nurturing firm development. The political and economic institutions of Shanghai, for example, were more effective in meeting the challenges of auto sector development than the institutions of either Beijing or Guangzhou. The Shanghai municipal government and a hierarchically organized business group coordinated the investment process, facilitated the transfer of technical and managerial knowledge between firms, and closely monitored the learning process. As the sector matured, however, the central government had to prevent parochial local interests from stifling competitive pressures, and foreign firms proved to be an unlikely ally. In many respects, the centre found foreign firms easier to control than its own localities.

Although the conventional wisdom is that Chinese entry into the WTO will have disastrous consequences for the Chinese auto industry, it could be exactly what is needed to counter the powerful sway of local politics. It is true that the competition facing Chinese-made cars will be severe, but the auto manufacturers will also have more flexibility than they have enjoyed in the past. Because the dramatic decreases in tariff barriers are now enshrined in international agreements that can only be changed at the risk of a tremendous loss in national prestige, the voices within China that have been arguing for more open competition will increasingly be able to prevail over the more parochial views of many local officials. Rather than being forced to do business with local firms for political reasons, assembly plants will be able to do business with whatever suppliers provide quality components, good service, and low prices. Proximity to the assembly plant and established ties may give an initial advantage to local suppliers in regions such as Shanghai – particularly given the relative strength of the supply network – but pressure from firms in other regions – and countries – will mean that geography will only get them so far.

As happens in all places that become increasingly integrated in the global economy, it may become more difficult to identify the cars rolling off the

Shanghai assembly lines as being uniquely 'Made in Shanghai' – or even 'Made in China' – but this is an outcome that is preferable to investing scarce resources in firms that are incapable of surviving without the support of local politicians. As many parents realize, development requires a delicate mixture of nurturing and discipline, and it is not always an easy balance to achieve. Shanghai proved to be very effective at the former, but for the latter, it needs some help from outside.

16

The Indian Passenger Car Industry and the South Asian Market: Global Auto Companies' Struggles in India

Yeong-Hyun Kim

Introduction

The 1991 liberalization opened up many sectors of the Indian economy to global capital flows, and its auto industry has attracted the bulk of foreign investment after it was deregulated in 1993. Ten of the world's leading auto companies have set up production facilities for passenger cars in India since deregulation. Over the past decade the Indian passenger car industry has witnessed a substantial increase in production, a wave of new models, and the inflows of global components suppliers. The decline of local companies was anticipated, and, indeed, some have seen their market shares shrink drastically in the past decade. The combined effects of these changes have led to a fundamental and extensive restructuring of the Indian passenger car industry, of which previous restructuring dates back to the early 1980s when Maruti Udyog, a joint venture of the Indian government and the Suzuki Motor Company, emerged as a dominant player in the market.

However, the recent restructuring in India does not match well the familiar story of large auto companies triumphing over small, incompetent local companies that is drawn on in much of the globalization literature currently available. Many of the ten global carmakers who have invested in India have been in trouble with the country's stagnant market, underdeveloped supplier base, regulative auto policies, and poor infrastructures, to name a few. In addition, their inability to export quantities of cars to neighbouring markets in South Asia has led to an overcapacity problem in the Indian passenger car industry. Indeed, two of the ten global firms have closed down their production lines, and others have been rumoured to be likely to follow these unfortunate examples. It has been widely known that global auto firms adapt to distinctive local settings rather than simply transferring their management practices to local operations (Abo, 1994; Boyer et al., 1998; Humphrey et al., 2001; Lung et al., 1999). Indeed, leading auto firms' ability and willingness to be adaptive to local differences have been recognized as a clear indicator of their success at the global level (Schlie and Yip, 2000). The aforementioned local conditions in India, however, seem to have neutralized many of the newly entered global auto companies' advantages and adapting efforts.

This chapter examines global auto companies' struggles for survival – let alone success – in India. Particular attention is paid to the small, stagnant passenger car market in India and, in a broader sense, the South Asian region. With its large population and emerging economy, India was expected to develop a fast-growing market for passenger cars, which was one of the reasons why the ten companies decided to invest in the country in the first place. However, its domestic market has yet to take off. Given the fact that most South Asian countries have been economically weak and/or politically at odds with India, the global auto firms' efforts to expand their sales outlets into the wider region have yielded, few tangible benefits. As a result, the lack of efficiency in production has become endemic for almost all of these auto firms and their components suppliers.

In what follows, I briefly review the history of restructuring in the Indian passenger car industry, which was highly regulated by its government before deregulation. I then examine the major reasons why ten of the global auto firms decided to invest in India and the problems that they have encountered in their Indian operations. Particular attention is paid to the country's overcrowded passenger car market, where a double-digit market share seems impossible to achieve for most of the newly entered global companies. Following this, I take a closer look at the auto companies' efforts to export their products to neighbouring markets in South Asia. The fifth – and final – section concludes with the summary of research findings and implications for future studies on global auto companies' operations in emerging markets with low demand and poor neighbours.

Primary information on the passenger car industry and global auto companies' operations in India was collected from two sources. One data source includes the Automotive Component Manufacturers Association of India (ACMA) and Society of Indian Automobile Manufacturers (SIAM). These two institutions provided statistical data on the annual production, sales, and export of passenger cars in India. The other source includes personal interviews and follow-up email exchanges with managers in global auto companies' operations in India for the information on individual companies' adaptations and struggles in India. Among the ten global companies investing in India, Fiat India at Mumbai, Honda SIEL India at Delhi, and Ford India and Hyundai India at Chennai were selected for personal interviews which were conducted between 2000 and 2002. In addition to these data sources, a series of semi-structured interviews with government officials in Department of Heavy Industries at Delhi helped collect information on India's auto policies after deregulation.

The re-restructuring of the Indian passenger car industry

The history of the passenger car industry in India is roughly divided into four phases (see Figure 16.1). The first phase started in the late 1920s when

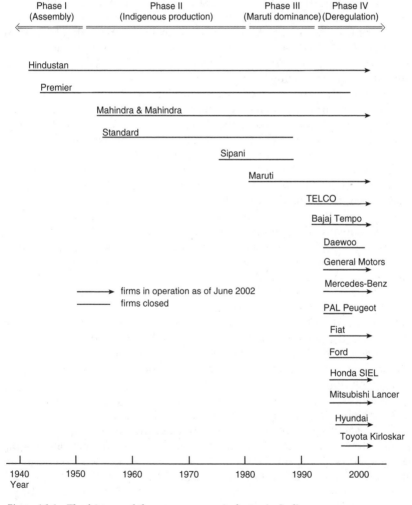

Figure 16.1 The history of the passenger car industry in India

foreign companies – namely General Motors and Ford – set up assembly plants in Mumbai (Bombay), Kolkata (Calcutta), and Chennai (Madras). Later, several local companies, including Hindustan Motors, Mahindra & Mahindra, Premier Automobiles, and Standard Motor Products, entered the industry to replace the foreign assemblers.

After more than two decades of assembly, the Indian auto industry finally started indigenous production in 1952. During the second phase – which lasted for three decades – the Indian passenger car industry made little progress in production volume and technology. The lack of dynamics during this phase was attributed mainly to the Indian government's auto policies, such as capacity licensing, entry restriction, foreign exchange allocation, restriction on foreign collaboration both in technology and finance, and price control (Mohanty et al., 1994; Narayana, 1989). The Economist Intelligence Unit (1994; 119) notes that the Indian passenger car industry during this period was 'stagnated by stifling controls, imposed production limitations, and crippling taxes'.

The third phase was marked by the entry and subsequent dominance of Maruti Udyog in the passenger car market in the 1980s (Chatterjee, 1990; D'Costa, 1995; Venkataramani, 1990). Maruti was initially set up by Sanjay Gandhi, the second son of then Prime Minister Indira Gandhi, in the mid-1970s. The company sought to manufacture fuel-efficient, low-cost, indigenous 'people's cars', but it was soon plagued by various political scandals (Mainstream Publications, 1977). After Sanjay Gandhi's accidental death, Maruti became nationalized in 1980, but it continued to underperform. In 1981 the Indian government decided to form a joint venture with the Suzuki Motor Company of Japan for financial and technological collaboration.

Although Suzuki was not a major carmaker either in Japan or in international markets, it made an immediate impact on the Indian auto industry that was at this time woefully behind international standards (Chatterjee, 1990; Gulyani, 2001). The industry's annual production volume grew from 59,135 units in 1981 to 192,069 in 1992, and most of this growth was achieved by Maruti. The company captured more than half of the passenger car market in the second half of the 1980s and around 80 per cent in the early 1990s. Maruti's role in changing the landscape of the Indian automobile industry and its components industry in the 1980s was considered to be a 'revolution' (Venkataramani, 1990).

The fourth – and final – phase started with the comprehensive deregulation of India's once highly regulated auto industry. The Indian economy faced a massive balance-of-payment crisis in 1991. After the International Monetary Fund (IMF) bailed it out, the Indian government, under the guidance of the IMF and World Bank, was forced to liberalize and deregulate its economy in an unprecedented manner (Joshi and Little, 1996; World Bank, 1996). Like most other manufacturing industries, the auto components sector was deregulated in 1991, and the automotive vehicles sector was deregulated in 1993 (Mohnot, 2001; Ohri, 1997). The deregulation of the auto vehicle sector allowed two local firms that had been specialized in light commercial vehicles, namely TELCO and Bajaj Tempo, to enter the passenger car industry. In addition, foreign auto firms, which had long been denied by the government's preventive licensing procedures, were now allowed to invest freely. Given the apparent potential, India attracted ten of the world's major carmakers shortly after deregulation. These included Daewoo, Mercedes-Benz (later renamed Daimler-Chrysler), Fiat, General Motors Opel, Ford, Honda, Hyundai, Mitsubishi, PSA Peugeot Citroën, and Toyota. Most of these companies had their plants located close to one of the three traditional auto manufacturing centres, namely Delhi, Mumbai and Chennai (Figure 16.2). While Delhi's emergence as an auto centre was greatly helped by Maruti's success,

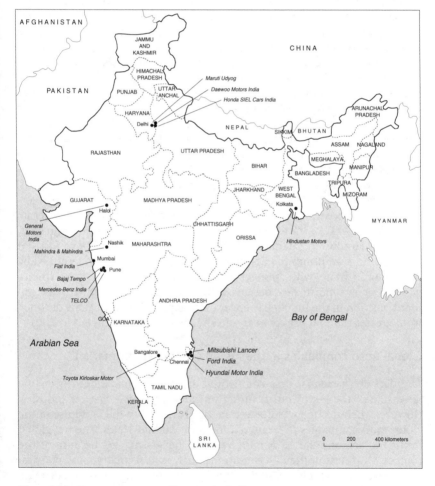

Figure 16.2   Passenger car manufactures in India

Mumbai and Chennai alike housed firms for light commercial vehicles and auto components.

Although the Indian government did not require foreign auto companies to associate with local partners, most of them started by entering into joint ventures with Indian firms (Table 16.1). Hyundai Motor Company, a South Korean carmaker, was the only company to start its Indian operation as a wholly owned subsidiary. However, most other companies seem to have followed Hyundai India's ownership model by increasing their shares in joint ventures over the years, as numerous managerial tensions between foreign and local partners in the joint venture have emerged (interview data, 2001). The total number of carmakers, foreign and local ones combined, peaked at 16 in the late 1990s, but with three companies (Daewoo India, PAL Peugeot, and Premier Automobiles) having closed down since, 13 companies are currently competing in the Indian passenger car market.[1] These global companies' local operations have significantly elevated India's passenger car production volume over the past decade. In fiscal year 2001–02, 13 carmakers together produced 687,784 units, compared with 243,869 units in 1993, when the passenger car sector was deregulated for the first time.

These new entrants have prompted the '*re*-restructuring' of the Indian automobile industry after Maruti had done the first round of restructuring back in the 1980s. They have introduced new models with much more stylish designs and sophisticated functions than the ones that Indian consumers used to see. They have also introduced a variety of auto financing systems to expand their consumer bases. A number of components manufacturers with global reach have invested in India to serve their assemblers' local operations, and they have factored in the restructuring of the assembler–supplier relations in the Indian auto industry (Humphrey and Salerno, 2000). In the wake of the ten global companies' investment, local companies, including Hindustan, Mahindra & Mahindra, and Premier, have lost out once again. In addition, the dominance of Maruti has been undermined by those new entrants with stronger international presences, better technologies and more sophisticated designs. Although Maruti still maintains a dominant position in the Indian passenger car industry, its market share declined from greater than 80 per cent early in the 1990s to 50.1 per cent in 2001.

Global auto companies in the Indian passenger car market

The decline of smaller, less competitive local firms has indeed been the downside of the recent restructuring of the Indian passenger car industry. However, their decline was not automatically linked to the rapid rise of the global auto companies that entered India in the mid-1990s. The ten global firms' Indian subsidiaries or joint ventures have struggled because of the country's business-unfriendly conditions, such as its regulative auto policies, underdeveloped supplier base, small and stagnant market, and inadequate

Table 16.1 Global auto companies' investment after deregulation

Global companies	Local partners	Foreign equity (%)	Establishment	Production capacity (units)	Changes in foreign stake
Daewoo*	DCM	51	1994	72,000	Daewoo to 91.6%
DaimlerChrysler	TELCO	76	1994	9,000	DaimlerChrysler to 100%
Fiat	Premier Automobile	51	1995	60,000	Fiat to 97%
Ford	Mahindra & Mahindra	50	1995	50,000	Ford to 92%
General Motors	Hindustan Motors	50	1994	25,000	General Motors to 100%
Honda	SIEL	60	1995	30,000	Honda to 99%
Hyundai	—	100	1996	120,000	
Mitsubishi	Hindustan Motors	10	1995	30,000	
Peugeot*	Premier Automobile	32	1994	60,000	
Toyota	Kirloskar	74	1997	50,000	Toyota to 80%

Note: * Daewoo India and PAL Peugeot became defunct in 2001 and 1999, respectively.

Sources: Compiled from AutoIndia.com (2001) and interviews with local auto industry analysts.

infrastructures (Kim, 2001). It is true that most emerging markets tend to pose similar problems to global auto firms problems (Humphrey et al., 2001), but India has been one of the more difficult locations for multinational firms. In my interviews with managers in four of the global companies who have invested in India, the lack of demand for passenger cars, in both the domestic market and the regional market, stood out as one of the most challenging problems that they had suffered. This section examines the ten global firms' market failure in India, while the section that follows examines that in the South Asian regional market.

As stated earlier, the raw potential of India's large population, along with the new opening of its untapped market, served as a major attraction for those ten assemblers to the country (interview data, 2002). A number of market forecasts made shortly after deregulation forecast that India was one of the fastest-growing markets in the developing world (*Automotive News*, 1995; Chrysler, 1995; Economist Intelligence Unit, 1994 and 1995; Knibb, 1997). Its sheer size of population led many auto experts and journalists to estimate that there would be millions of potential car buyers in the near future. This prospect of high growth rates was justified on two grounds – one is that the emergence of sizable middle class was projected, which was clearly an encouraging factor for auto firms (Chrysler, 1995; Vachani, 1997). An unprecedented explosion of demand for cars would be highly likely to occur in India, according to these forecasts, if these middle-class households, with help from newly created auto financing systems, traded up from two or three wheelers to passenger cars. An *Automotive News* article (1998: 26) stated that

> According to projections making the rounds of Western auto capitals following the 1991 economic liberalization program of then-Prime Minister Narasimha Rao, India's 'middle class' numbered in the scores of millions – some said as high as 350 million – all with rising incomes and large savings. And all, according to the prevailing wisdom, were thirsting for the chance to buy the latest American, Japanese or European cars.

The other is that India's well-known uneven income distribution was viewed as a positive factor in securing a substantial demand for passenger cars (Abrenica, 1998; Dargay and Gately, 1999). Although the country's average living standards had been amongst the lowest in the world, according to this account, its upper and upper-middle class, who could afford cars, would still be large enough to support all of the new entrants in the deregulated passenger car industry. An article in *Business Week* (Kripalani, 1996: 47) predicted that

> At least 2 million Indian households can buy a car with six month's wages. By 2000, provided economic growth is maintained at 6% to 7% a year, demand for passenger cars could reach 2 million units annually,

some estimate. Those are the numbers that keep foreign investors plugging away, hopeful their day will come.

It might not be the case that all ten global carmakers believed in these plainly out-of-reach projections about the Indian passenger car market when they decided to make some investment. Some might have invested to simply establish an early presence in this emerging market so that they can 'be in place and ready to grab a slice of the cake when it should eventually take off' (Schlie and Yip, 2000: 351). Given the strong presence of Japanese carmakers in the Southeast Asian region, India might have been considered to be a vital market, next to China, that American and European companies should focus on at the start of their Asian operations (Abrenica, 1998).

Along with its huge market potential, the Indian government's regulation of the import of completely built units (CBU) was another important reason why global auto manufacturers set up full-fledged assembly plants in India. In contrast to China, India did not place any limits on foreign ownership. Instead, it imposed a punitive tariff rate of 132 per cent on imported cars at the time of deregulation, which effectively aimed both at banning the import of foreign cars and at pressing global firms to develop their supplier bases in India. The high tariff rates on finished automotive components, ranging between 40 and 70 per cent in the 1990s, also forced these foreign companies to source components from locally-based suppliers.[2]

Whether or not the initial projections were unrealistically optimistic, the entrance of the ten global carmakers promptly made the Indian passenger car market very crowded. Local companies, including Hindustan, Mahindra & Mahindra, and Premier, have watched their market shares dwindle over the past decade, and Premier was indeed put out of business late in 1999. Meanwhile, the closing of Peugeot PAL – the Premier and Peugeot joint venture – might have been an early indication that global companies may not be immune to failure either in this crowded market. Following Daewoo India's phasing out of production lines in the middle of its parent company's bankruptcy in South Korea in 2001, there are currently 13 carmakers producing passenger cars or sports utility vehicles in this country. The market would have been less crowded for these companies to compete in, if the demand for cars had grown as fast as many had expected.

As Table 16.2 shows, Maruti was the only firm to sell more than 100,000 cars in 2001, despite the fact that its market share has declined since deregulation. The globally known auto firms have sold much smaller numbers than they initially projected. GM India, for example, sold a mere 8,010 cars, while Ford India sold 15,323 in 2001, although their annual production capacities were 25,000 and 100,000 units, respectively. The lack of efficiency in production has become endemic amongst all of these global companies' Indian subsidiaries and their components suppliers. The highly advertised 'burgeoning middle class', if there was any, has not yet been linked to

Table 16.2   Passenger car sales in India, 1981–2001

Manufacturers*	Sales (units) 2001	Market shares (%)				
		2001	1995/96	1990	1985	1981
Indian firms						
Maruti Udyog**	348,969	50.1	67.0	53.5	40.1	
TELCO	79,990	11.5	2.6			
Mahindra & Mahindra	57,188	8.2	13.9	13.9	16.9	22.2
Hindustan Motors	17,803	2.5	6.7	12.4	19.1	42.0
Bajaj Tempo	4,933	0.7	0.0			
Premier Automobiles***			4.9	20.2	23.9	35.9
Global firms' subsidiaries						
Hyundai Motor India	83,937	12.0				
Toyota Kirloskar Motor	28,016	4.0				
Daewoo Motors India***	21,573	3.1	2.2			
Ford India	15,323	2.2				
Fiat India	13,520	1.9				
Honda SIEL Cars India	10,229	1.5				
General Motors India	8,010	1.2				
Mitsubishi Lancer	2,452	0.9				
DaimlerChrysler India	1,271	0.2	0.1			
PAL Peugeot***			2.5			
Total	691,836	100.0	100.0	100.0	100.0	100.0

Notes

* Sipani and Standard Motors each held insignificant market shares in the 1980s.
** Joint venture of the Indian government and Suzuki.
*** Premier Automobiles and PAL Peugeot closed in 1999, while Daewoo Motors India closed in 2001.

Sources: Compiled from ACMA (2000), Narayana (1989: 217); and data provided by Society of Indian Automobile Manufacturers.

a demand for passenger cars. Middle-class Indian households have instead been content with the purchase of home electronics, such as fans and televisions. A huge market potential might still exist, but few seem to know when it will materialize – or even *whether* it will eventually materialize. Unless neighbouring markets in South and Southeast Asia become highly fond of 'made-in-India' cars, 13 companies still seem too many to compete in this small market.

Exports to the South Asian market

The lack of demand for passenger cars in the domestic market might have been less devastating for the global auto companies' Indian operations if sizable markets had been found in neighbouring countries in South Asia. The

South Asian region consists of seven countries, including Bangladesh, Bhutan, India, the Maldives, Nepal, Pakistan, and Sri Lanka. These countries, with the exception of the Maldives and Sri Lanka, belong to the low-income group of the World Bank's classification of economies, which is referred to the poorest of the poor with a gross national income per capita of US$755 or less in 2001 (World Bank, 2003). This severe, prevalent poverty has certainly limited the region's demand for passenger cars, although South Asia is one of the most populous regions in the world (Table 16.3).

Alongside the lack of purchasing power as a result of the low living standards, the lack of any substantial history of economic cooperation between India and its neighbouring countries has made it very difficult for the global auto companies to expand their markets into this wider region. Numerous political tensions between the countries in the region – most recently the India–Pakistan nuclear crisis and the India–Bangladesh border clash in 2002 – have prevented South Asian countries from developing any sorts of long-term economic relationship among themselves.

Indeed, the seven countries agreed to form the South Asian Association for Regional Cooperation (SAARC) in 1985, hoping to increase international trade among member countries and, consequently, to improve their economic status in the world (Pigato et al., 1997; Shome, 2001; United Nations, 1999). This agreement developed into the South Asian Preferential Trading Arrangement (SAPTA) in 1995, as the seven countries wanted to keep up with more advanced regional blocks in Europe, North America, and Southeast Asia. However, this trading agreement has not yet led to a significant increase in intra-regional trade of South Asia. The SAPTA has hosted annual preferential trade negotiations among member countries ever since, yet the bulk of the exports from individual members is still headed for developed countries outside the region. India's major export destinations in 2001, for example, included the United States, the United Kingdom, Hong Kong, Germany, and Japan in that order. While the United States has been its

Table 16.3 Economies in South Asia

	Population, 2001 (million)	*GNI per capita, 2001 (US$)*	*Imports from India, 2001 (US$ million)*
Bangladesh	133.4	370	1,087
Bhutan	0.8	590	16
India	1,016.0	460	—
Maldives	0.3	2,040	46
Nepal	23.6	250	434
Pakistan	141.5	420	219
Sri Lanka	19.6	830	547

Sources: IMF, World Bank.

number one trading partner to date, the six South Asian neighbours have combined to account for a mere 5.4 per cent of India's total exports and 0.9 per cent of its imports (IMF, 2002).

The limited trade volume between India and its neighbours has been mirrored by the country's passenger car exports in the region. The passenger car industry in India has never been known for exporting quantities of cars to international markets (Table 16.4), while industries of chassis, auto rickshaws and scooters have found markets in developing countries in Asia and Africa. In fiscal year 2001–02, the 14 auto companies (comprising five Indian firms and nine global ones) combined to export a mere 53,656 cars, earning much less than US$100 million. Up until the mid-1990s, when some of the global auto companies had only just started their operations in India, Maruti had been the only exporter in the passenger car sector. Maruti, under the brand name of Suzuki, exported a small number of entry-level models to several European countries, including the Netherlands, the United Kingdom, Finland, Sweden, Greece, and Italy (Maruti Suzuki, 2003).

Most of the newly entered global auto companies joined Maruti in exporting cars in the late 1990s when they came under pressure to balance their foreign exchanges under the Memorandum of Understanding with the Indian government. These efforts led to a small increase in the exports of passenger cars from India in the second half of the 1990s. The Indian passenger car industry recorded a big jump in exports in 2001–02, when Ford India managed to export a relatively large number of CKDs for the Ikon, a model designed specifically for emerging markets. Although this company has not yet emerged as a leading player in the Indian market, Ford India is the number one exporter among the 13 currently operating auto companies in India.

Table 16.4   India's passenger car exports*

	Exports (units)
1992–93	16,029
1993–94	18,835
1994–95	22,933
1995–96	31,838
1996–97	39,645
1997–98	32,993
1998–99	28,122
1999–00	28,419
2000–01	27,035
2001–02	53,656

Note: * Data collected for the fiscal year ending 31 March.

Source: Society of Indian Automobile Manufacturers.

Accounting for more than half of the car exports from India, Ford India plans to continue its focus on overseas markets (interview data, 2002). However, its export destinations have been very limited, because Mexico and South Africa have been the only two overseas markets for its made-in-India CKDs. In 2002 Ford India announced its plan to export CKDs and components to Brazil and China, but South Asian markets were not on their short list to pursue.

Compared to Ford India, Hyundai Motor India has developed more diversified – and somewhat regionally oriented – export strategies. The company started exporting cars in late 1999, when the company managed to ship out a mere 20 cars. Pressurized by both the Indian government's export obligations and a desperate need for economies of scale, the company sought to develop dealer networks in markets overseas. It has since become the third major exporter in the Indian passenger car industry behind Ford India and Maruti. Hyundai exported 6,092 cars in 2001, and South Asia (excluding India) absorbed only 382 cars, accounting for 6.3 per cent of the company's total exports. Its major export destinations included Indonesia, Algeria, Nepal, and Morocco. According to a series of interviews conducted with Hyundai Motor India, the company continues to work to increase its sales volume in regional markets. Although Hyundai is well aware of the low level of demand in South Asian countries, noted a marketing manager, the company believes that its sales volume should be much higher than the current figures, which range from 0 in Pakistan, Bhutan, and the Maldives, to 10 in Sri Lanka, and 340 in Nepal.

Apart from Ford, Maruti, and Hyundai, few auto firms in India have been able to export any substantial volume of cars. The Department of Heavy Industries, which is in charge of the passenger car industry, projects that the industry's export turnover should be doubled over the next four years (United Nations ESCAP, 2002), but it would be highly unlikely to meet this high expectation unless South Asian countries with large populations, such as Pakistan, absorb a significant portion of India's passenger car production.

Pakistan reports the production of 39,573 passenger cars in the fiscal year 2000–01 (United Nations ESCAP, 2002), but its production is restricted to assembling imported CKDs rather than manufacturing cars with locally-sourced components. The Pakistani market has long been dominated by Japanese carmakers, such as Suzuki, Toyota, and Honda in order of market share. However, these companies have imported CKDs from their Southeast Asian operations rather than Indian ones. In addition, the models that they have introduced to Pakistani consumers are very different from those produced in India. For example, Toyota's Pakistani operation, named the Indus Motor Company, has marketed the Corolla, while its Indian joint venture has produced the Qualis, a sports utility vehicle. The fact that the Pakistani car market is more or less integrated into the Southeast Asian market highlights the isolation of the Indian auto industry in the region. Alongside the political tension between the two countries, this makes it even more difficult for the Indian passenger car industry to find markets among its neighbours.

While car exports to overseas markets, particularly South Asian markets, have been less than phenomenal, the auto components sector has shown a comparatively impressive performance in exports in the past decade. Since the 1991 deregulation, the sector's export has grown at an average annual growth rate of 9.4 per cent in US dollar terms and of 29.1 per cent in Indian rupee terms (ACMA, 2001). In fiscal year 2000–01, auto suppliers' export earning reached US$417 million, although this figure included exports of parts for other vehicle types, such as scooters, tractors, and auto rickshaws.

This success of the auto components industry can be attributed to a few related factors, based on my interviews with managers in the four auto companies, industry analysts, and government officials. Firstly, large global auto components manufacturers that followed their assemblers to India, such as Delphi India and Visteon India, have ensured that their Indian operations have specialized in producing a limited number of items for global markets. Visteon India, for example, recorded an export earning of US$75 million during the fiscal year 2001–02, while only two items – namely the alternator and the starter motor – combined to account for approximately 90 per cent of its income (interview data, 2002). Secondly, those carmakers that have not been able to export quantities of CBUs or CKDs have focused instead on exporting auto parts. This has been the case for many companies, including Fiat India, Honda SIEL, and DaimlerChrysler India, because they have been required to balance their imports and exports. In an effort to neutralize foreign exchange, a large volume of 'genuine parts' have been exported to their operations around the world. Thirdly, and finally, the Indian auto components industry in general has been significantly upgraded through technical and financial collaborations with foreign companies over the past decade. As a result, local suppliers as well as global suppliers' joint ventures have become very competitive in international markets, and their improved competitiveness has led to a steady increase in auto components exports from India (Kim, 2002).

Conclusion

This chapter has examined global auto companies' struggles for survival in India, a market with a population of more than one billion but with low levels of demand for passenger cars and politically-distant, impoverished neighbours. Ten of the world's leading carmakers crowded into this market soon after the Indian government announced deregulation in 1993. At that time India was hailed as one of the fastest-growing markets in the developing world, and most global carmakers wanted access to it. The entrance of the ten global auto companies has caused an extensive restructuring of the country's passenger car industry, which had long been protected and regulated. In general local firms have lost a large proportion of their market shares, while some of them have been phasing out their production lines.

The decline of local firms, however, has not necessarily coincided with a rapid rise of all of the global carmakers' operations in India. To date, they have achieved much less success than had initially been expected. Indeed, many of them have experienced a great deal of difficulty in their Indian operations. Based on interviews with managers in global auto companies' local operations, a wide range of problems, reflecting India's economic conditions and regulative government policies, have posed them daunting challenges, but low demand in the market has been a most challenging condition that they have encountered in India. Their market failure has resulted in inefficiency in production throughout the country's passenger car industry and auto components industry. Their chances to expand markets into neighbouring countries in South Asia has been extremely limited, as most countries in the region are equally impoverished. To make matters worse, frequent political tensions between India and its neighbours have slowed down talks on regional economic cooperation, such as the SAPTA.

Although local conditions in emerging markets have posed formidable challenges for global auto companies, as those in India have, companies have managed to overcome uncertainly and adversity in Eastern Europe, Latin America, and Southeast Asia. The evidence from the ten global carmakers' operations in India, however, indicates that their abilities to dominate, transform, and/or adapt to local conditions cannot be assumed in all other emerging markets. Given the constraints in the domestic market and in the regional market, the eight global carmakers' local subsidiaries alike, with two already out of business, will continue to struggle for their survival, let alone to achieve large market shares and profits.

Notes

1 Introduction: In Search of a Viable Automobile Space

1. The cumulative number of bilateral investment treaties for instance quadrupled from less than 500 in 1990 to around 2000 in the year 2000 (UNCTAD, 2001: 7). Likewise bilateral treaties on taxation increased threefold (ibid.).
2. With one notable exception: Switzerland.
3. Chapter 2 will tackle this problem further by looking at the outcome of regional integration agreements for the actual trade and investment patterns. On the basis of these outcomes (not on the intentions of governments), regions will be labelled as more 'open' or more 'closed'.
4. Figure 1.2 excludes around 14 more modest RIAs in the Caribbean, the Andes and Central America, the Middle East, West Africa and the Pacific.
5. Except for the bilateral free trade agreement with Israel, which is matched by parallel deals with Mexico and Canada. The political motives of this agreement make it a very separate case. The United States is also negotiating a bilateral agreement with Jordan for comparable reasons.

2 The Faster Lane of Regionalism

1. This chapter is a shorter version of a much more extensive contribution, including also the 'go-it-alone' countries contained in this book. The original article can be obtained from: rtulder@fbk.eur.nl. The views expressed in this chapter are personal. Valuable input come from Fabienne Fortanier, Stefanie ten Napel, Didier Campion, Alan Muller and Marlies Overbeeke.
2. A distinct other meaning of 'open regionalism' is the question of open access: whether any country willing to abide by the rules of the RIA may join (World Bank, 2001: 99). Leading RIAs like the European Community, ASEAN or SADC have experienced an increasing membership, whereas Mercosur has a number of associated members and NAFTA is negotiating whether or not to admit new Latin American countries. In that sense all RIAs at the moment are relatively open, although no new entrant has yet received easy access to any RIA. As such all RIAs can equally be considered relatively closed.
3. Under the WTO Safeguards Agreement, members had to phase out existing arrangements within a period not exceeding four years, but they had the ability to retain one such measure for a period not extending the end of 1999. The automobile VRA between the EU and Japan was the one chosen for elimination under the longer deadline and it was effectively terminated on 31 December 1999.
4. Within the EU, motor vehicle distribution must conform to specific legislation as a condition of its exemption from anti-competitive proceedings. The regulation is known as the Block Exemption Regulation on the Selective and Exclusive Distribution of Cars, which was renewed in 1995 and extended until September 2002. This regulation seeks to safeguard consumers' access to vehicle and parts supply in any EU member state at favourable terms. It provides dealers with enhanced freedom to acquire additional franchises and to resist the imposition of sales targets by manufacturers. Although the franchise agreement can provide for

exclusive geographical zones, it is prohibited for dealers to reject sales to a consumer who is a resident of another EU member state – the so-called prohibition against parallel imports.

5. The European Commission has sanctioned and imposed hefty fines against Volkswagen in January 1998 (90 million euro) and the Dutch importer of Opel cars in July 2000 (43 million euro) for serious infringement of the competition law for having obstructed the proper operation of the Single Market. In July 2000, the fine against Volkswagen, although reduced, was upheld by a decision of the European Court of First Instance.

6. Japanese vehicle manufacturers which had invested significantly in Canada complained that they did not benefit from the same tariff exemption as the vehicle manufacturers grandfathered under the Auto Pact (Ford, GM, Daimler-Chrysler, Volvo and GM-Suzuki) which were able to import duty free some vehicles (Jaguars, Saabs and Isuzus).

7. NAFTA's automotive rules of origin provide for at least 50 per cent of a light vehicle's net cost (excluding cost of royalties, sales promotion, packaging and shipping, and limiting the cost of interest) must be of value originating in North America for the period 1994–97. From 1998 through 2001, this value will increase to 56 per cent and in 2002 it will reach 62.5 per cent. All other vehicles must meet a requirement of 50 per cent for the 1994–97 period, 55 per cent between 1998 and 2001 and 60 per cent thereafter.

8. National content requirement is established at 34 per cent between 1994 and 1998 and it will be reduced by one percentage point each following year to 29 per cent in 2003, and eliminated in 2004. Automotive manufacturers are required to achieve trade balancing requirements established as a percentage of the value of direct and indirect imports of auto parts which manufacturers incorporate into their production in Mexico for sale in Mexico.

9. Mexico has granted a delay of four years for implementing this provisions in order to facilitate adjustment and rationalization within the accreditation sector.

10. The extra-regional import ratio is equal to 100 minus the intra-regional import ratio for the region concerned.

3 Multinational Carmakers' Regional Strategies

1. This chapter is based on the results of the first and the second GERPISA international research programmes (Boyer and Freyssenet, 2002; Freyssenet and Lung, 2000). Michel Freyssenet has been co-director of these programmes, with Robert Boyer (*Emergence of New Industrial Models*, 1993–97) and Yannick Lung (*Between Globalization and Regionalization: the internationalization of the auto industry*, 1997–2000). The authors have largely benefited from the debates within the international network, but they remain responsible for any errors.

2. Carmakers' international strategies are analysed in depth in two collective GERPISA volumes edited by Freyssenet, Shimizu and Volpato (2003a and 2003b).

4 The Dynamics of Regional Integration in the European Car Industry

1. Source: GATT/OMC, CCFA.
2. Current data are available at the European Commission website: http://europa.eu.int/comm/competition/car_sector/distribution/
3. Available at: http://europa.eu.int/comm/competition/car_sector/price_diffs/

7   NAFTA: The Process of Regional Integration of Motor Vehicle Production

1. This chapter is based on a previous long paper presented by Carrillo, Hinojosa and Waldman (2001). The author is grateful for the valuable comments of Yannick Lung, Susan Helper and Jorge Alonso, as well as the assistance of Humberto Garcia. CONACYT and El Colegio de Mexico supported the present study.
2. In addition, socialized health care and pensions led to big savings as these costs grew in the United States.
3. 1999 alone saw a merger between Daimler-Benz and Chrysler, the acquisition of Volvo by Ford and a global alliance between Nissan and Renault.
4. Besides this core, there are four areas that contain significant numbers of firms in all tiers: Southern California, the Northeast; the mid-Atlantic and the horseshoe-shaped belt around southern Lake Michigan.
5. SIC change to NAICS as part of the NAFTA homologation statistics process (*2002 NAICS codes*).

10   Recreating an Automobile Space by Regional Integration: The CIS Perspective

1. Armenia, Azerbaijan, Belarus, Estonia, Georgia, Kazakhstan, Kyrgyzstan, Latvia, Lithuania, Moldova, Russia, Turkmenistan, Ukraine and Uzbekistan.
2. The Financial System of the Russian Federation. Banking. http://www.russian embassy.org, 21 March 2000.
3. Targeting seven countries: Argentina, Brazil, China, India, Poland, Russia and Turkey.

11   The Limits to Regionalism: The Automotive Industry in the Southern African Development Community

1. For perspectives on regional integration in southern Africa see Kalenga (2000), Lewis (2001) and McCarthy (1999).
2. South Africa is also part of the long standing Southern African Customs Union with its four smaller neighbours (Table 11.1).
3. South Africa produces nearly 80 per cent of the passenger cars produced in Africa and approximately 70 per cent of the commercial vehicles. Outside of southern Africa the only other significant producers are Egypt and Morocco.
4. Indeed SADC was founded as the Southern African Development Co-ordinating Conference (SADCC) in 1980 mainly to counter the economic and political weight of apartheid South Africa in the region. At that time it comprised nine member states and of the current SADC membership excluded Congo (DRC), Mauritius, Namibia, Seychelles and South Africa.
5. See 'Trade gap with SADC widens' (*Business Report*, 19 June 2002).
6. A ceasefire was reached between the MPLA government and UNITA rebels in 2002. However, the gains from peace are yet to be realized.
7. For further detail on the history of automotive development policy see Black (1994) and Duncan (1997).
8. See Republic of South Africa (1999).
9. Local content levels range between 6 and 15 per cent consisting mainly of peripheral components (Survey data).
10. See for instance 'Avoid dumping in our domestic market and protect jobs', *The Herald*, 21 March 1997.

11. Tariffs on passenger cars were increased to between 100 and 120 per cent; to 90 per cent for commercial vehicles and to between 30 and 80 per cent for components.
12. The origins of this investment are unusual in that it resulted in part from a trade policy wrangle within the Southern African Customs Union. As a member of SACU, Botswana is subject to the provisions of the Motor Industry Development Programme. When this was introduced in 1995, Hyundai Motor Distributors had been operating a semi knocked down operation supplying vehicles to the South African market. The plant was given a temporary special concession to continue with this operation subject to moving to full CKD assembly within a specific timeframe.
13. Data on exports from South Africa in this section include other members of SACU.
14. The survey results contained in this chapter are based on interviews conducted with executives in the Zimbabwean automotive industry during 1999. For further detail see Muradzikwa (1999).
15. This is considered to be a problem by component producers exporting to African markets outside of South Africa, which to some extent constitute a natural market for Zimbabwe because of its location and more developed manufacturing sector. Producers of batteries, tyres and exhaust systems were most affected.
16. See 'SACU Position in Respect of Motor Vehicles and Components', unpublished report.
17. These are the certificates which allow exporting firms to rebate import duties.
18. Used vehicles can only be imported into South Africa under permit of which very few are issued.
19. South Africa has, for instance, played a leading role in the New Partnership for African Development (Nepad), an ambitious initiative to resolve African developmental problems in partnership with the developed world.
20. Much of the automotive industry has been excluded from the initial agreement but is to be included in follow-up negotiations.

12 Maghrebi Integration and the Automobile Industry: Past Failures and New Perspectives

1. Before its privatization, the capital of the Société Marocaine de Construction Automobile was split between the Moroccan state (38 per cent), private investment companies, private Moroccan interests, and Fiat and Peugeot. Current plans call for its complete privatization. In 2003, the state sold its stake to Renault, which took control of the company.
2. The SOMACA is involved in passenger cars (Fiat and Simca), with Berliet and Star Auto (Volvo) being involved in commercial vehicles. Renault (in 1966) and Opel and Austin (in 1969) were authorized to set up assembly lines.
3. This programme assumed the abolition of customs tariffs on CKD kits; the elimination of import duties; lower VAT rates; higher integration rates; and relatively lower sales prices for local consumers.
4. This primarily involved certain engine parts (pistons, cables, radiators, filters), components in the transmission and suspension systems, brakes, wheels, the car's body and internal fittings.
5. Since the late 1980s, a company with private and public capital (Fatia) has been in charge of producing vehicles (like the Uno) meant to be sold in the domestic market. The absence of a clear public strategy, administrative and financial

barriers and security problems – all of these factors put an end to the project. Declared bankrupt, the company awaits a purchaser.

6. Commercial trade data are taken from the Chelem-CEPII database. The automobile branch combines three categories (elements from motor vehicles, passenger cars and commercial vehicles) that integrate other means of ground transport (bicycles, motorcycles, rolling train stock).

7. The three main French carmakers have been solidly established in the Maghrebi market since the 1920s (Loubet, 2000).

14   'Avoiding the Neighbours': The National/Global Development Strategy of the Korean Automobile Industry

1. The author wishes to thank Jean-Raphael Chaponnière, Kim Do Hoon, Christian Mory and Frédérique Sachwald for their support.

2. See the first chapters of the book.

3. From 1962 to 1986, it signed 57 technical licensing agreements with 31 firms from nine countries.

4. On the early history of the industry, see Kim and Lee (1980) and Kim (1998).

5. From an index 100 in 1970 to 238 in 1979, in comparison with a 34 per cent increase in Brazil and a 13 per cent fall in Argentina (nonagricultural wages only).

6. The tax ratio was estimated between 40 and 80 per cent in 1986, depending on the car type, in comparison with 20–28 per cent in Japan and 5–8 per cent in the United States (Rennard, 1992).

7. There were 3,750 strikes and lockouts in 1987, a higher figure than the total for the ten preceding years!

8. In the eight months following the end of the Japanese car import ban, Korea has imported a total of eight cars!

9. Sturgeon and Florida (1999) estimated the rate of capacity utilization of assembly plants in Vietnam at about 8–11 per cent, on average!

10. In 1987, the cost of Hyundai's advertisement campaign in the US reached US$600 per car sold. At the same time, BMW spent US$1,000 per car and the US carmakers around US$200 per car! (*Korea Automotive Review*, October 1988).

11. Several (true) stories of flying hoods or brake failure have generated a negative brand image in the late 1980s, when the Korean car park became large in North America.

12. In 1995, Korean sales in the EU doubled to 250,000 units, due to Daewoo's massive entry on the European market, which had been delayed until that year because of its separation agreement with GM.

13. For instance, both firms shared strong ambitions in India and in China. Hyundai also had FDI projects in three other countries in which Daewoo operated – Romania, Poland and Vietnam. But the Romanian project failed and the others were blocked by their respective governments.

14. As explained above, Korean firms initially gave a low priority to East Asia because of the overcapacity already built by a large number of carmakers who tried to gain an early-mover advantage at the same time, in Thailand, Vietnam, Indonesia or China.

15. The ratio of the cash flow on interest paid fell from 1.5 in 1994 to 0.9 in 1997 for the largest Korean firms. While the country's short-term foreign debt (less than one year) grew from US$40 billion to almost US$100 billion between 1993 and 1996 (sources: French Embassy in Korea; OECD).

16. On a notification basis. The September 1998 'Foreign Capital Inducement Act' completely liberalized FDI in South Korea.

17. Renault bought 70 per cent of the company assets for US$560 million to be paid over a ten-year period.
18. The contract was signed in April 2002. Daewoo's more profitable assets were transferred to a newly created company controlled 67 per cent by GM and other partners. GM will pay US$251 million for its own stake of 42 per cent and it will assume US$573 million of Daewoo Motors' debts.
19. In 2000, Renault announced plans to take 15 per cent of the Korean market by 2005.
20. Korean cars' largest foreign markets in 1998 were: the United States, Australia, Italy, Poland, the United Kingdom, Spain, Germany, Netherlands, Canada and Greece.
21. The ASEAN nations and China, Japan, South Korea and Taiwan.
22. Chaponniere and Lautier, 1994; Lautier, 1993.
23. In terms of output.

15 Going Local: Foreign Investment, Local Development, and the Chinese Auto Sector

1. The broader study from which this chapter is drawn (Thun, forthcoming) includes two additional localities, Changchun and Wuhan, but these cases from this version were excluded from this chapter due to space restrictions (for more details, see also: Thun, 2003). Unless otherwise noted, the information in the chapter is based on interviews conducted by the author between 1996 and 2003. Over 150 interviews were conducted with firm managers (both foreign and Chinese) and government officials (both central and local).
2. These outcomes, of course, are specific to the auto sector, and the same institutions can cause problems for sectors with different characteristics. Segal and Thun (2001) analyse how local institutional structures in China effect development outcomes across sectors.
3. Although the Guangzhou Municipal auto office announced in 1992 that it planned to develop 36 key supply firms in the Guangzhou municipality, interviewees reported that only 15–20 per cent of these projects actually came to fruition. It is difficult to confirm some of this evidence from published sources, however, because auto supply firms do not release profit and loss statements and statistical yearbooks only publish aggregate figures.
4. In Guangdong province as a whole, for instance, four different cities were supporting ten different assembly operations. Total investment was almost twice as high as in Shanghai, but was dispersed across the ten assembly operations and 879 parts firms. On lack of government control see Yan Yue, ' "Guangbiao" liyi zai jie zongshu', *Shanghai Qiche Bao*, 31 May 1998, p. 11.
5. On the central government's inability to control entry in the auto sector, see Huang (2003).
6. Market-preserving federalism provides the realization of this idea in theory, if not in practice; Montinola, Qian and Weingast (1995).
7. Shanghai spent two years were spent negotiating with four prospective partners – GM, Toyota, Nissan and Ford – and then, once GM was chosen from these four, another year and half was taken to negotiate the JV agreement. At every step of the process, the negotiators used the threat of central government disapproval to gain leverage. Although people involved in the negotiations would not specify the final terms of technology transfer, they would comment that GM 'could not

have gone much further'. GM wanted to build cars in China, and it was willing to pay in order to do so.

8. Over 90 per cent of the 50-odd firms within the group were JVs, and those that remained 100 per cent SOE manufactured relatively minor parts (such as springs).

9. 'Shuzihua Zhongguo Qiche' [Statistics for the Chinese Auto Sector], Zhongguo Qiche Bao [China Auto Daily], 7 January 2003, p. 3.

16   The Indian Passenger Car Industry and the South Asian Market: Global Auto Companies' Struggle in India

1. PAL Peugeot and Premier Automobiles stopped their production lines in late 1999, while Daewoo Motors India closed down in 2001. Meanwhile, Skoda, Volkswagen's Czech operation, started exporting a limited number of passenger cars to the Indian market in late 2001.

2. Through several rounds of negotiations with the World Trade Organization, however, quantitative restrictions and tariffs on imported CBUs, completely-knocked-down (CKD) kits and auto components have been significantly relaxed and lowered in recent years.

References

Abe, A. (2000) 'Different sectors, different story of globalization – Japanese automobile and banking industries', International Studies Association, 41st Annual Convention, Los Angeles.

Abo, T. (ed.) (1994) *Hybrid Factory: the Japanese Production System in the United States*, New York: Oxford University Press.

Abrenica, J.V. (1998) 'The Asian automotive industry: assessing the roles of state and market in the age of global competition', *Asian-Pacific Economic Literature*, vol. 12, no. 1, 12–26.

Amsden, A. (1989) *Asia's Next Giant: South Korea and Late Industrialization*, New York: Oxford University Press.

Anpo, T., Itagaki, H., Ueyama, K. and Kawamura, T. (1991) *Japanese Production System in USA: 'Usage' and 'Application for Localization'*, Tokyo: Toyo Economic Shinpo Press.

Ansal, H. (1990) 'Technical Change and Industrial Policy: The Case of Truck Manufacturing in Turkey', *World Development*, vol. 18, no. 11.

Association of Indian Automobile Manufacturers (AIAM) (1999) *The WTO Regime and Its Implications for the Indian Automobile Industry*, Delhi: AIAM.

Atkinson, G. (1999) 'Developing global institutions: lessons to be learned from regional integration experiences', *Journal of Economic Issues*, June.

Audet, D. and Van Grasstek, C. (1997) 'Market access issues in the automobile sector', in OECD, *Market Access Issues in the Automobile Sector*, Paris: OECD.

Audet, D., Van Tulder, R. and Ten Napel, S. (this volume) 'The faster lane of regionalism'.

Auto News (1998) 'Adjusting to India's market realities', 1 June, p. 26.

Automotive Component Manufacturers Association of India (ACMA), various years, *Facts and Figures: Automotive Industry of India*, New Delhi: ACMA.

Balassa, B. (1961) *The Theory of Economic Integration*, Homewood, IL: Irwin.

Baldwin, R. (1996) 'The political economy of trade policy: integrating the perspectives of economists and political scientists', in R. Feenstra, G. Grossman and D. Irvin (eds), *The Political Economy of Trade Policy*, Boston, MA: MIT Press.

Bangemann, M. (1992) *Meeting the Global Challenge: Establishing a Successful European Industrial Policy*, London: Kogan Page.

Banville, E. de and Chanaron, J.J. (1991) *Vers un système automobile européen*, Paris: Economica.

Baron, D. (2000) *Business and its Environment*, 3rd edition, Upper Saddle River: Prentice Hall.

Bartlett, D. and Seleny, A. (1998) 'The political enforcement of liberalism: bargaining, institutions, and auto multinationals in Hungary', *International Studies Quarterly*, vol. 42, 319–38.

Beck, P.M. (1998) 'Revitalizing Korea's chaebols', *Asian Survey*, vol. 38 no. 11, November.

Bélis-Bergouignan, M.C. and Lung, Y. (1994) 'Le mythe de la variété originelle: L'Internationalisation dans la trajectoire du modèle productif Japonais', *Annales. Histoire, Science Sociales*, vol. 49, no. 3, 541–67.

Bélis-Bergouignan, M.C., Bordenave, G. and Lung, Y. (2000) 'Global strategies in the automobile industry', *Regional Studies*, vol. 34, no. 1, 41–53.

Bellak, C. (1997) 'The contribution of the restructuring of (large "Western") MNCs to the catching-up of (small "Eastern") countries', *Development and International Cooperation*, vol. XIII, nos 24–5, 181–216.

Bennett, D. and Sharpe, K.E. (1979) 'Transnational corporations and the political economy of export promotion: the case of the Mexican automobile industry', *International Organization*, vol. 33, no. 2.

Bensunsan, G. and Bayon, M.C. (1997) *Estrategias sindicales frente al TLC: México, Estados Unidos y Canadá. El Sindicalismo del sector automotriz mexicano*, research report, Mexico: FLACSO.

Bergsten, F. (1997) 'Open regionalism', *Working Paper* 97-3, Institute for International Economics.

Bhagwati, J. (1993) 'Regionalism and multilateralism: an overview', in J. de Melo and A. Panagariya (eds), *New Dimensions in Regional Integration*, Cambridge: Cambridge University Press.

Black, A. (1994) *An Industrial Strategy for the Motor Vehicle Assembly and Component Sector*, Cape Town: UCT Press.

Black, A. (2001) 'Globalization and restructuring in the South African automotive industry', *Journal of International Development*, vol. 13, no. 6, 779–96.

Bogomolova, T. and Tapilina, V. (1999) *Income Mobility in Russia in the mid-1990s*, Economic Education and Research Consortium, Russian Economic Research Program, Working Paper no. 99/11.

Boisseau du Rocher, S. (1998) *L'ASEAN et la construction régionale en Asie du Sud-Est*, Paris: L'Harmattan.

Bonin, H., Lung, Y. and Tolliday, S. (eds) (2003) *Ford 1903–2003: the European History*, Paris: Plage.

Bordenave, G. (2003) 'Ford of Europe, 1967–2003', in H. Bonin, Y. Lung and S. Tolliday (eds), *Ford 1903–2003: the European History*, Paris: Plage.

Bordenave, G. and Lung, Y. (1996) 'New spatial configurations in the European automobile industry', *European Urban and Regional Studies*, vol. 3, no. 4, 305–21.

Bordenave, G. and Lung, Y. (2003) 'The twin strategies of internationalization strategies of US automakers: GM and Ford', in M. Freyssenet, K. Shimizu and G. Volpato (eds), *Globalization or Regionalization of the American and Asian Car Industry?*, Basingstoke: Palgrave Macmillan, 53–94.

Boyer, R. (1999) 'La politique à l'ère de la mondialisation et de la finance: le point sur quelques recherches régulationnistes', *L'année de la régulation*, vol. 3, 13–75.

Boyer, R. and Freyssenet, M. (1999) 'L'avenir est à nouveau ouvert. Stratégies de profit, formes d'internationalisation et nouveaux espaces de l'industrie automobile', *Gérer et Comprendre, Annales des Mines*, June, 21–30.

Boyer, R. and Freyssenet, M. (2000) 'Fusions-acquisitions et "stratégies de profit": une nouvelle approche', *Revue française de gestion*, no. 131, 20–8.

Boyer, R. and Freyssenet, M. (2002) *The Productive Models: the Conditions for Profitability*, London and New York: Palgrave Macmillan.

Boyer, R. and Saillard, Y. (eds) (2002) *Regulation Theory: the State of the Art*, London and New York: Routledge.

Boyer, R., Charron, E., Jurgens, U. and Tolliday, S. (eds) (1998) *Between Imitation and Innovation: the Transfer and Hybridization of Productive Models in the International Automobile Industry*, Oxford: Oxford University Press.

Brunat, E. (1999) 'Conversion militaire, transformation globale et Paix démocratique en Russie', *Diagonales Est-Ouest*, no. 62.

Buckley, R.M. and Gurenko, E.N. (1997) 'Housing and income distribution in Russia: Zhivago's legacy', *The World Bank Research Observer*, vol. 12, no. 1, February, 19–32.

Bungsche, H. and Heyder, T. (2003) 'After the loss of Japanese autonomy: the merger of Nissan/Renault and Mazda/Ford in comparison', *Eleventh Gerpisa International Colloquium*, Paris, 11–13 June.

Calmon, F. (1999) 'Keeping the faith', *Automotive World*, UK, December.

Camuffo, A. and Volpato, G. (1999) 'From lean to modular manufacturing? The case of the Fiat "178" world car', *IMVP-MIT Globalization Research*, Boston: MIT.

Carrillo, J. (1993) *La Ford en México: Reestructuración industrial y cambio en las relaciones sociales*, Doctoral Thesis, El Colegio de México.

Carrillo, J. (2002) 'Las paradojas de la integración en Norteamérica. Evolución industrial y pérdidas de ventajas', in E. De la Garza (ed.), *Impactos de la integración productiva en NAFTA*, FLACSO (Mexico: FLASCO).

Carrillo, J., Hinojosa, R. and Waldman, J. (2000) 'An uncertain trajectory in regional integration: the future of motor vehicle production in North America', paper presented at the 8th International Colloquium of Gerpisa, Paris, mimeo, June.

Carrillo, J., Hinojosa, R. and Waldman, J. (2001) *La Integración Norteamericana y Desarrollo: Impactos del TLC en la Reestructuración Industrial y el Empleo. El Caso de la Industria Automortiz en México*, Tijuana: COLEF (report).

Carrillo, J., Mortimore, M. and Alonso, J. (1999) *Competitividad y Mercados de Trabajo Empresas de Autopartes y de Televisores en México*, Plaza y Valdéz: UACJ y UAM.

CCFA (1997) *La présence asiatique en Europe*, Paris: CCFA.

CCFA (various years) *Repertoire mondial des activités de production et d'assemblage de véhicules automobiles*, Paris: CCFA.

Chanaron, J.J. (1985) 'L'industrie automobile en Afrique: le continent oublié', *Afrique/Asie*, no. 354, 2 August, 41–56.

Chanaron, J.J. (1998) 'Lada: viability of Fordism?', in M. Freyssenet, A. Mair, K. Shimizu and G. Volpato (eds), *One Best Way?*, Oxford: Oxford University Press, 440–51.

Chanaron, J.J. (2001) 'Managing technological and organizational innovations and core competencies: lessons from the automotive industry', *International Journal of Automobile Technology & Management*, Special Inaugural Issue, vol. 1, no. 1, 128–44.

Chanaron, J.J. and Jullien, B. (1999) 'The production, distribution and repair of automobiles: new relationships and new competencies', in Y. Lung, J.J. Chanaron, T. Fujimoto and D. Raff (eds), *Coping with Variety*, Aldershot: Ashgate.

Chandler, A. (1977) *The Visible Hand: the Managerial Revolution in American Busines*, Cambridge, MA: Belknap Press.

Chaponniere, J.R. (1997) *Korea: Open for Business*, Financial Times Management Reports, Hong Kong.

Chaponniere, J.R. and Lautier, M. (1994) *Une nouvelle donne industrielle dans le sud-est asiatique*, Rapport pour le ministère de l'industrie, Grenoble.

Chaponniere, J.R. and Lautier, M. (1995) 'Breaking into the Korean market – invest or licence', *Long Range Planning*, vol. 28, no. 1.

Chatterjee, B. (1990) *Japanese Management: Maruti and the Indian Experience*, New Delhi: Sterling.

Chrysler, M. (1995) 'Asia/Pacific outlook: hot, hot, hot', *Ward's Auto World*, December, 89–91.

Chung, M.-K. (2003) 'The chance of a peripheral market player: the internationalization strategies of the Korean automobile industry', in M. Freyssenet, K. Shimizu and G. Volpato (eds), *Globalization or Regionalization of the American and Asian Car Industry?*, Basingstoke: Palgrave Macmillan.

Chusho Kigyo Kinyu Koko (Small to Mid-size Finance Corporation) (1997) *Establishment of a New System of the Divisions of Labor between Japan and ASEAN Countries in the Electric Appliance Industry*, no. 97-3, June.

Chusho Kigyo Kinyu Koko (Small to Mid-size Finance Corporation) (1998) *Automobile Industry Trends in ASEAN and Effects to Our Domestic Small to Mid-size Parts Manufacturers*, Chusho Koko Report, no. 98-1, April.

Chusho Kigyo Kinyu Koko (Small to Mid-size Finance Corporation) (1999) *Japanese Small to Mid-size Companies go through the Economic Crisis in Asia*, report by Japan Finance Corporation for Small Businesses no. 99-2, July.

Cohen, E. and Lorenzi, J.H. (2000) *Politiques industrielles pour l'Europe*, Paris: La Documentation Française.

Cook, M.L. (1998) *Trade Union Strategies under NAFTA: the United States Automotive Sector*, New York: Cornell University.

Council on Foreign and Defense Policy (1998) *Russia vs. Corruption: Who Wins?*, analytic report, Moscow.

Cowles, M. (1995) 'Setting the agenda for a new Europe: the ERT and EC 1992', *Journal of Common Market Studies*, vol. 33, no. 4, 501–26.

Cusumano, M. (1985) *The Japanese Automobile Industry*, Cambridge, MA: Harvard University Press.

Dargay, J. and Gately, D. (1999) 'Income's effect on car and vehicle ownership, worldwide: 1960–2015', *Transportation Research Part A*, vol. 33, 101–38.

Dasgupta, R. (2000) 'The dowager's last days', *HIMAL*, July, 20–7.

D'Costa, A.P. (1995) 'The restructuring of the Indian automobile industry: Indian state and Japanese capital', *World Development*, vol. 23, no. 3, 485–502.

Degryse, H. and Verboven, F. (2000) *Car Price Differentials in the European Union: an Economic Analysis*, Investigation for the Competition Directorate-General of the European Commission, London: Centre for Economic Policy Research.

Dent, C.M. (1997) *The European Economy – the Global Context*, London and New York: Routledge.

Department of Commerce/United States Trade Representative (1997) *Report to President William Jefferson Clinton and the Interagency Enforcement Team Regarding the U.S.–Japan Agreement on Autos and Auto Parts* (18 April 1997), Washington, DC: International Trade Administration, Office of Automotive Affairs.

Department of Trade and Industry (1998) *Current Developments in the Automotive Industry*, Republic of South Africa.

Department of Trade and Industry (2001) *Current Developments in the Automotive Industry*, Republic of South Africa.

Derhak, J. (1998) *NAFTA and the Canadian Automotive Industry*, Los Angeles: University of California.

Doh, J. (1998) *The Impact of NAFTA on the Auto Industry in the United States* (report), Ankara.

Doner, R.F. (1991) *Driving a Bargain: Automobile Industrialization and Japanese Firms in Southeast Asia*, Berkeley and Los Angeles: University of California Press.

Duncan, D. (1997) *We are Motor Men*, Scotland: Whittles Publishing.

Dunning, J.H. (1992) *Multinational Enterprises and the Global Economy*, New York: Addison-Wesley.

Dunning, J.H. (1997) 'The European Internal Market Programme and inbound foreign direct investment' (pts 1 and 2), *Journal of Common Market Studies*, vol. 35.

Duruiz, L. (2003) 'Ford in Turkey: the partnership with Ford Otosan Company', in H. Bonin, Y. Lung and S. Tolliday (eds), *Ford 1903–2003: the European History*, Paris: Plage.

Duruiz, L. and Yentürk, N. (1992) *Facing the Challenge: Turkish Automobile, Steel and Clothing Industries' Responses to the Post-Fordist Restructuring*, Boston, MA: Ford Foundation.

Dyer, D., Salter, M.S. and Webber, A.M. (1987) *Changing Alliances*, Boston, MA: Harvard Business School Press.

Economist Intelligence Unit (EIU) (1994) 'The Indian motor industry: liberalisation takes effect', *International Motor Business*, 3rd Quarter, 119–36.

Economist Intelligence Unit (EIU) (1995) 'A review of the automotive sector in India', *International Motor Business*, 3rd Quarter, 68–88.

Economist Intelligence Unit (EIU) (2002) *World Investment Prospects: The Next FDI Boom*, New York/Hong Kong: EIU.

Eden, L. and Maureen, A.M. (1994) 'Made in America? The auto industry in the 1990's', *Working Paper* No. 31, Center for Trade Policy and Law, The Norman Patterson School of International Affairs, Carlenton University.

Ellegard, K. (1995) 'The creation of a new production system at the Volvo automobile assembly plant in Uddevalla, Sweden', in A. Sandberg (ed.), *Enriching Production*, Aldershot: Avebury.

Ellison, D.J. et al. (1995) 'Product development performance in the auto industry: 1990s update', *Working Paper 95-066*, Harvard Business School.

Ertürk, B. (1998) *Automotive Aftermarket, Turkey*. Industry Sector Analysis, Tradeport.

Ethier, W. (1998) 'Regionalism in a multilateral world', *Journal of Political Economy*, December.

European Commission (1999) *Etude sur le libre échange et la transition économique dans la région méditerranéenne*, DG 1B A4, Brussels: EC.

European Commission (2001) 'EU priority proposals for regulatory reform in Japan', Brussels, 12 October.

Flowers, E.B. et al. (1999), 'The new foreign investment. Restructuring Korean chaebols for wealth maximization', *Conference on International Trade and Capital Flows in Economic Restructuring and Growth*, Inha University, October.

Flynn, M. (1998) 'The General Motors trajectory: strategic shift or tactical drift?', in Freyssenet et al., *One Best Way? Trajectories and Industrial Models of the World's Automobile Producers*, Oxford: Oxford University Press.

Foreign Investment Promotion Center (FIPC) (1999) *Current Situation at Automobile-Building Enterprises: Development Perspectives*, Ministry of Economy, Russian Federation.

Freyssenet, M. (1995) 'La production réflexive, une alternative à la production de masse et à la production au plus juste?', *Sociologie du travail*, no. 3, 95.

Freyssenet, M. (2003) 'Renault: globalization, but for what purpose?', in M. Freyssenet, K. Shimizu and G. Volpato (eds), *Globalization or Regionalization of the American and Asian Car Industry?*, Basingstoke: Palgrave Macmillan.

Freyssenet, M. and Lung, Y. (2000) 'Between globalization and regionalization: what is the future of the automobile industry?', in J. Humphrey, Y. Lecler and M. Salerno (eds), *Global Strategies and Local Realities*, London: Macmillan Press.

Freyssenet, M. and Lung, Y. (2001) 'Les stratégies de régionalisation des constructeurs automobiles', *Sciences de la Société*, no. 51, 51–80.

Freyssenet, M., Mair, A., Shimizu, K. and Volpato, G. (eds) (1998) *One Best Way? Trajectories and Industrial Models of the World's Automobile Producers*, Oxford: Oxford University Press.

Freyssenet, M., Shimizu, K. and Volpato, G. (eds) (2003a) *Globalization or Regionalization of the American and Asian Car Industry?*, Basingstoke: Palgrave Macmillan.

Freyssenet, M., Shimizu, K. and Volpato, G. (eds) (2003b) *Globalization or Regionalization of the European Car Industry?*, Basingstoke: Palgrave Macmillan.

Frigant, V. and Lung, Y. (2002) 'Geographical proximity and supplying relationships in modular production', *International Journal of Urban and Regional Research*, vol. 25, no. 4, 742–55.

Froud, J., Haslam, C., Johal, S., Jullien, B. and Williams, K. (2000) 'Les dépenses de motorisation comme facteur d'accentuation des inégalités et comme frein au développement des entreprises automobiles: une comparaison franco-anglaise', in G. Dupuy and F. Bost (eds), *L'automobile et son monde*, Paris: Editions de l'aube.

Fujimoto, T. (1999) *The Evolution of a Manufacturing System at Toyota*, Oxford and New York: Oxford University Press.

Gaddy, C.G. and Ickes, B.W. (1998) 'Beyond a bailout: time to face reality about Russia's "virtual economy"', unpublished paper, Pennsylvania State University, June, The Brookings Institution, Washington DC.

Gaddy, C.G. and Ickes, B.W. (1999) 'Stability and disorder: an evolutionary analysis of Russia's virtual economy', *Working Paper*, no. 276, November.

Gilpin, R. (2001) *Global Political Economy: Understanding the International Economic Order*, Princeton, NJ: Princeton University Press.

Ginsburgh, V. and Vanhamme, G. (1989) 'Price differences in the EC car market: some further results', *Annales d'économie et de statistique*, nos 15/16, 137–49.

Gorski, K. (1999) 'Inorodnii avtomobil', *Kommersant Dengi*, no. 11, 29 April.

Guiheux, G. and Lecler, Y. (2000) 'Japanese car manufacturers and component makers in the ASEAN region: a case of expatriation under duress – or a strategy of regionally integrated production?', in J. Humphrey, Y. Lecler and M. Salerno (eds), *Global Strategies and Local Realities*, London: Macmillan Press.

Gulyani, S. (2001) *Innovating with Infrastructure: the Automobile Industry in India*, New York: Palgrave.

Guojia, X.Z. (1997) *Zhongguo Qiche Shichang Zhanwang 1998*, Beijing: Zhongguo Jihua Chubanshi.

Gwenell, L.B. and Villareal, A. (1993) *Mexican–US–Canadian Automotive Trade Issues*, CRS Report for Congress, Washington, DC.

Haggard, S. (1990) *Pathways from the Periphery: the Politics of Growth in the Newly Industrializing Countries*, Ithaca: Cornell University Press.

Halberstam, D. (1986) *The Reckoning*, New York: Morrow & Company.

Hao, J. and Lin, Z. (1994) *Changing Central–Local Relations in China: Reform and State Capacity*, Boulder, CO: Westview Press.

Harwit, E. (1995) *China's Automobile Industry: Policies, Problems, and Prospect*, Armonk, NY: M.E. Sharpe.

Havas, A. (1995) 'Hungarian car parts industry at a crossroads: Fordism versus lean production', *Emergo*, vol. 2, no. 3, 33–55.

Havas, A. (2000a) 'Changing patterns of inter- and intra-regional division of labour: Central Europe's long and winding road', in J. Humphrey, Y. Lecler and M. Salerno (eds), *Global Strategies and Local Realities: the Auto Industry in Emerging Markets*, Basingstoke: Macmillan Press.

Havas, A. (2000b) 'Local, regional and global production networks: reintegration of the Hungarian automotive industry', in Christian Von Hirschhausen and Jürgen Bitzer (eds) (2000) *The Globalization of Industry and Innovation in Eastern Europe*, Cheltenham: Edward Elgar.

Hayashi, T. (1989) 'Development and international divisions of labor for the automobile industry in East Asia', *Economic Management Theories*, vol. 8, nos 1/2, Yachiyo Gakuin University.

Heller, D. and Orihashi, S. (2003) 'Pooling capabilities abroad for global competitive advantage: investigating Ford–Mazda cooperation in Southeast Asia', *International Journal of Automotive Technology and Management*, vol. 3, nos 1/2, 122–43.

Helper, S. (1991) 'Strategy and irreversibility in supplier relations: the case of the U.S. automobile industry', *Business History Review* 65, Winter, 781–824.

Helper, S. (1994) 'Three steps forward, two steps back in automotive supplier relations', *Technovation*, vol. 14, no. 10, 633–40.

Helper, S. and MacDuffie, J. P. (2000) 'E-volving the auto industry: e-commerce effects on consumer and supplier relationships', paper prepared for *E-business and the changing terms of competition: a view from within the sectors*, Haas School of Business, UC Berkeley, 24 April.

Helper, S. and Sako, M. (1995) 'Supplier relations in Japan and the United States: are they converging?', *Sloan Management Review*, vol. 36, no. 3, Spring, 77–84.

Herrigel, G. (1996) *Industrial Constructions: the Source of German Industrial Power*, Cambridge: Cambridge University Press.

Herzenberg, S. (1996) 'Whither social unionism? Labor–management relations in the U.S. and Canadian auto industries', prepared for the conference on *North American Labor Movements: similarities and differences*, Center for International Affairs, Harvard University, 31 January.

Huang, Y. (1998) 'Between two coordination failures: automotive industrial policy in China and Korea', Harvard Business School, *Working Paper*, Boston, MA.

Huang, Y. (2003) *Selling China: Foreign Direct Investment during the Reform Era*, New York: Cambridge University Press.

Hugon, P. (2001) 'Régionalisation et pouvoirs en Asie de l'Est', *Economies et sociétés*, série P, no. 36.

Humphrey, J. and Oeter, A. (2000) 'Motor industry policies in emerging markets: globalisation and the promotion of domestic industry', in J. Humphrey, Y. Lecler and M. Salerno (eds), *Global Strategies and Local Realities*, London: Macmillan.

Humphrey, J. and Salerno, M. (2000) 'Globalization and assembler–supplier relations: Brazil and India', in J. Humphrey, Y. Lecler and M. Salerno (eds), *Global Strategies and Local Realities*, London: Macmillan.

Humphrey, J., Lecler, Y. and Salerno, M.S. (eds) (2000) *Global Strategies and Local Realities: the Auto Industry in Emerging Markets*, London: Macmillan.

Hyun, Y.S. (1998) 'Globalization of Daewoo Motor: From joint-venture to most aggressive globalization', *Actes du GERPISA*, no. 22.

Ikeda, M. and Nakagawa, Y. (2001) 'Globalization of the Japanese automobile industry and reorganization of Keiretsu suppliers', *Actes du GERPISA*, no. 33, 29–40.

Inoue, R., Urata, S. and Kohama H. (1990) *Industrial Policies of East Asia: For the New Development Strategies*, Japan Trade Promotion Bureau.

International Monetary Fund (IMF) (2002) *Direction of Trade Statistics*, Washington, DC: International Monetary Fund.

Ishiro, K. (1991) 'Current situation and parts supply in Taiwan', Kayoko Kitamura version, *Current Situation and Parts Supply of NIES Equipment Industry*, Asia Economic Research.

Itagaki, H. (1997) *Japanese Economic Production System and East Asia: Hybrid Factories in Taiwan*, Korea and China: Minelva Books.

Ivashchenko, N. and Savchenko, I. (1997) 'Restructuring the Russian economy: problems and tendencies', *Paper EU TACIS/ACE, Centre for Economic Reform and Transformation (CERT)*, Herriot-Watt University, Edinburgh.

Iwagaki, M. (1986) 'The state of China's automobile industry', JETRO, *China Newsletter*, no. 63, 9–16.

JAMA (2003) *Motor Vehicle Statistics* (http://www.japan auto.com/statistics)

Jenkins, R. (1987) *Transnational Corporations and the Latin American Automobile Industry*, London: Macmillan.

Jetin, B. (1999) 'The historical evolution of supply variety: an international comparative study', in Y. Lung et al. (eds), *Coping with Variety: Flexible Productive Systems for Product Variety in the Auto Industry*, Avebury: Ashgate.

Jetin, B. (2003) 'The internationalization of American and Asian automobile firms: a statistical comparison with the European companies', in Freyssenet et al. (eds),

Globalization or Regionalization of the American and Asian Car Industry?, Basingstoke: Palgrave Macmillan.

Johnson, C. (1982) *MITI and the Japanese Miracle: The Growth of Industrial Policy, 1925–1975*, Tokyo: Tutle.

Joshi, V. and Little, I.M.D. (1996) *India's Economic Reforms, 1991–2001*, Oxford: Oxford University Press.

Jovanovic, M.N. (1997) *European Economic Integration – Limits and Prospects*, London and New York: Routledge.

Judet, P. (1986) *Les nouveaux pays industriels*, Paris: Les Edition, Ouvrières.

Jürgens, U. (1998) 'The development of Volkswagen's industrial model, 1967–1995', in M. Freyssenet, A. Mair, K. Shimizu and G. Volpato (eds), *One Best Way? Trajectories and Industrial Models of the World's Automobile Producers*, Oxford: Oxford University Press.

Jürgens, U. (2004) 'Characteristics of the European automotive system: is there a distinctive European approach?', *International Journal of Automotive Technology and Management*, vol. 4, no. 1/2.

Kalenga, P. (2000) *Regional Trade Integration in Southern Africa: Critical Policy Issues*, Development Policy Research Unit, University of Cape Town, Working Paper 00/42.

Kawakami, M. (1995) 'Capital and technological introduction from Japanese corporations in the Taiwan automobile industry', *Asia Economy*, vol. 36, no. 11, Asia Economic Research.

KDI (1991) *Consequences of the Opening-up of the Market for the Korean Subcontracting System*, KDI Seoul (in Korean).

Kim, C.K. and Lee, C.H. (1980) 'Ancillary firm development in the Korean automotive industry', *KIEI Working Paper*, Seoul.

Kim, L.S. (1998) *Imitation to Innovation: the Dynamics of Korea's Technological Learning*, Cambridge, MA: Harvard Business School Press.

Kim, Y.-H. (2001) 'Rich carmakers and poor carbuyers: global automobile manufacturers in India', colloquium, Department of Geography, Ohio University.

Kim, Y.-H. (2002) 'More difficult than expected: global auto firms' local adaptations in India', colloquium, Department of Geography, Miami University.

Kitamura, K. (1997) 'Advancement of industrial structure in East Asia and Japanese industry', *Asia Economic Research*.

Knibb, B. (1997) 'Trade and investment issues in the automobile sector', in *Market Access Issues in the Automobile Sector*, OECD Proceedings, Organization for Economic Co-operation and Development, 101–26.

Kripalani, M. (1996) 'A traffic jam of auto makers', *Business Week*, 5 August, 46–7.

Krueger, A. (1993) *Political Economy of Policy Reforms in Developing Countries*, Cambridge, MA: MIT Press.

Kumar, P. and Holmes, J. (1997) *Diffusion of HR/IR Practices under Lean Production and North American Economic Integration: the Case of the Canadian Automotive Parts Industry*, Montreal: Queen's University Press.

Kumar, P. and Holmes, J. (1998) 'The impact of NAFTA on the auto industry in Canada', in S. Weintraub and C. Sands (eds), *The North American Auto Industry under NAFTA*, Washington, DC: The CSIS Press, Center for Strategic and International Studies.

Kumon, H. (1992) 'Japanese automobile factories in Taiwan', *Social Labour Research*, vol. 39, nos 2/3, Social Science Dept of Hosei University.

Kumon, H. (2003) 'Nissan: from a precocious export policy to a strategic alliance with Renault', in Freyssenet et al. (eds), *Globalization or Regionalization of the American and Asia Car Industry?*, Basingstoke: Palgrave Macmillan.

Lamming, R. (1993) *Beyond Partnership: Strategies for Innovation and Lean Supply*, New York: Prentice Hall.

Lanzarotti, M. (1992) *La Corée du Sud: une sortie du sous-développement*, Paris: PUF.

Laplane, M. and Sarti, F. (1997) 'The re-structuring of the Brazilian automobile industry in the nineties', in *Actes du GERPISA*, no. 20.

Laplane, M. and Sarti, F. (2000) 'Profit strategies in MERCOSUR: adaptability to changing conditions as a key factor for competition in unstable markets', in *Actes du GERPISA*, no. 29.

Laplane, M. and Sarti, F. (2002) 'Costs and paradoxes of market creation: evidence and argument from Brazil', *Competition and Change*, vol. 6, no. 1, 127–41.

Larsson, A. (2002) 'The development and regional significance of the automotive industry: supplier-parks in Western Europe', *International Journal of Urban and Regional Research*, vol. 25, no. 4, 767–84.

Lautier, M. (1993) 'La Corée du sud, une stratégie d'entrée agressive', in *La compétitivité des groupes automobiles mondiaux*, Paris: Eurostat.

Lautier, M. (1997) 'Les stratégies d'industrialisation automobile en Asie de l'Est', in GEMDEV, *Etats, Politiques publiques et développement en Asie*, Paris: Khartala.

Lautier, M. (1999) 'Les paradoxes des restructurations industrielles en Corée du Sud', *Revue Tiers Monde*, no. 160.

Lautier, M. (2001a) 'The international development of the Korean automobile industry', in F. Sachwald (ed.), *Going Multinational: the Korean Experience of Direct Investment*, London: Routledge.

Lautier, M. (2001b) 'Investissements etrangers et réorganisation industrielle en Asie', *Mondes en développement*, vol. 29, nos 113–14.

Layan, J.B. (2000) 'The integration of peripheral markets: a comparision of Spain and Mexico', in J. Humphrey, Y. Lecler and M. Salerno (eds), *Global Strategies and Local Realities*, London: Macmillan.

Layan, J.B. and Lung, Y. (1997) 'La globalisation de l'industrie automobile laisse-t-elle une place aux intégrations régionales périphériques? Le cas de l'industrie automobile', in F. Célimène et C. Lacour (eds), *L'intégration régionale des espaces*, Paris: Economica.

Layan, J.B. and Lung, Y. (2001) 'European regional integration and relocation of productive activities in the car industry', in J. Carrillo, N.A. Fuentes and A. Mercado Garcia (eds), *Libre comercio, integración y el futuro de la industria maquiladora. Produccion global y trabajadores locales*, Secretaria del Trabajo y Prevision Social, Mexico.

Layan, J.B., Lung, Y. and Mezouaghi, M. (2001) 'Entre mondialisation et régionalisation: quelles voies possibles pour l'industrie automobile algérienne?', in M.Y. Ferfera, M. Benguerna and M.A. Isli (eds), *Mondialisation et modernisation des entreprises. Enjeux et trajectoires*, Algiers: Casbah Editions.

Lecler, Y. (2002) 'The cluster role in the development of the Thai car industry', *International Journal of Urban and Regional Research*, vol. 25, no. 4, 799–814.

Lewis, J. (2001) *Reform and Opportunity: the Changing Role and Patterns of Trade in South Africa and SADC*, Africa Region Working Paper Series no. 14, Washington, DC: World Bank.

Li, A.D. (1997) *Jiating Jiaoche Youhuo Zhongguo*, Beijing: Zuojia Chubanshe.

Lieberthal, K. and Lampton, D. (eds) (1992) *Bureaucracy, Politics and Decision Making in Post-Mao China*, Berkeley and Los Angeles: University of California Press.

Lieberthal, K. and Oksenberg, M. (1988) *Policy Making in China: Leaders, Structures, and Processes*, Princeton, NJ: Princeton University Press.

Locke, R. (1995) *Remaking the Italian Economy*, Ithaca: Cornell University Press.

Loubet, J.L. (2000) 'Leçon du passé: l'automobile française n'a pas vu l'existence d'un espace méditerranéen', paper presented to the international colloquium *L'espace économique de la Méditerranée occidentale: enjeux et perspectives*, Bejaia, Algeria, 25–26 June.

Loubet, J.L. (2003) 'The cautious and progressive internationalization of PSA Peugeot Citroën', in M. Freyssenet, K. Shimizu and G. Volpato (eds), *Globalization or Regionalization of the European Car Industry?*, Basingstoke: Palgrave Macmillan.

Lung, Y. (2000) 'Is the rise of emerging countries as automobile producers an irreversible phenomenon?', in J. Humphrey, Y. Lecler and M. Salerno (eds), *Global Strategies and Local Realities*, London: Macmillan.

Lung, Y. (2001) 'The coordination of competencies and knowledge: a critical issue for regional automotive systems', *International Journal of Automotive Technology Management*, vol. 1, no. 1, 108–27.

Lung, Y. (2002) *Coordinating Competencies and Knowledge in the European Automobile System*, CoCKEAS final report for the European Commission, 5th Framework Programme, Thematic network (HPSE-CT-1999-00022), Pessac: IFReDE, Université Montesquieu-Bordeaux IV.

Lung, Y. (2004) 'The changing geography of the European automobile system', *International Journal of Automotive Technology and Management*, vol. 4, no. 1/2.

Lung, Y., Chanaron, J.-J., Fujimoto, T. and Raff, D. (eds) (1999) *Coping with Variety: Flexible Productive System for Product Variety in the Auto Industry*, Avebury: Ashgate.

Lung, Y., Salerno, M.S., Zilbovicius, M. and Carneiro Dias, A.M. (1999) 'Flexibility through modularity: experimentations with fractal production in Brazil and in Europe', in Y. Lung, J.-J. Chanaron, T. Fujimoto and D. Raff (eds), *Coping with Variety*, Aldershot: Ashgate.

Mainstream Publication (1977) *Maruti to Mafia: the Sanjay Gandhi Story*, New Delhi: Shaheed Prakashan Press.

Malkov, Y. (1994) *The Passenger Cars Market in Russia*, Moscow: American Embassy.

Mann, J. (1989) *Beijing Jeep: How Western Business Stalled in China*, New York: Simon & Schuster.

Matlack, C. (1999) 'AvtoVAZ: anatomy of a Russian corporate wreck, gangs of thugs and insider networks are choking AvtoVAZ', *Business Week*, 8 February, p. 20.

Mattli, W. (1999) *The Logic of European Integration: Europe and Beyond*, Cambridge: Cambridge University Press.

Maurel, F. (coord.) (1999) *Scénario pour une nouvelle géographie économique de l'Europe*, Rapport du Plan, CGP. Paris: Economica.

Maxcy, G. (1982) *Les Multinationales de l'automobile*, Paris: PUF-IRM.

McCarthy, C. (1999) 'Polarised development in a SADC Free Trade Area', *South African Journal of Economics*, vol. 67, no. 4, 375–99.

McKinsey (1998) *Productivity-led Growth for Korea*, chapter on the automotive industry, Seoul and Washington, DC: McKinsey.

McLaughlin, A.M. and Maloney, W.A. (1999) *The European Automobile Industry: Multi-level Governance, Policy and Politics*, London and New York: Routledge.

Mezouaghi, M. (2001) 'L'industrie automobile ukrainienne en transition', in Y. Lung (coord.), *Le développement de l'industrie automobile en Ukraine*, Recherche pour l'UEPLAC (Programme TACIS), IFREDE-CRITEC, Université Montesquieu-Bordeaux IV.

Mezouaghi, M. (2002) 'Les enseignements des approches de système national d'innovation: les économies semi-industrialisées', *Revue Tiers-Monde*, no. 169, 189–212.

Michelli, J. (1994) *Nueva manufactura, globalizanión y producción de automóviles en México*, Mexico, UNAM.

Mohanty, A.K., Sahu, P.K. and Pati, S.C. (1994) *Technology Transfer in the Indian Automobile Industry*, New Delhi: Ashish Publishing House.

Mohnot, S.R. (2001) *Automobile Industry 2001 and Beyond*, New Delhi: Centre for Industrial & Economic Research, Industrial Techno-Economic Services.

Montiel Hernández, Y. (2002) *Un mundo de coches. Nuevas formas de organización del trabajo. Estudios de caso*, Mexico: CIESAS.

Montinola, G., Qian, Y. and Weingast, B.R. (1995) 'Federalism, Chinese style: the political basis for economic success in China', *World Politics*, vol. 48, no. 1, 50–81.

Moore, D. (2000) 'The Price is Right', *Automotive World*, March.

Mori, M. (2001) 'New development of ASEAN automobile industry', *Jidosha Kogyo* (Automobile Industry), vol. 35, JAMA.

Mortimore, M. (1998) 'Getting a lift: modernizing industry by way of Latin American integration schemes; the example of automobiles', *Transnational Corporations*, vol. 7, no. 2, August.

Muller, A. and Van Tulder R. (2002) 'Macro intentions, micro realities: a two-level strategic approach to the Single European Market', *Multinational Business Review*, Fall, 1–10.

Muradzikwa, S. (1999) 'Competitiveness of the Zimbabwe automotive industry in an integrating region', paper presented at the Industrial Strategy Project Regional Research Workshop, Gauteng.

Narayana, D. (1989) *The Motor Vehicle Industry in India: Growth within a Regulatory Policy Environment*, New Delhi: Oxford and IBH Publishing Co.

Nedimoglu, F. (1995) 'Evaluation of suppliers of automotive sector on the way to customs union', paper presented to the Automotive and Suppliers Symposium, 3–4 November.

Nelson, D. (1996) 'The political economy of U.S. automobile production', in A.O. Krueger (eds), *The Political Economy of American Trade Policy*, Chicago: University of Chicago Press.

Norberto, E. and Uri, D. (2000) 'La révolution des petites cylindrées Le marché nouveau des "voitures populaires" au Brésil', *Les Actes du GERPISA (Université d'Evry-Val d'essonne)*, no. 29.

Nye, J. (2002) *The Paradox of American Power: Why the World's Only Superpower Can't Go It Alone*, New York: Oxford University Press.

Odaka, K. (1983) *The Motor Vehicle Industry in Asia*, Singapore University Press.

OECD (1994, 1998, 2001) *Economic Survey: Korea*, Paris: OECD.

OECD (1995) *Regional Integration and the Multilateral Trading System – Synergy and Divergence*, Paris: OECD.

OECD (1996) *Regionalism and its Place in the Multilateral Trading System*, Paris: OECD.

OECD (2000) *Regulatory Reform in Mexico*, Paris: OECD.

Ohri, V. (1997) 'Developments in India's auto industry', in *Market Access Issues in the Automobile Sector*, OECD Proceedings, Organization for Economic Co-operation and Development, pp. 127–31.

Ozawa, T. (1994) 'The southerly spread of America's automobile industry, flexible production and foreign direct investment as a corporate restructuring agent', *World Competition*, vol. 17, no. 4, June.

Pauly, L. and Reich, S. (1997) 'National structures and multinational corporate behavior: enduring differences in the age of globalization', *International Organization*, vol. LI, no. 1, Winter, 1–30.

Pavlínek, P. (2002) 'Restructuring the Central and Eastern European automobile industry: legacies, trends, and effects of foreign direct investment', *Post-Soviet Geography and Economics*, vol. 43, no. 1, 41–77.

Peigyo, K. (1994) 'Labor policies in Taiwan and establishment of "self-labor movement": labor movements in the 80s', *Economic Theories*, issue 8, Kyoto University.

Perrin, S. (2001) 'Korean direct investment in North-America and Europe: patterns and determinants', in F. Sachwald, *Going Multinational*, London: Taylor and Francis.

Pigato, M., Farah, C., Itakura, K., Jun, K., Martin, W., Murrell, K. and Srinivasan, T.G. (1997) *South Asia's Integration in the World Economy*, Washington, DC: The World Bank.

Pingle, V. (1999) *Rethinking the Developmental State: India's Industry in Comparative Perspective*, New York: St Martin's Press (Chapter 4: The Automobile Industry, pp. 85–120).

Pries, L. (1999) 'Die Globalisierung der deutschen Autohersteller und deren Sogeffekte fur die Automobilzullieferer', in H. Kilper and L. Pries (eds), *Die Globalisierungsspirale in der deutschen Automobil industrie*, Munich: Ed. Rainer Hamupp Verlas.

Pries, L. (2003) 'Volkswagen: accelerating from a multinational to a transnational automobile company', in M. Freyssenet, K. Shimizu and G. Volpato (eds), *Globalization or Regionalization of the European Car Industry?*, Basingstoke: Palgrave Macmillan.

Raff, D. (1998) 'Models, trajectories and the evolution of production systems: lesson from the American automobile industry in the years between the wars', in Freyssenet et al., *One Best Way? Trajectories and Industrial Models of the World's Automobile Producers*, Oxford: Oxford University Press.

Reinhart, N. and Peres, W. (2000) 'Latin America's new economic model: micro responses and economic restructuring', *World Development*, vol. 28, no. 9, 1543–66.

Rennard, J.P. (1992) *Semi-industrialisation et nouvelles approches de l'économie mondiale, le cas de l'industrie automobile en République de Corée*, PhD thesis, Université Grenoble II.

Republic of South Africa (1999) *Board on Tariffs and Trade: Mid Term Review Proposals for the Motor Industry Development Programme*, Government Gazette, Pretoria.

Rhys, D.G. (1996) *The Automotive Industry Sector in Africa*, Tunis, United Nations Industrial Development Organisation, Interregional Expert Group Meeting on the Automotive Industry.

Richet, X. and Bourassa, F. (2000) 'The reemergence of the automotive industry in Eastern Europe', in C. von Hirschhausen and J. Bilzer (eds), *The Centralization of Industry and Innovation in Eastern Europe* (Cheltenham: Edward Elgar), 59–95.

Rodriguez-Pose, A. and Arbix, G. (2001) 'Strategies of waste: bidding wars in the Brazilian automobile sector', *International Journal of Urban and Regional Research*, vol. 25, no. 1, 134–54.

Rodrik, D. (1999) *The New Global Economy and Developing Countries: Making Openness Work*, Washington DC: ODC.

Roldan, M. (1997) 'Continuities and discontinuities in the regulation and hierarchization of the world automotive industry: reflections on the Argentinean experience (1960's–1990's)', *Actes du GERPISA*, no. 20, 49–85.

Romijn, H., Van Assouw, R., Mortimore, M., Carrillo, J., Lall, S. and Poapongsakorn, N. (2000) 'TNCs, industrial restructuring and competitiveness in the automotive industry in NAFTA, MERCOSUR and ASEAN', in *Interregional Project on the Impact of Transnational Corporations on Industrial Restructuring in Developing Countries*, UNCTAD, Geneva, pp. 117–70.

Rubenstein, J.M. (1992) *The Changing U.S. Auto industry: a Geographical Analysis*, London and New York: Routledge.

Ruigrok, W. and Tate, J.J. (1996) 'Public testing and research centres in Japan: control and nurturing of small and medium-sized enterprises in the automobile industry', *Technology Analysis and Strategic Management*, vol. VIII, no. 4, 381–406.

Ruigrok, W. and van Tulder, R. (1995) *The Logic of International Restructuring*, London and New York: Routledge.

Ruigrok, W. and van Tulder, R. (1999) 'A two-way street in Asia: EU–US trade cooperation in the automobile and auto parts industries', in R. Steinberg and B. Stokes (eds), *Partners or Competitors? The Prospects for U.S.–European Cooperation on Asian Trade*, Lanham, MD: Rowman & Littlefield Publishers Inc.

Sachwald, F. (ed.) (1993) *European Integration and Competitiveness: Acquisitions and Alliances in Industry*, Aldershot: Edward Elgar Publishing.

Sachwald, F. (1995) *Japanese Firms in Europe*, Luxembourg: Harwood Academic Publishers.

Schlie, E. and Yip, G. (2000) 'Regional follows global: strategy mixes in the world automotive industry', *European Management Journal*, vol. 18, no. 4, 343–54.

Scott, A. (ed.) (1997) *The Limits of Globalization*, London: Taylor & Francis.

Segal, A. and Thun, E. (2001) 'Thinking globally, acting locally: local governments, industrial sectors, and development in China', *Politics and Society*, vol. 29, no. 4, 557–88.

Sei, S. (1989) 'Production system and technological standards of the Taiwan automobile parts industry', *Annual Report of the Economic Research*, Kanto Gakuin University.

Semenov, D. (1998) 'The market for automotive parts and accessories in the Republic of Belarus as of May 1998', *Business Information Service for the Newly Independent States* (BISNIS).

Shaiken, H. (1990) *Mexico in the Global Economy: High Technology and Work Organisation in Export Industries*, Monograph Series no. 33, Center for US–Mexican Studies, University of California, San Diego.

Shaiken, H. and Herzenberg, S. (1987) *Automation and Global Production: Automobile Engine Production in Mexico, the United States and Canada*, Center for US–Mexican Studies Monograph Series, No. 26, San Diego, University of California.

Shanghai Qiche Gongye Shi Bianweihui (1992) *Shanghai Qiche Gongye Shi*, Shanghai: Shanghai Renmin Chubanshe.

Shapiro, H. (1994) *Engines of Growth: the State and Transnational Auto Companies in Brazil*, Cambridge: Cambridge University Press.

Shimizu, K. (1999) *Le Toyotisme*, Paris: Repères, La Découverte.

Shimokawa, K. (1985) 'Japan's keiretsu system: the case of the automobile industry', *Japanese Economic Studies*, vol. 13, no. 4, Summer, 3–31.

Shimokawa, K. (1990) 'Taiwan automobile industry in the transition phase', *Economist*, 24 July.

Shimokawa, K. (2000) 'Development of direct investment and international divisions of labor of Japanese automobile industry in the Asia region', *Keiei Shirin*, vol. 35, no. 3.

Shimokawa, K. (2002) 'Re-evaluation of the international divisions of Labour in Japan's automobile industry in Asia', *Actes du Gerpisa*, no. 34.

Shome, P. (2001) *India and Economic Cooperation in South Asia*, New Delhi: Indian Council for Research on International Economic Relations.

Sid Ahmed, A. (1992) 'Maghreb, quelle intégration à la lumière des expériences dans le Tiers-Monde?', *Revue Tiers-Monde*, no. 129, 67–97.

Sintserov, L. (2000) 'Latest developments in the Russian automobile industry', *La Lettre du Gerpisa*, no. 145, 9–10.

Sogo Kyoiku Kikaku (Total Education Planning) (1997) *Asia Automobile Market Data Book.*

Soskice, D. (1999) 'Divergent production regimes: coordinated and uncoordinated market economies in the 1980s and 1990s', in Herbert Kitschelt et al. (eds), *Continuity and Change in Contemporary Capitalism*, Cambridge, UK; New York, NY: Cambridge University Press.

Stallings, B. and Peres, W. (2000) *Growth, Employment and Equity: the Impact of Economic Reforms in Latin America and the Caribbean*, Washington, DC: Brookings Institution Press for UN/ECLAC.

Starobin, P. and Kravchenko, O. (2000) 'Russia's middle class', *Business Week*, website, http://www.businessweek.com/2000/00_42/b3703093.htm.

Storper, M. (1997) *Regional World: Territorial Development in a Global Economy*, New York: Guilford Press.

Sturgeon, T. (1997) *Globalization and Jobs in the Automotive Industry*, a research project funded by the Alfred P. Sloan Foundation, research note no. 1, Cambridge, MA: Massachusetts Institute of Technology, October.

Sturgeon, T. and Florida, R. (1999) *The World that Changed the Machine: Globalization and Jobs in the Automotive Industry*, final report to the Alfred P. Sloan Foundation, Cambridge, MA: Massachusetts Institute of Technology.

Sugiyama, Y. and Fujimoto, T. (2000) 'Product development strategy in Indonesia: a dynamic view on global strategy', in J. Humphrey, Y. Lecler and M. Salerno (eds), *Global Strategies and Local Realities: the Auto Industry in Emerging Markets*, London: Macmillan Press.

Sun, N.Y. (1995) *Zhongguo Qiche Jixing*, Beijing: Zhongguo Tongji Chubanshe.

Takayasu, K. (2002) 'Global expansion and Asia strategies in the vehicle assembly industry', *Pacific Business and Industries*, vol. II, no. 4, 2–26.

Ten Napel, S. (1998) *SADC and the TNCs: Crossing Borders?*, MA Thesis, Erasmus University, Rotterdam.

Tezer, E. (1995) 'Automotive industry and customs union', paper presented to the *Automotive and Suppliers Symposium*, 3–4 November.

Thun, E. (forthcoming) *Changing Lanes in China: Foreign Direct Investment, Local Government, and Auto Sector Development*, New York: Cambridge University Press.

Thun, E. (2003) 'Local development and the Chinese auto sector: a political economy analysis', *Actes du GERPISA* (Université d'Evry-val d'Essonne), no. 37.

Tigre, P.B., Laplane, M.F., Lugones, G. and Porta, F. (1999) 'Technological change and modernization in the MERCOSUR automotive industry', *Integration and Trade*, vol. 3, nos 7/8, 123–46.

Tizaoui, H. (2001) *La mondialisation de l'industrie tunisienne. Les industries automobiles en Tunisie*, Tunis: Publication de la Faculté des Sciences Humaines et Sociales de l'Université de Tunis I.

Tizaoui, H. (2003) 'L'ascension fulgurante de la sous-branche des faisceaux de câbles automobiles en Tunisie: une hyperspécialisation ou une adaptation socio-spatiale à la mondialisation', *Working Paper*, Tunis: Faculté des Sciences Humaines et Sociales de l'Université de Tunis I.

TMMOB (1993) *Turkish Automobile Industry Productivity Analysis*, Congress of Industry, November, Bursa.

Tulder, R. van and Ruigrok, W. (1998) 'European cross-national production networks in the auto industry: Eastern Europe as the low end of European car complex', *Working Paper 121*, MIRE, May.

Tulder, R. van and Ruigrok, W. (1998) 'International production networks in the auto industry: Central and Eastern Europe as the low end of the West European car complexes', in J. Zysman and A. Schwartz (eds), *Enlarging Europe: the Industrial Foundations of a New Political Reality*, IAS–International and Area Studies, University of California at Berkeley, 202–38.

Tulder, R. van and Ruigrok, W. (1999) 'The integration of Central and Eastern Europe in car production networks', *Actes du Gerpisa*, no. 25, 119–54.

Tutak, R.J. (1999) 'Russia: wrong turn at the crossroads?, Russia Outlook', *World Automotive Manufacturing, Financial Times*, October, pp. 15–18.

UNCTAD (1999) *World Investment Report 1999 – Foreign Direct Investment and the Challenge of Development*, New York and Geneva: United Nations.

UNCTAD (2001) *World Investment Report 2001: Promoting Linkages*, Geneva: UNCTAD.

UNCTAD (2003) *World Investment Directory: Volume VIII – Central and Eastern Europe*, New York and Geneva.

United Nations (1999) *Socio-Economic Profile of SAARA Countries: a Statistical Analysis*, New York: United Nations.

United Nations Economic and Social Commission for Asia and the Pacific (ESCAP) (2002) *Development of the Automotive Sector in Selected Countries of the ESCAP Region*, Trade and Investment Division, United Nations ESCAP (ST/ESCAP/2223).

United States Trade Representative (1997) *1997 National Trade Estimates*, Washington, DC: USTR.

United States Trade Representative (2000) Annual Review of Automotive Framework Agreement, Washington DC: USTR.

Upton, D. and Seet, R. (1995) 'Shanghai Volkswagen', *Harvard Business School* case no. 1-695-080, Boston, MA: Harvard Business School.

Vachani, S. (1997) 'Economic liberalization's effect on sources of competitive advantage of different groups of companies: the case of India', *International Business Review*, vol. 6, no. 2, 165–84.

Venkataramani, R. (1990) *Japan Enters Indian Industry: The Maruti–Suzuki Joint Venture*, New Delhi: Radiant.

Vigier, P. (1992) 'La politique communautaire de l'automobile', *Revue du Marché Unique Européen*, nos 3 and 4, 73–126.

Wade, R. (1990) *Governing the Market: Economic Theory and the Role of Government in East Asian Industrialization*, Princeton, NJ: Princeton University Press.

Walder, A. (1995) 'Local governments as industrial firms: an organizational analysis of China's transitional economy', *Harvard University*, no. 95, 2.

Ward's (2000) *World Motor Vehicle Data*, Detroit.

Weintraub, S. (1998) 'Incomes and productivity in the auto industry in North America', in S. Weintraub and C. Sands (eds), *The North American Auto Industry under NAFTA*, 221–40.

Weintraub, S. and Sands, C. (eds) (1998) *The North American Auto Industry under NAFTA*, The CSIS Press, Washington, DC: Center for Strategic and International Studies.

Wilkins, M. and Hill, F.E. (1964) *American Business Abroad: Ford on Six Continents*, Detroit: Wayne State University Press.

Womack, J. and Jones, D. (1996) *Lean Thinking*, New York: Simon & Schuster.

Womack, J.P., Jones, D.T. and Roos, D. (1990) *The Machine that Changed the World*, New York: Rawson Associates (Macmillan Publishing Co.).

World Bank (1993) *The East Asian Miracle*, Oxford: Oxford University Press for the World Bank.

World Bank (1996) *India: Five Years of Stabilization and Reform and the Challenges Ahead*, Washington, DC: World Bank.

World Bank (2001) *Trade Blocks*, Oxford: Oxford University Press for the World Bank.

WTO (2000) *Mapping of Regional Trade Agreements*, WT/REG/W/41, 11 October.

Yin, J., McGee, R. and Doowon Lee (2001) 'WTO Trade Disputes and Its Future Development: An Empirical Analysis', Paper submitted to Association of International Business, Sydney.

Yoshimatsu, H. (2002) 'Preferences, interests and regional integration: the development of the ASEAN industrial cooperation arrangement', *Review of International Political Economy*, vol. 9, no. 1, 123–49.

Zemplinerová, A. (1998) 'Impact of foreign direct investment on the restructuring and growth in manufacturing', *Prague Economic Papers*, vol. 7, 329–45.

Index